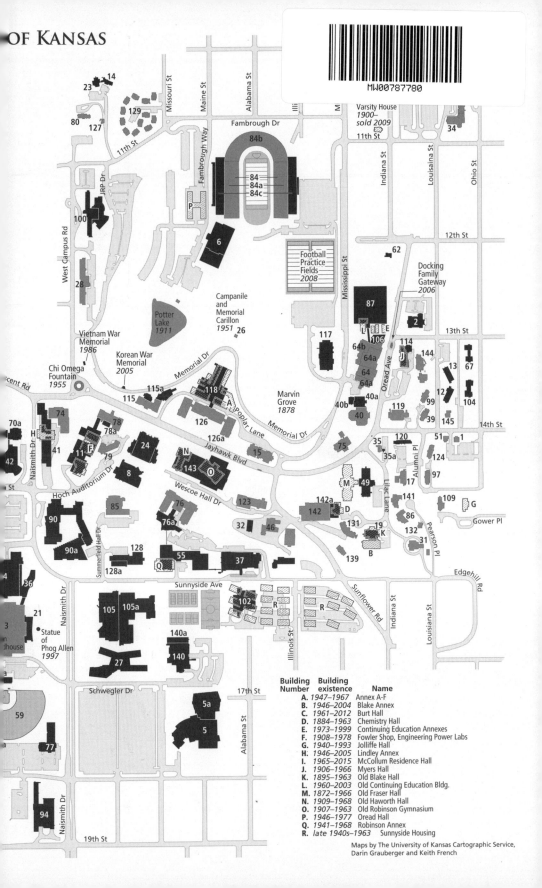

OF KANSAS

Varsity House
1900–
sold 2009

Football
Practice
Fields
2008

Campanile
and
Memorial
Carillon
1951

Docking
Family
Gateway
2006

Potter
Lake
1911

Vietnam War
Memorial
1986

Korean War
Memorial
2005

Chi Omega
Fountain
1955

Marvin
Grove
1878

Statue
of
Phog Allen
1997

Maps by The University of Kansas Cartographic Service,
Darin Grauberger and Keith French

Building Number	Building existence	Name
A.	1947–1967	Annex A-F
B.	1946–2004	Blake Annex
C.	1961–2012	Burt Hall
D.	1884–1963	Chemistry Hall
E.	1973–1999	Continuing Education Annexes
F.	1908–1978	Fowler Shop, Engineering Power Labs
G.	1940–1993	Jolliffe Hall
H.	1946–2005	Lindley Annex
I.	1965–2015	McCollum Residence Hall
J.	1906–1966	Myers Hall
K.	1895–1963	Old Blake Hall
L.	1960–2003	Old Continuing Education Bldg.
M.	1872–1966	Old Fraser Hall
N.	1909–1968	Old Haworth Hall
O.	1907–1963	Old Robinson Gymnasium
P.	1946–1977	Oread Hall
Q.	1941–1968	Robinson Annex
R.	late 1940s–1963	Sunnyside Housing

MW00787780

"The legacy of the University of Kansas is of an academic community constantly seeking to raise the expectations we have for ourselves, the aspirations we have for our state, and the hopes we have for our world. . . . It is also a legacy of achievement in the face of adversity, befitting the Kansas motto, *Ad astra per aspera*, and reflecting the lofty dreams and boundless ambitions that come to each of us when we stand atop Mount Oread."

Bernadette Gray-Little,
Chancellor of the University of Kansas

"I have reviewed this updated history of the past fifty years of KU and found it to be accurate, thorough, and exceptionally informative and interesting. Alumni and other friends of KU will find it to be a wonderful resource, full of facts and thoughtful observations about this treasured university."

Delbert M. Shankel,
Chancellor Emeritus of the University of Kansas

"As a 'KU 150: Boundless' project, this book provides a fifty-year perspective on the history of our university. The chapters should highlight memories for those that lived it, and a better understanding of the significance of changes at KU to those of us who have come to call it home."

Charles Persinger,
Director of University Ceremonies and Special Events

THE UNIVERSITY OF KANSAS 1865–2015

TRANSFORMING THE UNIVERSITY OF KANSAS

TRANSFORMING THE UNIVERSITY OF KANSAS

A History, 1965–2015

EDITED BY

John L. Rury and Kim Cary Warren

Foreword by Chancellor Bernadette Gray-Little

University Press of Kansas

All photographs courtesy of University Archives, Spencer Research Library, University of Kansas, unless otherwise noted.

Published by the University Press of Kansas (Lawrence, Kansas 66045), which was organized by the Kansas Board of Regents and is operated and funded by Emporia State University, Fort Hays State University, Kansas State University, Pittsburg State University, the University of Kansas, and Wichita State University

Library of Congress Cataloging-in-Publication Data
Transforming the University of Kansas: a history, 1965–2015 / edited by John L. Rury and Kim Cary Warren ; foreword by Chancellor Bernadette Gray-Little.
   pages   cm
   Includes bibliographical references and index.
   ISBN 978-0-7006-2118-7 (cloth : alk. paper) — ISBN 978-0-7006-2160-6 (ebook)
1. University of Kansas—History. I. Rury, John L. II. Warren, Kim Cary.
LD2688.T73   2015
378.009781'65–dc23
2015013866

British Library Cataloguing-in-Publication Data is available.

Printed in the United States of America

10 9 8 7 6 5 4 3 2 1

The paper used in this publication is recycled and contains 30 percent postconsumer waste. It is acid free and meets the minimum requirements of the American National Standard for Permanence of Paper for Printed Library Materials Z39.48-1992.

Contents

Abbreviations

KUEA	University of Kansas Endowment Association
KUMC	University of Kansas Medical Center
LHS	Lawrence High School
LJW	*Lawrence Journal-World*
OIRP	Office of Institutional Research and Planning
ROTC	Reserve Officer Training Corps
UDK	*University Daily Kansan*

Illustrations

Chapter 5

Chapter 6

Chapter 8

Foreword

BERNADETTE GRAY-LITTLE

THE red roofs of the University of Kansas appear on the horizon long before you reach Lawrence.

Sitting atop Mount Oread, the campus stands as a monument to the determination of the state's earliest settlers to build for the future. Even as the land was riven by civil war, they knew Kansas could not truly prosper without a university. And as a "city on a hill," our university has also reflected both society's hopes and its fears. The changes experienced by our nation and world over the past five decades have been experienced, and even amplified, at KU. As a result, much like the history of the United States, the last 50 years at the University of Kansas have been marked by tremendous accomplishments and by tremendous challenges.

The national debate over the Vietnam War created deep divisions in the community. Meanwhile, the civil rights movement rightfully brought change to a university that, though founded by those dedicated to equality, had not always lived up to its ideals. Shifting political climates altered who pays for college, increasing the burden on students and families. And political interests have at times threatened the academic freedoms vital to the success of all universities.

Throughout these and other challenges, this academic community has remained committed to KU's noble mission of lifting students and society by educating leaders, building healthy communities, and making discoveries that change the world. Tens of thousands of Jayhawks have walked down the Hill and into the world, taking up leadership positions around the world and in their communities, from Fortune 500 companies to the corner pharmacy.

The legacy of the past 50 years at the University of Kansas is reflected in all those whose lives were changed by what they learned here. It's also present in the lives of the countless people who may never even have set foot on a KU campus, yet have still benefited from

Chancellor Bernadette Gray-Little.

the knowledge and talent of our faculty, staff, and alumni. In every field of human endeavor, and in virtually every nation on Earth, you can find a KU graduate. And, in many instances, these Jayhawks are sharing research and creative works created at the university, from new treatments and cures, to new works of art and culture.

The legacy of the University of Kansas is of an academic community constantly seeking to raise the expectations we have for ourselves, the aspirations we have for our state, and the hopes we have for our world. Succeeding generations have built on the accomplishments of those who came before, all in service of KU's mission as a flagship university.

It is also a legacy of achievement in the face of adversity, befitting the Kansas motto, *Ad astra per aspera*, and reflecting the lofty dreams and boundless ambitions that come to each of us when we stand atop Mount Oread.

Preface and Acknowledgments

KIM CARY WARREN AND JOHN L. RURY

I N commemorating the sesquicentennial anniversary of the University of Kansas's founding, this book reflects upon the last 50 years of people, politics, and institutional developments that have made KU into the distinctive institution that it is today. Its authors consider KU's history since 1965, a pivotal year in many respects. Picking up where Clifford S. Griffin left off in his momentous study, *The University of Kansas: A History,* we have examined critical moments in the university's history over the past half century, a time of conflict over the means and purposes of education, dramatic expansion, and transformation in institutional identity. Many American universities experienced similar developments, but KU's story is unique in many respects and is told in the chapters to follow.

No longer just a teaching-oriented institution in a small town located between Kansas City and Topeka, the University of Kansas has undergone remarkable changes during this time. As the book's title, *Transforming the University of Kansas: A History, 1965–2015,* suggests, this era was one of transformation, a process wrought by many contributors. It saw the growth of undergraduate majors and the rapid expansion of graduate programs. Students rebelled and articulated new demands to address their diverse interests as well as their social causes. Faculty members repositioned themselves and their departments on the national and international stage, especially with respect to research and scholarship. The roles of university staff and administration evolved rapidly in response to changing curricular and extracurricular expectations, along with the development of digital technology. And the university's leaders provided vision and direction to mark a course of continued advancement.

By the time the twentieth century closed and the twenty-first century began, KU had established itself not only as the state's flagship university, but also as a leader in research and technological innovations. In the new millennium, in 2001, the Robert J. Dole Institute for Public Service and Public Policy broke ground in order to bring a host of national and international speakers to campus. At the medical school, a new $52 million building attracted millions of dollars in grant funding and some of the nation's top researchers at the Robert E. Hemenway Life Sciences Innovation Center. The Edwards Campus, originally founded in 1990 with the donation of 36 acres of land by Clay Blair III, a KU alumnus, contributed $500 million to the Johnson County economy within its first 21 years. KU has welcomed growing numbers of international students, in addition to enabling thousands of undergraduates to study abroad and gain a wider appreciation of the world.

Although the university continues to take pride in its service to the state of Kansas, satellite campuses have allowed for extensive outreach unforeseen in earlier years. The Lawrence campus maintains its traditional role as the heart of KU, while programs in Kansas City, Wichita, and Salina offer professional degrees and services to the broader community, especially in medical fields. The campus in Overland Park has helped make KU a metropolitan university that serves both sides of the Kansas-Missouri state line. Boasting 28,000 students and more than 2,000 faculty on five campuses, KU's presence is felt far beyond its immediate environs.

IN THE FOOTSTEPS OF CLIFFORD GRIFFIN

In the essays that follow, KU scholars have drawn upon a wealth of information, taken from university archival collections, oral history interviews, student yearbooks and other publications, and alumni sources, to paint a picture of KU over the past five decades. Each author has focused on a particular thematic aspect of KU's history in order to capture the essential changes that have taken place in this period.

Although there have been several books written about KU, its alumni, athletics, and history, one stands out as the authoritative book of record for the university's first century: Clifford S. Griffin's *The University of Kansas*, published in 1974 (a mere nine years after KU's centennial celebration). A professor of history at KU from 1959 to 1996, Griffin mined university archival material to trace KU's history from its embryonic days as a preparatory school and as it grew into a major institution of higher learning. Griffin starts with KU's humble origins and traces the gradual expansion of the university, detailing the many struggles that paved the way. He also described the inevitable

Clifford Griffin was the author of KU's history for the university centennial.

tension between the university's mission to serve the public while also cultivating the most elite talent from across the state and the nation. Just as Griffin's volume chronicled KU's first century (1865–1965), *Transforming the University of Kansas* proposes to stand as a scholarly and institutional book of record for the past 50 years (1965–2015).

ORGANIZATION OF THE BOOK

This collection of essays is organized thematically, so that each chapter provides a 50-year perspective on key events and leaders concerned with at least one important theme in the university's development. Each author is a KU faculty or staff member, whose field of study is reflected in the chapter that s/he has written. The topics reflect important dimensions of change in higher education since the 1960s, and events at the University of Kansas in particular. The chapters have been organized into three broad topical categories: Leadership and Politics; Teaching and Research; and Students, Protest, and Sports. In this way, we hope to lend a bit more coherence to the wide diversity of people, events, and circumstances that a volume such as this necessarily considers. While this book is not an omnibus history such as Griffin's, it does offer a good deal of insight about changes that have occurred in this large and complex institution and the historical circumstances that contributed to them.

To begin, John Rury, a historian of education, provides a chronological overview of KU's growth and development during this period and how it fit into the larger context of higher education nationally. While KU was known for both athletic and academic accomplishment well before this time, it was transformed from a somewhat bucolic college into a major research university in relatively short order. Historically drawing students into the arts and sciences along with pre-professional programs, the university grew rapidly into a center of graduate training and research. These changes occurred at other institutions, of course, but took a particular path at KU. In describing these developments, Rury sets the stage for the chapters that follow.

Chapter 1, written by Susan Twombly, professor of higher education, lays out the major agendas of eight chancellors beginning with Clarke Wescoe and ending with Bernadette Gray-Little. By incorporating their own memos and other correspondence into her chapter, Twombly captures the distinctive spirit of each chancellor as s/he faced crises, budget shortfalls, student unrest, and pressure from the legislature, in addition to moments of pride and joy with each start of the school year.

As Twombly argues, chancellors could not lead the university without the support of the state, so Burdett Loomis, political scientist, examines, in Chapter 2, the continuous tussles and negotiations that have characterized KU's relationship with Kansas politicians. Employing personal interviews as well as institutional records, Loomis provides insight into the personalities and key decision makers that have not been emphasized in previous studies about KU. Loomis shows how annual debates about funding for KU kept the university at the forefront of arguments about educational priorities in the statehouse and on campus.

In Chapter 3, James Woelfel, professor of philosophy and humanities and Western Civilization, explains that KU has always kept undergraduate education as a core priority, even as the university has expanded its research agenda. While KU introduced several innovations in learning, including an Honors Program and the Colleges-within-the-College, it also paid attention to the needs of the majority of students focused on earning their general education requirements and marching toward their degrees in a timely fashion. Woelfel explains how programs aimed at the top tier of students joined large-scale curricular reforms meant to affect all students in order to make KU's undergraduate experience inventive yet still obtainable within four to five years.

Chapter 4, written by Megan Greene, a historian of modern China and director of KU's East Asian Studies Center, focuses on the international community of learners in Lawrence and around the world. Greene explains how the development of federally funded Title VI area studies programs and the expansion of study abroad opportunities made KU students and faculty think of themselves as contributing to a larger, more global body of scholarship. The rapid growth of international students, especially in the 1960s, diversified the student body and brought more attention to KU's international interests in the humanities and the sciences.

Joshua Rosenbloom, an economic historian, returns readers to the themes of a transformed university outlined at the beginning the volume. In Chapter 5, Rosenbloom explains exactly how the university used the pursuit of external funding to sponsor research projects that gained national attention and sponsorship for the university. With an enthusiastic and aggressive approach, individual faculty and students, as well as programs and departments, brought new research funding to KU and thus pushed the university to realize its current status as a research institution.

Students' experiences are at the heart of KU's history, and William Tuttle, professor emeritus of American Studies, focuses on the years of student activism during the civil rights, women's rights, and antiwar protest eras. Tuttle's Chapter 6 especially draws on student publications and city newspapers to detail the complex and confrontational campus atmosphere as KU students accelerated social activism, making a name for Lawrence as a political "hot bed," especially in the 1960s and 1970s but also beyond.

In Chapter 7, Kathryn Nemeth Tuttle, associate vice provost emerita, also examines student life, showing that activism manifested in various ways, including student demands for more diverse academic programs and representation on university committees that made decisions directly affecting them. Tuttle shows that student protest turned into new leadership roles at KU and then created different pathways for students to become empowered in university-wide decision making and in the creation of innovative curricular and extracurricular programs.

Student athletes, as well as their coaches and fans, are the focus of Chapter 8, written by Bernie Kish, lecturer in sport management. Kish examines KU's long history of athletic achievement in basketball and football, as well as its tradition of building excellence in programs in track and field, baseball, and other sports. The 1972 Title IX decision barring sex discrimination in educational programs receiving federal assistance created a turning point in KU athletics, opening new avenues for female, as well as male, athletes and coaches.

Through essays and photographs, readers of *Transforming the University of Kansas* will explore KU's past through a variety of perspectives—administrators, politicians, faculty, staff, students, and community members. Although none of these groups was ever in complete agreement with all of the others about the direction of the university, readers will find that each of these constituencies felt that KU's success reflected their own, invested astutely in the growth of the university, and saw rapid changes during the past five decades.

Scholarship is an integrally collective enterprise, and this book is the result of a great deal of collaboration. It began four years ago with a discussion between the editors about university history, a conversation that has grown expansively over time. It has been generously supported by the university, starting with Chancellor Bernadette Gray-Little and the KU-150 Sesquicentennial Committee, particularly Charlie Persinger, Liz Kowalchuk, Jonathan Earle, and Bill Crowe. The research for the book has received enormous assistance from the staff of the University Archives at the Spencer Research Library, especially Becky Schulte, Letha Johnson, and Kathy Lafferty, who guided researchers through archives and hundreds of documents and photographs. Deb Teeter, Virginia Nichols, and the staff at KU's Office of Institutional Research and Planning also were very accommodating, specifically with regard to the institution's changing statistical profile. Fred Woodward, Chuck Myers, and Kelly Chrisman Jacques of the University Press of Kansas have been helpful guides to the publication process.

Our keen and highly adept research assistants, Angela Murphy, JoJo Palko, and Battsetseg Serj, provided invaluable support to the book's authors and editors, tracking down sources, helping identify photos, and drafting captions. Most of the material used and cited in the book was found in KU's unusually rich and far-reaching archival collection, but additional sources were utilized from the Department of Athletics, the Medical Center Library, the Booth Hall of Fame, the Hall Center for the Humanities, the School of Law, the School of Architecture, Design and Planning, the School of Education, and the Department of History. We would like to thank Darin Grauberger of the Geography Department's cartography lab for preparation of maps for the end-papers. Thanks also to Pam LeRow for creating the index.

It is also important to acknowledge our gratitude to the dozens of individuals who took time to share memories of their KU experiences in the form of oral history interviews. All of these conversations were arranged by the chapter authors in connection with topics in their respective essays, and some individuals were interviewed for more than one chapter. These interviews were a critical dimension of the research, representing sources of information and insight that would not otherwise be available to future generations. They have added significantly to our comprehension of KU and the meaning it held for Jayhawks everywhere. Without the assistance of the people who shared their memories with us, this facet of the study would not have been possible.

The greatest debt of gratitude goes to our chapter authors, who have worked tirelessly to complete the research and writing for this volume, staying on track to meet a deadline imposed by the 2015 start of the sesquicentennial celebration. We met periodically in lively, productive writing seminars to discuss work in progress, attended by Angela, JoJo, and Letha as well. Each of the authors embraced the task of writing the history of the past 50 years at KU with devotion and resolve, revealing historical details and insights that none of us anticipated. Without their dedication, knowledge, and skill, this book would not have been possible.

Finally, we would like to thank our other colleagues, friends, and family members who have also supported this project, whether happily or not, for the past several years. We hope this acknowledgment of our appreciation and affection will be a small recompense for the sustenance and care that they have provided through thick and thin.

INTRODUCTION

Decades of Transformation
Fifty Years of KU History

JOHN L. RURY

THE University of Kansas has grown and developed dramatically
since 1965, reflecting changes that have shaped many American
institutions of higher education, as well as local events. While change
has occurred throughout KU's past, this period has been especially
transformative in many respects. Starting with a time of conflict and
turmoil on college campuses—and at KU in particular—the University
of Kansas has emerged as a multifaceted and mature research institution, striving to keep pace with its national and international peers.
True to its historical mission of instruction, the university has continued to emphasize excellence in teaching, offering nationally recognized programs of study that serve students from across Kansas and
around the world. And it has enhanced its service to the state and
region in myriad other ways, ranging from the geological survey to the
training of police and firefighters to the development of assessments
for public schools, among many others. On the eve of its sesquicentennial, it stands as one of the nation's major public research universities,
building upon achievements of the past to prepare for the future.

The road to KU's present stature, however, has not been smooth.
In the decades since the mid-1960s, it has experienced turbulent student unrest, rapid and largely unplanned growth, a sharply increased
emphasis on research productivity, an onslaught of digital technology
advances, and many other changes. The university has been subject to
criticism from regional and national accrediting agencies, from politicians and journalists, and from its own students and staff members.

Looking across Jayhawk Boulevard to Bailey Hall in the mid-1960s. The leafy central campus offered a decidedly collegiate atmosphere.

It has contended with periodic and unanticipated losses of funding, mounting costs of instruction, changing information requirements, and shifting student and public expectations about the collegiate experience. Rising tuition has brought greater public scrutiny of higher education, and KU has been affected by this as well. Gone were the days when the campus was considered a quiet sanctuary. With ever more students attending college and higher education becoming a much larger enterprise, institutions like KU were often in the news during this period and not always in a positive light.[1]

On the other hand, KU has long enjoyed a fine reputation as an academic institution, earning praise for the high quality of its faculty and students. It has extremely loyal and accomplished alumni, and Jayhawks are nationally known for their scholastic and professional accomplishments, as well as athletic prowess. But a critical aspect of the university's success has been its ability to respond confidently to the problems it has faced and to prepare effectively for the future. The university has been fortunate in finding leaders who have addressed the dilemmas of their times and prepared for those to come. Not all have fared equally well, but the overall record is one of largely success-ful adaptation to the ever-shifting landscape of higher education. The university also benefited from many other resourceful and imagina-tive administrators, faculty members, and students who have helped it to meet the challenges of each period in its development. This book chronicles their history and the questions they collectively faced, along with many other developments that marked the times.

This introduction is devoted to describing the major changes that the university has experienced during the past 50 years, highlighting the principal challenges it encountered. In this respect, it provides an overview of KU's recent history and also sets the stage for the remain-der of the book. Each of the chapters to follow deals with a separate theme in the university's development, ranging from leadership and politics, to curriculum and research, international connections, stu-dent life, and athletics, and touching upon many additional issues. The authors approach these topics in somewhat different ways, but all help to place KU within a larger context and all focus on changes that shaped the university across the period. KU evolved from a state uni-versity wracked by dissension and spontaneous growth to one striving to realize its full potential as a research and teaching institution. To appreciate the magnitude of this change, however, it is necessary to revisit a time of considerable uncertainty and turmoil.

A TIME OF GROWTH AND CONFLICT, 1965–1975

KU was a widely respected institution in 1965, but it was entering a period of manifold change, much of it quite difficult. Like many other universities, it faced rapid growth in enrollments and a rising tide of student protest and conflict. Enrollments doubled in the 1960s and graduate and undergraduate programs proliferated. Curricular experiments were tried and research funding was increased. At the same time, however, state funding failed to keep pace with growth and there was turnover at the highest levels of university leadership. A lack of planning characterized the university response to many of these challenges.

The 1960s became a time associated in the public mind with stu-dent unrest at American colleges and universities, and this was cer-tainly true of KU. Lawrence was a focal point of protest against the war in Vietnam and in support of civil rights for African Americans, women, and other groups facing discrimination and exclusion in American life. As William Tuttle and Kathryn Nemeth Tuttle demonstrate in Chapters 6 and 7, the years between 1965 and the 1990s witnessed a wave of student activism connected directly to these issues, cresting in a dramatic series of incidents in the spring and summer of 1970, when the Kansas Union was struck by arsonists and the national guard was summoned to Lawrence. This placed the university prominently among the national sites of large-scale student protest, a notoriety that KU administrators and city leaders hardly relished. Yet it also demonstrated that opposition to racism, sexism, imperialist war, and many other forms of cruelty was alive and flourishing in America's heartland. Protesters in Lawrence recalled the city's antislavery origins, a local tradition of inspired resistance to oppression dating back to John Brown and earlier.

All this, of course, proved quite shocking to many Kansas residents, who had difficulty imagining that such disorder could occur in a traditionally rural midwestern state, even if most KU students grew up in urban or suburban settings.[2] As Burdett Loomis indicates in Chapter 2, it did little to enhance the university's public image, at least among the state's largely conservative electorate. It did make Lawrence an appealing destination, however, for young people interested in alternative lifestyles and political activism, contributing to a growing counterculture movement in the Oread neighborhood just east of the campus.[3] This was a particular mark of distinction for the university, one that some Kansans may not have appreciated.

There was a lot more occurring at KU during the 1960s and 1970s besides student protest, however. It was also a time of frenetic growth for almost all institutions of higher education, and in this regard the University of Kansas was not an exception. The university's overall pattern of growth can be seen in Table I-1. In 1960, KU's Lawrence enrollment was 8,711, and in the next 20 years it nearly tripled. Growth was distributed across both graduate and undergraduate programs. Enrollment also grew at the University of Kansas Medical Center (KUMC), if a bit slower than in Lawrence. Perhaps most notable, the number of graduate programs more than doubled during this period, with increases especially evident at the doctoral level. This was a point of concern registered by members of the visiting committee of the North Central Association in 1969, who commented that such "rampant expansion" was largely uncoordinated and had occurred with relatively meager resources. They observed that the quality of new doctoral programs was highly uneven, and that library resources lagged behind the

The Kansas Union ablaze in the night, an iconic image from the tumultuous spring of 1970.

Table I-1: University Enrollment, 1965–2013

Year	Laurence Head Count	Proportion Undergraduate	Proportion Multicultural*	Proportion Resident	Proportion International	KUMC Head Count	Proportion Female	Proportion Full Time	Residing on Campus
1965	13,565	79.1%	na	73.3%	4.7%**	1,199	36.5%	79.2%	33.6%
1970	17,947	79.4%	na	69.8%	5.6%**	1,446	40.1%	76.9%	26.6%
1975	21,738	76.1%	na	78.2%	5.6%**	1,803	43.4%	75.8%	20.5%
1980	24,466	79.4%	na	73.4%	5.9%	2,279	48.4%	74.7%	29.1%
1985	24,774	73.3%	19.8%	70.3%	6.8%	2,367	48.5%	76.7%	26.3%
1990	26,436	73.7%	18.7%	65.6%	7.3%	2,473	50.8%	78.4%	21.3%
1995	25,036	72.2%	23.3%	67.3%	7.1%	2,603	50.8%	77.6%	18.4%
2000	25,920	76%	18.9%	67.7%	6.1%	2,409	52.9%	78.9%	19.9%
2005	26,934	77.6%	20.7%	69.8%	5.6%	2,690	50.9%	79.9%	18.2%
2010	26,266	75.6%	23.9%	69.1%	8.1%	3,196	49.4%	86.2%	17.9%
2013	24,435	76.7%	26.7%	65.5%	9.2%	3,349	49.8%	86.4%	20.7%

*Includes African American, Asian American, Hispanic American, and American Indian students, as well as international students; data on students in each of these groups are unavailable prior to 1985.

**Estimates made from limited data or proximate year.

The new Fraser Hall under construction, 1966. The old one, a campus landmark, had been built in 1872.

rapid escalation in graduate work. Rising numbers of students were taught by graduate teaching assistants (GTAs), and too many graduate students held GTA appointments as a sole source of support.[4] In short, growth had occurred in a somewhat pell-mell fashion, and insufficient attention was given to quality of instruction, at both the graduate and undergraduate levels.

KU was hardly the only institution to experience such growing pains, as similar problems were evident at many universities during the 1960s. Much of this was due to demographic change associated with the postwar baby boom generation, but it also reflected improved high school graduation rates and a growing interest in going to college.[5] The physical plant expanded as well, especially with respect to student housing and classroom space. When another North Central Association accreditation team visited in 1975, its report noted that many of the problems reported five years earlier had not been effectively addressed. The libraries continued to struggle in cataloging growing acquisitions, and laboratory facilities for teaching and research were described as "austere." Contending with growth and campus controversies, the university had failed to make much headway in resolving some of the major questions it faced as an institution of higher learning.[6]

A Medical School lecture in 1972, using blackboards to display diagrams and concepts to a large lecture class, in an era before digital technology was used in classrooms.

Turnover in university leadership during this period did not help matters. Chancellor W. Clarke Wescoe's departure in 1969 came just as the university entered a time of heightened conflict and controversy, and his successor, Laurence Chalmers, remained in office just three years. As Susan Twombly suggests in Chapter 1, these changes contributed to a sense of uncertainty on campus. Chalmers had led the university through a tumultuous time but was widely viewed as ineffective. By the time Archie Dykes arrived in 1973 as his replacement, the university's public reputation had suffered considerably, especially within the state.[7]

This did not mean, however, that important academic reforms were forgotten or that faculty research failed to move forward. As Joshua Rosenbloom notes in Chapter 5, a number of significant research initiatives gained momentum in the 1960s and continued to advance into the following decade, most of them initiated under Chancellors Frank Murphy and Wescoe. Additionally, under Wescoe's leadership, the

Two KU students take in a rainy football game in 1972.

University of Kansas Endowment Association (KUEA), the nation's first such organization at a state university, launched a major fund-raising campaign, Program for Progress, ultimately raising nearly $20 million (about $120 million in 2013 dollars). It was the second-largest total for such a campaign in the country then, clearly demonstrating the willingness of alumni and others to support the university. This would be an especially important facet of KU's success in years to come.[8] In the 1960s, the university also attempted a bold experiment in curriculum reform, popularly referred to as "Colleges-within-the-College." In an effort to personalize student experiences on a rapidly expanding campus and to allay the alienation of large classes, students were assigned to residential colleges where they could build relationships and work together on common problems. As James Woelfel indicates in Chapter 3, however, it was not adequately supported by the university. The idea had been tried at Wayne State, Florida State, Michigan, and other institutions, but it encountered significant implementation problems at KU. This was yet another sign of the difficulties endured during this period.[9]

If the university did relatively little to enhance its academic reputation during the later 1960s and early 1970s, Jayhawk athletic teams certainly helped to keep it in the national limelight, as Bernie Kish

shows in Chapter 8. Basketball, of course, was the university's traditional strength, and under Coach Ted Owens the Jayhawks won five
conference titles in nine years and advanced to the Final Four of the
NCAA tournament in 1971 and 1974. The football team also contributed to the university's athletic renown. After finishing second in the
Big Eight in 1967, it won a conference title the following year and
played in the Orange Bowl, narrowly losing to Penn State. The team
also went to bowl games in 1971 and 1975. As a result of these exploits,
the Jayhawks remained familiar to sports fans across the country.[10]

REGAINING MOMENTUM: 1975–1985

Under the leadership of Chancellor Archie Dykes, the university
gained a measure of stability that it had lacked since the late 1960s.
Dykes focused on restoring KU's reputation across the state and with
the legislature in Topeka, and, as indicated in Table I-2, state funding
for the university increased substantially. At the same time, KU began
to address many of the problems that had been noted in accreditation
reports, particularly in 1974. There was a more consistent approach
to planning, and university facilities underwent significant enhancement. Even though enrollments continued to grow, reaching almost

Table I-2: University Funding Sources, State Appropriation and Tuition,
1965–2013 (in thousands)

Year	Lawrence Appropriation (in 2013 dollars)	KUMC Appropriation (in 2013 dollars)	Tuition & Fees Total (in 2013 dollars)	Tuition & Fees Percentage
1965	$12,675 ($93,737)	$5,848 ($43,248)	$3,880 ($25,403)	17.1%
1975	$30,945 ($133,994)	$18,483 ($80,032)	$11,679 ($50,571)	19%
1985	$76,673 ($166,078)	$40,860 ($88,505)	$25,646 ($55,551)	25.1%
1995	$107,562 ($164,497)	$78,870 ($120,617)	$61,668 ($94,310)	36.4%
2005	$136,397 ($162,774)	$101,620 ($121,272)	$145,194 ($173,273)	51.6%
2013	$141,003	$106,352	$262,515	51.5%

Ivy-covered Marvin Hall in 1970.

The Regents Center in the 1970s. Faculty members greeted prospective students in a converted elementary school classroom.

27,000 in Lawrence and Kansas City combined by 1980, expansion was much slower thereafter. This permitted renewed attention to improving the quality of teaching and scholarship, which enhanced the lives of students and faculty alike, a theme taken up methodically by Dykes's successor, Gene Budig. When yet another accreditation team visited the university in 1984, signs of progress were readily evident, although a number of important troubles remained.[11]

Shortly after he arrived in Kansas, Dykes realized the magnitude of problems faced by the university. Public confidence in the institution had declined, an issue faced by much of higher education in the later 1970s, and political support had weakened. Dykes was especially worried about the future prospects of flagship research universities such as KU, which needed greater support than other institutions to pursue excellence in teaching and scholarship. The state's funding formula, driven largely by enrollments, did not take into account the higher cost of graduate programs, especially at the doctoral level. And demographic projections indicated that a decline in enrollments was quickly approaching with the end of the baby boom era.[12]

Dykes set to work on all these fronts, but particularly on the public relations and political questions, soon becoming a popular spokesman for higher education and KU in particular, as noted in Chapters 1 and 2. University budgets were gradually enhanced and faculty salaries improved somewhat. A Center for Research in the Humanities was established at the urging of influential faculty members. Significant enhancements were made to the Medical School and University Hospital in Kansas City, Kansas.[13] In 1975, KU further augmented its presence in the greater Kansas City area by offering classes at a former elementary school in the Shawnee Mission School District. Named the Regents Center, it enrolled more than 1,300 students in its first year, marking a fast start to the university's presence in booming Johnson County. By the mid-1980s, enrollments had outgrown this original site and the university was searching for a new campus near the newly built Johnson County Community College in Overland Park.[14]

A year after Dykes left KU in 1980 for a leadership position in the insurance industry, Gene Budig arrived as chancellor to face a number of issues that still remained unresolved. The faculty was getting older, and since so many had been hired during the rapid growth of the 1960s and 1970s, the university was approaching high "tenure density," permitting relatively few new hires. Research funding had increased but lagged other institutions nationally and even within the Big Eight, KU's geographic peer group. Although the KUEA had managed to sustain much of the momentum generated by the Program for Progress, remaining a national leader in university fund-raising, it had gone more than a decade without a major campaign (total asset figures are provided in Table I-3). A similar period had passed since a major curricular reform was undertaken at KU, and the economic recession of the early 1980s threatened to wipe out gains in state funding that had been realized in the 1970s.[15] At the same time, certain groups of students remained restive about issues dating to the 1960s,

Table I-3: KU Endowment Association, Total Assets (in thousands)

Year	Dollar Amount (in 2013 dollars)	Year	Dollar Amount (in 2013 dollars)
1965	$13,234 ($97,872)	1995	$420,337 ($642,523)
1970	$27,021 ($162,235)	2000	$952,400 ($1,288,433)
1975	$47,358 ($205,358)	2005	$1,143,517 ($1,326,006)
1980	$80,806 ($228,451)	2010	$1,261,077 ($1,347,254)
1985	$151,620 ($328,262)	2013	$1,562,679
1990	$258,945 ($461,627)		

UN ambassador George H. W. Bush speaking with KU students in 1972.

especially discrimination against minority groups, defined in terms of race and ethnicity and gender and sexual orientation.[16]

A number of these issues surfaced in the North Central Association accreditation report of 1984, but the question of minority students received especially critical attention. Noting that these students often felt isolated, the visiting team suggested that "there is not enough cultural and social support in the university environment to help them succeed academically." The visitors also reported that some students believed that "the curriculum mainly reflects majority cultural views and history" and "is silent on minority perspectives." Much of the faculty, meanwhile, was "seen as insensitive to minority concerns." The report also noted that the university had made very slow progress in attracting minority faculty members. Students were reportedly often unaware of the university's Office of Minority Affairs, and the accreditation visiting team suggested that it be given a considerably larger role in freshman orientation.[17] On questions of diversity, it seems, KU still had a ways to go, with respect to both students and the faculty that served them.

The Budig administration began to address these questions, initiating an effort to revise the university's core curriculum to feature a greater emphasis on social and cultural diversity, among other questions. Greater emphasis was placed on hiring minority faculty members, although budget problems and tenure density made this difficult. Budig also launched a major fund-raising effort, Campaign Kansas, undertaken to address budget questions and strengthen the university's endowment, a principal source of resources to enhance the campus and attract more faculty and students. Starting in 1988, some $265 million was raised by 1992, exceeding most of the campaign's goals and pushing the endowment's total assets past $326 million ($550 million in 2013 dollars). KUEA's success helped the university achieve a more secure financial footing, providing it with more than $44 million in 1991 ($75 million in 2013 dollars).[18] As indicated in Table I-3, the endowment's assets roughly doubled in size in the ten years following 1985, a considerably higher rate of growth than the previous decade.

The university had many academic strengths that needed enhancement as well, including nationally prominent programs in applied and clinical psychology, medicinal and pharmaceutical chemistry, and remote sensing engineering, among others. Fund-raising helped to highlight and enhance KU's points of scholarly distinction. Area studies programs focusing on Latin America, Africa, and East Asia also were quite vibrant, along with the study of languages, as Megan Greene shows in Chapter 4. Library resources were ranked first in the Big Eight by the mid-1980s, bolstered by the growing collections of the Spencer Research Library and the Spencer Art Museum, which opened in 1968 and 1977, respectively. As a consequence, KU became well known for the quality of its faculty in various humanist disciplines, buoyed by KUEA resources, the success of area studies, and a newly endowed Hall Center for the Humanities in 1982.[19]

KU students in the 1980s began to see some of the benefits of automated record-keeping, as registration gradually shifted away from the laborious process of "enrollment," registering in person at Hoch Auditorium or Allen Fieldhouse, enduring long lines and interminable waits in occasionally insufferable heat. Familiar institutions such as the KU Information Service or Joe's Donuts on Ninth Street made student life easier, and widely frequented campus haunts such as The Hawk provided memorable diversions for many.[20] The basketball Jayhawks continued to be successful, even if their football brethren experienced relatively few triumphs during these years. Annual contests against the University of Missouri and Kansas State, however, rarely failed to generate a good deal of excitement and even capped an occasional victorious season.[21]

A computer science lab in Snow Hall in the 1980s.

The days of mass and sometimes violent protest remained a vivid memory in the 1980s, as groups of students and faculty demanded changes in the curriculum, better services for minority students, and greater minority representation on the faculty and staff. At the same time, KUEA came under attack from students calling for divestment from companies doing business in South Africa.[22] For the most part, however, students were increasingly career oriented, and enrollments in business and professional schools grew faster than in such popular majors of earlier years as education and the liberal arts.[23] The student body was changing, and not necessarily in ways that much of the faculty and the university's more-activist alums may have cared for. For many other Kansans, on the other hand, the career and professional orientation of many KU students was doubtless just fine.

BUILDING A NATIONAL PROFILE: 1985–1995

The decade following 1985 was a time of relative stability, at least regarding growth, when the university was able to focus on addressing concerns about quality of instruction, research, and service, the core elements of its mission. Gene Budig's 14-year tenure as chancellor provided a degree of consistency in leadership that KU had not known since the Ernest H. Lindley years in the 1920s and 1930s. It also was a

Anschutz Science Library under construction, 1989.

time of rapid technological change, as personal computing and integrated information systems became ubiquitous, permeating the campus. Fire wrecked a familiar campus landmark and Dutch elm disease
destroyed the fulsome canopy over Jayhawk Boulevard, but more than
$100 million (about $185 million in 2013 dollars) in new building
altered the material footprint of the university. Fund-raising stepped
up with a major capital campaign, and the number of unclassified staff
members increased substantially. Additionally, and not least, the men's
basketball Jayhawks won a national championship in 1988, heralding
another era of cage excellence in the venerable arena nicknamed
"The Phog."

Automation of registration turned out to be just one of the early
steps in a much-larger transformation of information processing and
retrieval at KU during these years. In 1987, the library's catalog was
placed online, totaling more than 1.4 million records. Mainframe computing capacity was enhanced, partly with private donations through
KUEA. At the same time, the entire campus was wired and "micro-
computing" was introduced in stages, eventually linking the Lawrence
and KUMC campuses. By 1993, more than 5,000 desktop computers
had been distributed to offices across the university, launching a minor
revolution in the way that students, faculty, and staff members did their
work.[24] At about the same time, the university community began using
a new electronic form of communication that went by the odd name of

Table I-4: Lawrence Campus, Staffing Profile, 1975–2013

Year	Full-Time Faculty Members	Faculty Administrators	Unclassified Professional and Academic Staff	Classified Employees	Student Employees
1975	890	45	750	1,680	3,716
1985	967	46	775	1,639	3,883
1995	999	31	1,081	1,646	3,998
2005	955	41	1,966	1,411	4,532
2013	1,095	48	2,141	1,206	4,782

Data from 1965 are not available for these categories; there were approximately 670 full-time faculty members at that time.

"e-mail." Even though students had to hike over to the computer center to sign up for an account in 1994, it grew rapidly in popularity.[25]

The staffing configuration of the university changed during these years in a number of respects, as indicated in Table I-4. Enrollments edged upward in the early 1990s, and the size of the tenure-track faculty failed to keep pace. Restive over relatively low salaries, the faculty narrowly defeated a proposal to unionize, as pointed out in Chapter 1. Between 1984 and 1992, the proportion of the instructional staff in tenure-track positions declined from 64 to 57 percent, and the number holding GTA appointments increased from 26 percent to about a third.[26] Reflecting their greater numbers, GTAs across the campus agitated for a collective bargaining agreement in the 1990s, which the university opposed. In 1995, however, the right of GTAs to be represented by a union and bargain for wages and other benefits was granted in an arbitration hearing, leading to the first such contract in the university's history.[27] At about the same time, on the other hand, the total number of tenure-track faculty members increased to nearly a thousand, slightly more than ten years earlier. Somewhat lighter teaching loads—to allow for more research—and additional students meant that their share of the university's instructional obligations went down.

Also during this period, the number of unclassified staff members witnessed a 28 percent increase, adding nearly 200 new positions. Many of these were advisers or counselors for students or administrative assistants working in offices across campus, along with technology support services. Research staff expanded even more dramatically, by nearly 60 percent, to 100, while the classified staff grew by 138, an 8 percent increase.[28] Altogether, the number of people employed by

The pedestrian plaza in front of Wescoe Hall became known as "Wescoe Beach" and was a prime location for students to meet, hang out, and discuss issues of the day.

KU was increasing steadily and labor relations on campus were becoming more complicated. A growing human resources department kept track of all this. In pursuit of greater efficiency and accountability, the university became more bureaucratic and businesslike or corporate. In this respect, KU's experience reflected national trends, as the size and complexity of its organizational structure kept pace with peer institutions.[29]

University employees and students needed places to work and learn, of course, and this era also saw many physical enhancements to the Lawrence campus. Some 34 projects were undertaken in a nine-year period, including such major additions as the Anschutz Library in 1989, the Dole Center for Human Development in 1990, and the Lied Center in 1993 and major renovations of both the Kansas and the Burge Unions in the same year. Hoch Auditorium burned in 1991 with an estimated $31 million in damages ($53 million in 2013 dollars) and had to be rebuilt. Additionally, the Regents Center moved to the new Edwards Campus in Overland Park, providing the university with an expanded presence in suburban Kansas City. The university also offered courses at the Capitol Center in Topeka, to serve both ends of the state's northeast "growth corridor" at the close of the century.[30] These new facilities all enhanced KU's capacity to provide high-quality instruction and world-class research and service to a wider clientele in northeast Kansas. They also made the campus a bit more congested, especially on the crowded south slope of Mount Oread.

All of this required money, and during these years the university budget increased steadily as well. In constant dollars, KU education expenditures increased by 16 percent in the ten years following 1985,

Hoch Auditorium burning, June 15, 1991.

and capital outlays also grew with the flurry of construction projects in the early 1990s.[31] The state's funding framework shifted away from strictly enrollment-driven formulas, but appropriations failed to keep pace with growth in employment or credit hours. KUEA fund-raising helped, of course, but most of the resulting resources were earmarked for particular purposes. Faculty and staff salaries kept pace with inflation, yet still lagged behind those of peer institutions. To keep abreast of rising costs, in that case, the university relied increasingly on tuition as a source of revenue. Between 1984 and 1994, the proportion of KU's budget drawn from tuition and fees grew from 25 to nearly 37 percent, about a 50 percent increase.[32] This is clearly evident in Table I-2. If students were gaining a higher-quality learning experience from the many enhancements made during these years, they were paying for a bigger part of it.

General education had been revamped in 1987, with greater attention to questions of diversity and equity, but students still exercised considerable discretion in how they satisfied requirements. As in the past, KU's academic culture was characterized by a good deal of decentralization, allowing colleges and schools significant autonomy in curricular terms. Efforts were made to rehabilitate or eliminate programs with low enrollments or tenuous faculty support, with majors such as

A quilting exhibition at the Spencer Museum in 1981.

atmospheric sciences, comparative literature, history and philosophy of science, and geophysics being phased out or merged with other programs.[33] The Budig administration proposed the creation of "teaching professorships" to honor faculty members who exhibited outstanding commitment to and skill in classroom instruction. KU had traditionally celebrated outstanding teachers with annual awards, but this was a new level of recognition. With KUEA funding, these became "Chancellor's Club" chairs awarded to faculty members with demonstrated accomplishment in this regard, in addition to their other professional obligations, including research.[34]

KU had long featured a relatively open admissions policy, especially for Kansas residents, which sometimes meant that it did not fare well in comparisons with more selective institutions, particularly those on either coast. It still enjoyed a good academic reputation, however, and was consistently rated highly by various college guides read by prospective students and parents. One national publication described it as among the nation's best state universities, calling it the finest of the Big Eight. KU had the biggest library system of its regional peers and was still cited for its accomplished humanities faculty. The university's traditional strengths in clinical psychology and in human development and disability studies, including special education, continued to

A student celebrates his heritage with a sombrero during the 2003 commencement.

be important, along with research in the pharmaceutical disciplines. Professional school programs in law, medicine, engineering, education, and social work were well regarded in their respective fields.[35] Even though KU was hardly a leader in research funding during the Budig years, the quality of its academic offerings continued to be formidable.

Despite its many academic strengths, the university still contended with questions of diversity and equity. The proportion of KU students from suburban Johnson County and similar areas grew steadily in the late 1980s and early 1990s, and minority student numbers increased slowly. In 1991, the Budig administration created a $1 million fund for scholarships to recruit and support minority students. Minority faculty members were in even shorter supply.[36] The 1994 North Central Association accreditation team noted the need for added attention to this question, which would continue to be a focal point for the university in years to come.[37] As William Tuttle and Kathryn Nemeth Tuttle show, active groups of minority students helped to animate the Lawrence campus student body, with organizations for Asian American, Native American, African American, and Hispanic American students holding regular meetings and occasional marches or rallies to make their voices heard. For the most part, these students and their faculty/staff

Hillary Clinton speaking with reporters on Campanile Hill, October 1992.

supporters campaigned for a greater presence in the curriculum and additional resources for the study of their history and culture.[38] Not all of KU's other students appreciated the significance of these questions, however. In 1992, one reported being "shocked by the polarization of the minority students and the white students," and "that KU was so dominated by white suburbanites." He became active in helping establish an organization to help bridge differences across predominantly black and white Hellenic organizations.[39] Efforts such as this were emblematic of issues facing the campus. It took time, but eventually the university community responded.

There was also continued attention to women's rights and questions related to sexuality on the campus, as seen in Chapters 6 and 7. A consensual sexual harassment policy was adopted in 1994, following an incident involving a student and faculty member in the law school.[40] The year 1992 was declared the "year of the woman" at the Democratic National Convention, and Hillary Clinton spoke to a crowd of more than 10,000 students in the fall at KU, focusing to a large extent on women's issues.[41] The Emily Taylor Women's Resource Center, which had opened in the 1960s, expanded its offerings of seminars and lectures on women's issues. A small but vocal group of students also advocated for the recognition of issues facing gay, lesbian, and transsexual

Coach Roy Williams speaks with players during a game, 1995.

students and faculty members, issues that had been debated since the late 1970s.[42] Beginning in the late 1980s, the campus Gay-Lesbian Alliance began holding annual Gay Pride Week celebrations, following national developments in the gay rights movement.[43] Questions related to gender and sexuality would continue to be important topics of contention on campus in the years to come.

Finally, the late 1980s and early 1990s was a momentous time in KU athletics. First, the whole Jayhawk nation celebrated the surprising success of the 1988 men's basketball team, which won the national championship under Coach Larry Brown, propelled by a remarkable performance by Danny Manning. Brown left shortly afterward, and Manning followed him to the NBA, but the proud Jayhawk basketball tradition continued under the tutelage of Roy Williams, who arrived from North Carolina in 1988. Under his leadership, KU won five Big Eight titles in seven seasons and went to the NCAA Tournament each year except his first, when it was on probation. At the same time, the women's basketball team also experienced a good deal of success, advancing to the NCAA tournament six times and the Women's National Invitational Tournament once under the guidance of longtime coach Marian Washington. The football team was also a highlight during these years, going to the Aloha Bowl in Hawaii in 1992 and 1995, beating Brigham Young University and UCLA, respectively. Annual contests with Kansas State and Missouri, of course, continued to be high points of the fall semester.[44]

PURSUING EXCELLENCE IN RESEARCH AND TEACHING, 1995–2005

In 1994, Gene Budig left KU to become president of major league baseball's American League, and in late 1995 Robert Hemenway was appointed as the university's 16th chancellor, having served in a similar role at the University of Kentucky. Arriving in 1996, Hemenway moved quickly to address a range of issues at KU, including an effort to streamline and focus the university's management of external research funding. He also launched initiatives to improve teaching and make the institution more "student friendly," and KU succeeded in gaining greater control of tuition and improving admissions criteria. Following in Budig's footsteps, he undertook a major fund-raising campaign with KUEA. As an overall goal, Hemenway asserted that KU should aim to become one of the 25 best public research universities in the country, while acknowledging that the competition for such recognition was steep. At the same time, he guided KU through a number of

Chancellor Hemenway (right) speaks with longtime KU radio announcer Max Falkenstien.

troubling episodes regarding questions of academic freedom and the politics of education.

As Joshua Rosenbloom demonstrates in Chapter 5, the Hemenway years witnessed a substantial increase in research funding at KU, expressed both in absolute terms and as a percentage of all federally sponsored research at American universities. This was partly a result of consolidating responsibility for development and management of externally funded research in a single entity, the University of Kansas Center for Research. As Rosenbloom shows, this process began almost immediately upon Hemenway's arrival and was complete within a year, along with other changes in the administration of research activities, devoting significantly greater resources to new initiatives and improved proposal development and grant management.[45] The result was a momentous and sustained enhancement of research activity on KU's principal campuses in Lawrence and Kansas City, substantially improving the university's standing among its institutional peers.

Hemenway also undertook a reorganization of the university's central administration, establishing a provost model of leadership that permitted focusing resources on academic priorities. Following months of meetings, focus groups, and interviews with faculty, staff, and students, the change was made in 1997, as longtime Vice Chancellor for Academic Affairs David Shulenburger assumed the role of provost. With oversight over all operational aspects of the institution, the provost's office could set priorities intended to advance the cause of excellence in research and teaching. Some observers suggested that the change also made KU more "student centered" in that the administration could be more open to student concerns.[46] The goal was to make the university more responsive to the ever-changing world around it.

Hemenway's administration pressed forward on other fronts too. As Burdett Loomis points out in Chapter 2, working closely with the legislature and Governor Bill Graves, KU and other Kansas Board of Regents institutions secured passage of a measure giving the university greater control of tuition revenues, a long-standing goal of university leaders. This permitted added flexibility in the use of these funds to address academic priorities and opened the door to further revenue enhancement through tuition and fees.[47] Greater faculty involvement in teaching had been evident as the number of professorial positions increased and reliance on GTAs for teaching undergraduate students declined. Altogether, lower-division credit hours taught by GTAs decreased from 42 to 24 percent between 1993 and 2002.[48] Also during this period, KU and other Regents institutions succeeded in gaining

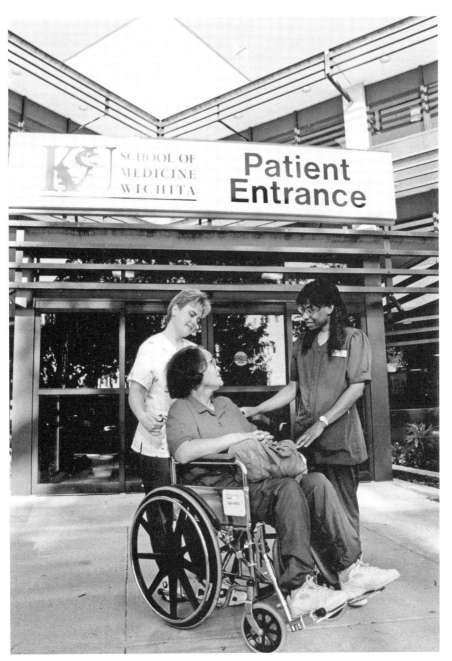

At the School of Medicine, Wichita campus, a patient with staff members.

approval of "qualified" admissions criteria, which set clear guidelines for admission to the university.[49] Beginning in 2001, this barred students with very weak academic preparation from being admitted to the university, although they still could attend community colleges and transfer to KU if successful. All of these steps helped to enhance KU's reputation as a flagship public research institution and affirm its status in the national rankings that had become so critical at the time.

Hemenway also worked with the legislature to gain greater autonomy for the University of Kansas Hospital, allowing it to compete more effectively with other health care providers in Greater Kansas City. In 1998, the hospital became an independent entity, receiving no funding from the state.[50] Hemenway aimed to significantly augment research at KUMC and helped to initiate a push for the Medical School to become designated as a National Cancer Center, an ambitious goal that would take seven years to achieve. Much of the work in raising the research profile of the school was accomplished under the leadership of Dr. Barbara Atkinson, who became dean in 2002 and executive vice chancellor of the Medical Center campus in 2004.[51] This would pay significant dividends in the years to come.

On other fronts, Hemenway's administration took decisive steps toward improving the quality of teaching at KU. In 1997, the chancellor oversaw the founding of the Center for Teaching Excellence (CTE), which was charged with providing KU faculty members with resources to improve teaching. Distinction in instruction had long been a focal point at KU, of course, but the establishment of CTE gave it added significance. In the years to follow, CTE hosted regular faculty workshops and other events to discuss instructional enhancements and launched an annual "Teaching Summit" at the start of the academic year.[52] In 2003, a report by the National Survey of Student Engagement, conducted in conjunction with a project titled "Documenting Effective Educational Practice" (DEEP), cited KU for specific strengths, including a highly collegial environment, an emphasis on excellence in undergraduate teaching, and data-driven decision making. In particular, the DEEP Report noted the role of CTE in promoting sustained reflection on the quality of teaching and continual improvement, along with the support of the university's senior leadership. Indicative of this, the report also noted that Chancellor Hemenway himself regularly taught a course in American literature to undergraduates.[53]

As was true in other eras of KU's history, state funding had shifted notably by the end of this period, partly due to the economic downturn associated with the 2001 attack on the World Trade Center. But

Students at the 2002 commencement.

the resources available to the university increased substantially because of other sources of revenue. The impact of these developments
can be seen in Tables I-2 and I-3, which show continued growth in
both tuition as a source of revenue and the total assets of KUEA. In the
decade beginning in 1993, per-student per-year state appropriation
funds declined from $6,100 to $5,600 in inflation-adjusted dollars,
a loss of some $12 million. At the same time, tuition increases added
$26 million, and annual support from endowment sources increased
from $55 million to $83 million in 2003 dollars. Research and training activities funded from external sources nearly doubled, growing
from $128 million to $257 million in the same period, again in constant 2003 dollars. And finally, funds from "Crumbling Classrooms"
legislation in 1996 contributed $48 million to renovations on campus,
including conversion of JR Pearson Hall from a dormitory to a new
home for the School of Education, improvements to studios, stages,
and other facilities of the Music and Theater programs in Murphy
Hall, and a long list of other projects. Capping all of this, the Hemenway administration launched a major fund-raising campaign in 1998,
Kansas First, which collected more than $650 million by the time it
ended in 2004 (about $800 million in 2013 dollars). As a part of it, the
Dole Institute of Politics was dedicated on the university's West Campus on July 22, 2003, built with donations and support from KUEA.[54]
Despite gradually declining state support, assets available to KU grew
considerably, enabling the university to add faculty members, improve
the campus environment, and provide greater support to students
needing assistance.

    Budget woes did prove upsetting to students, however, as tuition
hikes were widely discussed and debated. In 2002, 200 students gathered to protest proposed tuition hikes in front of Wescoe Hall, noting that one proposal had KU tuition doubling in the space of four
years. Some even complained to the Regents.[55] But university leaders,
especially David Shulenburger, reached out and gained the approval
of student representatives for the increases. The results included enhancements to the quality of instruction.

    A new generation of faculty and the growing popularity of the In-
ternet contributed to changes in teaching and learning.[56] In 1999,
KU started using Blackboard, an online portal for course materials
and student discussion of questions that instructors posed for them.
Online resources for the libraries expanded rapidly, including e-books
and journal articles, which were rapidly integrated into courses across
the campus, especially by younger faculty members. Over $4 million

was used to upgrade classroom technology after 2003, and additional resources were used by the various schools and colleges to augment these funds. In 2003, the Kyou (now myKU) portal was opened on the university's webpage, providing a convenient point of reference for students and faculty in one place for all sorts of vital information.[57] One important facet of the World Wide Web was that all of the growing array of KU services and information resources that were made available in this fashion could be accessed from anywhere. In this respect, KU truly was becoming global.

Building upon the work of previous administrations, Hemenway continued the push to achieve greater diversity among KU's faculty and staff. Additional funding was devoted to need-based tuition scholarships, totaling an additional $5 million by 2004. This contributed to an 11 percent increase in minority students in the same period, a record increase for KU at the time. The number of minority faculty members grew as well, by nearly 40 percent in a ten-year span, from 10 to 14 percent, and women on the faculty increased from 29 to 39 percent.[58] While the numbers of such students and faculty members still remained low, especially compared to many of KU's peer institutions, the campus environment was slowly becoming more multicultural in ways that were plainly visible. KU still had a ways to go, but progress during these years demonstrated that change was possible.

Some aspects of life at the university remained much the same, of course. Students still enjoyed their many social diversions, and in 2003 KU was named number 9 on *Playboy* magazine's list of the nation's party schools. It was the university's first appearance on the list since 1987, when it ranked 26, but the honor was dubious to say the least.[59] Also that year, the university produced the first calendar featuring "KU Women of Distinction," a response to similar publications featuring pictures of KU coeds that had appeared since at least the late 1990s.[60] Organizations such as the Black Student Union, the Hispanic American Leadership Organization, the Asian American Student Association, and the First Nations Student Association represented the diverse interests of various minority groups in the student body, celebrating cultural milestones and agitating for curricular diversity and other causes.[61] Queers and Allies, the principal gay, lesbian, bisexual, and transsexual group on campus, upheld the annual tradition of Gay Pride Week and other activities, often drawing a crowd of more than a thousand for the Drag Show.[62] Added to this, of course, were the traditional haunts and pastimes of KU students across generations, including an expansive Greek community, although business at Joe's

The view from inside Joe's Bakery in the 1970s.

Donuts declined steadily until it finally closed in 2007.[63] Altogether, a wide array of events and social activities defined a campus scene that continued to be vibrant into the twenty-first century.

Whatever their differences, however, KU students still had reason to cheer with the success of KU athletics, especially the men's basketball team. This started with the university's affiliation with the newly formed Big 12 in 1996, which added four Texas schools to the old Big Eight conference. With the guidance of Coach Roy Williams, the men's basketball Jayhawks won four conference championships in seven years and advanced to the national championship game in 2003, losing to Syracuse. Following that game, Williams left the university to become head coach at North Carolina, his alma mater. He was replaced by Bill Self, who helped to continue KU's winning tradition. The university's football team experienced success toward the end of this period under the leadership of Coach Mark Mangino, who arrived at KU in 2001. The gridiron Jayhawks went to the Tangerine Bowl in 2003 and the Fort Worth Bowl in 2005, losing the first and winning the second.[64]

The Hemenway administration also had to contend with questions of academic freedom and educational policy in an increasingly conservative state political environment. Controversies erupted over the teaching of human sexuality at KU and biological science in the public schools of Kansas, both occurring during the opening years of the new century. The first of these issues concerned a class taught by Professor Dennis Dailey of the School of Social Welfare, Human Sexuality in Everyday Life, which upset certain students and state politicians in 2003. The university, however, firmly stood by the principle of Professor Dailey's academic freedom to conduct his course in the manner he saw fit.[65] A year later, statewide elections for the Kansas Board of Education resulted in a 6–4 majority for religious conservatives, who rejected the theory of evolution as a matter of principle. Chancellor Hemenway had appointed a task force that led to creating a Center for Science Education, with faculty representation from both the sciences and education. Started in 2001, the new center was intended in part to inform public discussions of science and its role in education, in ways that would augment the cause of scientific integrity in education throughout the state, a mission especially pertinent after 2004. Ideological conflict with conservative politicians would continue to be an issue at KU in the years to come.[66]

TRANSITION TO BOLD ASPIRATIONS, 2005–2015

When Robert Hemenway announced his decision to step down as chancellor, a national search brought Dr. Bernadette Gray-Little to Lawrence in 2009 from the University of North Carolina to succeed him. Having served as provost and chief academic officer at Chapel Hill, she was the first woman and the first African American to serve as chancellor at KU. Her appointment marked a new chapter in the university's history and symbolized its commitment to diversity and openness to change. Following a time of transition, under her leadership the university continued to build upon the legacy left by Hemenway and his predecessors, moving forward in research, teaching excellence, and service to the state. Gray-Little also helped launch a major fund-raising campaign, Far Above, which quickly exceeded records established by earlier KUEA campaigns (see Table I-3 for figures). Even though her impact on KU is still not complete, there can be no doubt about her determination to see the institution reach new heights in the years ahead.

The years immediately following 2005 marked a number of important changes in the university's leadership. Provost David Shulenburger left KU in 2006 for the National Association of State Universities and Land-Grant Colleges in Washington, DC, and was replaced by Richard Lariviere, who arrived from the University of Texas. After helping to shepherd the university through state budget cuts following the economic downturn of 2008 and leading organizational changes in graduate studies and fine arts, he left KU to take the presidency of the University of Oregon. Lariviere's departure permitted Chancellor Gray-Little to appoint a new provost, and the post was eventually filled by Jeffrey Vitter, a distinguished computer scientist who had held a similar position at Texas A&M. With Vitter's arrival in 2010, KU had a new team at the highest levels of leadership.[67]

As the new chancellor and provost started preparing for a revitalization of KU's pursuit of teaching and research excellence, the academic world was shocked in 2011 by news that two members of the prestigious American Association of Universities (AAU) were compelled to drop their memberships. This was an extraordinary development, signaling a new degree of competitiveness among institutions for status and resources. KU had been a member of the AAU since 1909, but in recent years the association's emphasis on federally funded research as a key element of evaluation had placed the university in the lower tier of its members.[68] This lent greater urgency to planning for KU's future and especially to strengthening the university's research profile. To this end, Provost Vitter initiated a faculty-led process for identifying strategic goals, expressed in four cross-disciplinary topical themes to guide future investments in research and teaching. New funding was made available for seed grants to teams of researchers working within these areas, and forums were established for the presentation and discussion of research. The university also secured funding from the state for new "Foundation" professorships, intended to bring outstanding scholars to KU.[69]

The KUEA campaign associated with Chancellor Gray-Little, titled Far Above, was well timed to contribute to these efforts. Although the campaign had been started before her arrival at KU, she soon became a highly visible public spokesperson for it. Publicly launched in 2012, within a year it had already raised $900 million, setting a pace to easily surpass its announced goal of $1.2 billion. With the decline in state funding during the national economic recession, KUEA had become an ever-larger contributor to the university's success, representing about 10 percent of the budget in recent years. Endowment contributions to KU surpassed $100 million in 2004 and reached $124 million in 2014.[70] While generally equivalent in constant dollars, these figures

Spring blooms in front of Stauffer-Flint.

were considerably more than KUEA had provided to the university in the past. Like many other public research institutions, KU has relied increasingly on private contributions to remain competitive with its national peers. The results are evident in Table I-3. While Kansas has remained a leader among state universities in endowment resources and successive campaigns since 1988 have sustained a high rate of growth in KUEA assets, its position in 2014 was hardly as commanding as in earlier times.[71]

The quest for recognition was enhanced significantly in June 2012 when the National Cancer Institute (NCI) recommended that KU's Cancer Center be designated as an NCI center, marking a milestone that had taken nearly a decade to be reached. The Medical Center had received state funding to support its application for this designation, along with more than $100 million in private donations through the KUEA. Leading research faculty members were hired in this process, significantly adding to the university's academic profile. The NCI designation promised to make KU and the region a destination for cancer treatment and research, augmenting the Medical Center's other strengths in cardiac care, neurosciences, head and neck surgery, and other specialties. It also promised to make the university even more competitive for federally funded research.[72]

Other initiatives launched during this period included a major revision of the university's undergraduate core requirements, the first
in nearly 25 years. As James Woelfel explains in Chapter 3, this process resulted in a simplified framework for fulfilling requirements in
six broad areas, described as learning goals, which could be satisfied
by a range of courses and learning experiences. One practical effect
was to reduce the number of credit hours needed to meet university
core expectations, bringing KU into line with other national research
universities and making it easier for students to complete programs of
study in a timely fashion.[73]

The KU student body continued to evolve during these years, as the
number of international students increased and the university drew
applicants from new parts of the country, particularly Texas and the
Southwest.[74] Marking a long-term trend, the number of students described as nontraditional, those with families or who were at least three
years older than class norms, passed 2,500, or more than one in ten
undergraduates.[75] Although the KU campus was officially "dry," which
meant that alcohol was not served in the unions or elsewhere, students
followed national trends with respect to binge drinking, consuming
large quantities of alcohol in a single evening. In 2008, Lawrence Memorial Hospital saw more than 1,500 alcohol-related patients, nearly
300 of whom could definitely be identified as KU students. The university announced a policy of informing parents of alcohol and drug
violations on campus and an alcohol assessment process for freshmen.[76] Enrollment fluctuated in the wake of demographic changes in
the region's college-age population, but the academic profile of the
entering classes at KU improved during these years. The long-term
trend of drawing students from suburban Johnson County continued
to be evident, and by 2009 more than 40 percent of Kansas undergraduates came from several school districts there.[77] While KU continued
to draw students from all over the state, it become even more closely
associated with urban and suburban counties, particularly those within
the state's northeast quadrant.

If student festivity was becoming a problem, Jayhawk athletics certainly gave fans plenty to celebrate. Under Bill Self's tutelage, the
men's basketball Jayhawks won an unparalleled ten consecutive Big 12
championships and added a national title in 2008. They maintained
the nation's longest streak of successive NCAA tournament invitations
and appeared again in the national title game in 2012. The football
program also experienced unprecedented success under Coach Mark
Mangino, going 12–1 in 2007 and defeating Virginia Tech in the

Construction has altered other sides of Mount Oread, but the north campus has maintained a park-like character.

Orange Bowl. In 2008, the Jayhawks posted another winning season and defeated Minnesota in the Insight Bowl. The Lady Jayhawk basketball team also experienced strong seasons in 2012 and 2013, advancing to the Sweet Sixteen of the NCAA Tournament in both years under the leadership of Coach Bonnie Henrickson.[78] The university's debate team added to the winning record by taking a national championship in 2009, sustaining KU's long tradition of success in that competitive domain as well.[79]

CONCLUSION: AN ERA OF TRANSFORMATION

In the past 50 years, the University of Kansas has taken great strides in its development as a national public research university. It has dealt with the rapid expansion and student unrest in the 1960s and 1970s, the budgetary vicissitudes of the 1980s, and the technological revolution of the 1990s. In more recent years, it has suffered sizable cutbacks in state support and political controversy over the use of social media

President Barack Obama speaks at the Anschutz Sports Pavilion, January 22, 2015.

by the faculty and staff, along with student discontent over sexual violence and related issues.[80] These events are reminders that the university remains a public institution in a highly charged political environment, a fact of life unlikely to change in the foreseeable future.

Reflective of this, the university welcomed President Barack Obama
to Lawrence in January 2015 for a speech highlighting themes from
the State of the Union address he had delivered two days earlier.
Speaking to a crowd of more than 7,000 at the Anschutz Sports Pavilion, he emphasized the importance of equal pay, affordable child care,
and education, including affordable higher education, to the nation's
future. The president highlighted his Kansas roots and expressed his
admiration for the winning Jayhawk tradition in basketball. It was a
historic moment for the university community, regardless of political
views. More than a century had passed since a sitting president had
visited KU, and the university had changed a great deal during that
time.[81] Today, KU stands as a major international research institution,
reflecting many of the principles outlined in the president's speech.

KU has emerged in the twenty-first century as a stronger and
more-accomplished institution, but one facing new challenges as
the landscape of higher education continues to change. As recent
events have suggested, the university has little choice but to enhance

its capacity as a research institution at the same time that it strives for excellence in teaching and service. It has grown substantially in the number of staff members, while holding numbers of students and tenure-track faculty members more or less constant for more than 30 years, all evident in the statistical tables accompanying this account. This has enabled KU to keep pace with changing national standards for student support services, research and technical support, and other critical functions. Much of this has been paid for by rising tuition, especially in recent years, with students shouldering a greater share of the cost of their education, although endowment funds have been important too. Still, KU has continued to push forward in efforts to diversify its student body, along with the faculty and staff, to keep pace with a rapidly changing national population. The university has built an enviable record of international scholarship and teaching and draws students from around the world, but it faces growing pressure to expand its reach in these respects as well. If the past is a guide, the KUEA will doubtlessly contribute a great deal to this, but it too will likely face an increasingly competitive environment for raising funds.[82]

In short, while the university has come a long way since the mid-1960s, its journey is far from complete and likely never will be. In the years ahead, its leaders, along with faculty, staff, and students, will have to continue addressing the many problems that KU must face to remain a well-regarded international research university. Working together, with the support of Jayhawks everywhere, history has shown that the possibilities for success may be quite promising indeed.

Part 1

LEADERSHIP & POLITICS

CHAPTER 1

"Lift the Chorus Ever Onward"
Leading the University

SUSAN B. TWOMBLY

O N the occasion of KU's 100th birthday, Chancellor Clarke Wescoe
assured the university community that KU was ready to face the
challenges of its next century, a time that would impose increasing
demands on universities. In meeting these challenges, he warned that
KU must strive to maintain a balance among its "three basic commitments: to education, to research and to service." The allure of research
was great, he noted, but only as "a way of making teaching more immediate and meaningful" and not as an end in and of itself.[1]

While later chancellors may have demurred on the role of research,
Wescoe identified a major challenge facing him as well as his successors: how to build and solidify KU's place in the top tier of national
public research universities while simultaneously providing a stellar
undergraduate education to an expanding and diversifying student
body, in a state where adequate funding had been a consistent problem. KU has had 17 chancellors in its 150-year history; eight have
served since 1960.[2] Collectively, these leaders have led the transformation of KU from a relatively small, loosely configured university to a
complex, bureaucratic, more corporate-like organization with satellite
campuses in Overland Park, Wichita, Salina, and Topeka.

This growth and development has occurred in a local context
characterized by times of significant protest and various problems in
uniting the Medical Center and Lawrence campuses and in a national
context valuing access to higher education for all and increasing emphasis on and competition for research dollars and for rankings. Most

The view of Mount Oread while walking to campus from Daisy Hill in 1963.

significant, these 50 years have been characterized by a state economic climate in which there has been, compared to other states with top-tier universities, modest financial support for higher education. This has often manifested itself in cycles of a few good years followed by one or two austere years. Sustained progress has been a challenge in this unpredictable environment, and the fact that progress has been made at all is due in no small part to the chancellors who have led the university. As Thomas Burish, KU alumnus and Notre Dame provost, said in a recent speech at KU, leading in this environment has required a great deal of grit.[3]

Leading a university is a job like no other. In this setting, the president or chancellor of a university is *primus inter pares,* the first among equals. In the words of Chancellor Budig: "So nobody really runs it [the university]. . . . Nobody *can* really. . . . It is operated through shared governance."[4]

With all of these limitations, the role of the president or chancellor remains critical. Organizations need leaders to "coordinate their activities, represent them to their various publics, and symbolize the embodiment of institutional purpose."[5] The chancellor, then, is first and foremost an important symbol of KU and what it stands for. The chancellor sets the vision and exerts more influence than anyone else on campus. That said, it is actually difficult to attribute specific acts or accomplishments to individual chancellors. They are often judged by the university's overall accomplishments and successes (or failures).[6]

This chapter tells the story of the eight individuals who have presided over the university's transformation over the last 50 years. It will attempt to capture in brief the vision, leadership style, challenges, and accomplishments of each. Of course, the chancellor does not lead the university alone. During the past 50 years, KU has been blessed with many other outstanding leaders who have also shaped the institution.[7]

W. CLARKE WESCOE:
"K.U.'S SINGING CHANCELLOR," 1960–1969

W. Clarke Wescoe, KU's tenth chancellor, was known as its "singing chancellor," a medical doctor who wrote and sang songs on ceremonial occasions.[8] Reflective of how things have changed since 1960, Wescoe did not interview for the chancellorship or even know with certainty that he was under consideration for the position. His name was unanimously recommended to the Board of Regents by a faculty committee, which expressed such confidence in Dean Wescoe that an additional search was not deemed necessary.[9]

Wescoe was filled with "unbounded optimism" as he began his term as chancellor. He accepted, with enthusiasm, the challenge of providing an elite education in an open-access university. Enhancing a scholarly faculty, internationalizing the university, expanding research, and addressing building needs brought on by tremendous growth in numbers of students were his other goals.[10]

For Wescoe, educating thousands more students meant doing "it better than ever before," which KU would do by providing a humanistic education that teaches humans to live with themselves. Students, he believed, should be treated as adults and not as "hot house plants," educated in environments that protect them from the rough-and-tumble world of conflicting ideas. He expressed confidence "that the educational preparation and maturity of its students will insure a calm and reasoned approach to all ideas."[11]

Shortly after taking office, Wescoe made changes to the administrative structure of the university, noting that it had not changed since 1939. These developments, approved in 1963, created the position of provost/executive vice chancellor for each of the Lawrence and Medical Center campuses. Thus began a lengthy evolution in the role of the chancellor as the external face of the university and executive vice chancellors as the chief administrators of their respective campuses.[12]

One change that proved both significant and lasting was the establishment late in Wescoe's term of a new university governance structure, consisting of a Faculty Senate, a Student Senate, and a University

Chancellor Wescoe attending an athletic event with scholarship donor Benjamin Stansbury.

Senate.[13] Wescoe was ambivalent about this. Publicly, he celebrated the fact that the system ensured that faculty became a vital part of the administrative structure, playing a key role in the escalating crises late in his term, while warning that decision making would be slowed.[14] For him, the governance system and its codified rules and committee structures symbolized the end to a university run by "the gentleman's code of conduct," which was no longer adequate for an increasingly complex institution with significant problems.[15]

Wescoe faced growing student unrest with the uncertainty of most of his contemporaries. Early in his term he had warned that rapid growth would challenge university harmony. It is not clear that he was adequately prepared to deal with the practical implications of the challenges, especially after 1965. In response to a sit-in in his office in the spring of 1965 regarding civil rights, Wescoe supported the arrest of students who refused to leave. He suspended the arrested students but then reinstated them. Although sympathizing with the protesters' ideals, he rejected their methods. As a result of this protest, significant changes were made at KU addressing many of the protesters' concerns.

As student protest escalated in the spring of 1968, the Senate Executive Committee agreed to add students to the University Senate, which the Regents approved in 1969.[16] As later statements would indicate, Wescoe was becoming increasingly impatient with protests, but still he shocked everyone by abruptly notifying the Board of Regents that 1968–1969 would be his last at KU. He told those gathered at 1968 Fall Convocation that the time was right for "a new voice, a new face and a new approach."[17] He was 48.

Wescoe faced a difficult last few weeks on the job that would set the stage for his less fortunate successor. The spark was the 1969 ROTC Tri-Service Review, which was called off when it was met with about 100 protesters. Members of the Board of Regents in attendance insisted that the protesters be arrested, but no one would reveal their names publicly. Wescoe would leave office in a few weeks, and his successor was left to deal with the issue.[18]

By nature optimistic, Wescoe in his final farewell to graduates in May 1969 expressed his pent-up frustration that the "excesses and irresponsibility of a few" were discrediting an entire movement that was questioning old values and methods of education.[19] And yet he ended on a positive note, nostalgic for the university he called home, the university to which he had given almost two-thirds of his working career and his loyalty.

The university grew and prospered in many ways during Wescoe's term. Not only were there more students, they were, as Wescoe frequently noted, also better students. Faculty numbers increased significantly, from 573 to 917. New schools of architecture and urban design and social welfare were established. Under the guidance of Dean George Waggoner, the Colleges-within-the College were created and study abroad was expanded, as were interdisciplinary programs.[20] The system of shared governance formed and adopted under Wescoe has remained a KU mark of distinction ever since.

Sponsored research more than doubled on the Lawrence campus. The library expanded from just over 800,000 volumes to almost 1.5 million. Spencer Research Library opened in 1968.[21] Wescoe continually lavished praise on KU's loyal alumni and other supporters. In honor of KU's Centennial in 1965, Wescoe announced an $18.6 million capital campaign ($134 million in 2013 dollars), titled Program for Progress. Despite the Vietnam War and general mood of the country, $21 million was raised ($140 million in 2013 dollars) by the campaign's end in 1969. It was the second-largest campaign for a state-assisted university at the time.[22]

Most notable were changes to the physical shape and look of the campus. Benefiting from generous federal assistance, Hashinger, Ellsworth, McCollum, and Oliver residence halls were built, creating beds

Four chancellors pose together: Franklin Murphy, Archie Dykes, Clarke Wescoe, and Raymond Nichols in 1974.

for 2,750 students. Stouffer Place was built for married students. Notable indeed was the demolition and replacement of Old Fraser Hall, the very symbol of KU. Also, despite increasing unrest, students agreed to assess themselves a fee to support construction of what would become Watkins Memorial Health Center and the humanities building that would become Wescoe Hall. The Lawrence campus master plan developed under Wescoe set the central principle guiding planning to this day: undergraduate liberal arts education at the campus's center, with graduate and professional schools on the outer ring.[23]

E. LAURENCE CHALMERS: "LARRY," 1969–1972

E. Laurence Chalmers was installed as KU's 11th chancellor on September 15, 1969, stepping into what was undoubtedly the most turbulent three years in KU's history.[24] Although KU had experienced increasing levels of protest and even violence in the years prior to his arrival, Chalmers did not anticipate the depth and extent of events to come: a subpoena to release the names of protesters from the spring of 1969; the bombing of Summerfield Hall in December 1970; the

Cleanup at the Kansas Union following the fire in 1970.

burning of the Kansas Union on April 20, 1970; and the deaths in July of two men, one a student and the other a young black man and former student from Lawrence. Shortly thereafter, Chalmers was forced by the Board of Regents to fire Gary Jackson, assistant dean of men, for allegedly buying ammunition. Then, in 1972, a group of women students calling themselves the February Sisters took over the East Asian Studies building, and finally students protested and were arrested as ordered by the Kansas attorney general in May 1972.[25] Chalmers's own account of the "19 Days and Nights" in the spring of 1970 portrays a university on the brink of chaos.[26]

Chalmers was 40 years old when appointed chancellor. He came to KU from Florida State University, where he rose from assistant professor through academic and administrative ranks, serving as dean of the College of Arts and Sciences and vice president for Academic Affairs.[27] He faced a formidable task. He followed in the footsteps of the popular Chancellor Wescoe and faced funding challenges and the lingering question of the identities of the protesters at the ROTC Tri-Service Review the previous spring.[28] Before even setting foot on campus, the primary question he got from the press was how he would deal with student protest. A headline in the *Topeka Capital Journal* on March 13,

Chancellor Chalmers at home with his family, 1969.

1969, captured the essence of his response to those pre-arrival questions: "Dissent Is Healthy If Orderly."[29]

Chalmers was chancellor for three troubled years in KU's history.
He survived at least one vote by the Board of Regents to fire him at
the end of his first year and continued scrutiny by the Regents after
that, and he resigned before the start of the 1972 academic year. The
public reason given for his resignation was emergency divorce pro-
ceedings initiated by his wife; some suspect he was fired for lying to the
Regents.[30] Observers of the "turbulent years" tend to view Chalmers as
either contributing to the turmoil because of his alleged agreement
with the protesters and his lenient approach to them or as a deft administrator who saved KU from worse destruction and injury.[31] Time
and distance have added weight to the latter interpretation. Most accounts of the Chalmers years focus on disruption and overlook what
was accomplished during his short tenure as chancellor.

Chalmers believed students of the 1970s were different—that they
were concerned about and involved in world problems. He described
students as "democratic, intelligent, committed and humane (as opposed to communistic)." He agreed with their objections to the Vietnam War and supported their freedom to protest and speak, but he

drew the line at violence.[32] These views no doubt did little to inspire confidence in the Board of Regents.

Under the best of circumstances, leadership of colleges and universities in the late 1960s was a challenge.[33] From the very beginning, Chalmers was "intrigued by a combined student-faculty governing body . . . developed out of willingness."[34] He called the new system of shared governance the "most significant creation of the 1968–1970 biennium." For Chalmers, consensus was essential to governing a university.[35] At the same time, he spoke emphatically about the need for accountability "to reexamine the use of every dollar that has been allocated to the University" and for assessment of student learning.[36]

Although some suggest it was Chalmers's inability to make decisions rather than a belief in shared governance that shaped his reliance on it, his actions generally seemed to support his words, particularly with respect to the role of the new Senate Executive Committee in responding to escalating disruption in the spring of 1970.[37] He argued against violence because it threatened academic freedom, defended controversial professors, and sought input on important decisions about dealing with protests.[38] He was seemingly less sympathetic to calls for gender equality than he was to calls for ending the war. He came down hard on the February Sisters, who occupied a building to demand, among other things, an affirmative action program, that a woman be named to fill a vacant senior administrative position, an end to discriminatory employment practices, and the creation of a women's studies program. Insensitive though he may have been at the time, the February Sisters got much of what they demanded. In defending his views to Henry Bubb, chair of the Board of Regents, Chalmers described himself as a pragmatist in doing what was necessary to achieve institutional goals as long as it was legal and moral.[39]

Chalmers does not get sufficient credit for all that was accomplished during his brief tenure. Despite significant protest activity, student and faculty life continued on. Students took classes taught by faculty and graduated. Buildings were built and remodeled, the Kansas Union among them. Alumni gave money. The Wichita Campus of the KU Med Center opened in 1971. He defended academic freedom and fought proposed cuts to the graduate research fund.[40]

By all accounts, his most remarkable accomplishment was that of holding the university together in the spring of 1970 with no loss of life or more significant property damage than a burned Union and a slightly damaged computer center. Although Chalmers himself was out of town on the day the Union burned and the immediate crisis was

Chancellor Chalmers with the Jayhawks at Homecoming, 1971.

diffused by others, Chalmers is rightfully given credit for negotiating
the subsequent May 10, 1970, emergency convocation giving students
the choice to continue or to end coursework and take the grades they
had earned at the time. Chalmers worked with the University Senate
to formulate the options presented to students.[41] More than a burning

Union was at stake. Nationally, protests against the Vietnam War had escalated. The shock of student deaths at Kent State University reverberated throughout Lawrence. Other universities were closing, and there were reports of Lawrence citizens arming themselves. Despite growing tension, the Kansas Regents declared that universities would remain open. KU students, meanwhile, were threatening to "Shut 'er down! Strike!"[42] Collectively, these events put Chalmers in a very difficult spot. As Chalmers's successor, Raymond Nichols, remembered: "He [Chalmers] saved us from a Kent State situation. We didn't have a murder or death on campus. We had one boy shot in the neck when he challenged a student who was using a spray can to write something on the library wall. That was not bad. . . . There were crowds every night, every place. Merchants downtown had men with high powered rifles stationed in their businesses." Nichols noted, "The Chancellor [Chalmers] controlled, in a sense, the destiny of this university."[43]

Chalmers tinkered with administrative changes and solidified the system of shared governance that has existed to this day. Drawing on recommendations from various committees (and undoubtedly the 1969 North Central Association accreditation report), the Lawrence position of dean of faculties was upgraded to vice chancellor for academic affairs, responsible for all aspects of the academic mission of the university, and graduate studies and research were combined under a new vice chancellor position.[44] At the Medical Center, the position of provost was replaced by a vice chancellor for health affairs. An Office of Affirmative Action also was created.

When Chalmers resigned at the end of the 1971–1972 academic year, reactions were more mixed than one might have expected. In particular, a number of regional newspapers, the *LJW* not among them, were very positive about the way Chalmers had handled events thrown at him. The *Wichita Eagle*, for one, proclaimed, "Students are the losers."[45]

RAYMOND F. NICHOLS: "MR. KU," 1972–1973

In the wake of Chalmers's resignation, Raymond F. Nichols, executive secretary of the university, was named interim chancellor. A Kansan by birth and Jayhawk by education, Nichols had spent more than 50 years on Mount Oread, first as a student, then as "right-hand man" to six chancellors, and then as vice chancellor for finance. Upon reaching the mandatory retirement age of 65, his title reverted to executive

Raymond Nichols.

secretary.[46] Less than two months into his term as interim chancellor,
this loyal Kansan, raised by a single mother on the Kansas prairie eat-
ing "mush and milk," was officially named KU's 12th chancellor by the
Board of Regents.[47]

A modest man, Nichols was just what the university needed following the previous tumultuous years. Although he did not have a PhD
and was not a faculty member, he was the man who would bring stability to KU.[48] Among the issues he faced were the budget, addressing
public views of KU as a dangerous place, and capital improvements.
He combated negative perceptions by answering hundreds of letters
to students and parents about the situation at KU.[49]

Nichols urged faculty to readjust their curricula to be responsive to
national hiring needs, responded to federal government regulations,
adopted an Affirmative Action Plan endorsing "the University's earlier
commitment to equal opportunities for admission and employment,"
and established a new Office of Instructional Resources and the Office
of Institutional Research and Planning.[50] The year was an active one
on the building front. The Space Technology Center that bears his
name, the State Geological Survey Building, the new humanities building to be named for Wescoe, the new student health facility, and the
expansion of Learned Hall were completed or were nearly complete.[51]

Governor Robert Docking and Chancellor Nichols talk during a space technology conference.

Reflecting on his own term, Nichols noted that "the timing was just perfect. . . . The students were tired of all the parading and demanding. . . . I had no problems with faculty; it was unbelievable."[52] Upon his retirement, he was named chancellor emeritus, but most knew him as Mr. KU.[53]

ARCHIE R. DYKES: "THE MOST POPULAR MAN IN THE STATE OF KANSAS," 1973–1980

In April 1973, the Board of Regents announced Archie Reese Dykes as the 13th chancellor of the University of Kansas. Dykes had emerged as the unanimous choice of the Board of Regents after a six-month search.[54] Despite the calm of Nichols's year, an air of instability still hung over Mount Oread. Dykes was the fourth chancellor in five years. His first press conference was held under tight security for fear of student demonstrations over fee allocations. By the end of this term he was known as the "Most Popular Man in the State of Kansas."[55] Notwithstanding this, the disruptions of the Chalmers years were over and it was up to Dykes to repair KU's public image. In this, by most accounts, he succeeded.[56]

Archie Dykes was born in a small town in Tennessee in 1931, making him 42 at the time of his appointment.[57] He came to KU "with a burst of energy and a million-dollar smile." He was a very effective spokesperson for KU and higher education because he "cultivated an exemplary relationship with the legislature and worked long and hard to involve all of Kansas in adult education programs." Dykes was famous for walking the grounds, taking notes and then notifying staff the following day of things needing attention.[58]

Undergraduate education was one of Dykes's top priorities. "Few matters are more crucial or more pressing in American higher education than the development of more meaningful and stimulating undergraduate teaching and learning," he told those at his inauguration. One way of doing this was to create "an academic setting where students can have close, personal relationships with individual faculty members."[59] As the economy struggled in the mid-1970s, he stressed the need for greater connection between national manpower planning and university curricula and for making a college degree useful while retaining the importance of the arts and sciences. He decried an education that was "too narrow" or did not prepare professionals to think critically or humanely.[60] Dykes was also committed to lifelong,

Chancellor Archie Dykes.

or continuing, learning, which he called the "dominant educational trend of our time." He saw this as a way for KU to "reach out into the state to serve educational needs only it can fill." Dykes understood that it was important that citizens of the state and nation shared the hopes of the university. Research and graduate education seemingly occupied a lesser place in his priorities.[61]

Dykes's record as a leader is full of paradoxes. He was at once "a man who paid attention to the smallest detail, yet who had moved to decentralize his authority so as to unburden his office of many bureaucratic demands on his time."[62] He expected much of his staff but would put off an important meeting to talk with a prospective student. At the same time, he was not seen as being very student centered. He had stressed in his inaugural address that participation by all in decision making was an obligation and yet chafed at constraints on his authority. More than anything specific about his administrative style it was his personal touch, his ability to persuade and to help people understand what KU was trying to achieve, that defined his leadership style and won him accolades. It was his "character and personality" that made him a force in the legislature. While Chalmers embraced

Chancellor Dykes speaking at a community event.

shared authority, Dykes complained that the chancellor was expected to achieve goals without exercising control. Administrators, in turn, were "exhausted by Dykes' continuing demands."[63]

He faced two particular administrative challenges. One involved "a whirlpool of problems" at the KU Medical Center; the second was the challenge of responding to increasing federal requirements. The Med Center took a considerable portion of Dykes's time in his early years. Recognizing its importance to the university, he engaged in an effort to tie the two campuses more closely together. It was a theme that would reappear later.[64]

The 1970s were years of burgeoning federal requirements: affirmative action and labor relations among them. Dykes bristled at the attention and resources compliance required, calling them a threat to university autonomy.[65] Sounding a familiar refrain, he argued that the sooner the university got its own house in order, the "quicker the bureaucratic armies of accountants, auditors, and analysts will disappear."[66]

He, like other chancellors, reorganized the central administration. Most notable, he created parallel administrative structures: an executive vice chancellor for each campus. He appointed Del Shankel to the post on the Lawrence campus and William Rieke to the post at the Med Center.[67] Del Shankel had high hopes "that this would really be the chief officer for the campus and would be essentially in charge of everything on the Lawrence Campus." To his dismay, "after about three years, Archie decided he wanted to change some things" and rearranged the structure to have some positions that had reported to the executive vice chancellor now report directly to the chancellor.[68] Dykes's efforts marked yet another step, although not an entirely successful one, in the direction of creating and consolidating what would eventually become the position and role of executive vice chancellor and provost to oversee internal affairs while external matters consumed more of the chancellor's time and effort.

Although rumors that Dykes was leaving KU were common, his resignation on June 4, 1979, was a surprise.[69] He suggested that after being a chancellor for a total of 13 years, he was ready for a change. Praise for Dykes's accomplishments was widespread. The list of accomplishments includes increasing the budget from $98 million to $250 million; 20 major building projects on both the Lawrence and the Medical Center campuses (including the Law School, the Visual Arts Building, the A. R. Dykes Library, and the current version of the Bell Hospital at the Medical Center); establishing the School of Nursing; increasing faculty salaries; increasing student enrollments by 30 percent to more than 26,000; expanding adult/continuing education; "seizing control of the beleaguered School of Medicine in Kansas City and [taking] KU's medical school in Wichita under his wing"; and establishing the Regents Center to advance lifelong learning and cement KU's place in the Kansas City area. Perhaps his greatest accomplishment was that of restoring a positive public image of the university.[70]

Despite all of the positive things that happened, Dykes's term was not untroubled. He dealt with the problems at the Medical Center campus, the Pearson Integrated Humanities Program, unauthorized trips by two KU professors to Iran, and protests about freedom of speech on campus.[71] He also implemented a system of faculty evaluation. The North Central Association report of its 1974 reaccreditation visit noted that there were no women in top administrative posts.[72] Frances Degen Horowitz was appointed vice chancellor for research and graduate studies in 1978. She was the first woman appointed to a senior academic administrative position (except for Emily Taylor) in this 50-year period. Likewise, his record on affirmative action was reportedly weak, and KU found itself under federal government scrutiny for Title IX violations.[73]

In contrast to his predecessors, Wescoe and Chalmers, Dykes was not widely praised for his relations with students or for addressing the general needs of the academic community. The arrests of 12 students for displaying banners at the 1980 commencement (prohibited by Regents policy) certainly did not help his reputation for relations with students. He was further described by some faculty as "a hard-nosed, two-fisted administrator" who was "totally insensitive to the needs of the faculty and the students."[74] While Dykes may have been these things, the fact that faculty salaries increased significantly during his term suggests that he was not completely insensitive to faculty concerns. He went on to assume a successful career as CEO of Security Benefits Insurance Company.[75]

DELBERT M. "DEL" SHANKEL:
ACTING CHANCELLOR, 1980–1981

Del Shankel was named acting chancellor shortly after Dykes announced his resignation. As an astute *UDK* reporter noted: "His title may be 'acting' chancellor, but his term has been far from just a caretaker administration."[76]

Delbert Shankel.

Like Nichols, Shankel had held numerous administrative positions at KU before being appointed acting chancellor, and he was certainly a well-known quantity when tabbed by the Regents to fill the position. He had moved into administrative positions early in his career, beginning in 1964 as acting chairperson of the Department of Microbiology. He then became assistant and then associate dean and acting dean of the College of Liberal Arts and Sciences. In 1974, Chancellor Archie Dykes named Shankel to the post of executive vice chancellor for the Lawrence campus, a position from which he resigned in 1980 shortly before Dykes announced his resignation.

Shankel's goal was "to leave the institution at the end of the year in at least as good a shape as I found it," which, as it turned out, was not such an easy task.[77] When he described his work style, he noted that he would "seek all the advice I can, have all the facts I can get, take time to assess the situation, make a decision I'm comfortable with, and then take responsibility for that decision."[78] He indicated that he would give renewed attention to support of the arts as a major goal.[79]

Banners advocating freedom of speech welcomed Shankel at opening convocation in August 1980. He chose not to have the protesters arrested, arguing that no one but the stage party actually saw the banners. The banner incident and several other free speech issues occupied a good bit of Shankel's attention. By choosing not to have protesters arrested, Shankel scored his first victory with students and faculty. Soon thereafter, charges leveled against the protesters were dropped, and the Regents charged each university with developing its own freedom of expression policy. In February 1981, the banner incident finally came to a conclusion with adoption of a policy that promoted a climate conducive to freedom of speech with as few restrictions as possible.[80]

The university also weathered a series of charges reported in the *Kansas City Times* alleging academic problems in the Athletics Department and drug abuse by athletes and allegations of mismanagement and poor housekeeping at the Medical Center.[81] There was also continuing fallout from two professors who had traveled, without authorization, to Iran during the previous school year, resulting in an unsuccessful proposal to put tenure decisions and faculty discipline in the hands of the legislature.[82]

GENE A. BUDIG: "BATTER UP," 1981–1994

Gene A. Budig, a native of McCook, Nebraska, was named KU's 14th chancellor on March 20, 1981.[83] Only 41 at the time of his appointment, Budig had already served as president of two other major universities, first Illinois State University and then West Virginia University. He left a job in the Nebraska governor's office in 1967 to become an assistant professor of higher education and administrative assistant to the chancellor at the University of Nebraska; thus his rise through the professorial and administrative ranks was rapid. In 1972, he was named president of Illinois State, a position he held until he was appointed president of West Virginia University in 1977.[84]

Several themes stand out in Budig's vision for higher education and his goals for KU. One of his goals was to raise KU into the ranks of the top ten research universities in the country. To accomplish this, he planned to invest in faculty, both the number of them and in their compensation. Advancement also required investment in libraries and scientific equipment. Repairing relations with the state was Dykes's goal; making KU a top state priority was Budig's.[85]

Budig took great pride in being a "teaching" chancellor (he regularly taught a graduate seminar), and over the course of his chancellorship he supported various initiatives to enhance the learning

Chancellor Budig (right) with Lt. Governor Shelby Smith in 1983.

environment, including establishing several endowed teaching awards. He devoted efforts to improving academic advising, rewarding outstanding teaching, and building the honors program. A revised general education program was approved in 1985 after a failed attempt by his vice chancellor for academic affairs, Deanell Tacha, to implement a core curriculum. He also believed it important to diversify the student body.[86] His message to students, which he repeated often, was that the university offered a wide range of opportunities, but that getting an education was up to each of them.[87]

Yet another prominent theme in Budig's view of education was his concern for freedom of speech and gender, racial, and disability equality, which grew stronger over the course of his term. The motivating events changed. In 1983, it was a series of incidents in which members of the Jewish, African American, and gay and lesbian communities had been harassed.[88] In 1988, the provocation was an invitation by a professor of journalism for members of the Ku Klux Klan to speak on campus. Despite calls for the appearance to be canceled, Budig and his executive vice chancellor, Judith Ramaley, argued that suppression of views had no place in a university. The Ku Klux Klan members spoke at an open forum on free speech. In 1990, it was the "pizza incident," in which an African American pizza delivery woman was attacked by a fraternity member. He tried to find the silver lining in these events, viewing them as teachable moments for all members of the community to learn about tolerance.[89]

Like his predecessors, Budig admitted that running a university is complex. "No one person ever speaks for all of the university constituents," he explained. "The chancellor has an obligation to express values and to point out directions. Realization of those ends comes through a process." At the same time, he recognized that being chancellor of a university was different from being head of a corporation: "This is not like running General Motors Corporation. . . . A budget document from KU is a collegial document . . . produced in consultation with representative faculty, staff and students."[90]

Budig sought to strengthen the role of the executive vice chancellors of the Medical Center and Lawrence campuses. Kay Clawson was appointed as executive vice chancellor of the Medical Center campus, reportedly in an effort to head off an attempt by the legislature to privatize the hospital, taking it out of the hands of the Medical Center.[91] The university had long struggled to establish a strong provost position and a clear administrative structure.[92] In 1987, he appointed Judith Ramaley to serve as executive vice chancellor for the Lawrence campus. These appointments seem to have marked a subtle shift toward investing more authority in each executive vice chancellor/provost for managing the campus, although the vice chancellor for academic affairs position continued on the Lawrence campus. Ramaley was the first woman to serve at the executive vice chancellor level.

Toward the end of Budig's term, the North Central Association accreditation team praised KU's governance and administrative structure and processes. If there was a criticism it was that shared governance was so strong "it is difficult to think of 'the administration' independent of the governance structure and process." The team noted that the university was still very decentralized.[93]

As with any chancellorship that lasts 13 years, the Budig years were filled with ups and downs, crises and successes. Early in his term, the major challenges were financial and athletic. Budig was "sobered by the state of the national economy." In 1982, a national economic downturn and statewide deficit forced KU to cut almost 5 percent of its budget, forcing staff reductions at the Medical Center.[94] In 1987, the faculty narrowly defeated a vote to unionize. Then, in 1989, the Kansas legislature agreed to fund the first year of the Margin of Excellence, a multiyear plan to raise faculty salaries to the average salaries of peers (helping to avert a second vote by faculty to unionize).[95]

As the chapter on athletics will show, athletics successes and failures also surprised Budig at the end of the decade. In addition, the campus

Chancellor Budig in 1983 outside the Regents Center in Overland Park.

experienced the firing of two tenured professors and persistent challenges on the Medical Center campus.

During his term, KU was struck by a disaster of a different kind. On
a stormy June day in 1991, historic Hoch Auditorium was struck by
lightning and dramatically burned. It was not insured, but Governor
Joan Finney provided $18 million to help rebuild the building with
state-of-the-art classrooms. The restored building opened in 1997.

Budig's accomplishments are notable. Primary among them were
building and fund-raising. The Boots Adams Alumni Center, renovations to the libraries, an addition to Haworth Hall, the Dole Building,
the Edwards campus, the Anschutz Science Library, the Lied Center
for the Performing Arts, and a rebuilt Budig Hall/Hoch Auditoria are
among the lasting building projects of his term. Major donations from
the Hall Family Foundation in support of the humanities and a successful capital campaign marked Budig's term. Campaign Kansas, the
"largest fund-drive in KU history" up to that time, began in 1988 and
concluded in 1992 having raised more than $265 million ($430 million in 2013 dollars), well exceeding its goal.[96]

On the student rights front, Budig joined the protest over the US
Department of Defense policy banning "homosexuals from becoming commissioned officers," which was contradictory to the university's antidiscrimination policy. He chipped away at the Kansas open

Lied Center construction site, 1991.

admissions policy by supporting modifications: an earlier application deadline and establishing a recommended high school curriculum. Minority student enrollment increased during his term, and the number of named professorships grew to 135 from 49 in 1981.[97]

For all of Budig's commitment to teaching and the undergraduate experience, student leaders gave him mixed reviews. Specifically, he was not as involved "in the hands-on-aspect of student life" as some would have liked, noted David Epstein, 1987 student body president.[98] Despite this perception, Deanell Tacha, vice chancellor for academic affairs, said, "I will never forget hours of meetings in which the chancellor said, 'We will take it from everywhere but the academic programs.' . . . He fought to avoid cuts but "when he had to take what he had to take, he knew exactly how to prioritize." Students would come first.[99]

Budig resigned at the end of the 1993–1994 academic year to assume his "dream job" as president of Major League Baseball's American League, a post he held from 1994 to 1999, when the position was abolished. Those who worked with and for Budig praised him for his commitment to diversifying the campus and his success at gaining financial commitments from the legislature (Margin of Excellence), bolstering the libraries, raising funds, and restoring the Medical

Center's financial stability. Even though he had served as president of two other universities, his wife, Gretchen, told Alumni Association reporters, "We've become Jayhawks."[100]

DEL SHANKEL: "THE ULTIMATE PINCH HITTER,"
1994–1995

When Budig resigned, Del Shankel was once again called on to fill the interim position. Reference to Shankel as pinch hitter was particularly apt. In addition to having served as acting chancellor, Shankel served in numerous administrative positions for Budig.[101]

In 1994, the university was in better shape than it had been in 1980, and Shankel was optimistic that his second term as acting chancellor would be better than the first. In an effort to consolidate gains from the Budig years, one of Shankel's major initiatives would be "an effort to improve students' undergraduate experience."[102] Other priorities of his and of Executive Vice Chancellor Ed Meyen included the Edwards campus and the Capitol Center in Topeka, improving the freshman/sophomore experience, expanding capacity for technology transfer, enhancing diversity, and improving public understanding of KU. The Blueprint for Diversity, a plan to increase diversity, was developed, and the Multicultural Resources Center was opened.[103]

At its April 1995 meeting, the Board of Regents officially designated Shankel as KU's fifteenth chancellor. At Shankel's official retirement celebration, David Shulenburger, vice chancellor for academic affairs, said that Shankel would "be remembered as being the great pinch hitter of all time."[104]

ROBERT E. HEMENWAY: "A MAN OF MANY HATS,"
1995–2009

Robert E. Hemenway, chancellor of the University of Kentucky at Lexington, was named KU's 16th chancellor on January 7, 1995. He officially took office on June 1. Like Budig and Shankel, Hemenway was a midwesterner, having grown up in Nebraska.[105]

Hemenway worked his way up the academic ladder, beginning as an assistant professor at the University of Kentucky in 1966 and then moving to the University of Wyoming in 1968, where he was promoted to associate professor. In 1973, he returned to the University of Kentucky,

Chancellor Bob Hemenway helps an undergraduate move into a scholarship hall during "move-in day" in 1999.

where he was promoted to full professor and then assumed the role of chair of the English Department in 1981. In 1986, he moved to the University of Oklahoma as dean of arts and sciences, before returning in 1989 to the University of Kentucky as chancellor of the Lexington campus. At KU, Hemenway continued to teach: American Literature at 7:30 in the morning.[106] Over the course of his 14-year term at KU, Hemenway became known for his many distinctive hats—especially for the tam he wore in winter months and for the plainsman straw hat he sported at commencement—and for his warm smile and daily walks around the campus, for assisting students on "move-in" day, and for reinvigorating campus traditions such as "the walk down the hill."[107]

Despite the success of the Budig years, Hemenway faced significant challenges in 1995. These included managing the aforementioned budget shortfall that hit in May, filling the position of executive vice chancellor of the Medical Center, and dealing with a heart transplant program that eventually closed. In addition, the North Central Association visiting reaccreditation team had identified a host of significant challenges, including deferred maintenance, recruitment and retention of women and minority faculty, open admissions, inadequate technology, concern about growth of external satellite locations such

Chancellor Hemenway congratulates graduates in Memorial Stadium at the 2002 commencement.

as the Topeka Capitol Center, graduate admissions and graduate student stipends, and library space.[108]

Hemenway's basic values were summed up early: "In one sense the university is a simple place. If there weren't any students at the university, there would be no need for a chancellor, there would be no need for a faculty, no need for a staff, no need for this grand physical plant you have in Lawrence. You start with the basic reason for being and that is students." Preserving quality classroom experiences would guide any budget-cutting exercise. He was also committed to recruiting minority faculty and students.[109]

Hemenway described his leadership style as relaxed and consultative. But he was, more so than his predecessors, explicitly goal oriented. He recognized the need for universities to be accountable, and his challenge was "how to take a good university and make it an even better university during a time that seems hostile to higher education." He wanted to raise KU's rank among research universities and laid out the ten characteristics of a top research university.

Thus he began his chancellorship with ten goals that guided his actions for his first five years. They included, in the student area, increasing minority student enrollment and recruiting and retaining

women and minority administrators, bringing to 100 the number of
National Merit Scholars on campus, and ensuring an international experience for students. He sought to increase research funding to $120
million. He restructured administration and aimed to improve salaries. Enhancing patient care at the Med Center, reallocating funds for
libraries and buildings, and enhancing the Edwards campus rounded
out his goals.[110]

One of Hemenway's most significant early actions was a major administrative reorganization. Several actions proved to be particularly
important. He combined the job of executive vice chancellor and that
of vice chancellor for academic affairs into one provost position with
supervisory responsibility for the Lawrence campus (a step previous
chancellors had not taken). Then, in what may have been his "single most important decision," he appointed David Shulenburger, vice
chancellor for academic affairs and professor of business, to the position.[111] Together, Shulenburger and Hemenway would lead KU's Lawrence campus for ten years. In 2001, the provost gained the title executive vice chancellor and provost for the Lawrence campus, clarifying
that the provost was "both chief academic officer and chief operating
officer."[112] Hemenway hired Vice Admiral Don Hagen, former sur-
geon general of the US Navy, as executive vice chancellor of KU Med
Center. When Hagen stepped down in 2004, he appointed Barbara
Atkinson, executive dean of the School of Medicine, to the position of
executive vice chancellor of the Medical Center and executive dean.[113]

Two other organizational changes proved significant. In 1996, the
Center for Research, which had primarily served the School of Engineering, was expanded to become the KU Center for Research, the operation overseeing funded research on the Lawrence campus. Then,
in 1998, the KU Hospital was separated from the Medical Center and
established as a public authority with its own board of directors, providing much-needed flexibility to both.[114]

In 2000, Hemenway initiated a strategic planning process that resulted in Initiative 2001, a plan to guide the university for the next
five years. The four pillars of Initiative 2001 were building premier
learning communities, serving Kansans, acting as one university, and
serving as the research university for the greater Kansas City area.[115]
Among Hemenway's priorities were boosting the quality of KU students and improving their educational experience to yield higher
retention and graduation rates. He supported the Regents' qualified
admissions policy requiring Kansas, as well as out-of-state, students to
meet minimum standards as measured by ACT scores, class rank, or

KU leadership in Johnson County, 1998: Provost David Shulenburger, Dean Robert Clark of the Edwards Campus, Dean Deborah Powell of the School of Medicine, Executive Vice Chancellor Donald Hagen, and Chancellor Hemenway.

completion of a college preparatory curriculum. This policy marked yet another step toward more selective admissions. To improve retention and graduation rates, a host of co-curricular activities and support services were implemented, including a university-wide advising center, the writing center, and the Center for Teaching Excellence. The Global Awareness Program was initiated to make global experiences available to all students (internationalizing KU was a top Hemenway priority—see Chapter 4). Collectively, this set of activities was credited with improving KU's freshman retention rates from 74 percent in 1993 to 83 percent for freshmen entering in fall 2003 and six-year graduation rates from 56 percent to 58 percent.[116]

Hemenway's quest for additional resources was aided in 2001 when the mechanism for funding Regents institutions changed. Beginning in 2001, KU received a block grant from the state and also control of tuition dollars. The Regents asked each campus to come up with a five-year plan that included tuition increases. Since KU would retain control of its tuition dollars, increases were one way of gaining the funds necessary to fund improvements.[117] Convincing students of the need for tuition increases was a matter of some importance and not a sure thing.

In response to the Board of Regents mandate that students be consulted in the tuition planning process, Shulenburger created an ad hoc committee on tuition, co-chaired by a student and a faculty member and consisting of equal numbers of each group plus staff members. In the end, the students were convinced that the quality of the education offered at KU was worth tuition increases, some of which would go to providing financial assistance to students in need. In exchange for their support, students gained a commitment from Shulenburger to spend the money as planned. This decision was followed in 2007 with the four-year fixed or guaranteed tuition model.[118]

Other accomplishments included obtaining $64 million for the Crumbling Classroom Initiative, resulting in infrastructure and capital improvements. Under Hemenway, sponsored research dollars increased by 120 percent. He initiated the Wheat State Whirlwind Tour, an annual weeklong bus tour to introduce about 40 new faculty members and administrators to the history, geography, economy, and culture of their adopted state.[119] KU First, a capital campaign with the target of raising $500 million, launched in 2001 and ended in 2004 having raised a total of $653 million ($796,908,132 in 2013 dollars).[120] Last but not least, KU literally got a new identity: a new logo, set of visual identity standards, and official colors.[121] As a chancellor who embraced the role of college athletics, he dealt with a number of challenges on this front, which are highlighted in Chapter 8.

He provided moral leadership as well. In 1999 and 2005, he staunchly defended the teaching of evolution in Kansas public schools in the face of efforts by the Kansas State Board of Education to displace it. He and Shulenburger defended the right of Professor Dennis Dailey to teach a popular human sexuality course in the face of attacks by legislators.[122]

In 2005, KU received reaccreditation by the Higher Learning Commission of the North Central Association with absolutely no concerns.[123] Although Hemenway remained upbeat, the next five years would bring their ups and downs. His goals remained steadfast: "to ensure KU continues its considerable rise as a national teaching and research university until it is unquestionably one of the 25 best public universities in America."[124] First, Provost Shulenburger announced in 2005 that he would step down at the end of the academic year. After remarkable stability in the provost position, Shulenburger's departure set off a series of personnel changes in that post. In 2006, Hemenway hired Richard Lariviere, dean of liberal arts and sciences at the University of Texas at Austin, to fill the vacancy. Lariviere would stay for three years before leaving to become president of the University of Oregon.

One of the most significant accomplishments of this time, and perhaps of Hemenway's entire chancellorship, was the decision to seek designation as a National Cancer Center. Hemenway officially launched a strategy to secure such designation in 2005. Roy Jensen was hired to be director of the KU Cancer Center in 2004 and would become director of KU's National Cancer Center. Hemenway kept the issue of Cancer Center funding in front of the Regents, despite mixed reactions on and off campus.[125]

If laying the groundwork for designation as a National Cancer Center was his crowning achievement, it was also the Medical Center that presented one of his greatest challenges in his last few years as chancellor. One of KU's goals for 2007–2008 was "completion of affiliation between Saint Luke's Hospital and KUMC; also affiliation agreement between the KU Hospital Authority and KU Medical Center." Both affiliation agreements were ultimately achieved after months of difficult negotiation and some shrill public criticism.[126]

In May 2008, Hemenway initiated a new strategic planning process, but then he abruptly announced in December of that year that he would retire in June. At his retirement press conference, he noted significant accomplishments: being on course to achieve designation as a National Cancer Center; achieving records for enrollment, ACT scores and diversity of students, and faculty and staff and donor giving; more than doubling research funding; and "riding the crest of what arguably has been the singularly most successful year in KU history in terms of performance by our students and faculty."[127]

BERNADETTE GRAY-LITTLE: BOLD ASPIRATIONS, 2009–

May 29, 2009, was a momentous day in the life of KU.[128] At 3 PM that day, the Board of Regents announced that Bernadette Gray-Little, executive vice chancellor and provost at the University of North Carolina at Chapel Hill, would become KU's seventeenth chancellor. Gray-Little is the first woman and African American to hold the chancellorship. She grew up in Washington, North Carolina, a segregated community on the Pamlico River. Gray-Little joined the faculty at the University of North Carolina at Chapel Hill in 1971. She spent the next 38 years at UNC moving through the academic and administrative ranks to a position of campus-wide leadership.[129]

The new chancellor's inaugural goals were to increase the number of KU students who graduate on time, improve KU's scholarly profile, and increase funding. To this end, one of her first acts was to charge three task forces: one on retention and graduation, one on admissions standards, and one on research engagement. Like her predecessors, she sought to raise KU to be among "the very top tier of the nation's best institutions."[130] Key to enhancing KU's scholarly profile was obtaining National Cancer Institute designation as a National Cancer Center, providing the facilities and support for research, and attracting the best graduate students. Under Gray-Little, the normally gradual pace of developments accelerated in 2010 when she hired Jeffrey Vitter, former provost at Texas A&M, to be executive vice chancellor and provost. Together, they initiated several large-scale projects and significantly ramped up the speed of change.

Beginning in 2010, both the Lawrence and the Medical Center campuses engaged in strategic planning exercises. The result was Bold Aspirations, an umbrella under which both plans fit but which is most often associated with the Lawrence Campus plan. On the Lawrence campus, Bold Aspirations became a plan to guide KU through from 2012 to 2017, which relied heavily on the recommendations of Gray-Little's three task forces and Hemenway's 2008 planning process. KU's ambition to become a top-tier university would be accomplished

Chancellor Bernadette Gray-Little at her inauguration in 2009.

by raising excellence in undergraduate and graduate education, by training leaders, and by harnessing the scholarly expertise of its faculty to make discoveries that would lead to healthy communities and change the world. To do this, KU would make "the strategic choices necessary to transform itself and achieve its vision." Raising retention and six-year graduation rates to 90 percent and 70 percent, respectively, and improving graduate education were set as goals. Essential to these goals was recruiting better students, providing them with the tools to succeed, and reviewing and revising the general education curriculum.[131] Gray-Little also became the first chancellor in this era to explicitly focus on improving graduate education.

A second major initiative, Changing for Excellence, guided by outside consultants, is seeking to transform and increase efficiencies in business practices that will generate funds for carrying out some of the university's bold aspirations. The third major initiative (also part of the strategic plan) was the design and implementation in fall of 2013 of the KU Core Curriculum. The first major revision of general education in almost 30 years, the KU Core represents the first set of truly university-wide requirements.[132] In April 2012, Gray-Little formally launched Far Above, a $1.2 billion capital campaign that is scheduled to conclude in June 2016.[133]

The urgency to engage in so many major initiatives in such a short period of time may have been motivated by two trends. Despite obvious advances during the previous decade, on two very public measures, enrollment and ranking in *U.S. News and World Reports*, KU began to slip between 2008 and 2012. In 2008, enrollment hit an all-time high of 30,004 students, 26,826 of whom were on the Lawrence campus. By 2011, enrollment on the Lawrence campus had declined to 24,577. Rankings among public research universities also slipped. In 2008, KU was tied for 40th; by 2012 it had slipped to 51st.[134] Some of KU's lower ranking is attributed to its lack of selective admissions requirements, which leads to lower retention and graduation rates, important *U.S. News* measures. Additional explanations include the increased competition for a declining population of traditional-aged college students in the Midwest, a decline in grant activities, and declining state funding for higher education. KU had proposed adopting a more selective admissions policy to the Regents in 2011 and was invited to do so in December 2011. An admissions proposal, raising KU's admissions standards, went to the Board of Regents in May 2012, was approved in June 2012, and will go into effect in 2016.[135]

In 2011, the University of Nebraska was voted out of the AAU. Although federal research expenditures had increased significantly

Four chancellors: Del Shankel, Bernadette Gray-Little, Robert Hemenway, and Archie Dykes, in 2009.

under Hemenway, there was renewed concern that KU would also be in danger of being excluded from this historic and prestigious set of universities. While making gains in faculty salaries relative to its peers by the end of the decade (2009), salaries have once again begun to slip or barely hold steady in comparison to peers.[136]

Gray-Little's first four years have seen other challenges. A ticket scandal in the Athletics Department broke soon after her arrival and led to the arrest and conviction of several employees. Dissatisfaction among some faculty in the School of Medicine was widely publicized. Gray-Little navigated a leadership change in both of these areas. Athletics conference realignment also cast a shadow early in her term. Additionally, in the face of the economic recession of 2008 and an increasingly conservative state government, her term has been constrained by cuts to higher education budgets leading to lower salary increases for a longer time than at any other during the 50-year period. Increasingly, the cost of faculty raises are born by student tuition. In 2014, in response to a controversial tweet by a journalism professor, the Board of Regents passed a very unpopular social media policy that many find anathema to academic freedom on campus.

Finally, in 2012, KU got what it had been seeking for seven years: designation as a National Cancer Center.[137] In the fall of 2013 there was more good news. First-year student enrollments reversed several years of decline when 4,000 new students arrived on Mount Oread and the KU Core launched on time. Despite lukewarm support from the state legislature, KU under Gray-Little was well on its way to achieving the bold aspirations it has set for itself.

VISION, LEADERSHIP, AND CHANGE

For anyone who wonders what the chancellor actually does, this brief review of chancellors has shown that they have first and foremost set the vision and direction for the university and then have fought to secure support—financial and human—to carry out their visions. Residence halls on Daisy Hill would probably have been built by the late 1960s regardless of who was chancellor at the time. On the other hand, the KU National Cancer Center would not have become a reality without Hemenway's vision and accompanying efforts to secure necessary funding. KU would likely not have such a strong international and liberal arts emphasis without the vision and support of its chancellors and other administrators. Likewise, its unique system of faculty, student, and staff governance might not exist were it not for the fact that Chancellor Wescoe recognized the need for it and that Chancellor Chalmers admired and supported the new structure when he easily could have squashed it.

The chancellors have "lifted the chorus" to push the university "ever onward." Each chancellor has had the general goal of making KU a better place, in the eyes of the state and the nation. Each, especially since Budig, has explicitly talked about raising KU's stature as a national public institution (earlier, KU's status was generally assumed), among the top tier of research universities. However, a cornerstone of each chancellor's vision consistently has been improving the students' educational experience, especially for undergraduates.

Chancellors have emphasized different aspects of this vision, whether it be Colleges-within-the-College; study abroad; educating students to forge a better, more tolerant society; protecting classroom activities in times of budget cuts; building premier learning communities; or energizing the educational environment through the KU Core. All have emphasized a broad rather than narrow curriculum and furthered KU's historic emphasis on the liberal arts. Although Chancellors Murphy and Wescoe, in particular, attempted to promote KU's research agenda, it was Hemenway and Gray-Little who explicitly attempted in their strategic plans to make both undergraduate education and research top priorities. Gray-Little's Bold Aspirations build on this dual focus and have prioritized undergraduate education alongside attention to graduate education and research. Whether and to what extent the chancellors' visions have been realized has depended on forces outside (for example, state and federal funding) and inside (personnel) the university. Increasingly, implementing change on the Medical Center and Lawrence campuses has depended on the abilities and actions of the executive vice chancellors/provosts, who carry out the vision of the chancellor while at the same time bringing their own to the task.

The times have dictated different approaches to leadership, different organizational structures, and different strategies to achieving the vision. Wescoe and Chalmers had very personal relations with students and faculty. They were hands-on leaders. As the university has grown and become more complex, the chancellor has become more of an external leader while the job of running the campus has been delegated to the executive vice chancellor. Before Hemenway, chancellors were driven by vision and broad goals. Since Hemenway and to some extent under Executive Vice Chancellor Ramaley and Provost Meyen under Budig, chancellors have had specific plans, goals, and strategies for accomplishing their visions. Gray-Little and Vitter's Bold Aspirations strategic plan drives decision making. In an era in which higher education is under much criticism for everything from high cost to lack of outcomes for students, KU has become more laser-focused on its priorities and more businesslike in how it achieves them. Students have become tuition-paying customers and markets. Faculty are urged to get grants to support themselves and their work. Efficiency has become a primary guiding value. The KU Core is outcome driven; among its rationales are flexibility and reduction of time to degree. The chancellor's vision "to lift students and society by educating leaders, building healthy communities, and making discoveries that change the world" is enacted through very specific goals and strategies.[138] In this climate, the challenge is to not let the parts overtake the whole at the risk of losing the larger sense of direction and the values and purpose that drive and have characterized KU.

In the ever-changing economic climate that buffets KU, none of the chancellors could have been as effective in their jobs without the financial support of KU's loyal alumni and supporters. Each and every chancellor has lavished praise on this group for generously donating to KU. In all of this, the KUEA has been the chancellors' silent partner, developing and carrying out four capital campaigns in this 50-year period, each of which exceeded publicly stated goals. Rarely has the KUEA itself, at least in the chancellors' public speeches, received the formal recognition for its significant contribution to the growth and success of KU in the last 50 years. Wescoe first used the KUEA to organize and carry out Program for Progress, which raised over $21 million. At the time, it was the second-largest campaign for a public university, and it was the first run by KUEA. Although KU did not engage in capital campaigns during the Chalmers and Dykes years, the KUEA ensured a continuous and steady flow of donations to support KU's mission of excellence in teaching, research, and service. After 20 years with no campaign, each chancellor since Budig has led a capital campaign, each more ambitious, even when adjusting for inflation, than the previous: Campaign Kansas in 1988 ($263 million), KU First in 1998 ($653 million), and Far Above in 2008 ($1.2 billion). In 2013, KUEA provided nearly $120 million in direct financial support to KU.[139] The frequency, level, and extent of fund-raising would not have been possible without KUEA's organizational and financial skills.

A university rarely "stride[s] boldly into the future." Rather it inches forward, building on its past as it does so.[140] Surprisingly, the issues facing the eight chancellors have remained remarkably consistent over time. Preparing KU for its next 50 years may be an even more daunting task than that facing Wescoe in 1965, of how to provide a high-quality undergraduate education to the masses of baby boomers. The pressing question facing Chancellor Gray-Little and her successors is and will be how to prepare KU for a somewhat uncertain future in which costs continue to rise (including tuition), the state's portion of overall funding continues to decline, and new forms of online education challenge traditional notions of where and how higher education occurs. Many argue that the current model of higher education is unsustainable; history would suggest otherwise. Although Chancellor Gray-Little and her successors may feel less confident about the future than Wescoe, this history of the chancellors suggests that, regardless of the challenges, a set of values and traditions has and will continue to sustain KU and its leaders in their quest to offer excellent teaching and learning, research, and public service to the state, the nation, and the world.

CHAPTER 2

The University and Government
Managing Politics

BURDETT LOOMIS

> We were driving to the regular Wednesday meeting of KU and Med
> Center officials in Kansas City. It was snowing like crazy, and the Turn-
> pike was icy. Archie [Dykes] was at the wheel, as usual, and, as usual, he
> was driving too fast. We hit an icy patch and spun out, into the median
> strip, and just sat there. A truck came along, and pulled us out. Archie
> started the car right back up, and off we went, still going too fast. But
> we got to the meeting.
> —Mike Davis, former KU general counsel and Law School dean

Although Chancellor Archie Dykes represented an extreme example,
University of Kansas chancellors typically must speed through their
days. There is so much to do, and so little time. Chancellors may be
most visible at ceremonial events and athletic contests, but a major
part of their job revolves around working with the state legislature and,
increasingly, the federal government, in dozens of distinct ways. In the
late 1970s, Chancellor Dykes was often rushing to the University of
Kansas Medical Center (KUMC) as part of a mandate from the Regents to make significant changes in how that important element of
the university operated. In his peripatetic, hands-on style, he personally oversaw a major shake-up at KUMC, which fundamentally altered
how it related to the central administration and how it served the state,
especially in rural areas.

Thirty-five years later, in the wake of enormous groundwork laid
by Chancellor Robert Hemenway and carried forward by Chancellor

Bernadette Gray-Little, KUMC gained federal designation as a National Cancer Center. Bob Hemenway drove more carefully than Archie Dykes, and Bernadette Gray-Little ultimately came to employ a driver, to use her time more effectively, but both paid inordinate attention to the Med Center and the KU Hospital as they successfully pursued this highly significant status for the institution.

The KU of 2015 differs greatly from that of 1965, but the interactions between a major state university and governmental actors, while changing dramatically over time, have continually shaped the role of the chancellor and the nature of the institution. This chapter will focus on many of the struggles and alliances between state and federal governments and the university, largely by exploring two broad and interrelated themes. The first emphasizes how the evolving, growing university of the past 50 years changed its relationships with the state and federal governments. The University of Kansas in 1965 was in the early days of an immense growth spurt, moving from about 13,000 students to more than 25,000 in 1980. This coincided with the development of myriad governmental policies, concerning issues such

Governor George Docking and Mary Docking with Chancellor Frank Murphy, 1956.

as student aid, research funding, construction subsidies, and a host of regulations that dictated a steady increase in connections to both Topeka and Washington, DC. Subsequently, KU has steadily placed greater emphasis on its research mission and related revenues, along with sharp tuition increases, while relying less on state governmental appropriations. The state-assisted university of the post-2000 period interacts with both state and federal entities in more and increasingly complex ways than in prior times. This presents a distinct set of challenges for KU as it wrestles with managing and taking best advantage of its multiple, overlapping ties to government.

The second theme addresses the substance and styles of KU's chancellors and top administrators as they have interacted with governors, legislators, and, to a lesser extent, federal officials. A key part of these interactions flows from how all the chancellors worked inside the university to prepare for outside lobbying on a host of issues. Another factor was how they worked with the Board of Regents, which articulated the higher education policy that framed many of the specific actions, strategies, and tactics of the university. Each chancellor has labored within a particular context of politics and policy, complemented by wide differences in styles, but all with the goal to move the university forward in myriad ways.

GOVERNMENT AND THE UNIVERSITY: 1965–2015

In the early 1960s, the state of Kansas remained strongly tied to its historic roots as a rural state, with a barebones budget of about $400 million (about $3 billion in 2013 dollars), which provided very modest support to K–12 education (a local obligation), maintained the essential and extensive road system, and funded five universities (soon to be six with the addition of Wichita State). Kansans did not expect too much from their government, and this expectation was met. Democratic governor Robert Docking (1967–1975) summarized this perspective with his catchphrase "Austere, but Adequate."[1] In 1965, the Kansas legislature remained among the most badly apportioned in the country. The state Senate had not been seriously reapportioned in 80 years, and the House was even worse. The state constitution dictated that each of Kansas's 105 counties would receive a minimum of one representative in the 125-member chamber, leaving metropolitan areas, especially Wichita and the Kansas City suburbs, grossly underrepresented. Given this malapportionment, it is remarkable—and a testimony to a century of state legislators—that the University of Kansas had been generally well supported. Still, as the university enrolled ever-larger numbers of students from Johnson County, the overwhelmingly rural orientation of the legislature was becoming increasingly problematic.

In the early 1960s, there were tangible signs that the state recognized that the baby boomers would need or demand far more investments in education, from kindergarten through graduate school. In 1965, Republican governor William Avery and the Republican-dominated legislature passed a sales tax increase that was driven by his desire to increase aid to K–12 education and enhance the state's community colleges.[2] The same baby boom bubble of students that was rapidly expanding elementary and secondary education was starting to test the capacity of higher education as well.

It is unclear how a badly malapportioned legislature would have reacted to these burgeoning pressures, but Kansans did not have to find out. By 1966, a series of national and state court cases had created a "one-person, one-vote" standard for apportionment that would profoundly change the nature of Kansas politics.[3] The first legislative session (1967) held in the wake of reapportionment and redistricting included 47 House members from the four most urban counties, up from the previous total of 22. And these numbers would only increase over the years, especially for Johnson County, whose House numbers rose from 10 in 1967 to 21 (20 percent of all seats) in 2013. Reapportionment, while extremely significant for Kansas politics and implicitly for higher education policy making, did not mean that urban/suburban districts dominated or that rural influence completely waned. But the balance of power had shifted, and this was central to the growth and evolution of KU from an undergraduate-oriented institution that served the state's needs for collegiate and professional education to a multifaceted, research-focused university in the twenty-first century.

In the wake of reapportionment and a move to modernize state government in the late 1960s and early 1970s, led by Representatives Pete McGill (R-Overland Park) and Pete Loux (D-Wichita), along with Senator Robert Bennett (R-Johnson County), Kansas government morphed from its nineteenth-century configuration in the early 1960s to a more modern structure within a decade. These changes were solidified when the moderate, policy-oriented Republican Bennett narrowly and unexpectedly won the governorship in 1974, defeating Attorney General Vern Miller, a conservative Democrat who had won notoriety for, among other things, conducting drug busts in Lawrence (sometimes by leaping out of a police car's trunk). Although Bennett

Pierre Salinger, press secretary to Presidents Kennedy and Johnson, speaking at KU about the press and government, 1972.

served only one term, sandwiched between the eight-year Democratic regimes of Robert Docking and John Carlin, his reforms as senator and governor produced a stable, moderate-conservative governing tradition in Kansas, which lasted largely unchallenged until the 2010 election of conservative Republican Sam Brownback.

Despite day-in, day-out partisan politics, rural-urban conflicts, and even the introduction of social issues over the 1965–2010 period, Kansas actually experienced great stability. Governors, whether Democratic or Republican, faced a legislature that was ultimately controlled by a moderate-conservative majority that produced bipartisan coalitions, especially when it came to annual budget bills. This generally worked to the advantage of the university, in that chancellors and KU lobbyists could build strong long-term relationships with responsible officeholders. Over time, KU could educate key committee chairs and top legislative leaders about its needs and opportunities, as with the Med Center and the expansion of research capacity. Moreover, governors from rural areas, such as Democrat John Carlin (1979–1987) and Republican Mike Hayden (1987–1991), understood the importance of the university to the entire state, in large part because they had served in key committee and party leadership roles in the legislature. Thus, as we shall see, KU chancellors could create lasting linkages within a generally predictable political environment.

The valuable stability of a moderate-conservative Kansas governing coalition came to an end in the elections of 2010 and 2012. In 2010, US senator Sam Brownback easily won the governorship; he campaigned on a platform of lower income taxes, which he argued would provide a "shot of adrenaline" to the lagging Kansas economy. In 2012, the legislature passed a radical tax bill, eliminating income taxes for many small businesses and individual proprietorships, while reducing income taxes for most other Kansans. Predictably, this resulted in a substantial drop in state revenues; in 2014, there was no sign that lower tax rates had spurred the state's economy. Moreover, in 2012, Brownback and his right-wing allies campaigned vigorously against several moderate GOP state senators and won most of these races. When the legislature convened in 2013, both chambers were firmly controlled by far-right majorities. The long-term implications of this change are not clear, but what is certain is that the university's previous, stable relationship with legislators and governors over a 40-year period has been dramatically altered. For KU in particular and higher education in general, this has placed into question the level of overall state support that could be expected.

Charles Oldfather, university counsel and professor of law in the 1960s and an accomplished musician.

Beyond the political climate in Topeka and across the state, various broad trends affected the relationship between the university and state and federal governments. As of 1965, federal funds represented only a sliver of the university's budget. Likewise, the ensuing waves of federal regulations were yet to wash over the university; these would affect everything from financial aid to the privacy rights of students to research funding and would require compliance with a web of complex rules and reporting requirements. By 2014, federal funds from all sources, although difficult to calculate, provided, either directly or indirectly, a significant portion of the university's budget, largely through student financial aid and grants for research, training, or other purposes. Internally, this meant that administrative resources were required to address federal reporting requirements and other expectations. Most notable, perhaps, was the steady growth of the University Counsel's office. It grew from one part-time lawyer, Professor Charles Oldfather in 1965, to a phalanx of attorneys and support personnel that worked in Lawrence or at the Med Center in 2014. Thus, in the words of University Counsel Jim Pottorf:

> Currently, the office has four full-time attorneys at KUMC: a health law attorney, an employment law attorney, a contracts attorney, and a risk manager/health law attorney. We also have a paralegal and an administrative assistant there. In the Lawrence office we also have four full-time attorneys: two litigators/employment law attorneys, a higher education/ employment law attorney, and "generalist" who provides most of our support to the university's research enterprise in Lawrence. We also have the university tax analyst, an office manager, and an administrative assistant. Finally, there is an attorney at the Kansas Law Enforcement Center who is appointed 25 percent as an associate general counsel and 75 percent as chief academic officer for that organization. I am the 10th attorney in our office. While there has been significant growth in the last 14 years, it roughly corresponds to the growth in federal law and regulations covering many aspects of university operations.[4]

Lobbying was yet another realm of expanding activity. Although KU had employed a federal government representative since the 1970s, that individual had either been a part-time contract lobbyist in DC (Bob Woody) or had resided in Lawrence, traveling to Washington once or twice a month (Keith Yehle). In 2012, the university hired Jack Cline as its DC lobbyist; he lived in Washington and had had similar experience at another major research university. Representing KU in Washington had become a full-time job with a permanent base in the capital.

As federal funding has risen, state monies for Regents' institutions, as a percentage of the total state budget, have fallen steadily from the late 1960s to 2015, dropping from 24.3 percent in 1969 to the 12 percent range by 2012.[5] Moreover, the state's share of funding for KU gradually, then precipitously, fell over the 1985–2014 period, as evident in Table I-2 in the Introduction.

Although the university continued to rely on state appropriations for the lion's share of its instructional funding until the early years of the twenty-first century, it rapidly increased tuition to the point that, by 2005, the largest block of funding came from tuition and fees. And the gap has continued to widen, especially in the wake of KU's successful, long-term campaign to control tuition funds, which won legislative approval in 2002 (see below). While this meant the university could expand its budget, albeit at greater cost to students and their families, this major change dramatically shifted its reliance on the state. As *LJW* publisher and longtime critic/observer Dolph Simons, Jr., noted in 2014, "In 2003, the state of Kansas provided 27 percent of KU's operating budget. Today, the state provides 17.6 percent of the university's operating fund. In 2003, tuition funds provided 21 percent of the university's operating funds. This year, tuition dollars account for 32.4 percent of those funds."[6]

Politically, one implication for many conservative state legislators has been that the state's obligation to fund the university is substantially less than it once was, given KU's capacity to raise tuition. In many ways, this trend mirrors those in many other states, as universities become state-assisted, rather than relying on direct funding from annual budgets.[7] In addition, KU's growing ability to raise private money through the KUEA and increase its external research funding provide additional rationales for the state to reduce both its share of the university budget and the proportion of overall state appropriations that flow to KU. It is ironic—and perhaps perverse—that the very success of the university in attracting federal research funds and KUEA's proficiency in raising large sums of private money has meant that legislators and governors can apportion fewer state dollars to KU and other public universities.

In sum, the university's relationships with both state and federal governments have changed substantially. State funding, while still significant, has declined in relative importance; federal funding from multiple sources has grown very rapidly but has necessitated that the university increase its administrative staff to manage related requirements and standards of performance. These trends mean that chancellors have faced changing circumstances in both Topeka and Washington, DC, as they have guided the institution from its smaller, service-to-the-state identity of the late 1950s and early 1960s to its complex balance of undergraduate, graduate, and professional education with the growing research expectations of the twenty-first century.

PERSONALITIES, POLITICS, AND POLICIES:
CHANCELLORS AND THE PUBLIC SPHERE

Over time, chancellors have come to rely on more staff members as they deal with legislators, governors, and federal officials. Still, only the chancellor can truly speak for the university, and such statements set the tone for relations with all levels of government. Examining how chancellors have dealt with these obligations offers revealing insights into how the university has evolved with respect to its external relationships over the past half century.

The Chancellor as Public Figure: From Murphy to Nichols (1950s–1973)

To understand the linkages between KU and the state government, one cannot begin in 1965. Rather, the appropriate starting point is the late 1950s and the remarkably public battles between two Kansas giants: Democratic governor George Docking (from Lawrence) and Chancellor Franklin Murphy, a vocal opponent of the governor and a Republican.[8] Docking consistently challenged Murphy's view of the university as an institution that served the state and society in multiple ways, including through cultural enrichment and research productivity. The chancellor, in turn, became increasingly combative, fearing that the progress he had helped engineer in the early 1950s would be reversed by a governor who viewed education through the lens of an "auditor." Moreover, the governor, in 1957, banned the chancellor, along with other college leaders, from presenting their budget proposals to the legislature, arguing that they were becoming nothing more than politicians. Indeed, over the remainder of his tenure at KU, Franklin Murphy remained in the political crucible, both speaking and editorializing against the cuts proposed by George Docking and his budget director, Jim Bibb.

Murphy's dramatic resignation on March 17, 1960, effective immediately, ended the personal conflict, which had intensified since 1956, when Murphy publicly supported the Republican nominee, Warren Shaw, against Docking. Their continuing battles over budgets and vision ended with their respective departures from the Kansas political scene by 1961. In a larger sense, the Murphy-Docking era (1956–1960) interjected an unseemly amount of politics into the relationship between the university and the state, as well as leaving up in the air the question of what kind of university KU would become. The personal nature of their differences was a major element in the selection of KU Medical School dean Clarke Wescoe to succeed Murphy as chancellor.

Wescoe was Murphy's clear choice for the chancellorship, given his success as Medical School dean in the wake of Murphy's promotion from that position in 1950. Wescoe was widely admired, and the Regents were set to recommend him with a 6–3 vote.[9] Wescoe expressed dismay at the divided vote and stated that he would not accept the

Chancellor Wescoe flanked by Governor Docking and Provost George Wolf a few weeks before stepping down in 1969.

position under such circumstances. It appeared that the divisiveness of the Murphy-Docking era would continue to affect relations between the state and the university. Various participants in the process explained to him, however, that three regents felt obliged to cast a negative vote in deference to the governor, but that this single vote would represent the full extent of their obligation to Docking. This proved to be the case; Clarke Wescoe later reported that during the remainder of his tenure as chancellor the regents voted unanimously to back his proposals. With the 1960 election of a new governor, Republican John Anderson, the overt, partisan politics in the relationship between the KU chancellor and the governor was put to rest.

Clarke Wescoe's energetic, accomplished approach to the chancellorship allowed the university to leave behind, quickly and relatively painlessly, the legacy of the contentious Murphy-Docking relationship. That did not mean that the 1960s would be an easy time for Chancellor Wescoe, but it did allow the university to grow steadily, even as George Docking's son Robert, an heir to his father's fiscal conservatism, began his first of four two-year terms as governor in 1967. In many ways, as a political actor within the state and as the chief representative of the university, Wescoe both continued Murphy's initiatives and diverged substantially from his predecessor's more direct, sometimes confrontational approach, as he pursued KU's interests. Still, as chancellor, he did insert himself into policy debates, even on thorny and controversial issues. For example, in 1963 as the legislature was preparing to meet, he called for enhanced state funding of the university, a typical request for any chancellor. But in addition to the funding request, he proposed instituting a statewide sales tax, which he labeled "the only quick, continuing source of a substantial amount of state revenue."[10]

The sales tax did become law, and in a general way the university benefited from this new revenue stream, even as it confronted the budgetary austerity of Governor Robert Docking. Wescoe's tenure witnessed steady growth in student numbers and budgets, as well as numbers of faculty members, and the chancellor, with modest administrative support by the standards of later eras, was continually on the move. As he reflected on his tenure as chancellor and as dean of the KU Medical School, he noted, "For the past 18 years my children really haven't had a father. I have gone as long as 37 days without ever sitting down to dinner with my family."[11]

As chancellor, Wescoe was by definition heavily involved with state policy making, but given his professional and administrative position, his advice was also valued at the national level. His work in Washington included consulting on the implementation of Medicare and participating in the Johnson-Nixon transition process in late 1968, as well as testifying on various legislative proposals before Congress. As more federal programs, such as student aid, research funding, and construction assistance, came to affect universities, Wescoe participated in significant ways as a national educational figure, one whose stature transcended the state.

Chancellor Wescoe earned near-unanimous plaudits and many expressions of regret in the wake of announcing his retirement in September 1968, effective at the end of the academic year. This outpouring demonstrated his success in playing a statewide role both as KU's chancellor and as a well-regarded advocate for higher education.[12]

Clarke Wescoe's increasingly tense last months at KU presaged the brief and tumultuous career of his successor, Lawrence Chalmers. The protesting of and eventual cancelation of the spring 1969 military officer induction ceremony (see Chapter 1) demonstrated that the anti–Vietnam War movement that had swept through many other campuses across the nation would not spare KU and Lawrence. Indeed, Chancellor Chalmers, who went through a national recruitment process in contrast to Wescoe's ascension, was never able to place his mark

Senator Robert Kennedy campaigning at KU, March 18, 1968.

upon the university during his three-year tenure. If Franklin Murphy had made clear decisions in pursuing a political fight with Governor George Docking, Chancellor Chalmers had little choice in defending the university amid protests and violence in Lawrence. Murphy brought the university into politics, while Chalmers led an institution that had politics thrust upon it.

Alone among KU's chancellors over the past 50 years, Lawrence Chalmers found it impossible to chart a conventional course in terms of pursuing enhanced budgets, capital improvements, and other policies that might advance the particular interests of the university. Other authors in this volume detail the issues that he was forced to address. Fairly or not, the Chalmers era was judged a failure by many state policy makers, regardless of where responsibility might reasonably have been placed. Moreover, his brief, stormy tenure left many legislators, to say nothing of Governor Robert Docking, skeptical about the character of the university, even as it continued to grow during this period.

To rebuild important relationships between KU and state policy makers, the Regents made two crucial personnel decisions. First, they appointed longtime KU administrator Ray Nichols, who had served five previous chancellors as executive secretary, to become interim

Exterior damage to the Kansas Union, April 1970.

chancellor for the 1972–1973 academic year. Nichols was an ideal selection,[13] a well-known administrator who understood both the internal and the external politics of the university. Still, the selection of a
new permanent chancellor, who would face a skeptical legislature and
a host of emerging problems, was crucial to the university during the
brief Nichols administration.

Mr. Fix-It: The Hands-On Style of Archie Dykes

Archie Dykes served a relatively short time—seven years—as KU's
chancellor, but his energetic style, minute attention to detail, and willingness to address difficult problems allowed him to make an indelible
mark upon the university and the state. Many previous chancellors—
including Franklin Murphy and Clarke Wescoe—had been major public figures within the state, but the Chalmers-Nichols years had, for
various reasons, diminished the statewide luster of the KU chancellor.
Archie Dykes restored the visibility of this role, albeit in his unique
way. As longtime KU administrator (and former chancellor) Del Shankel observed, "Archie was highly detailed-oriented, and emphasized
personal relationships. He saw Kansans as his constituents, a little like

Governor Robert Bennett visiting a KU class in 1973.

an electoral politician."[14] Given this outlook, the chancellor could understand how legislators thought about the university, and attitudes became generally positive during his tenure. At the same time, he was fortunate to work for four years with Governor Robert Bennett, who loved the details of policy. "Bennett was a policy aficionado, who could get deeply into the bowels of the budget," noted Shankel, "which gave him a great capacity to understand the university as an institution."[15]

Additionally, Dykes enjoyed excellent relations with key legislative leaders. Representative Mike Hayden (R-Atwood), as a member and then chair of the House Ways and Means committee, worked closely with him, as the chancellor frequently visited the capitol and often hosted Hayden and other legislative leaders at his residence. Republican Speaker Joe Hoagland, from Johnson County, would regularly stop by as he drove to and from Topeka. And when the chancellor was not personally engaging legislators, his do-everything assistant Rick Von Ende, would be at the capitol, chatting with lawmakers during and after their legislative sessions. Although he was never given the title of KU lobbyist, that is exactly the role that Von Ende filled between 1974 and 1986. A graduate student who was working part-time in KU public relations operations (under former Speaker John Conard), he was tapped by Ray Nichols to fill in as executive secretary, an appointment that Dykes made permanent in 1973. The energetic Von Ende was the ideal person to serve as the chancellor's eyes and ears. He noted, "Archie had an incredible need to know everything that was happening that might affect KU, especially in the university."[16]

Chancellor Dykes with Kansas City, Kansas, Mayor Richard Walsh at the KU Medical Center.

While the chancellor maintained a busy schedule, which included courting legislators, Von Ende became KU's full-time representative at the statehouse during the session. Dykes did have some major policy goals, such as gaining control of the Med Center, but his overarching concern lay with the budget. Although state budget director Jim Bibb, a legendary and powerful figure, and the Regents had the most influence in setting levels of salaries and operating and other expenses, there remained room for KU to argue for its own projects and funding within the legislative process. Von Ende testified regularly before the appropriations committees in both chambers and worked closely with Lawrence legislators, such as Representative John Vogel and Senators Reynolds Schultz, Arnold Berman, Jane Eldredge, and Wint Winter, Jr., all Republicans, save Berman. The Dykes/Von Ende duo had to be careful in seeking too many resources for KU, given the Regents' aim to have all institutions treated fairly, though not identically, in accord with their distinct missions.[17]

Overall, the combined lobbying of Archie Dykes and Rick Von Ende proved successful. Von Ende recounted that in 1978 Chancellor Dykes asked him to come up with a total figure of new KU funding for programs and capital projects since he arrived in Lawrence in 1973; that sum approached $175 million, including the Lawrence campus and the Medical School facilities in Kansas City and Wichita.[18] This latter endeavor was especially significant in buttressing KU's status with legislators from Sedgwick County and the western part of the state.

Bennett's interest in budgets and policy was important as he worked with Dykes to address a host of problems with the KU Hospital and Medical School. This was no easy task, as physicians and their practices dominated the KU Hospital. While technically under the authority of the university, the physicians had tremendous autonomy, often to the disadvantage of KU. A story from the Chalmers era illustrates this lack of control. The chancellor and Keith Nitcher, KU's vice chancellor for business and financial affairs, were headed to Topeka for a Board of Regents meeting, and the morning of the meeting Nitcher called the Med Center to ask for a copy of its budget. He was informed that the chancellor and his party could pick it up at the Lawrence West exit on the Kansas Turnpike, which they did.[19] The fact that the chancellor's office did not have a copy of this important document, along with its unceremonious delivery, underscored the often-tenuous relationship of KU's central administration to the Medical School.

While working for the legislature, Marlin Rein accompanied several legislators to the Board of Regents offices for what he would describe as a "Come to Jesus meeting."[20] Tempers flared as legislative leaders admonished the Regents to ensure that the university would regain administrative control of the Med Center, something that former KU Medical School deans Murphy and Wescoe had maintained, given their experience there. As Rein recounted, "Archie got the message," and he immediately instituted weekly meetings at the Med Center, at which he would preside. Steadily, Dykes strengthened his administrative hold there by integrating various departments and other units and having them report to his office. Dykes's attention to detail was crucial, and after his departure the Med Center moved back toward less accountability—a problem that the next two chancellors would have to address.[21]

*The Budig-Hemenway Era: The State University
Becomes the State-Assisted University*

From 1981 through 2010, save for Del Shankel's second stint as "pinch hitter," the University of Kansas was led by two chancellors: Gene Budig (1981–1994) and Robert (Bob) Hemenway (1995–2009). Although they were stylistically different and approached the chancellor's job in distinct ways, their nearly 30 years of KU leadership in dealing with state and federal issues constitutes a single arc of KU's movement from a state university to a state-assisted institution, a path similar to that of many other public research universities.[22]

As chancellor, Archie Dykes had proven a great ambassador to the state and a successful task-oriented leader, as suggested by his work with the Med Center, though this issue would still require assiduous attention from both Budig and Hemenway. Moreover, Dykes's relatively brief seven-year tenure did not address many fundamental issues, such as building and maintaining a strong, well-paid faculty, attracting more research funding, and regularizing the ways in which the university related to legislators and administrators in Topeka and Washington.

If, as chancellor, Archie Dykes was omnipresent around the state and at the state capitol, Gene Budig's presence was far less flashy and far more nuanced. As one former administrative colleague concluded, "Gene was very cautious. You had to jump through a lot of hoops to do anything."[23] Such a deliberate style meant that when KU acted during his tenure, it did so with great preparation and a high probability of success. With a background that included a doctorate in education, significant experience in newspaper publishing and high-level state politics (as a staff member for the governor of Nebraska), and stints as the chief executive of two large state universities (Illinois State and West Virginia), Budig took over KU's administrative reins with a remarkable background, considering that he was just 41 when he became the 14th chancellor. In many ways, Gene Budig could not have been better prepared for the job.

Budig's experience showed in how he established relationships with many powerful individuals in the state. For example, he grew up in McCook, Nebraska, about 60 miles north of Atwood, Kansas, the hometown of Mike Hayden, who served as House Ways and Means chair, speaker, and governor during the Budig era. Given Atwood's far northwest Kansas location, its high school students often went to McCook, a regional hub, for various competitions and events. Moreover, as Hayden recounted, "I was from a baseball family, and we hit it off right away," which was natural, given Budig's abiding interest in the game.[24] "We had a great relationship," Hayden said, "and overall KU did real well in the Legislature over those years (1981–1990)."

Likewise, with his background in regional newspaper publishing, Budig quickly established a strong relationship with the prickly-but-influential publisher of the *LJW*, Dolph Simons, Jr. Although good personal ties could not shield him completely from Simon's editorial

Chancellor Budig (center) meets with legislators at the annual KU luncheon in 1988.

slings and arrows, in general the hometown paper did not take issue with the chancellor's actions, a state of affairs that did not extend to his successor.

It would be an understatement to observe that Gene Budig was a cautious man as chancellor; that was his nature. But like other chancellors over the past half century, he labored energetically and tirelessly on behalf of KU, and many of those efforts were directed at working with public officials. Although one top-level KU administrator concluded that Budig thought he only needed to know, personally, about six key individuals in the state, that was a considerable overstatement. Rather, as chancellor, Budig institutionalized KU's governmental relations operation. He inherited uber-lobbyist Rick Von Ende and worked effectively with him until personal issues led to Von Ende's ouster in 1986. Still, Von Ende's dynamic, highly personal style of lobbying was better suited for the Archie Dykes era than for the more reserved style of Gene Budig.

To replace Von Ende, in 1986 Budig called upon veteran state legislative fiscal specialist Marlin Rein, who had come to the university in 1983, after nine years in Topeka. Rein brought a host of assets to his job as chief KU lobbyist. He had extensive background with the hospital, both in Topeka and in his initial three years at KU; holding a

Governor John Carlin (center) meeting with KU students in 1984.

master's degree in Public Administration from KU, he also had strong professional and personal contacts in the state budget office and the legislature. In particular, he had a long-standing individual relationship with Mike Hayden, perhaps the single most important Kansas politician of the 1980s. As Rein put it, "I knew how the system worked and how you could work it. I had great respect for the legislature and these were personal friends."[25]

Rein made good use of his skills and contacts in representing the university, as did his associate, Jon Josserand, who joined him in 1991 after serving in state government. Rein worked closely with Budig and Keith Nitcher, KU's chief budget officer, along with other top administrators, to craft well-developed, factually sound proposals that they could present to the regents, the governor, and the legislature as being in the best interests of the state and the university. Rein and his team would try to make their proposals "a win for everyone." This often meant working with Douglas County legislators, such as Republican senator Wint Winter, Jr., and Democratic representative John Solbach, to champion KU's interests in Topeka without antagonizing other legislators, especially those from rural areas. In practice, the Lawrence-area legislators sought to build broad coalitions in which KU, with its northeast Kansas/Johnson County base, would work with legislators across the state. That is partly how the Edwards campus came into existence; in a key 1989 appropriations conference committee, Rein convinced the conferees to put the campus back into the budget by loading "the bill up with lots of stuff for K–12 and community colleges,"[26] which

Chancellor Budig (right) and Governor Joan Finney at the signing of Hoch Bill in 1992.

rural legislators favored. Moreover, the funding of the Edwards campus led to the first instance of KU being permitted to capture tuition money for its own use, an important precedent for the comprehensive powers it would later gain.

This is not to say that Gene Budig was not important to KU's success in Topeka. Although his legislative testimony would often be dry, with key points duly numbered so as not to omit anything, his answers to legislators' often well-formed questions, such as those from House Ways and Means chair Gus Bogina, were on point and sometimes laced with humor. In the end, to the extent that he was a politician, he practiced retail politics, not the wholesale variety of Archie Dykes. Whether on the phone, or in his office, or at a KU basketball game, Budig was effective with those who could help the university. One close observer noted that if an individual was not a strong supporter of KU, he (or she) did not merit much consideration from the chancellor. He left relations with such individuals in the capable hands of Marlin Rein and Douglas County lawmakers.

Indeed, during the 1970s and 1980s, the Douglas County legislative delegation often functioned as highly significant representatives of the university. While such a description applied to most legislators, the most important figure was Wint Winter, Jr., who served in the state Senate between 1983 and 1994. A former KU football player and the son of Republican state senator (Ottawa) Wint Winter, Sr., a farmer, banker, and diehard KU supporter, Winter noted, "Early on [in my Senate career] effective advocacy for KU was the most important outcome each year."[27] As a Republican member of the Senate Ways and Means Committee, Winter was in an ideal position to protect KU's interests, especially within the Republican-controlled body. Even as he took on other important issues with increased seniority, Winter could use his Ways and Means position and seat on conference committees to do his best for KU. Moreover, this also meant that the chancellor often had a direct line to a key legislator. This did not mean that the university could get all that it wanted, in terms of capital projects, salary enhancements, and increased operating expenses, but the generally moderate nature of the legislature in the 1980s did mean that Winter, Rein, and others could team together for consistent levels of success, depending on the state's fiscal condition.[28]

Typical of the cooperative efforts between KU and its legislative supporters in the 1980s was the campaign to pass the "Margin of Excellence" bill in 1988, within the context of a broad Board of Regents' initiative to increase faculty salaries, thus making them more competitive nationally. Taking advantage of a strong state financial position, the Regents made an aggressive three-year proposal, calling for excellence within a national higher education context. The program was ultimately approved, with $30 million going to KU in the Margin of Excellence's first two years.[29] For Senator Winter, the key was that the regents' proposal "provided a hook" for KU and other universities to argue in favor of enhanced funding; after that, he noted, he urged the chancellor to lobby more effectively across the state, especially in rural areas, bringing the power of KU alums to bear. In short, he pushed KU to build a strong "grass-roots" effort among influential constituents in legislators' districts. Such lobbying, he noted, was far more likely to succeed, at least then, than having particular legislative leaders attempt to push Senate Ways and Means chair Bogina to do it. With the support of Governor Mike Hayden, who actively supported the initiative, those who had a vision for strengthening higher education ultimately triumphed.

During the Budig years, KU and the Board of Regents constantly struggled with the legislature over retaining tuition funds generated by rising enrollment, as well as what the proper levels of tuition should be. The Board of Regents continued to stick to its core policy goal of

Chancellor Budig (right) with Governor Mike Hayden, 1990.

"high accessibility and low cost" for in-state students, but the legislature, most notably Representative Gus Bogina (R-Johnson County), the Ways and Means chair, opened the door to tuition increases beyond historic norms.[30] Throughout the Budig era, there were continuing adjustments within a three-cornered set of negotiations among state government, the Board of Regents, and the university. KU came to control somewhat more of its own tuition funds, but only as a result of a well-organized lobbying effort that included the chancellor, the provost, Keith Nitcher, Marlin Rein, and Jon Josserand (with the latter two representing the university on a daily basis in Topeka), along with the Board of Regents.

Gene Budig, the cautious gradualist, worked consistently to move KU down the road to becoming a more research-oriented university, lobbying the legislature consistently for better funding, Upon his arrival at KU in 1981, according to one account, "Budig's goals as chancellor were to attract and retain the nation's best educators, expand the University's libraries and physical plant, improve services and increase efficiency at KUMC, and, naturally, to loosen the purse-strings of the state legislature."[31] In his steady way, Chancellor Budig accomplished those goals, and far more. But in departing, he left the critical tasks of resolving structural issues at the Med Center and KU Hospital and gaining full control of revenues (whether from research, tuition, or the KU Hospital) still to be resolved.

In contrast to Budig's style, Robert Hemenway was practically spontaneous. In a 2014 interview, former governor Bill Graves (1995–2003) recounted a modest, but telling, story of how Hemenway operated as chancellor:

> I remember one day when I was governor, and Bob Hemenway was proposing to build a new scholarship hall, on the east edge of the campus. The University wanted to tear down some old, decrepit houses, and was running into problems from the State Historical Society. It turns out that in an obscure section of legislation, the governor has the right to overturn the ruling of the director of the historical society. I was in Lawrence one day, and Hemenway grabbed me and got me into his car, and we drove down to the prospective site. The houses really were a mess, and I agreed to approve the demolition. And Bob got his scholarship hall built.[32]

If Gene Budig demonstrated a cautious personal style, which overlapped with his approach to administration, his successor (after Del Shankel's second stint as interim chancellor), Robert (Bob) Hemenway, proved more outgoing and more goal oriented, sometimes at the risk of alienating prospective supporters. That is, Hemenway focused more on accomplishing large goals than on making steady progress across a wide array of issues. As veteran KU lobbyist Marlin Rein observed, "He would look at a problem, say 'Why not?' and move ahead."[33] And even with the growth of KU's public relations machinery, increasingly centralized in the chancellor's office, Hemenway was often more spontaneous than the often-staid Budig. Overall, both styles worked well at the university, with Budig's cautious progress laying the groundwork for Hemenway's major accomplishments. These included winning control of tuition funds and dramatically reforming the Med Center/KU Hospital, as well as continuing Budig's initiatives by embarking upon a major expansion at the Edwards campus and increasing the research capacity of the university.

Hemenway, a former English professor who, like Budig, continued to teach as chancellor, had served as dean of arts and sciences at the University of Oklahoma and as chancellor for six years at the University of Kentucky. Although he did not have as much experience as Budig as a higher education chief executive, his background at similar major state universities prepared him well for working with the Kansas state government. Hemenway had the relative good fortune to work

Big Jay visits the legislature to celebrate a basketball victory over Kansas State in 1975.

with two pro–higher education governors, Bill Graves and Kathleen Sebelius. In addition, at least for the first few years of his tenure, from 1995 to 2000, the state's economy, mirroring that of the country's, performed very well.

After assuming the chancellor's position in 1995, Hemenway demonstrated his big-picture mentality, as he sought to fundamentally change the relationship between KU and the state in (1) restructuring the KU Hospital and the Medical School so as to create far more independence from the state for the hospital, while leveraging new funds to improve services, medical education, and national rankings; and (2) obtaining control of tuition rates and cash flow for the university. Both tuition control and the status of the KU Hospital and Med School had received substantial attention from Chancellors Dykes and Budig, but they remained difficult, contentious issues. These questions required continuing work for the chancellor, his top staff, the Board of Regents, and legislative leaders, because in each instance a major goal was to increase the fiscal independence of the university from the state. Doing this would likely benefit KU, to be sure, but might also be seen as weakening state control over the university and denying sources of KU-generated funds to the state.

Upon arriving at KU in 1995, Hemenway sought to radically restructure the Med Center and Hospital. By 1996, he and his administration laid out a plan to move the hospital outside the control of the state, a proposal filled with a variety of challenges. In a series of steps that mirrored the approach of previous chancellors, Hemenway took his time, built a strong team to lobby state government, and, most important, developed a strong argument on behalf of the changes he proposed. Such preparation might seem routine, but—in one form or another—it reflects what virtually all KU policy advocates report when asked how the university is most effective in pursuing its preferences. In their own ways, the Dykes team and the Budig team did much the same thing in building well-reasoned cases to achieve major changes.

KU's most pressing obstacle in seeking independence for the Med Center was that the hospital provided a substantial source of revenue to the Regents system and, indirectly, to the state. "The hospital was a cash cow for the Regents," stated former KU lobbyist and Med Center veteran Marlin Rein. "Income was siphoned off to support non-hospital purposes; they became general use funds, and the legislature treated these funds interchangeably. So, when the hospital produced more revenue than the Med Center could use, state funding went down, which meant that the excess funds could go to other institutions."[34]

Former president Bill Clinton, Senator Bob Dole, and Chancellor Hemenway at the Dole Institute in 2004.

Simply put, as former provost David Shulenburger observed, "If the hospital made money, it was taken by the state. If it lost money, the university had to eat it."[35] In broader policy terms, given the complexity of major academic hospitals, KUMC truly needed to win managerial independence from the state, not just to defend itself, but to embark upon entrepreneurial expansion and modernization that could propel it into the top ranks of academic medicine. As Hemenway put it, privatization was essential "so that the hospital could function as a private business but support the mission of the medical center."[36]

Over the course of three years, between 1996 and 1999, Hemenway, Shulenburger, and Rein, along with Don Hagen, the chancellor's choice to lead KUMC, built a case for restructuring with the legislature. Key supporters included influential Republican senators Dick Bond (Johnson County), Dave Kerr (Hutchinson), and Steve Morris (Ulysses). While Bond could legitimately be called a "moderate," Kerr and Morris were traditional Kansas conservatives, from far beyond the Kansas City metro area. Kerr, in particular, as chair of the Ways and Means Committee, was crucial to any plan that would shift significant funds. Given Rein's long-term, trusting connections to both the Med Center and the legislature, the university was able to assure skeptical lawmakers that creating an independent entity would best serve the state. The restructuring of 1999 did not end health policy politicking for the Med Center, as the 2000–2010 period witnessed "some real growing pains." In the end, the new entity benefited both the university and the state, to the point that Rein could conclude, "Although we got some relief from the state over the previous twenty years, the hospital might not have survived; it just wasn't all that great. But by 2014 it's the best facility between Denver and St. Louis."[37]

If Hemenway took the lead in pushing for the KUMC restructuring, he needed to be convinced that KU should seek to capture control of its tuition and then significantly raise its rates. "That wasn't the Chancellor's project," noted former provost Shulenburger. "It took me forever to convince him that it was necessary. Bob Hemenway was a populist. He wanted to keep tuition rates low."[38] Indeed, the fight over tuition represented the last chapter in the redefining of the university as a major research institution, one that would also do a good job of educating undergraduates. This was a slight shift away from a primary focus on provision of a liberal education to students from across the state. "If we stuck with low tuition," Shulenburger stated, "we were destined to remain poor [financially]," and that implied educational mediocrity.

Again, KU needed to convince the legislature that it should give up control of tuition funds, so that the university could place itself in a position to compete with its peers. The campaign for higher tuition was multifaceted, with Shulenburger and others convincing the Regents, KU students, and, not insignificant, *LJW* publisher Dolph Simons, Jr., who editorialized in favor of the move. In addition, the Kansas State administration went along with the KU proposal, which helped convince legislators and the Regents. Shulenburger and the provost of Kansas State traveled across the state, visiting legislators in their homes. KU also effectively employed its alumni network across the state, arguing that increasing salaries, reducing class sizes, and enhancing computer access were crucial to improving KU's competitive position. In the end, the Board of Regents tasked the university with pursuing the legislation, which was passed in 2002 as part of a five-year plan. All Regents institutions benefited from this development.[39]

Ironically, the capture of tuition funds, while sold largely in terms of improving undergraduate education, provided the university with both the revenues and the flexibility to grow in directions that ultimately moved institutional priorities more toward scientific and professional education and an increasingly corporate management style. Department chairs and deans had decreased autonomy, as hiring decisions increasingly reflected broad university priorities. And this trend

Former president Jimmy Carter at the Dole Institute dedication, 2003.

escalated in the post-Hemenway era with the implementation of an inclusive strategic plan.[40]

Moreover, with KUMC restructured and revitalized, the chancellor could turn to his final major project: obtaining a "major cancer center" designation for the Med Center. Hemenway would step down as chancellor before the National Cancer Center designation was announced in 2012, seven years after he had made it the university's top policy goal,[41] but the same project-oriented, step-by-step process was followed. The university's most important move came in recruiting Roy Jensen, a distinguished cancer research scientist, to head the effort. Not only did KU need to convince the National Cancer Institute and the Kansas congressional delegation of its Med Center prowess, but it required the solid backing of the Regents, the governor, and the legislature. In the end, everyone cooperated to make the effort a success.

One additional change, unique to KU within the Regents system, should be noted. In 2003, with the active backing of the provost, Chancellor Hemenway sought to detach KU's classified workers from the overall state system. As with tuition matters, he and Shulenburger concluded that the university needed more flexibility to address a whole range of classified-staff issues, ranging from salaries to working conditions. Administrators lobbied the Regents, the legislature, and the classified workers to win this significant policy change. As Shulenburger noted, "The Regents were always willing to treat KU differently if the other institutions had the chance to do the same."[42] In October 2003, the Classified Senate voted in favor of this policy, and the legislature gave its overwhelming approval in 2005; KU remains the only university within the state that has taken advantage of this option.

The amiable, seemingly low-key Bob Hemenway and his administrative team worked with state and national government officials in highly organized ways as he pursued these major projects, along with many others. His provosts—David Shulenburger and Richard Lariviere—proved effective emissaries to the legislature. As the chief operating officers of the university, they were effective in working closely with key legislators as they provided solid information on KU's activities and plans. Along with the university's paid lobbyists—Jon Josserand, Marlin Rein, Kathy Damron, and, for federal affairs, Keith Yehle—they complemented Hemenway's goal-oriented approach to serving as chancellor. They also benefited from the continuing, if increasingly challenged, power of the moderate conservative coalition that had controlled the state for almost 50 years.

Chancellor Bernadette Gray-Little: Sailing into Uncharted Waters

As an African American woman, Bernadette Gray-Little, becoming KU's 17th chancellor in August 2009, provided a very different face for the university. She would have just over a year to coexist with a traditional state legislature and its moderate-conservative majority, before the November 2010 elections would dramatically shift the character of Kansas politics. Naturally quiet and retiring, Chancellor Gray-Little slowly built the kind of relationships that Budig and Hemenway, in different ways, had established relatively quickly. The sudden emergence of an increasingly right-wing state government meant that any chancellor and KU administration would have found the politics of the post-2010 era to be very challenging.

Chancellor Gray-Little's most significant initial task was to maintain the momentum behind KU's bid for National Cancer Center designation. The National Cancer Institute had previously invited the university to bid for this status by September 2011, so a major part of her job was to make sure that the appropriate steps were effectively completed.[43] Preparation for the application included not only funding a host of major drug trials, but also lobbying the Kansas legislature and the Johnson County Board of Supervisors to encourage participation in the trials and propose an ultimately successful one-eighth-cent

Chancellor Bernadette Gray-Little with Governor Sam Brownback.

sales tax referendum, dedicated to supporting relevant research. In addition, the Kansas Bioscience Authority, created by the legislature to further support research and aid the commercialization of products from research, provided $29 million (eventually $50 million) to create state-of-the art research facilities and to recruit leading scientists for the cancer center.

Progress on many fronts—funding, research results, recruitment, and outside evaluation—continued up to and past the winning of the National Cancer Center designation in 2012. Given the extensive scope of this enterprise, Chancellor Gray-Little's mission, successfully completed, was to oversee the efforts and add her voice when appropriate. In many ways, her style was highly compatible with the team-oriented approach built by Roy Jensen and others.

While the university prospered on many fronts during Chancellor Gray-Little's initial five years, political backing for higher education—as measured in state support and expressed skepticism from state legislators—appeared to decline. The Kansas Board of Regents, while highly supportive, entered into the political fray in 2013–2014 by implementing a harsh social media policy. This came as a result of a "tweeting" incident, in which a KU journalism professor created a firestorm of controversy with a message in the wake of a mass shooting incident. In many of the highly publicized incidents from the past affecting KU, the Regents generally had deferred to the decisions of the chancellor and the university in how to address the issue. But in 2013, the Regents quickly enunciated a very tough-sounding, highly controversial policy that would allow a university administration to dismiss a tenured faculty member for various social media transgressions, including any that "adversely affect[ed] the university's ability to efficiently provide services."[44] Strangely enough, as state support as a percentage of the overall budget dramatically decreased in the early twenty-first century, the Regents responded by seeking to tighten restrictions on faculty members.

While state revenues fell significantly as a percentage of KU resources, the definition of what constitutes university success began to change. For example, in 2014, the university sought partial state funding for a major new medical education building at KUMC. Rather than using $25 million in refunds of erroneous federal charges for use on this project, the legislature only permitted the university to use bonding authority to help cover the $75 million cost. The state-of-the-art building would proceed, but with no direct state funding. Indeed, at the 2013 ground-breaking for KU's new, privately funded, School of Business building, Governor Sam Brownback commented, "We can do that on all the buildings at KU."[45] By 2015, as with the Medical Education building, the university could not expect much help from the state, even as it sold itself to state lawmakers as a research and professional institution that would serve as an economic engine for all of Kansas.

KU AND GOVERNMENT, 1965–2015: TOWARD THE STATE-ASSISTED UNIVERSITY

Given the national trends toward severe reductions in the funding of state universities and the corresponding decline of support in the Kansas legislature, the university under the trajectory of the Budig, Hemenway, and Gray-Little administrations has consistently moved away from reliance on state budgetary funding, drawing upon tuition and fees, increased federal research funds, and greatly enhanced private giving. This movement toward independence has been liberating in many ways, as chancellors no longer have to go hat in hand to Topeka to lobby for specific increases in funding for salaries, for maintenance, and for capital improvements. While attending to KUMC has remained one continuing aspect of chancellors' jobs, the nature of that attention has changed dramatically with the resolution of the KU Hospital's status on Hemenway's watch.

The openly partisan interactions between Chancellor Murphy and Governor Docking and the strained-past-the-breaking-point relations of Chancellor Chalmers and a host of legislators and other political figures were long replaced by well-developed working relationships among chancellors, their top staff, and legislators and governors, often mediated through the Board of Regents. The Kansas political context of the 2011–2014 period has challenged that conclusion, but the institutional importance of the university, including the Med Center, continues to be acknowledged to one degree or another by all state policy makers.

Still, the role of the KU chancellor within the state has changed dramatically. Chancellors Murphy and Wescoe were well-known, highly regarded state figures. Archie Dykes, through his mission of reconciliation and dynamic personality, also became a significant public figure in the 1970s. But beginning with Gene Budig and continuing with Bob Hemenway and Bernadette Gray-Little, the role of the chancellor as a major state public figure has diminished. The large, state-assisted

university simply requires a different mix of skills for its leaders than
that of mid-century chancellors. Communicating effectively at the
state and national levels will always be important, and on many occasions, only a chancellor's words or presence will suffice. But KU, like
other large state universities, has created a host of external-relations
positions to carry out much of this work, freeing the chancellor to
use her time as wisely as possible, within the context of the regulated,
complex organization that constitutes the public research institution
of the twenty-first century.

Part 2

TEACHING & RESEARCH

CHAPTER 3

The Idea of a Liberal Education
Continuity and Change

JAMES WOELFEL

Coming to KU was a big step in my life, and at the time, seemed like an immense challenge. . . . What I found here was a place that stimulated the lifelong intellectual endeavor that has sort of characterized me, I hope, ever since.

—Deanell Reece Tacha, c. 1968

The undergraduate curriculum at the University of Kansas has undergone many changes since 1965, typically in response to transformations in American society as well as in higher education itself.[1] Imparting a remarkable continuity and stability to those changes, however, has been the idea of a liberal education as the "soul" of what an American university is all about: an education that requires of students a wide exposure to human knowledge and culture, through "general education" courses in the liberal arts and sciences.[2] Throughout the 50 years we are examining in this book, KU has distinguished itself among research universities for maintaining its commitment to undergraduate liberal education. In 2013, the university saw the inauguration of a university-wide "core" curriculum reform, which is the most recent effort to implement the liberal idea.

The story of liberal education at KU since 1965 will be told here by illuminating briefly just a few of the highlights along the way from a much larger and more complex story. Beginning with a look at the vision and organization of general education at KU in 1965–1966, we will go on to examine:

- the important and creative role of the Honors Program, founded in 1955, in modeling a liberal education;

- the bold, ultimately unsuccessful experiment of the Colleges-within-the-College in the late 1960s and early 1970s;

- the academic impact of the movements for racial and gender equality and for student participation in university governance and curricular issues in the late 1960s and early 1970s and the general education reforms reflecting those developments;

- the failed efforts in the early 1980s to create a common university-wide general education curriculum, followed in the mid-1980s by the successful reform of general education in the College of Liberal Arts and Sciences (generally known as the College at KU), which was in place until 2013;

- the growing impact on KU of diversity, globalization, and information technology beginning in the 1990s, together with both external and internal pressures to improve retention and graduation rates in the early 2000s, which in 2013 resulted in the substantial rethinking and reorganizing of liberal education, known as the "KU Core."

Wescoe Hall under construction, 1973. It would become the center of humanities education on campus, despite its somewhat uninspiring appearance.

Many visitors to KU have advanced the ideals of a liberal education. Washington Post *reporter and columnist Bob Woodward meets with a class, February 2000.*

Clifford Griffin's history of KU's first 100 years includes a chapter entitled "The Quest for a Liberal Education," in which he tells the story of efforts at curricular reform from the 1920s to 1965. On a much more limited scale, I am continuing that story down to the present day. Griffin followed this chapter with a chapter on "Undergraduate Professional Education," covering the Schools of Business, Education, Engineering, Fine Arts, Journalism, and Pharmacy.[3] In what follows, I will be focusing on the College as the historic "home," main provider, and chief advocate and interpreter of liberal education at the university. However, I also want to highlight briefly the fact that the undergraduate professional schools have, in their general education and admission requirements, affirmed that it is their participation in a university context characterized by the idea of a liberal education that distinguishes them from purely professional or "trade" schools.

"THE TIMES, THEY ARE A-CHANGIN'": KU, 1965–1966

Like KU freshmen of every generation, many who began their studies in September 1965 were undoubtedly bewildered by the size and complexity of the university and fearful about whether they would succeed academically—and socially. In the fall of 1965, total KU enrollment on the Lawrence campus was 13,565, of whom 9,829 were undergraduates and almost three-fourths were residents of Kansas. Just over half of the undergraduates were students in the College, with the rest divided among the six undergraduate professional schools existing at that time. There were half again as many male as female students. A 3.0 grade-point average was a straight-A record, in a system in which an F subtracted 1 point. The course numbering system consisted of one- and two-digit numbers, with "H" added for honors sections.

Beginning in the fall and continuing throughout academic year 1965–1966, the university celebrated its centennial with a series of special events, including concerts and lectures by internationally renowned performers and scholars. With a kind of historical irony, Old Fraser Hall had succumbed to the wrecking ball in August 1965, after three years of protests and pleas from KU alumni to save the long-deteriorating building.

In the wider world, events of far-reaching significance were taking place that would have profound and long-lasting effects on the university. The African American struggle for freedom and justice continued unabated, and the women's movement was rapidly organizing and making its influence felt. By 1965–1966, both movements were actively represented at KU. The United States was beginning the escalation of its involvement in the Vietnam War, and a countercultural movement began to emerge that celebrated sexual and lifestyle freedom and challenged prevailing American values. Over the next ten years, these movements would have a dramatic impact upon KU—from academic programs and student life to university governance and state politics.

But the concerns immediately dominating the minds of student newcomers to Mount Oread in 1965 were very likely the perennial freshman questions about why they were at KU and what they were going to do here: What courses do I have to take to graduate? What am I going to major in? What sort of career do I want to pursue? The university's answer to the first of these questions was its general education curriculum, which consisted of required courses and proficiency examinations housed in the College. As the university's largest school, the College was in 1965, and still is, the gateway for a large majority of its entering students and the academic home for many throughout their undergraduate years.

Through the decades, the College has periodically restated the aims of a liberal education, but all the restatements have been variations on the theme of describing an education that is a broad, balanced, and comprehensive exposure to the liberal arts and sciences, together with intensive study in a specific field. Revisions of general education requirements have reflected ongoing discussion of the most effective and practicable ways to embody the idea of a liberal education—always in the wider context of developments in higher education generally and in response to changes taking place in the United States and the world.

GENERAL EDUCATION IN 1965–1966

Our story begins with the statement of the College's aims in the 1965–1966 KU catalog, articulated in two purposes. The first was "to forward the type of education rightly called 'liberal.' It stresses the value of intellectual proficiency and of ideas for their own sake, but it also aims at the cultivation of knowledge and clear thinking because of their practical value." The statement went on to specify the importance to all students who major in fields of study within the College of acquiring at least a basic acquaintance with a broad range of different fields of study. Singled out for special mention were "a reasonable mastery of written composition in English and proficiency in a foreign language." The aim of a liberal education was that students "will come to be more intelligent citizens and more reasonable human beings capable of full and well-ordered lives."[4] The second purpose was to provide a wide intellectual background as a foundation upon which students would concentrate in one of the College's many majors or in one of KU's undergraduate professional schools.

The general education requirements in place in 1965–1966 resulted from a substantial curriculum reform in the College undertaken in the late 1950s under the leadership of a new and innovative dean, George Waggoner, and implemented beginning in 1959. The College divided its general education curriculum between "underclass requirements" and "graduation requirements" for the bachelor of arts (BA) degree, a distinction that stayed in place until 1973.[5] Students who continued in the College after the first two years fulfilled both sets of requirements, while students in four of the undergraduate professional schools plus nursing were typically required to fulfill only the under-class requirements. The broad categories of inquiry in which students were required to take courses were simplified into the now-long-familiar three divisions: humanities (understood to include the arts), social sciences, and natural sciences and mathematics. Students fulfilled most of their general education requirements by choosing from a list of "principal" courses in each division: courses, according to the university catalog, "essential to an understanding of the conceptions and the techniques underlying the respective subject."[6] Other changes specifically affecting upper-class students in the College included raising the foreign language requirement to 16 credit hours or demonstration of equivalent proficiency.

The under-class requirements included nine hours of English, two of speech, the first course in a foreign language, a lab science, two semesters of a Western Civilization discussion class, and three from the list of principal courses, one in each of the three large divisions. Students who continued in the College to work for a BA degree were required, by their junior and senior years, to pass the English Proficiency and the Western Civilization comprehensive exams, demonstrate competence in a foreign language, take three courses in each of the three divisions, and complete a major consisting of not less than 20 nor more than 40 hours. Most of this should sound broadly familiar to generations of KU College alumni extending through the first decade of the twenty-first century, reflecting the stability and continuity of the College's general education curriculum even as it adapted in response to successive waves of social change and academic innovation.

In 1965–1966, students who wished to go on to receive a degree from the Schools of Business, Education, Journalism, Pharmacy, or Nursing spent their first two years in the College and fulfilled the under-class requirements before moving on. They were admitted to those undergraduate professional schools only as juniors and after having met their respective admission requirements.[7] By contrast, qualified students could directly enter the School of Engineering and Architecture (Architecture would later become a separate school) and the School of Fine Arts in their first year. However, both of those schools, in addition to specifying their own requirements, also expected students to complete a lesser core of general education requirements, typically including at least the two basic English courses and a course in speech and a basic distribution of one course each in the humanities, social sciences, and natural sciences and mathematics from the College's list of principal courses.

When we look at the statements of purpose and the general education requirements of KU's undergraduate professional schools, not only in 1965–1966 but through many years afterward, it is noteworthy that, whether "maximally" or "minimally," all of these schools acknowledged that the idea of a liberal education is essential to being a university, as opposed to a purely professional institution. As a somewhat later statement of the College's aims put it, the liberal education that students in KU's undergraduate professional schools received differed from "isolated specialization."[8] Journalism, Education, and, later, Social Welfare were quite explicit about it. For example, in 1965–1966, the School of Journalism's statement of purpose included the following: "Nearly 70 percent of the journalism student's education is in the liberal arts, where background courses in the humanities, social sciences, natural sciences, and other areas help develop the student's ability to interpret the significance of the day's events and the society in which he lives."[9] Under "Education of the Prospective Teacher," in the 1969–1970 catalog, the School of Education emphasized "a broad background in the arts and sciences, in addition to intensive preparation in the field or fields of teaching."[10] The early catalog description of the School of Social Welfare stated: "The undergraduate social work program in the School of Social Welfare is academically related to the College, emphasizing a strong liberal arts background."[11]

THE FEW, THE PROUD: THE HONORS PROGRAM

The University Honors Program is one of the great success stories of undergraduate education at KU. Inaugurated in 1955 with 31 students, in 2013–2014 it numbered 1,299 students, among them 382 freshmen. In *A Review of Fifty Public University Honors Programs*, published in 2012, the KU program was ranked second in the nation, based on curriculum, prestigious awards, retention and graduation rates, and study abroad programs.[12] Over the past half century, the Honors Program has been a model and stimulus for creating similar opportunities for all students—among them the Colleges-within-the-College, undergraduate research, study abroad, the growth of interdisciplinary courses and degrees, learning communities, freshman seminars, and senior "capstone" projects.

The College Honors Program, as it was called during its first four decades, expanded to include students from the undergraduate professional schools (most of which also had their own honors programs), and in the 1990s the name was changed to the University Honors Program to reflect the fact that it was by then officially a university-wide program. Before the Honors Program, KU had offered students informal opportunities to conduct honors-level work in their major departments, some as early as 1920. Professor Walter Sandelius, a Rhodes Scholar, first created such a program in political science. Qualified students could take a senior-level special honors course in his or her own field, culminating in an honors thesis under the supervision of the faculty member offering the course. English and geology also offered such opportunities, but by 1940 only 15 students had taken advantage of them. However, the prewar period also saw the creation of a scholarship program based entirely on merit and providing four-year support to outstanding male high school graduates from Kansas. The funds were provided by a Lawrence native and KU alumnus, Solon Summerfield, and in 1929 the first Summerfield Scholars began their studies at KU. The Watkins Scholarships for gifted young Kansas women were established after World War II, with funds made available through the legacy of one of KU's greatest benefactors, Elizabeth Watkins. The Summerfield and Watkins Scholars would provide the core of students for an entirely new, campus-wide Honors Program that was inaugurated in 1955.

The creator of the Honors Program was College dean George R. Waggoner, whose vision, enthusiasm, and restless energy also made him a pioneering figure in liberal education reform generally and a prime mover in the development of KU's study abroad programs.[13] Waggoner came to KU from Indiana University, where he had been associate dean of the College of Arts and Sciences. While at Indiana, he received a grant from the Carnegie Corporation to investigate special programs for exceptional students, and he came to KU with an active commitment to and considerable knowledge of honors education—along with the Carnegie grant.

Dean Waggoner also came to KU with a model of honors education developed by Joseph Cohen, a philosophy professor at the University of Colorado, who was a major influence on the emergence of honors programs throughout the nation. Cohen believed that honors students "needed to be induced to look at the world broadly" and in an interdisciplinary way—in other words, they needed to be offered a liberal education at an advanced level.[14]

Before the end of Waggoner's first year at KU, the faculty committee overseeing the College curriculum and Chancellor Franklin Murphy approved his proposal to create a "Gifted Student Program" on an experimental basis. In the fall of 1955, 31 Summerfield and Watkins Scholarship finalists entered the university with the opportunity to take larger course loads, enroll in upper-division classes as freshmen and sophomores, and fulfill general requirements and electives through a number of small, special honors sections of courses. In 1956 and 1957, the new program expanded with a wider pool than only

Professor Francis Heller in 1962.

Summerfield and Watkins finalists, more honors sections, and, for 20 of the best students, stipends as research assistants to faculty.

Examination of the faculty group involved in creating the Honor Program, the College Administrative Committee, provides an illuminating glimpse into the informal way that KU functioned administratively at the time. In 1955 and until 1966, the committee, consisting of eight faculty members, was the sole College-wide vehicle of faculty curricular governance.[15] Waggoner conveniently designated the members of the committee as faculty advisers to the new honors students. Francis Heller, who was elected to the committee shortly after Waggoner became dean, drily noted some years later that the committee readily agreed to the role of faculty advisers since it already had the flexibility to grant waivers and ratify students' programs.[16]

In 1957, Heller became both the first associate dean of the College and the first director of the Honors Program.[17] Under his direction, more honors sections of courses, three junior-level interdisciplinary seminars, and, on an invitational basis, a seminar for seniors were added. Heller described his policy as director as "keep[ing] the program informal. I shied away from rigid requirements, never formally dismissed a student from the program and opened its opportunities to students who . . . had shown that we should have selected them to begin with."[18]

Even by 1957 it was clear, Heller recalled, that the Honors Program was becoming "successful beyond all expectations." The young Honors Program was attracting and nurturing exceptionally good students. Between 1959 and 1970, five KU students were awarded Rhodes Scholarships. During that period, KU also boasted two Marshall Scholars and 12 Danforth Fellows. KU perennially ranked among the top ten universities in the number of Woodrow Wilson Fellows selected, 17 in 1970 alone. Between 1967 and 1970, 23 KU students received Fulbright Scholarships.[19]

In his reminiscences, Heller expressed the opinion that "the KU College's program . . . went into decline when our successors treated it as an appendage that could be entrusted" to people who were not tenured faculty and "appeared to have no support from the College office proper."[20] He traced the revitalization of the Honors Program to the appointment of Deanell Reece Tacha as vice chancellor for academic affairs in 1981.

However, the Honors Program hardly lay dormant during the 1970s. Philip McKnight of the School of Education, himself an honors graduate, was active as chair of the Chancellor's Honors Scholarship Committee in the late 1970s in urging program improvements: among them a university-wide honors program, more effective procedures for identifying and recruiting outstanding students, and creation of a newsletter. All these recommendations would sooner or later be implemented. Another very important development during this period was the inauguration of the freshman honors tutorials in 1977–1978, which have remained an essential part of the honors experience to the present day.

Deanell Reece Tacha was a 1968 KU honors graduate in American Studies who went on to a distinguished career in law and university administration, which included five years as a KU law professor followed by six years as the university's associate vice chancellor and then vice chancellor for academic affairs.[21] She was a strong and active advocate of both honors education and a core liberal education for all KU undergraduates.

In a later section, we will examine the core curriculum proposals of a landmark Commission on the Improvement of Undergraduate Education, which met throughout 1980–1981 under the leadership of Tacha (at the time serving as associate vice chancellor). The commission's recommendations regarding honors education reflected

Tacha's own commitment and would provide a basis for strengthening the Honors Program in the 1980s and 1990s. Recalling the vibrancy and achievements of the program's early years, the commission called for "a concerted effort to refocus attention on the potential for excellence among our undergraduates."[22] Toward that end, it noted that a new University Scholars Program was now funded and would be implemented beginning in the fall of 1981. This was, and remains, a "crème de la crème" group of 20 honors sophomores, each of whom was assigned a faculty mentor for the remainder of his or her undergraduate career, and who met as a group in a special spring sophomore honors seminar. The commission also recommended that the university request that KUEA provide, on a permanent basis, a limited number of undergraduate research grants, to begin in the summer of 1982. While special research opportunities had been made available to honors students since the program's earliest years, the new research grant program opened up more opportunities for them and also extended them to all KU undergraduates. Finally, the report called for a thorough review of the honors and scholarship programs, to "more effectively target scholarship funds" and "provide a clear focus for the University's efforts to assist and reward its undergraduate students."[23]

One of the most important events in the history of the KU Honors Program occurred in 1983 when the program acquired its own building. Nunemaker Center was built in 1971, funded by a gift of $350,000 from Irene Nunemaker of New York City as part of KU's $18.6 million Program for Progress capital fund campaign launched in 1966 by the university and administered through KUEA. One of the most interesting modern structures at the university, Nunemaker houses administrative and faculty offices, a room for student meetings, a library, an audiovisual room, a student lounge, classrooms, seminar rooms, and an apartment for campus visitors. Nunemaker Center has for over 30 years remained the "jewel in the crown" of the Honors Program at KU, providing a strikingly attractive multipurpose home for generations of honors students.

In the summer 1990 issue of the College newsletter, outgoing director Sharon Brehm announced that beginning in the fall one floor of McCollum Hall would be an honors residence for 60 to 80 honors students. Designating an honors residence "floor" continued, in Templin and Ellsworth Halls, and since the fall of 2014 Templin has housed the Honors Program residence. In his introduction to the 1990 newsletter, incoming director J. Michael Young articulated two central purposes of honors education. One, he said, in an age of increasing specialization,

The Nunemaker Center, home to the KU Honors Program.

is to help put students in contact with faculty, enable them to do honors work in their major fields, and provide the opportunity for undergraduate research. The other, however, is general education, the need for which is greater than ever: "As the pressure toward specialization . . . increases there is also a growing need for a counterbalance, for a lively program of general education. A second important function of the honors program, accordingly, is to support a wide range of courses designed to widen interests and broaden vision. As it has in the past, the honors program will provide broad, introductory courses. Hopefully, too, we will be able to offer a number of interdisciplinary honors seminars."[24]

Beginning in the 1980s, the Honors Program has had a succession of prominent and able faculty as its directors. In the first decade and a half of the twenty-first century, the program has achieved a level of success its founders could only imagine—in student numbers, curricular scope, faculty participation, scholarship funding, and research and study abroad opportunities and in its wide range of special events and activities and physical location, which has helped create and sustain a "small college" sense of community among its students. And with all the riches the program has offered students, it has through the decades also pioneered and modeled undergraduate opportunities

The Spencer Research Library, a gift from Helen Foresman Spencer in honor of her husband, Kenneth, under construction in 1967. The building houses noncirculating collections for undergraduate, graduate, and faculty researchers.

In 1990, Professor Michael Young became the director of the Honors Program. In 2014, his son, Professor Bryan Young, became director.

that have been extended to all KU students—from freshman seminars and learning communities to undergraduate research and capstone courses.

OXBRIDGE ON THE KAW:
THE COLLEGES-WITHIN-THE-COLLEGE

The early success of the Honors Program, creating as it did a small community of students within the wider university context, set the stage for a much bigger experiment in combining the advantages of a large research university with those of a small liberal arts college. Like the Honors Program, it was born of George Waggoner's creative vision of what a liberal education at KU could and should be. His ambitious aim was nothing less than a complete reorganization of freshman-sophomore education and administration in the College of Liberal Arts and Sciences. The timing seemed perfect: the inauguration of the bold new experiment would coincide with the celebration of KU's centennial in 1965.

During 1964 and 1965, the dean, his staff, and the College Administrative Committee worked out the plan for what would be called the Colleges-within-the-College (CWC). In late 1965, E. Jackson Baur of the Department of Sociology reported to the committee on a recent study of college undergraduates he had conducted in which the interviewing team found that "students in the typical classroom are a collection of competing strangers who are incapable of collaborating with one another in a pleasurable pursuit of scholarship" and concluding that "students who form a social group have greater potentialities for supporting and reinforcing the teaching efforts of professors than a classroom of anonymous individuals."[25] The College's proposal was included as one of the goals in KU's Program for Progress, the $18.6 million capital campaign announced in the spring of 1966 by KUEA. Chancellor Wescoe endorsed the proposal, which was widely publicized. With these high-level expressions of support at KU, the College submitted a proposal to the Carnegie Corporation for a three-year grant and was awarded $288,000 to help launch the new venture.

As with the development of the Honors Program, KU's experiment in liberal education was riding the crest of a national wave. In the 1960s, a number of large and midsize universities were developing similar programs to create, as KU's grant proposal put it, "effective suburbs within the university city."[26] Wayne State University led off in

Dean George Waggoner in repose by Potter Lake, 1957.

1959, followed by Florida State University, Michigan State University, the University of Michigan, Rutgers, SUNY at Stony Brook, the University of Kentucky, and Ohio State. An article in the September 9, 1966, issue of *Time* magazine reported on the new phenomenon of "living-learning clusters" and included KU's just-inaugurated CWC.[27]

The KU plan called for the creation of five colleges, the first to open in the fall of 1966, which by the fall of 1968 would include all freshmen and sophomores in the College. The university's press release in July 1966 envisioned that students would "live together, take many of their classes together, and share the same advisers and administrators."[28] Enthusiasts for the program anticipated that the new arrangements would foster closer student-student and student-faculty relationships and spur academic innovation.

The first of the colleges, fittingly called "Centennial," opened as a "pilot project" in the fall of 1966. The 450 students were selected at random from among those who were planning to enroll as freshmen that fall—225 men were assigned to three floors of Ellsworth Hall, and 225 women were assigned to three floors of the new Oliver Hall. Its administrative offices were in Oliver Hall, and the pattern of CWC administration was established: each college would have a representative from the College office, the dean of men, the dean of women, and

Assistant Dean Jerry Lewis (right) and Janice Lewis, sitting with local developer and former Jayhawk basketball player Bob Billings and Bev Billings.

the registrar, together with faculty advisers. The director of Centennial College was Jerry Lewis, assistant dean of the College, who would become the executive director of the entire CWC system.

Beginning in the fall of 1967, all freshmen entering the College were placed in Centennial and four newly created colleges: North, Corbin, Oliver, and Pearson. Of the 2,500 first-year students distributed among the colleges, 450 joined the original 450, now sophomores, in Centennial College. By 1968, all freshmen and sophomores in the College were enrolled in one of the colleges.

The CWC plan involved no fundamental curricular changes, and this was seen as an important advantage of the venture. Most freshmen and sophomores could be assumed to be taking many of the same introductory courses—those that fulfilled basic under-class requirements.[29] This pattern, together with advising college-by-college, would make "clustering" CWC students together into certain sections of large-enrollment basic courses feasible.

However, one of the envisioned purposes of the CWC that excited both student and faculty participants was that it would be a "laboratory" for academic experimentation and innovation. This produced two notable innovations: the Liberal Arts & Sciences (LAS) courses and the Pearson Integrated Humanities Program (PIHP). The former were born out of the desire for a rubric under which a particular college could introduce and teach courses for its students on any of a wide variety of topics reflecting current student interest and would be free of disciplinary boundaries. This meant a wide range of courses exploring anything and everything within the wide realm of the "liberal arts and sciences."

The other, very different, academic innovation is best seen within the context of George Waggoner's idea of the CWC. He envisioned that the five colleges might evolve to represent distinctly different philosophies of education—from very structured and traditional to very free and experimental—and he actively and enthusiastically encouraged such a development.

As a matter of fact, three of the colleges did develop distinct identities. One was North College, where there was a popular Eastern Civilizations course that the director and a number of the students wanted to see become an alternative to Western Civilization as a general education requirement. A second was Corbin College, renamed Nunemaker College in 1970, which created a distinctive Tutorial Program for honors students.[30] The third was the PIHP, whose traditionalist approach to liberal education achieved considerable notoriety. PIHP inspired devoted loyalty among some students, skepticism and criticism among other students and many faculty, and bitter opposition among still other faculty, parents, and alumni. It directly challenged the assumptions of the faculty's "liberal consensus" about liberal education and Waggoner's optimistic pluralism.

The director of Pearson College, Dennis Quinn, a popular English professor and 1968 HOPE award winner, together with Frank Nelick, also in English, and John Senior in classics (another HOPE winner, in 1974), created what might be called a "total immersion" experience for students selected for the PIHP: a fully integrated, four-semester Western "great books" program—covering the Greeks, the Romans, Christianity and the Middle Ages, and "the Moderns"—taught from a traditional Roman Catholic scholastic or Thomistic philosophical and theological perspective.[31] The three faculty were quite open about their traditionally Catholic approach to a liberal education. Early on, however, and increasingly over time, this orientation made the PIHP an object of suspicion, criticism, and hostility. Quinn, Senior, and Nelick—who combined charisma with an authoritarian approach in

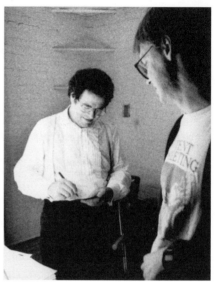

KU has hosted many guest speakers for   *Itzhak Perlman backstage at Hoch*
student audiences, including poet Allan   *Auditorium in 1990.*
Ginsberg, who reads from his book Howl.

the classroom—were accused of indoctrinating instead of educating and indeed of proselytizing for their faith to vulnerable students.

As part of the general trend of the College's encouragement of curricular experimentation, in 1971 the College Assembly approved allowing PIHP students to substitute the integrated program as an alternative to all their normal under-class humanities requirements (English, speech, Western Civilization, and the humanities distribution requirement). Students received six hours of humanities credit for each of the four semesters.

However, all new and experimental programs were approved conditionally for a one-year period and required evaluation at the end of that period. In the spring of 1972, the College's Committee on Evaluation and Advancement of Instruction submitted an extensive evaluation report and recommendation regarding PIHP. A large majority of committee members recommended that the PIHP be continued but put under "regularized curricular and administrative direction" by an interdepartmental advisory committee, which would include representatives from several specified humanities departments.[32] In correspondence and before the committee, Quinn vigorously repudiated the report and denied that a committee of the College had the right or the

TOP TO BOTTOM:

Gwendolyn Brooks, poet and Pulitzer Prize winner, at KU in 1991.

Writer Kurt Vonnegut, Jr., speaks at the Lied Center in 1995.

Scholar, writer, and feminist Angela Davis, 2012.

competence to evaluate the program.[33] In 1973, the College Assembly rescinded permission for students to use the PIHP as a substitute for the prescribed freshman-sophomore humanities requirements.

In time, the controversy surrounding the PIHP intensified and spread, amplified by media coverage. A Jewish student converted to Catholicism, four students made a "holy pilgrimage" to a Benedictine abbey in France, and a Unitarian minister in Kansas City organized an anti-PIHP group. The most substantive battle, however, took place between the Pearson triumvirate and KU faculty who vigorously opposed the program on academic and pedagogical grounds. That contest was over the breadth and boundaries of the "liberal consensus" about general education: How far does encouragement and tolerance of intellectual pluralism legitimately extend? May it encompass the "illiberal" without self-contradiction? What is the proper place of a clearly defined religious approach to education in a public, secular university in the context of a rather thoroughly secularized intellectual and academic world? These are questions that have continued to be debated in other academic settings and institutional contexts.[34]

In 1972–1973, the Ad Hoc Committee on the Future of the Colleges within the College, composed of seven KU faculty members and chaired by Frances Degen Horowitz, conducted a thorough examination of the CWC program.[35] Among their generally negative conclusions were that the "living-learning" arrangements had been largely discontinued after the second year because of the logistical problems of housing students by college; that involving more senior faculty had failed because of insufficient faculty and financial support; that random assignment of faculty advisers had been "disastrous"; and that CWC staff had experienced serious problems of role definition and lack of adequate information and budgetary control. The committee found the introduction of the LAS rubric to have been a positive contribution, but one that had come to enjoy successful independent status. Also cited in the report was a study and evaluation by E. Jackson Baur at the end of the first two years of CWC, which showed only marginal gains in overcoming student social isolation and negligible gains academically.[36]

The committee concluded by saying that "academically, the CWCs have made some contributions, but for a variety of reasons they did not develop as originally envisioned. . . . The CWC structure helped to generate interest in educational innovation. But, in most cases, the activities themselves were, or could be, relatively independent of the CWC structure." The report suggested that the lack of faculty participation was probably due to the fact that "the reward system never was related to the CWCs." While students liked aspects of the more personalized staff and faculty access of the CWC, and the CWC provided a "home structure" for some academic innovation, there was "a widespread feeling that many of these things could have been done better if conditions of adequate funding and more extended planning had obtained."[37]

The last mention of the CWC was in the 1974–1975 university catalog. Thus ended a noble but unworkable effort at providing the large majority of first- and second-year KU students with a "small college" experience in the midst of a large and rapidly growing public university. What endured, as represented by the creation of the LAS courses, was an impetus to academic innovation in an age when students were coming to expect more opportunities for learning that explored "real-world" topics in untraditional ways.

LIBERTY AND JUSTICE FOR ALL: CHANGING THE FACE OF LIBERAL EDUCATION

The period from 1965 to 1975 was a turbulent time of change at KU, as it was throughout the nation, with the convergence of the movements for racial and gender equality, the anti–Vietnam War movement, and the sexual liberation and countercultural lifestyle movements—all of which involved fundamental questioning of taken-for-granted American values and new visions of the future.[38] Hand in hand with these movements for greater equality and individual freedom came increasing demands for student participation in university governance, including curricular reform. In this light, it is instructive to look briefly at the establishing of academic programs in African and African-American Studies in 1970 and Women's Studies in 1972 and their lasting influence on the curriculum. Then we will examine the College's general education reforms implemented in 1973, focusing on the creation of the bachelor of general studies (BGS) degree, as a testimony to the new voice of students in curricular discussion and decision making.

The demand for academic programs variously called Black, African, or African-American Studies grew directly out of the emergence of the civil rights and Black Power movements in the 1960s. Its agenda included "the demand on behalf of African American students for an education pertinent to their experiences and heritage," which took the form of creating appropriate academic programs.[39] Writing in 1992, a student historian specifically described the national movement for such programs as representing "a call for the transformation of . . . liberal arts education and curriculum. This was aimed at ending the contradiction between the professed goals of a liberal arts education and the curriculum provided to accomplish this. . . . It was not the theory of a liberal arts education that failed, but the application of the theory and the focus of the courses."[40]

In the midst of the national and campus turmoil over racism during the late 1960s and the beginning of the 1970s, the university was moving toward the creation of a Department of African Studies. In the fall of 1968, William Tuttle of the History Department offered the first course in African American studies, Topics in Negro Life and History, with a class of 26 students evenly representing blacks and whites.[41] In 1970, Professor Jacob Gordon came to KU to organize a department and serve as its first chair.[42] In March 1972, his proposal for a degree program was approved by the Board of Regents. While black student demands played an integral role in creating KU's program, Gordon, together with supportive administrators and faculty, established it as a credible academic program. In 1986, the department name became African and African-American Studies.

The impact of this department on the idea and implementation of a liberal education at KU has been significant. At the widest level, the department dramatically enlarged the international scope of the university's curriculum through courses in cultures and languages, study abroad opportunities, research, and outreach focused on an entire continent that had been neglected. Similarly, the department established the essential role and importance of African American history, correcting traditional views of the United States and expanding the horizons of both students and faculty.

In 1971–1972, the Western Civilization Program introduced a unit on colonialism, using Frantz Fanon's *The Wretched of the Earth* as the primary text, which appeared on the reading list until 1985. In succeeding years, a unit on slavery and reconstruction and readings by African Americans Frederick Douglass, W. E. B. Du Bois, and Booker T. Washington were assigned. The first edition of the program's textbook, *Patterns in Western Civilization,* from 1991, contained a chapter by Jacob Gordon on African American history, and later editions added a chapter on the history of Islam, imperialism and colonialism, slavery, and postcolonial developments.

The movement for gender equality and empowerment of women at KU dramatically accelerated beginning in 1965. A few courses in

Marilyn Dell Brady and Deborah Dandridge, scholars of women's and African American history, as history graduate students at KU, 1985. Both held positions at the Kansas Collection in the Spencer Research Library.

women's studies had been taught at KU beginning in 1960, when Muriel Johnson, a faculty member in Human Development and Family Life, designed and taught KU's first such course, Women in Contemporary Culture. In 1965, a professor of speech, Will Linkugel, introduced a course called The Rhetoric of Women's Rights. However, the creation of an academic program in women's studies was one of the demands issued by women protesters, called the February Sisters, on February 4, 1972, resulting in a degree program founded in the fall, with English professor Janet Sharistanian as its first coordinator.

The Program in Women's Studies at KU was among the first in the United States. Also established was the Women's Studies Advisory Committee, consisting of faculty, librarians, staff, and students—a body that has continued to the present day. Women's Studies (renamed Women, Gender, and Sexuality Studies in 2008) followed a different path of institutional development from that of African and African-American Studies. From the outset, the latter sought and attained departmental status, but the former began and remained for most of its history an interdisciplinary program, headed by a coordinator (later called a director).

The important impact of Women's Studies on the university curriculum manifested itself immediately after its founding, with a rapidly increasing range of courses in humanities and social science disciplines on a wide array of gender-related topics. The 1972–1973 Western Civilization reading list included Elaine Showalter's *Women's Liberation and Literature*, to be followed in succeeding decades by readings from Mary Wollstonecraft, Elizabeth Cady Stanton, Margaret Fuller, Simone de Beauvoir, and Virginia Woolf. And as with African and African-American Studies, Women's Studies courses enlarged and enriched the options from which students could fulfill the non-Western culture and principal course requirements in the humanities and social sciences. After Women, Gender, and Sexuality Studies changed its name and became a department in 2008, its faculty and advisory committee pursued and obtained approval from the Board of Regents for a PhD program, which began in 2011.

While the CWC floundered, the College was reforming its general education curriculum, the most notable innovation of which was the introduction of the BGS degree. The reforms of the early 1970s clearly reflected the demands of student activists throughout the late 1960s for more student representation in university governance generally, and in curricular matters specifically, and for greater latitude and experimentation in the curriculum.

The College reforms of the early 1970s began by eliminating the long-standing separation between "under-class" and "upper-class" requirements and referring simply to "requirements for the B.A. degree." Among the familiar freshman-sophomore courses were a few changes. One was a new option for fulfilling the Western Civilization requirement: in addition to enrolling in the weekly discussion sections or simply passing the comprehensive exam, the program was now offering a limited number of lecture-discussion classes under different numbers. This change, mandated by the College Assembly as one of the era's experiments in general education, was a response to both student desire for help with the readings and decades-old faculty criticisms of minimally structured student exposure to important and often difficult texts, which led many to rely upon locally published summaries for the comprehensive exams. A hotly debated change concerned the foreign language requirement. Now, instead of attaining fourth-semester proficiency in one language, students had the option of taking two first-year semesters (ten hours) in each of two languages.[43]

Other changes in the catalog included a new three-digit course numbering system, replacing the long-standing use of one- and two-digit numbers. Also appearing for the first time was gender-inclusive language, doubtless reflecting important gains KU women had made. But the major innovation in the College reforms of the early 1970s was the introduction of the BGS degree, a clear realization of student desire for a more flexible and individualized degree program. Students could earn the BGS by taking a minimum of three courses from two different departments, in each of the three large curricular divisions. Of the 124-credit-hour total then required for graduation, 40 had to be in courses numbered 300 or above. BGS students could opt to take a major with more than the 40 hours permitted for the BA, a major in two departments, a special major, or no major at all.[44]

The original BGS, then, was a degree option stripped of the specific courses required of students working toward the BA, offering considerable freedom to students. As faculty skeptics pointed out, in practice the BGS became the default degree for many who wished to avoid foreign language, math, science, and Western Civilization requirements and for others whose grade-point average was not high enough to gain entry to various majors. However, it also made possible the attainment of a university degree by genuinely interested and educationally committed students in a variety of circumstances, such as nontraditional students who needed flexibility in meeting requirements. The BGS has endured as a College degree program and an attractive or practicable option for many KU students.

VISION AND REALITY:
GENERAL EDUCATION REFORM IN THE 1980S

Executive Vice Chancellor Robert Cobb appointed the Commission on the Improvement of Undergraduate Education in 1980. Chairing the commission was Deanell Reece Tacha, who would soon become vice chancellor for academic affairs. In 1981, the commission released a report of findings and recommendations, possibly the single most influential document on undergraduate education at KU in the past 50 years. Its six recommendations collectively addressed a wide range of key issues. Each included several concrete proposals—most with a time frame for study, approval, and implementation—for strengthening and improving the undergraduate learning experience. Among the specific proposals was a university-wide core curriculum for all undergraduates.

The commission noted that ACT scores were declining nationally, fewer students were receiving top scholarships, and writing and

Deanell Tacha, vice chancellor for academic affairs, was sworn in as a judge of the 10th US District Court in 1985. Two of the ceremony's speakers were Chancellor Budig (left) and Senate majority leader Bob Dole (right).

math skills were declining. In seeking to do a "total analysis" of the undergraduate situation, however, the commission preferred to use a qualitative method, relying "largely on the perceptions and analyses of members of the faculty" and soliciting letters from every member of the faculty. In concluding the introduction to their report, commission members said that they had "attempted to provide a composite documentation of guiding principles and specific details of a vision widely held among . . . faculty that this institution can provide a superior undergraduate education."[45] They prefaced their recommendations by placing them within the national higher education context, examining reports from other universities on the state of undergraduate education and efforts to improve it.

The commission concluded that the "general view" was that "undergraduate education is in crisis" because of the pressures and changes of the decade of the 1970s. Among these pressures, they observed, was "the inherent diversity of purposes of a multi-mission university serving the needs of the nation and a state," which had resulted in the neglect of undergraduate education. But a major pressure was "the staggering growth in the number of undergraduate students" in the 1970s—nationally from 7.5 million to 10.5 million between 1970 and 1980, and at KU from just under 18,000 to more than 24,000.[46] Other

Budig Hall and Hoch Auditoria in 1997, following reconstruction.

factors cited were greater freedom in academic choices and more liberal admissions policies, coupled with greater diversity in background
and preparation among students wanting to go to college.

The commission report went on to note that many colleges and
universities "have adopted some form of required curriculum," often
including basic skills courses, minimum competency standards, a foreign language requirement, and, in general, clearer and more rigor-
ous academic standards. Working within the context of these national
trends, the commission's efforts were nevertheless focused on "building upon the great history and traditions of undergraduate education
at this institution."[47] The report proposed, and elaborated in detail,
six responsibilities that KU should assume in providing the structures
and processes that would strengthen and enhance "high quality undergraduate education," which have continued to inform curricular
development at KU in years hence.[48]

Recommendation 2 was "to structure a university-wide curriculum
that allows for full development for professional school goals, but es-
tablishes an expectation of breadth of exposure to diverse disciplines
and of minimum ability to communicate verbally and understand
basic mathematical concepts." The commission began with an observation of the current situation and called for fundamental change:
"The University of Kansas undergraduate program has no common
requirements. . . . It is clear that we are not stating any common goals
which we expect of all those who seek an undergraduate degree at the
University of Kansas."

The commission went on to offer its own sketch of what the curriculum should include. Its members explicitly referred to it as a "core
curriculum," which, they said, "differs from distribution requirements
in its specification of subject matter areas without which the institution
believes that its undergraduates would be inadequately educated."[49]
Its only specific proposal was that each school should mandate continuous enrollment in the required English and math courses beginning
in the freshman year.

In August 1982, Vice Chancellor Tacha convened a university-wide
committee of faculty and student representatives to consider and make
recommendations concerning a core curriculum, inaugurating their
work with "an impassioned and persuasive statement of her views."[50]
The committee spent a great deal of time debating "basic skills" requirements, some arguing that assuring such skills must precede discussing other aspects of a core, while others promoted a computer
language as an essential skill.[51] The committee spent much of 1983

trying to reach a consensus on the content of the core but did not succeed in getting beyond specific concerns. There was also considerable "pushback" from some of the professional schools. The committee's final report concluded: "It safely can be predicted that the great core curriculum debate at the University of Kansas will continue for some months or years."[52]

Hard on the heels of Vice Chancellor Tacha's August 1982 appointment of the University Core Curriculum Committee came Dean Robert Lineberry's address to the September 1982 meeting of the College Assembly. Referring to Tacha's initiation of the process to explore the possibility of a university-wide core curriculum, he called upon the College to provide a model of "curricular excellence" as part of that process and announced: "Shortly, Dean [J. Michael] Young and I will be announcing the creation of a set of task forces within the College to generate a dialogue on our general education program."[53]

The College process began with the formation of "seminar groups" to discuss, during academic year 1982–1983, the general education requirements and generate ideas and issues to examine further. A Dean's Task Force on General Education, led by Young, was then constituted and began its work. By October 1983, the task force had produced a preliminary report focusing on "Foundations," basic skills in English and mathematics; "Breadth," which included substantial reduction of the number of principal courses and subdividing the broad divisional areas into more specific topical areas; and "Integration," which called for strengthening of the Western Civilization Program, requiring a course in a non-Western culture and the creation by each department of a "capstone course" required of all majors. The task force also recommended developing a program in "writing across the curriculum" and invited suggestions on effective ways to do that across the College.[54]

The Dean's Task Force continued its work over a two-year period, with recommendations considered by the College Committee on Undergraduate Studies and Advising in the fall of 1984 and then presented to the College Assembly in early 1985. On April 26, the committee's proposals, further revised in the light of votes at the College Assembly meetings, were distributed to all members of the College Assembly for a mail ballot, an up-or-down, "for" or "against" vote. The proposals were approved, and the College's revised general education curriculum went into effect in the fall of 1987.

Among the most important changes in requirements for the BA were a second-level course in mathematics, fourth-semester proficiency in one foreign language as the only language option, a basic

Students studying at the Anschutz Science Library in 1990. By 2012, patrons checked out nearly 165,000 items annually and accessed more than 3.3 million articles online.

course in oral communication or logic, nine principal courses now divided among specific topical groups in the three divisional areas, and a course in a non-Western culture. The Western Civilization requirement was retained, but both the Dean's Task Force and the College Committee on Undergraduate Studies and Advising had recommended ways to improve the program.[55] New requirements for students seeking the BGS degree were included, bringing it closer to the BA degree.[56]

The College's general education reforms remained in place, with minor revisions, until 2013. They offered a model of how to do it. They were achieved by a long, careful, and thorough process of discussion and decision making in which the aim was to enable the voices of as many faculty members and student representatives as possible to be heard. Convened as a committee of the whole, the College Assembly devoted six meetings in the spring of 1985—four in April alone—to full debate, with spirited and sometimes heated arguments on all sides. The College's reforms, while not university-wide, applied to most of KU's undergraduates—in the 1980s, 75 percent of the total number.

BOLDLY ASPIRING:
LIBERAL EDUCATION IN THE NEW CENTURY

KU emerged into the twenty-first century from a decade highlighted by new forms of activism on behalf of diversity and multiculturalism in the university community and the curriculum and intensified administrative efforts to attract and recruit minority students, faculty, and staff. The 1990s were also marked by the slow but steady transformation of university infrastructure, teaching, and research by advances in information technology for both students and instructors. It was the beginning of online course supplements and growing calls for "computer literacy" as essential to a liberal education. And after decades of varied attempts to improve advising, in 1997 the Freshman-Sophomore Advising Center was opened for business—surely a milestone for undergraduate education at KU in the past 50 years. With the dawn of the new millennium, undergraduate education received a further boost with the creation of the Center for Teaching Excellence. With its many programs and resources for instructors, it became the single most important stimulus to teaching improvement and innovation.

General education at KU at the turn of the century remained essentially what it had been since the College reforms of the 1980s. However, the new trends and challenges that had been emerging in

Historian Phillip Paludan with a class on the Civil War during a field trip to the
Oak Hill Cemetery, July 1991.

the 1990s, both nationally and locally, were exerting substantial pressure to reconsider the meaning and content of general education for
the new century. The assessment movement called upon colleges and
universities to develop standardized methods and measurable criteria
for evaluating student outcomes in their courses. The advances of the
technological revolution were now influencing every aspect of teaching and learning; students were becoming increasingly "wired," to the
laptop computer and to smart phones and tablets, and social media
had become an integral part of personal and social life.

Students and their parents, encouraged by the media and even by
some representatives of higher education, were increasingly viewing
higher education as career preparation—job training—a trend that

was only intensified by the 2008 recession. The numbers of majors in the liberal arts and sciences have steadily declined in favor of majors in professional schools such as business and engineering, on the pervasive but faulty assumption that students "can't get jobs" with a liberal arts concentration.[57] These developments have also clearly presented a challenge to the very idea of a liberal education.

The most immediately urgent challenge in the new century, however, was KU's low retention and graduation rates, which put it near the bottom of its peer public institutions in the elite Association of American Universities (AAU). Too many freshmen were dropping out of KU and too many students were failing to graduate within six years.[58] The 1990s and early 2000s saw an increasing preoccupation with national rankings (such as the annual list published by *U.S. News & World Report*) by colleges and universities across the country. Major research universities like KU have had to respond on three fronts—undergraduate education, graduate education, and externally funded research—with creative and strenuous efforts to correct and strengthen programs in order to improve in the rankings and avoid potential loss of AAU membership.

The reduction of the total number of general education hours became a crucial item in view of KU's concerns about retention and graduation, and nowhere more urgently than in the College, which

Undergraduates in class, 1999.

continued to be where a large majority of the university's undergraduates pursued their degrees. An official university priority became "graduation in four," but the College still required 72 credit hours of general education courses for the BA, an unusually high number when compared with KU's peer institutions. Internal studies showed that the effort to fulfill this in four or even five years—especially given the complexities created by transferring, having to work, trying to schedule required courses, or changing majors—was an important contributor to KU's unimpressive graduation rate. The formidable College requirements also discouraged some students at an early stage of their university education, thereby contributing to the unfavorable retention rate, and led others to fulfill many of the most basic requirements at nearby community colleges.

When Bernadette Gray-Little became KU's 17th chancellor in 2009, one of her first initiatives was to appoint a task force to examine ways to improve the university's retention and graduation rates. The following year, she was joined in her efforts by a new provost, Jeffrey Vitter, under whose leadership the university developed a comprehensive strategic plan called Bold Aspirations, which became the framework for reforms over the whole spectrum of KU's mission. The plan articulated six goals and multiple strategies for their realization: improvement of undergraduate education; increased support for graduate education; research innovation and funding; scholarly entrepreneurship and public outreach; recruitment and retention of a diverse faculty and staff; and creative management and enhancement of financial and physical resources, including a capital campaign. The first strategy focused on the university's tradition of liberal education expressed in the first goal: a university-wide core curriculum for all undergraduate students—the "KU Core."

The committee that undertook the review and reform of the general education curriculum began by soliciting opinions, via extensive e-mails, on what the aims or goals of a KU education for the twenty-first century should be. This was the first hint that the new curricular reform was no mere "reform." In 1999, Provost David Shulenburger had appointed two all-university committees: one to review, revise, and update a 1989 statement of the "Aims of General Education" into a statement reflecting new developments and the beginning of a new century, and the other to evaluate how well the university's general education assessment procedures were achieving their stated goals. In 2001, the Goals Committee produced "Six Goals of General Education," which began to appear in the KU catalog:

1. Enhance the skills and knowledge needed to research, organize, evaluate, and apply new information, and develop a spirit of critical inquiry and intellectual integrity;
2. acquire knowledge in the fine arts, the humanities, and the social, natural, and mathematical sciences and be able to integrate that knowledge across disciplines;
3. improve the core skills of reading, writing, and numeracy, and enhance communication by clear, effective use of language;
4. understand and appreciate the development, culture, and diversity of the United States and of other societies and nations;
5. become aware of contemporary issues in society, technology, and the natural world and appreciate their complexity of cause and consequences;
6. practice an ethic of self-discipline, social responsibility, and citizenship on a local, national, and international level.[59]

Given the ambitious, university-wide scope of the changes being envisioned in 2010, it is perhaps not surprising that the committee charged with developing the KU Core chose not to build upon this statement of goals but to start from scratch with a "grass roots" survey of all opinions on the aims of a KU education and progressively refine it into a new set of goals.

Also unsurprising, the new goals that emerged from this process looked very much like the 2001 "Six Goals of General Education." In their shortened forms, these were critical thinking and quantitative literacy; written and oral communication; breadth of knowledge; culture and diversity; social responsibility and ethics; integration and creativity. Each goal in the KU Core was then substantially elaborated: first into short bullet-point specifications, and then into long descriptions in terms of learning outcomes and the requirements for achieving them. The first three covered skills and knowledge acquisition that should be acquired during the freshman-sophomore years, and the last three explored areas of further study appropriate to the junior-senior level and culminating in a "capstone" experience. The KU Core also incorporated recent trends in higher education by encouraging and accrediting "educational experiences" alongside courses, as, for example, service learning, undergraduate research, and study abroad.[60]

As with the initial stage of setting aside KU's existing general education goals and creating new ones, so in filling in the core with courses the framers "de-privileged" all the existing requirements and leveled the playing field. While introductory English, mathematics, philosophy, and communication studies courses might seem to have had an obvious "edge" as fulfilling Goals 1 (critical thinking and quantitative literacy) and 2 (written and oral communication), courses in a variety of other departments and fields were also approved.

The KU Core required 36 credit hours of approved Core courses/ educational experiences of all students in the university—exactly half of the College total that had been in place for 25 years. Each of the schools was allowed to add or specify requirements but was discouraged from increasing the number of hours substantially beyond the 36. The College specified, for the BA, a course in college algebra, a laboratory or field experience, English 101 and 102, and a four-semester foreign language/culture requirement.[61] The smaller number of general education hours required, even with added College requirements, freed up more hours of the 120 now required for graduation for the student to take more courses in the major and electives.

The fact that all KU students now share what looks like a common liberal education was an impressive achievement, a fulfillment of the aspirations of those who had tried to create a university-wide core curriculum in the early 1980s. However, the traditional presuppositions and methods of curricular reform examined in this chapter were based on a broad consensus about what a liberal education looked like and a commitment to curricular continuity, which meant incremental revision rather than wholesale replacement. Crucially, that broad consensus assumed that liberal education was to be structured according to fields of study, such as the natural sciences, mathematics, social sciences, history, literature, philosophy, rhetoric, and fine arts.

The creators of the KU Core sought to create a new consensus— hence their desire to start the process from scratch and to adopt an entirely different model for constructing a core curriculum. The very term "core," which historically referred to a group of texts and/ or courses that it was believed should be required of every student, now referred to the six "core goals" that denote very broadly the skills, themes, and accomplishments deemed important in equipping KU graduates for life and work in the twenty-first century.[62]

The KU Core represented a model of university-wide liberal education that has the merit, in the large-research-university environment of the early twenty-first century, of perhaps being the only one possible. Faculty have long had a difficult time agreeing on what students should learn as part of a liberal education. This is especially the case at large research universities with many diverse fields and interests represented within the liberal arts and sciences, not to mention at the undergraduate professional schools. In trying to define and implement a liberal education, it was less difficult to obtain faculty agreement about broad areas of competence and learning than about particular fields of study and courses. The KU Core also accommodated student desires, going back, as we have seen, at least to the late 1960s and early 1970s, for greater flexibility and freedom in designing students' own undergraduate courses of study.

Skeptics might observe that the newer core model, by no longer privileging academic disciplines or curricular divisions, created a bewildering miscellany of courses that meet the criteria for fulfilling the requirements for most of the goals.[63] From the standpoint of the story of general education at KU, which has been the theme of this chapter, the KU Core can appear as though it consists entirely of a greatly expanded and revised principal course system in which courses from the three broad curricular divisions and the undergraduate professional schools often compete with one another to fulfill the same goals and outcomes.

The KU Core was inaugurated in tandem with other new Bold Aspirations undergraduate programs such as the First Year Experience. This included freshman seminars, an annual all-campus "common book," freshman learning communities, a one-hour course introducing students to the university, and substantial efforts to strengthen freshman recruiting, advising, and orientation. The hope was that together these measures would support first-year students in transitioning and being integrated into the intellectual life and community of the university, thus encouraging them to stay. The Core reduced a substantial general education responsibility and thereby freed students to pursue more courses to which they were more likely to bring motivation and interest.

As to the educational value of the Core, only time and the very imperfect results of future student and alumni surveys will tell. It is the latest—and thus far perhaps the most dramatic—chapter in the continuing story of liberal education at the University of Kansas. KU students and faculty in 1965 could hardly have imagined the national, international, and technological changes that have shaped the present day and its issues. Likewise, in 2015 we cannot likely imagine the changes that will have taken place when KU celebrates its bicentennial in 2065–2066. The university itself may look very different, and so may its undergraduate programs. However, perhaps we may allow ourselves to hope that in 50 years the ideal of a liberal education—a balanced and comprehensive undergraduate experience that is particularly valuable in preparing graduates for lifelong learning, personal fulfillment, responsible citizenship, and career achievement and satisfaction—will continue to be at the heart of what it means to be a university.

CHAPTER 4

The Global Dimension

J. MEGAN GREENE

IN 2008, the University of Kansas put up a new signboard along Interstate 70, westbound approaching Lawrence, proclaiming to all drivers that they were nearing the home of an "international research university." The signboard signaled that KU's internationalism had become a selling point worth proclaiming to the many Kansans and others who drive past. By the 2013–2014 school year, 25 percent of KU students were studying abroad, 9 percent were from other countries, and most of KU's faculty engaged in research activities with some sort of international dimension, ranging from subject matter to collaboration with foreign scholars. In addition, 255 KU students completed a Global Awareness Certificate, the number majoring in Global and International Studies was growing rapidly, and the number of students who imagined that their future careers would require knowledge of another part of the world was steadily increasing.

International is becoming the norm today, and few are the faculty and students at KU who are not touched in some way by an international experience. But this has not always been the case. The story of KU's internationalization began in the 1950s and early 1960s, much as it did for many institutions of higher learning across the country. It was spurred by a rising number of students and faculty who had experienced international travel and learned foreign languages during World War II and the Korean War and the growing availability of both government and foundation funding to support the study of foreign languages and cultures (particularly after the Russian Sputnik satellite was launched). To this was added the increasing allure of US institutions of higher education to students from around the world and a rising sense among American academics of the role that they could play in fostering development and democratization abroad. As at many peer institutions, KU's leadership and faculty responded to these trends along with the student body, and since the later 1950s KU has undergone a long and steady process of bringing students and scholars together from around the world.

AGENTS OF CHANGE

KU's first international student was a Welshman, James F. Harris, who attended the university for one year in 1874–1875; a KU student, Virginia Joseph, was among the first group of Fulbright Scholars in 1949; and an office to administer study abroad opened at KU during World War II. Therefore, it would be wrong to suggest that KU had no international engagement prior to the 1950s. However, the big push toward internationalization of the institution really took place in the period between 1958 and 1965, under the leadership of faculty and administrators who had joined the university in the years between 1945 and 1954. Two chancellors, Franklin Murphy (1951–1960) and W. Clarke Wescoe (1960–1969), were particularly influential in fostering an environment that encouraged the expansion of KU's international engagement.

Chancellor Murphy, who had himself studied abroad in Germany, started a major push for internationalization in 1958 when he simultaneously sought to strengthen the foreign language requirement for students in the College of Liberal Arts and Sciences from 10 to 16 credit hours and persuaded the Board of Regents and the legislature to sanction plans to develop a relationship with the University of Costa Rica (UCR) and expand course offerings in Slavic and Soviet Studies and East Asian Studies. According to Francis Heller, a political scientist who served as associate dean for the College, Murphy made a point of assuring the Board of Regents that KU would limit its international offerings to Latin America, Russia and Eastern Europe, and East Asia.[1] Murphy signed an agreement with UCR that served as the founding document for an exchange that would become a centerpiece of KU's international programs. Taken together, these acts signified a deep commitment to expanding KU's international dimensions, but Murphy wanted to involve both faculty and students, and by 1959 he had "appointed a committee to study and formulate the role of the University of Kansas in world affairs."[2]

After Murphy's departure for UCLA, the work of this preliminary committee continued under Chancellor Wescoe and culminated in the establishment in September 1961 of the University Committee on International Educational Affairs, which was also chaired by Heller and included Russian historian Oswald P. Backus, petroleum engineer Floyd R. Preston, and Thomas R. Smith, a geographer. The committee met throughout the 1961–1962 academic year and drafted a prospectus on international education in June 1962.[3] The committee's final report asserted that "a state university will not have fulfilled its obligation to its state in this, the 20th century, if it fails to provide for its students the kind of educational experience which will fit them for life in the 21st century." To do this, the report suggested that KU "accept, and act on, the proposition that the people it serves are no longer bounded by narrow local limits but that their needs, interests, and responsibilities are and will continue to be world-wide." It urged recognition "that the most demanding problem of our day and of our future will not be economic or technological but will be the absolute necessity for all peoples to learn to live together in a world that has been radically transformed." And it implored the university to "never lose sight of the fact that it is an integral part of the community, that its activities must always be related to and be a part of the community which it serves."[4] In other words, in the view of the committee, the people of Kansas were part of a shrinking world, and the university should serve them as they engaged with the new global context. The report went on to propose, among other things, that every KU student should be exposed to courses on international subjects and encouraged to study abroad, and that faculty should be encouraged to engage in international research.

The fact that Murphy started these initiatives in 1958 was surely not accidental. Public uproar over the 1957 Soviet Sputnik satellite had made global awareness a national concern. In September of the following year, the National Defense Education Act (NDEA) provided government funding to support the creation of area studies centers at American universities. KU received NDEA funding for East Asian Studies and International Studies from the start and has had continuous support from this source, later renamed the Title VI program, to support at least one—and usually several—of its area studies programs ever since. Over the years, this sort of funding has been used to enhance student language learning and study abroad with Foreign Language and Area Studies (FLAS) grants, to build foreign language library collections, to aid faculty hires in East Asian, Russian and East European,

KU student Noemi Tracy looking through the "door of no return" at the historic slave fort on Goree Island, Senegal, Africa, 2013.

and Latin American studies (the Kansas African Studies Center was not created until the 1970s), and to support faculty research.

Although Chancellors Murphy and Wescoe were both ardent advocates of expanding KU's international engagement, much of the legwork was done by committed administrators and individual faculty members. George Waggoner, for example, who was dean of the College from 1954 to 1974, played a key role in almost all of the internationalization efforts during his tenure. He was Chancellor Murphy's key collaborator in the development of the initial exchange program with UCR and was very active in international programs. Waggoner directed a number of nationally sponsored seminars to assist Central American universities in identifying and solving administrative and structural problems and led the development of many additional exchange programs with universities around the world. He also provided key moral and financial support for the activities of internationally minded faculty. Waggoner, along with a number of key faculty colleagues, displayed extraordinary energy and helped to transform the university by securing foundation and government grants and establishing new programs. Three faculty members who played key roles in this process during the 1950s and 1960s were George Beckmann,

The Chinese Student Association celebrating the Lunar New Year in February 2010.

J. Anthony (Toni) Burzle, and E. Raymond Hall, all of whom conducted research on international topics.

George Beckmann, a historian of modern Japan hired in 1954, was perhaps most active in seeking external funding to support the development of programs for international curriculum development and research at KU. He created the Department of Oriental Languages and chaired the East Asian Area Studies Committee (the precursor of the Center for East Asian Studies) from its inception in 1959 as part of the effort to secure NDEA funding. A few years later, he led the effort to secure Ford Foundation support to develop KU offices to serve international students and support study abroad, expand library resources, hire new faculty with expertise on international subject matters, and provide research support to those faculty. In the meantime, Beckmann went about expanding the East Asian curriculum by adding Chinese (Japanese was already being taught, although it was housed in the German Department) and building a faculty for East Asian Studies by traveling around the world to find his future colleagues. Beckmann was, by all accounts, a very tall figure with a great deal of presence and charm, and he used these attributes to good effect as he built his program. In 1960, he recruited Felix Moos, a young anthropologist then teaching in Japan, literally seeking him out in his classroom while on a trip to Japan and inviting him to join the KU faculty. A couple of years later, he sought out Grant Goodman, a historian of premodern Japan, at a cocktail party on the West Coast and offered him a job. These were but two of several important hires that were made over the course of the 1960s as Beckmann oversaw the expansion of East Asian Studies at KU.

Beckmann was able to hire new faculty in this way because he was extraordinarily successful in securing outside funding to support his initiatives. Perhaps most important were two $500,000 Ford Foundation grants that Beckmann secured in 1963 to support international programs at KU (about $7.6 million total in 2013 dollars). These grants were sufficiently large to permit the university to hire area studies librarians to oversee the development of foreign language collections, particularly those written in non-Latin scripts, and new faculty members, particularly in foreign languages. It also enabled KU to create a Center for Intensive English and an office to support foreign students; establish a cooperative intensive summer language program in Chinese, Japanese, Russian, and Polish; and provide release time and short-term research support for KU faculty working on international topics.[5] As part of a Ford Foundation grant, the post of associate dean of faculties was created in 1964, and Beckmann was given the position. A major aspect of his duties was administration of the grant and helping "the deans of colleges and schools and . . . the chairmen of departments and of foreign area programs in order to facilitate the kind of improvement and expansion that is required to enhance the University's capacity in meeting the many education challenges in the international fields."[6]

Toni Burzle, an immigrant from Munich, came to KU in 1945 to teach German language and literature. At the time he joined the German Department, it had only two faculty members, who had split all of the teaching duties between them. This was quite a heavy load because there was considerable demand for German, especially among returning GIs. By the late 1940s, Burzle had become engaged in serving foreign students and promoting study abroad. This involved programs such as the Kansas University Exchange Scholarship, the Foreign Student Hospitality Program, and the Fulbright Program, which he was instrumental in bringing to campus. He later became an adviser to the German and Austrian Fulbright commissions. Between 1951 and 1977, Burzle ran an institute for foreign scholars, funded by the State Department. Through this program, 50 to 75 foreign scholars came each summer to the KU Orientation Center for an eight-week course on American culture and English. Burzle also helped get KU connected to other State Department projects, such as the participation of the KU Brass Ensemble in a 1964 cultural presentation program that traveled to the Ryukyus, Ceylon, Laos, Malaysia, Indonesia, and Australia. Starting in 1968, at the request of the Command and General Staff College at Fort Leavenworth, Burzle created and ran an American culture and English language course for visiting foreign officers.

Of all these many initiatives, perhaps Burzle's most important contribution to the internationalization of the educational experience of KU students was the formation, in 1948, of the KU Direct Exchange Scholarship, through which KU students could spend a year in Germany, France, or England in exchanges with students from partner institutions, who would come to KU for the year. In 1960, he built on the foundation of the Direct Exchange by developing a series of summer language institutes in Europe, through which KU students could spend the summer doing intensive language study in France, Germany, or Spain. In that first year, any junior with at least a C average, who had taken at least two years of the relevant foreign language and achieved at least a B average in those courses, and who could afford the sum of $2,000 for the summer (about $15,700 in 2013 dollars) was eligible to participate.[7] By the 1970s, Burzle directed both the Foreign Study Programs (the precursor to the Office of Study Abroad) and the KU Orientation Center for Foreign Scholars, and he did so until his retirement in 1977.[8]

E. Raymond Hall, director of KU's Natural History Museum and chair of the Department of Zoology, also planted some important seeds in the 1940s and 1950s that fostered KU's place in a broader, more global community. Through a collaboration with Ruben Torres Rojas, of UCR, Hall helped develop the foundation for what would become KU's longest-standing and most successful relationship with a partner university abroad. That partnership, which was codified into an exchange in 1958, arose from a seemingly accidental increase in the number of Costa Rican students at KU in the mid- to late 1940s (5 of the 19 foreign students at KU in 1945 were from Costa Rica) and a museum collaboration that began in 1947 between Torres Rojas, a scientist and dean at UCR, and Hall, both of whom had interests in natural history museums.[9] By 1947, Hall and Torres Rojas were discussing the possibility of establishing a regularized faculty exchange program, and professors from various disciplines at each institution did start to travel back and forth. By the late 1950s, interest in Latin

History professor Charlie Stansifer and former president of Costa Rica Óscar Arias Sánchez in 1994.

George Waggoner, dean of Arts and Sciences, receives an honorary degree from Universidad de Oriente in Cumaná, Venezuela, for contributions to comparative education, university reform, and scholarly understanding throughout Latin America.

America and the study of Spanish was increasing in the United States, so the time was right for Chancellor Murphy of KU and Rector Rodrigo Facio of UCR to sign a comprehensive agreement between the two universities.[10] Although the foundation of this long-term relationship started in the sciences and social sciences, particularly zoology and anthropology, it was also very important to the development of both the Latin American Studies program and study abroad at KU. The first group of KU students to study abroad at UCR went in 1960, and by 1999 over 700 KU students had participated in the program.[11] Over time, George Waggoner and Anita Herzfeld came to manage the further development of the UCR exchange.

INSTITUTIONALIZING THE INTERNATIONAL

Although the University of Kansas had long exhibited an international dimension, the shifts that took place in the late 1950s and early 1960s were nonetheless considerable and laid the foundation for patterns of institutional development in the areas of study abroad, exchanges with institutions abroad, library acquisitions, faculty hiring, curricular development, and student recruitment that continue to be evident today. What motivated this turn toward the larger world? Certainly, major international events such as Sputnik and the 1962 Cuban Missile Crisis played a role, as did the new availability of funding to support initiatives in area studies, but KU publications from the 1960s suggest that there clearly was another important reason. KU staff and faculty saw themselves as ambassadors of American culture and understood their interactions with international students, visiting scholars, and faculty at institutions of higher education in other countries to have an important diplomatic dimension.

Perhaps this way of thinking owed something to KU's proximity to the People to People program, which was headquartered in Kansas City and aimed to build goodwill toward the United States and spread American values to other countries through interpersonal relationships between ordinary citizens. KU had its own People to People ambassadors and kept international students and visiting scholars informed about the activities of the People to People program in Kansas City.[12]

Just as the People to People program sought to educate foreigners about American values, so too did the Office of the Foreign Student Advisor (Burzle's office). The November 1965 edition of its *Newsletter*

Jodi Gentry and Aida Ramos Viera, graduate students, and Brent Metz, professor of anthropology, collaborate with villagers in Guatemala during the Sustainable Development Field School in January 2013.

provides a window into the university's thinking about the function and purpose of all of this international contact. Stuck right in the middle of the *Newsletter*, between a note on vacation housing and another on the International Film Festival, was a quotation from W. W. Rostow, one of the intellectual architects of US aid policy in the 1950s and 1960s: "It is the ability of a community to achieve consensus on the great issues and compromises on the lesser issues, which lie at the heart of the democratic process."[13] The KU Office of the Foreign Student Advisor clearly understood itself to be in the business of educating foreign students about democracy. It supported this agenda by doing such things as sending students to UNESCO conferences in Kansas City and to United Nations anniversary dinners held in such small Kansas towns as Chanute.

Study and research abroad, for American students and faculty as well as foreign students coming to KU, were ways of connecting the university to international networks that promoted peace and understanding. The same edition of the *Newsletter* also included an article reprinted from the October 2, 1965, edition of the *Asian Student* about a visit to Japan by Dr. Grayson L. Kirk, president of Columbia University,

Elie Wiesel (left), a survivor of concentration camps, author of over 50 books, and a political activist, was awarded the Nobel Prize in 1986 and visited KU during the 1988–1989 school year.

who had spoken on the importance of greater international under-standing as the basis for world peace. Knowing more about the wider world and building personal relationships with people across the globe was one way to help foster peace, and in the 1960s this goal must have seemed particularly salient to KU faculty and staff. As citizens of a changing world, these members of the KU community reshaped university activities—both instructional and others—to mirror the so-called softpower strategies for building international goodwill, such as the People to People, Sister Cities, and Peace Corps programs, which were popularized by the Eisenhower and Kennedy administrations.

The transmission of American know-how to the developing world and the establishment of programs of genuine intellectual exchange were also big motivators for KU faculty and staff in the 1960s. By March 1962, for example, KU's School of Engineering and Architecture had taken a leading role within a group of eight engineering schools in Kansas and neighboring states to draft a document entitled "A Program of Foreign Aid in Engineering Education," which made clear precisely how KU's engineering faculty members, along with other such faculty at engineering schools across the Midwest, envisioned

Jehan Sadat, widow of the late Egyptian president Anwar Sadat, speaks at a press conference before her 1986 lecture on the role of women in the Middle East.

their role in the world. It stated, "Because faculties of engineering schools have an opportunity and competence to assist educational institutions in countries with advanced technology, and because such activities properly pursued appear vital to us and to our country, several deans of . . . schools of engineering are seeking ways of pairing this potential for support with acknowledged needs at institutions in either Latin America or Africa."[14] The attitudes reflected in this document clearly demonstrate that KU faculty members believed they could play an important role in disseminating technical knowledge in developing countries and assisting them to develop. Fifteen engineering faculty members at KU expressed an interest in participating in the program.[15]

The presence of increasing numbers of international students on campus also had an impact on the character of KU and certainly led to changes in the administrative structure of the institution. In 1957, there were sufficient numbers of foreign students—197 of them—to justify hiring Clark Coan, who was then teaching government at Lawrence High School, as a part-time foreign student adviser.[16] Over the course of the early 1960s, the number of international students grew steadily, so that by the fall of 1965, KU had 542 international students from 85 countries. Of these, by far the most came from Asia (316, of whom 222

Archbishop Desmond Tutu visiting KU in April 1999.

were identified as being from the Far East and 94 were from the Near East). In addition, 88 students came from Central and South America, 77 from Europe, 45 from Africa, and 16 from Canada and Mexico (North America). Of these, 444 students were men (98 were women), 290 were graduate students, 191 were undergraduate students, and 60 were enrolled at the Intensive English Center. These students had available to them a number of clubs, such as the Japanese-American Club, the Arab-American Club, the African Students' Club, and the Centro de Estudiantes Venezolanos, all of which were established by students from abroad and were designed to serve the needs of new foreign students looking for connections to home and advice on how to navigate in their new setting. Although these clubs were designed by international students for other foreign students, they did sometimes put on events that exposed other KU students to cultural features of different countries.

To address the particular needs of foreign students, in 1965 KU created the Intensive English Center, which was later renamed the Applied English Center. In its first year, it had 60 students. It was created with some of the Ford Foundation funds that had been secured by Beckmann, and it was directed by Edward Erazmus.[17] The Office of the Foreign Student Advisor located in Strong Hall dispensed advice and information and helped students in various ways, such as providing blankets to those needing them and being a source of information about such topics as keeping receipts for taxes, how to get auto insurance, the Oskaloosa Rotary Dinner, good deals on Greyhound tickets, and similar questions.[18] In 1966, the Office of the Foreign Student Advisor was renamed the Office of the Dean of Foreign Students and was placed under the new administrative position of dean of International Programs. In 1971, the Office of the Dean of Foreign Students was moved yet again and placed under the Office of the Vice Chancellor for Student Affairs.

Study abroad was another area that witnessed enormous growth in the early 1960s, largely through the efforts of Toni Burzle, and it was surely the international activity that touched the largest number of KU students over the years. But it is worth remembering that study abroad was not the norm in the 1950s. In fact, the number of students participating in it was quite small in 1959 (12 students), but the number started increasing rapidly thereafter, and in 1968, 200 KU students studied abroad. The first group of students went to UCR on the newly established exchange program in 1960, and in that same year the first cohort of Summer Language Institute students (120 or more each summer, not all from KU) started attending the institutes in Europe. KU's rapidly rising study abroad profile and its leadership in creating programs serving students from other institutions led the New York–based Institute for International Education to recognize KU as one of five institutions to receive its Reader's Digest Award in 1964. KU was the only public university to receive the award that year.

Administrative structures continued to change periodically from the mid-1960s on, and new academic units, such as African and African-American Studies (established in the 1970s), were also created as KU continued to internationalize its curriculum. But the general contours of KU's engagement with the world had been established by the mid-1960s. Study abroad, engagement with partner institutions abroad, collaboration in all sorts of disciplines between faculty at KU and colleagues abroad, instruction in foreign languages and cultures, and a warm welcome for foreign students were becoming institutional norms by 1965.

As early as 1971, Dean of Foreign Students Clark Coan noted that the perceived exoticism of the international student had diminished as their numbers on campus had grown. Moreover, their self-sufficiency had also increased, as they ceased to be as dependent on or as engaged with the Dean of Foreign Students Office. Coan said, "When we had

Students from KU have traveled to many countries to engage in study abroad. This group participated in KU's long-running exchange with Costa Rica in the 1970s.

only 200 foreign students we would have good response to plans for trips: but now we have 800 and we have to really scramble to have a bus load of students."[19] With the increase in numbers, the function of the office gradually began to shift away from its earlier mission of teaching foreign students how to live in the United States and providing them with comforts that would enhance their stay, toward more bureaucratized assistance with forms and procedures needed by both the university and the Immigration and Naturalization Service. Nonetheless, Coan remained in office until 1990, becoming well known for the personal attention he paid to students and his remarkable ability to remember the names and personal details of hundreds of people his office dealt with over the years.

The presence of foreign students on campus did, however, continue to connect the university to major international events. In the 1970s, for example, the largest group of KU's foreign students came from Iran, as was the case at other institutions. At the time of the Iranian revolution in 1979, there were about 275 Iranian students at KU. As conflict heated up in Iran, political divisions among these students became evident, and, according to Clark Coan, they led numerous demonstrations with occasional fights breaking out between them over conflicting political views. After the US hostages were taken at the American Embassy in Tehran, Coan recalled that things deteriorated, and KU's

Iranian students were the victims of threats and harassment by other
KU students as well as others in Lawrence. To make matters worse,
as the United States cut off relations with Iran, US Immigration and
Naturalization Service agents came to campus to interview the Iranian
students, and they often asked for assistance from the Dean of Foreign
Students Office. This put the KU office in a difficult position because
its primary function was to support foreign students, and its staff did
not want to be perceived as acting on behalf of the government. The
number of Iranian students fell as a result of the rift in diplomatic relations between the two countries, but about 75, most of whom had not
been home in years, still remained at KU a decade later.[20]

At the same time, study abroad, although it experienced a bit of
a lull in the 1970s, was also becoming increasingly popular among
students at KU by the 1980s, as KU programs regularly attracted 200
to 300 students a year, along with many non-KU students. KU's long-
established pattern of encouraging study abroad impressed Mary Elizabeth Debicki (then Gwin) as she was being recruited from the University of Mississippi to lead the study abroad program in 1985, although
at first she had no interest in moving to Kansas. A New Yorker who
had made her home in Mississippi for a couple of decades, Debicki
thought Kansas was too far from home and unfamiliar to be worth
considering. But the colleagues she had come to know through the
International Student Exchange Program, of which both KU and Mississippi were members, finally convinced her to apply, and as she later
said, "It was so exciting to meet the faculty, to meet the people who
were involved in international education at that level at that time. I
just fell in love with KU." Debicki, a French instructor who had created the study abroad office at Mississippi in the 1970s, found that
KU, which had established its own such office in the 1950s, "was much
more forward-looking than a place like Mississippi. I was the whole
office in Mississippi. Here they had had a director. They had two study
abroad advisors and lots of student workers and a secretary and a very
active study abroad program."[21] Under Debicki's leadership, the variety of study abroad opportunities and the number of students taking
advantage of them steadily increased.

ORGANIZING THE INTERNATIONAL UNIVERSITY

By the late 1980s, during the tenure of Chancellor Gene Budig
(1981–1994), the KU administration had determined that all things

international at KU needed to be consolidated under a single roof. This was done under the leadership of George Woodyard, of the Spanish and Portuguese Department, who worked at KU from 1966 to 2005. He served in various administrative roles, including chair of his academic department. In the early 1980s, Woodyard, who was then working in central administration and had helped establish the Hall Center for the Humanities, proposed a Center for International Programs to the Board of Regents, which was approved in 1984. Through that center, Woodyard and Susan Gronbeck-Tedesco wrote grant proposals to support international studies, including faculty research projects abroad and a Fund for the Improvement of Postsecondary Education grant to take engineering students to study Spanish in Mexico.[22] By the late 1980s, Woodyard, who clearly had great vision, was advocating for the complete reorganization of KU's international initiatives. His efforts resulted in the creation of a new unit, International Studies, in Lippincott Hall, and he became its first and only dean in 1989. He remained in the position until 1996, when the unit lost its independent status and was placed under the direction of the Graduate School. The distinguishing feature of this unit was its goal of coordinating and promoting all things international, from the foreign student experience to study abroad to teaching and research on international subjects. It absorbed the Applied English Center and the Office of Study Abroad and worked closely with the area studies programs, granting them a status that allowed connections with the professional schools, something they could not easily do as units within the College. The International Studies Office undertook a variety of new initiatives, including starting overseas alumni chapters, facilitating rotations abroad for medical students, and applying for additional grants. From Woodyard's perspective, the whole enterprise was very successful but was ruined when Chancellor Robert Hemenway (1995–2009) decided that there should no longer be a separate dean of international studies and merged international studies with the Graduate School, where it languished until it was split off again. Woodyard, clearly quite disillusioned with the Hemenway administration, observed in a 2005 interview that "the chancellor talks a lot about how important it is to be international but they've stripped the influence out of the programs."[23]

Woodyard was not the only one to complain of a lack of vision or support on the part of KU's central administration in the mid-1990s. Mary Elizabeth Debicki, who had joined KU in 1986 and directed the Office of Study Abroad until 1996, expressed considerable concern in a 1995 annual report over a lack of institutional support for study abroad. In spite of the enthusiasm with which she had come to KU, by 1995 Debicki appears to have become quite frustrated in her job. Her 1995 annual report on the Office of Study Abroad indicated that she believed the institution and its faculty were simply not providing adequate support for international study. Her staff was too small and was underpaid and underappreciated, but worst of all, her sense was that the value of study abroad and the ways in which it connected to students' academic development was simply not widely recognized. "We know," she wrote, "that language majors are created as a direct result of time spent abroad. The Area Studies Centers realize the value to their programs of what we can help them to achieve. Why do other departments not jump at the chance to enhance their offerings in this competitive market? The encouragement *must* come from on high." Even more frustrating for Debicki, however, was the lack of interaction between the various units engaged in international activities. "There is NO standard for informing us of initiatives which are being discussed or undertaken. Rightly or wrongly we [at study abroad] feel we have something to offer to international programs both here and abroad and it is frustrating to *always* seem to be hearing of activities of other units on the fly. Taking time for coordinated planning would be time well spent."[24] In theory, it would seem that Woodyard's unit should have been the place for such coordinated planning to take place, but Debicki's comments do not appear to have been directed at him or at International Studies. Rather, they seem to have been meant for the university's central administration. In spite of Debicki's concerns over lack of support, however, her 1995 report makes it clear that her office was exceptionally active and that study abroad, although clearly over-taxed and understaffed, was certainly not waning.

With respect to foreign students, outgoing Associate Dean of Student Life and Director of Foreign Student Services Clark Coan observed in a 1990 interview that, over his 33 years at KU, the number of foreign students had increased tenfold, and demand was such that the number could go up as high as the university administration would permit. However, he recommended that the university stay at a level of just under 2,000 foreign students—the number it had reached in the late 1980s—because that was what its infrastructure could handle well, particularly in terms of English language instruction. An increase in the number of foreign students, he suggested, might diminish both the quality of the students and their educational experiences at KU.[25] In fact, the number of foreign students declined by 600 between 1993 and 1996, sparking concern among Coan's successors in International

Student and Scholar Services. Director Joe Potts, interviewed shortly after his arrival at KU in 1999, seemed concerned by the decline in international student numbers and felt that KU needed to develop a clear set of goals with respect to their recruitment.[26]

Perhaps part of the problem was that the 1990s were a difficult decade financially for the university, with declining state support and before the university embarked on a strategy of making up the difference with tuition revenues. Under such circumstances, some argued that KU's best strategy would be to focus on its existing strengths rather than expand into new ventures. Clark Coan, for example, was concerned that overextension of study abroad opportunities would lead to the demise of the study abroad program, and that expansion of area studies programs into new world regions would stretch resources too thin and therefore not benefit the university.[27]

By the late 1990s, however, the university seemed to be embarking on a path that would lead to both expansion and the rectification of some of the problems that Debicki and Potts had observed a few years earlier. In 1998, Provost David Shulenburger called for every student to have a "significant international experience." Potts enthusiastically said of this initiative, "Every department and unit on campus could and should be involved in one way or another."[28] The recently retired Debicki also expressed enthusiasm for the shift toward the international in 1998. "I'm kind of excited about some of the directions KU is taking. It was quite a shock to have a lot of the shake-ups that have taken place in the last few years. But I think it has a great future. I'm very happy to see the international aspects of KU being emphasized."[29] A strong international focus would, in fact, become one of KU's defining features in the new millennium, and by 2010 the university would be building its faculty, curriculum, and library resources in new world regions, such as the Middle East and South Asia, adding to its array of study abroad offerings and encouraging international engagement through a variety of new programs.

Shulenburger's push for students to have a "significant international experience" resulted in a rapid and dramatic increase in study abroad participation. Whereas 498 KU students participated in study abroad in 1996–1997, by 2000–2001 that number had more than doubled, rising to 1,141. In 2004, KU ranked fourth among public research universities for the number of students studying abroad, with a quarter of undergraduates having studied in a foreign country. Study abroad participation peaked in 2008–2009 with 1,468. Since that time, perhaps owing to the global recession, the number has declined somewhat, and in 2011–2012 it was 1,275.[30] Nonetheless, although the number of KU students has declined, it has remained the case for the past decade that approximately 25 percent of KU undergraduate students study abroad, a strong rate of participation.

Also in response to Shulenburger's call for a greater degree of internationalization, Diana Carlin, dean of International Programs, and Hodgie Bricke, assistant dean in the Office of International Programs, launched a new experiential certificate—the Global Awareness Program (GAP)—in 2004. The GAP program's first coordinator was Jane Irungu, a Kenyan PhD candidate in Education (she completed her degree in 2010), who would say to students, "Here I am, I'm from Africa, and I'm working right in the middle of America. You could find yourself in the same position. You need to know what's going on in these other parts of the world."[31] GAP attempts to help students toward this goal by offering them a certificate on their transcripts if they meet two of three requirements: study abroad; taking at least two terms of a modern foreign language and three internationally focused courses; or engaging in co-curricular activities with an international focus. Foreign students at KU can also get the GAP certificate by meeting a slightly modified set of requirements.

Shulenburger's renewal of KU's commitment to internationalization, as demonstrated by the push to send students abroad and to help them engage with the world by participating in internationally oriented activities and taking coursework on other parts of the world, helped bring KU important recognition from the National Association for Foreign Student Affairs (NAFSA) in 2005, when NAFSA awarded KU the Senator Paul Simon Award for Campus Internationalization. The NAFSA acknowledgment of KU also emphasized the importance of the university's long-standing and highly developed area studies programs, its rich and extensive foreign language offerings, and the emphasis on international engagement in its professional schools, particularly engineering and law, as additional reasons for its decision to make this award.[32]

In the twenty-first century, as that sign on I-70 attests, KU has made a point of identifying itself as an international university. Granted, this is surely partly because terms like "international" and "global" became buzzwords to signify modernity in the early twenty-first century. KU's current mission statement observes that "the university is dedicated to preparing its students for lives of learning and for the challenges educated citizens will encounter in an increasingly complex and diverse global community. More than 100 programs of international study and cooperative research are available for students and faculty at sites throughout the world. KU teaching and research draw upon and contribute to the most advanced developments throughout the United States and the world. At the same time, KU's extensive international ties support economic development in Kansas."[33] In other words, as was already quite apparent to the University Committee on International Affairs in 1961, the rest of the world matters in Kansas too. Buzzword or not, KU's internationalism rests on a strong legacy that has been steadily built over the past 60 years.

One measure of the steadiness of this growth is KU's success in supporting students pursuing prestigious external awards that permit them to study abroad. Already by 1960, Toni Burzle was putting out an extensive annual list of awards and deadlines in an effort to encourage students to find ways to afford study abroad for a term or a year. By the turn of the century, KU's Office of International Programs, its Office of Study Abroad, and the Honors Program, as well as its area studies centers and language departments, all engage in efforts to support study abroad. As of 2014, 443 KU students had earned Fulbright Awards, and there had been only one year since the inception of the Fulbright program in which no KU students won an award. Also as of 2014, 26 KU students had been named Rhodes Scholars, 9 had received the Marshall Scholarship, 60 had earned Gilman Scholarships, 70 had won Boren Scholarships, and 25 had won Critical Language Scholarships. All of these prestigious awards support study or research abroad for undergraduates, graduate students, or recent graduates. In addition, numerous alumni and retired faculty have sponsored scholarships to support KU students wishing to study abroad, most administered through the KUEA.

Another measure is in the sheer number of course offerings that engage international subject matter and are available to students on campus. By the second decade of the twenty-first century, KU was offering 40 (or more) foreign languages, many of which, like Uyghur, Tibetan, Wolof, and Kaqchikel Maya, are taught at very few other institutions in the United States. The dramatic expansion in the number of languages offered was largely the result of years of successful competition for Title VI funds by KU's area studies programs. When KU's newly created Center for Global and International Studies submitted its first Title VI grant application in 2010, it identified 61 pages worth of courses with at least some international content (including language courses), amounting to roughly 2,400 such classes being taught over a three-year cycle.

Tibetan students at KU during the 2010–2011 school year.

One shift over the years has been a change in the nature of interaction between KU faculty members and scholars at institutions around the world. Whereas, in the 1960s, many KU professors were guided by a sense of responsibility to share their expertise with scholars, citizens, and even governments around the world, by the turn of the century their relationships abroad tended to be on a more equal footing and to have a more genuinely collaborative character. That said, KU faculty members do continue to serve as consultants for development projects of various sorts around the globe, though often the line between aid and collaboration is perhaps more blurred than 50 years ago. A great example of a twenty-first-century KU project that has both domestic and international application and that is both collaborative and development oriented is the Community Toolbox created by Stephen Fawcett, a professor in applied behavioral science. The toolbox is a web resource that promotes community health and development and that has been used by communities all over the world seeking to tackle local health and development problems.

LOOKING TO THE FUTURE

When KU celebrates its bicentennial in another 50 years and another volume like this is written, its authors may discover that, with respect to internationalization, the second decade of the twenty-first century was another major turning point. In particular, 2013 and 2014 were filled with changes that may have an impact on the way that KU engages with the rest of the world. Three major developments are the implementation of the KU Core, the consolidation of the foreign language departments into a School of Languages, Literatures and Cultures, and the engagement of a private firm to increase the number of foreign students attending the university.

The KU Core, the common undergraduate curriculum introduced in the fall of 2013, takes a skills-based rather than a knowledge-based approach to general education. Whereas students in the College had previously been required to take the Western Civilization sequence as well as a non–Western studies course, and students taking the BA were required to take four semesters of a single language, now, according to the KU Core, all students across the institution are required to complete a two-course culture and diversity requirement. This new requirement can be partially fulfilled by study abroad, which could motivate students to study in a foreign country, but it can also be

partially fulfilled by a course on diversity in the United States. This
means that many KU students will be able to graduate having taken
only one course with content on a country outside the United States.
On the other hand, the reduction in the number of general education
requirements might mean that students feel they have more time to
devote to taking courses on international subject matters or to study
abroad, and the fact that the KU Core applies to all undergraduates
means that many students in the professional schools may find themselves taking an international course that they might never have otherwise considered. Students in the College still have a language requirement, although it can now be satisfied with three semesters in
one language and a single semester in a separate language—again, a
requirement that has the potential to lead students to experiment with
more than one language, though it also has the potential to leave students without mastery of any foreign language. It remains to be seen
if or how the KU Core will affect students' international engagement.

Similarly, in 2014 the College decided to meld the foreign language departments into a single School of Languages, Literatures and
Cultures, thus radically transforming an institutional structure that
had been, for the most part, established in the mid-1960s. This new
arrangement has the potential to foster transregional and interdisciplinary teaching and research collaborations and to raise the visibility
of KU's foreign languages among students. But it will almost certainly
lead, over time, to radical shifts in the organizational structure and the
relations among the foreign language departments. As with the KU
Core, the impact of these changes remains to be seen.

Finally, in a belated answer to Joe Potts's 1999 question about strategic planning with respect to foreign student recruitment, after some
years of recruiting foreign undergraduates more aggressively than in
the twentieth century, KU decided in 2014 to contract with Shorelight,
a firm that specializes in recruiting students from abroad. One aim
of undergraduate foreign student recruitment since 2000 has been
to help fill the revenue gap that has been created by declining state
support for higher education. Foreign undergraduates pay the higher
out-of-state tuition rate and are thus a valuable source of revenue for
the institution. The number of foreign students at KU in 2014 was
roughly 2,200, of whom about two-thirds were undergraduates, many
from China. The Office of International Programs plans to continue
recruiting students through traditional mechanisms, and indeed to increase the number of students it recruits, but also to gradually double
the number of full-paying foreign students on campus through the

Students making dumplings for the Lunar New Year in January 2014.

Shorelight program. So the goal, over the next five to ten years, is to reach a target of about 15 percent international students at KU.

KU's decision to contract with Shorelight marks a sea change in its approach to foreign student recruitment because it turns the process much more explicitly into a business venture than ever before. Shorelight will do the recruiting and, working with the Applied English Center and several KU academic departments, will help students through their first-year curriculum. Foreign students in the Shorelight Academic Accelerator Program will enroll in acculturation courses, English courses, and regular KU courses on such subjects as Introduction to American Studies, Kansas Landscapes, and math. For these services, Shorelight will be paid about half of the profits after student tuition has paid program expenses for the Academic Accelerator Program, and it will also earn a small percentage of the tuition that students will pay after they have fully matriculated at KU. Shorelight will bear the burden of helping these students to acclimate to KU and the American university system, and KU will ultimately benefit from the presence of larger numbers of full-paying international undergraduates who are well prepared to study at KU.[34]

If in the 1960s a major reason for bringing foreign students, most of whom were graduate students, to Kansas was to teach them about

American values and send them home as ambassadors for an American way of life, today a major reason for foreign student recruitment is to make it financially possible to continue to operate the university and thus to educate and serve the people of Kansas. So foreign student recruitment would appear to have lost its altruistic and developmentally minded (though also paternalistic) overtones and to have become a fairly mercenary endeavor, though the primary aim will surely continue to be to provide foreign students with the best possible education. Nonetheless, one by-product of this gradual doubling of the number of foreign students on campus will be the further internationalization of the student body, and of classrooms in all disciplines. If KU can develop a new set of strategies to help these students truly integrate into the university environment, then the potential for people-to-people exchange, mutual understanding, and increased enthusiasm for knowledge of other parts of the world among domestic KU students is enormous. KU will surely continue to internationalize in the future and, even with these seismic shifts that are taking place in 2013 and 2014, to build upon the foundation of the past 50 years.

CHAPTER 5

Forging a University
Research Mission

JOSHUA L. ROSENBLOOM

The university exists to accommodate and implement the whole human learning process, and this must include creative scholarship and
research. Thus research is not an optional activity of the university, not
merely a legitimate pursuit for those who may be interested and willing to dedicate their spare time, nor an assignment justified to either
the university or the professor by the resultant income in dollars and
publicity. Rather, research is an inescapable responsibility of the university and an inseparable part of its total educational function.
　　　　　　　　　　—"The Place of Research in the University"

By far the most visible features of the University of Kansas revolve
around its undergraduate education mission. As the quotation above
suggests, however, the university's commitment to research and creative scholarship is at least as important in defining KU's identity.[1]
Research has always been central to the university's identity; at his inauguration in 1890, Chancellor Francis H. Snow observed that it was
incumbent on the faculty "not only to teach the old truth, but also to
discover new truth."[2] As Clifford Griffin's history of KU's first 100 years
documents, the conviction that the university's role extends beyond
communicating existing knowledge to the production of new knowledge has been reaffirmed by every subsequent chancellor.[3]

Nationally and internationally, it is KU's role as a research university,
where faculty extend the frontiers of knowledge and the next generation of scholars is trained, that is its truly distinctive feature. According

Burt Hall nuclear reactor, School of Engineering, 1965, an important research facility for faculty and students alike.

to the US Department of Education, there are over 4,600 institutions of higher education in the United States today. At most of them, however, the primary focus is on teaching. Only about 300 institutions are classified as research universities, and just 108 of these—including the elite private universities and most major state flagship universities— are classified by the Carnegie Foundation as ones of "very high research activity." KU is one of these research-intensive universities.

Although KU's identity as a research university has very deep roots, the meaning of this commitment has changed dramatically in the last 50 years. In these years, the university's leadership has focused more intently on promoting research, and KU's contributions to advancing knowledge have become more prominent nationally and internationally. The transformations that KU has experienced in the last half century have not been unique. Since the late 1950s, larger societal forces have contributed to a growing emphasis on science and engineering and the expansion of higher education, resulting in a substantial broadening of the nation's research capability beyond the small group of elite private universities and select public campuses that dominated research and graduate training in the pre–World War II era.[4] The changes that took place at the University of Kansas were thus a local manifestation of a broader transformation of the country's university system.

Figure 5-1: Real Federally Supported University R&D
(millions of 2005 $)

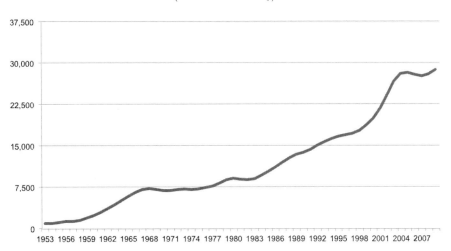

Among the forces that have affected KU since the early 1960s, the most important were a rapid expansion in federal funding for scientific and engineering research and the expansion of undergraduate enrollments caused by the postwar baby boom. Between 1957 and 1967, inflation-adjusted federal research and development funding for universities more than quadrupled (see Fig. 5-1). Meanwhile funding agencies focused on distributing these resources beyond the select group of universities that had dominated federal research support during and immediately after World War II. As federal funding grew, support also expanded beyond the physical sciences and engineering. In 1965, the formation of the National Endowment for the Arts and the National Endowment for the Humanities created new sources of funding to support scholars in the creative arts and humanistic fields of study. In 1968, the mandate of the National Science Foundation was expanded to explicitly incorporate funding for the social sciences.

Rising federal investments in science and engineering and in other fields of scholarship coincided with rapidly rising undergraduate enrollments as the first wave of the baby boom generation reached college age.[5] At KU, although rising enrollment placed substantial strains on the university, the new students also provided an important infusion of resources that helped support increases in faculty numbers,

The new Haworth Hall under construction in 1968, home to the university's Division of Biological Sciences.

new campus construction, expansion of graduate programs, and growing research capabilities.

The heady growth that characterized higher education in the decade after 1957 came to an end in the late 1960s. After 1968, the growth of federal funding for research and development slowed and became more unpredictable. Nonetheless, as the basis of American economic leadership shifted from manufacturing to innovation, science and engineering advances assumed a greater importance for government and industry alike. The increasing national focus on the sciences stimulated continued growth in both the demand for science and engineering research at the nation's universities and the resources to support the expansion of university research capabilities across the late twentieth and early twenty-first centuries.

While the evolution of federal and industrial research funding and broad demographic forces were important factors influencing KU's development after 1965, how these national forces affected the university was largely a function of the university's past history and of strategic and organizational decisions made by the institution's leadership and faculty in response to changing circumstances. The remainder of this chapter explores in more depth the interactions among these external and internal factors in transforming KU's research mission.

Because the impact of the changing climate for external funding was greatest in the natural and social sciences, the focus of this chapter will be primarily on these disciplines, and especially on those areas of research in which KU has attained the greatest distinction. The focus will not be exclusively on the sciences, however, as KU was able to build on its strong traditions in humanistic research to secure funding for what became the Hall Center for the Humanities. With support from both philanthropic sources and the National Endowment for the Humanities, the Hall Center has become by the early twenty-first century one of the leading centers supporting humanities research in the nation, if not in the world. Because of space constraints, this chapter must confine itself primarily to the larger, organized research efforts that have garnered national distinction for the university and will not attempt to provide a comprehensive account of the myriad accomplishments of individual KU faculty members over the past 50 years.

THE PLACE OF RESEARCH AT KU IN THE EARLY 1960S

By virtue of its history and aspirations in its first 100 years, the University of Kansas was positioned to respond to the opportunities that the infusion of new resources for university research has created since the late 1950s. In the early 1960s, KU could point to well-established and recognized areas of research strength in zoology, entomology, bacteriology, geology, and chemistry, as well as important applied research and service activities of the Kansas Geological Survey and the Kansas Biological Survey.[6] Moreover, in 1951, the legislature had, after repeated urging from Chancellor Deane Malott, authorized $300,000 ($2.6 million in 2013 dollars) annually to establish a General Research Fund.[7] Funds from KUEA, which helped to support faculty salaries and pay for buildings, specialized equipment, student tuition, and other expenses, were another key ingredient supporting the university's research activities, and one that would become increasingly important over time.

Nevertheless, as the university approached its centennial, its commitment and that of the state to the investments necessary to become a full-fledged research university remained somewhat tenuous. The amount authorized by the legislature for the General Research Fund had increased to only $304,000 by 1959 ($2.3 million in 2013 dollars). Moreover, a 1957 comprehensive survey of higher education in the state found that KU faculty reported spending 66 percent of their

Completed in 1960, Youngberg Hall originally housed the Center for Research in Engineering Science, which became the Center for Research, Inc., in 1962.

time on teaching and only 16 percent on research. In 1961, when Alvin Eurich of the Ford Foundation conducted another assessment at the invitation of the Board of Regents, he reported as well that "research effort is too low."[8]

In the fall of 1960, shortly after his appointment as chancellor, W. Clarke Wescoe appointed a committee to examine the place of research at KU. Chaired by William J. Argersinger, professor of chemistry and associate dean of the Graduate School, the committee proceeded deliberately, delivering a lengthy report in June 1962. After reiterating the central place that research must play in the university, the report turned to the major determinants of the university's research activity, describing in turn the role of the faculty, libraries, museums, nature reserves, the physical plant, and the administrative structures that supported research activities before offering its recommendations.

The faculty were, the committee observed, the key ingredient determining the quality and level of research activity at the university. Confronted, however, by a lack of "knowledge and understanding of why some university faculty members are dedicated to research and others are indifferent or even contemptuous toward it," the committee urged a focus on selecting new faculty members inclined toward research, creating an atmosphere conducive to research by limiting demands for service and administrative tasks and placing a greater emphasis on research in promotion decisions.

If the committee's recommendations maintained a level of generality, its review of the university's support of the libraries and research collections was more pointed. While noting the relatively generous support that the libraries had received in the previous decade, the committee clearly noted the growing demands placed on library staff and budgets by a profusion of new publications, the addition of new programs and research areas, and anticipated growth in enrollment, all of which would require further commitments of resources.

Similarly, the committee pointed out the inadequate support that was provided to the university's research collections. "Staff in our museums is in several cases almost tragically short," its report declared. "From the standpoint of number of specimens and potential research importance, two of our most important research collections are the Museum of Invertebrate Paleontology and the Snow Entomological Museum. . . . Each is well known throughout the country not only for its importance . . . but for its inadequate staff."[9] Materials in these collections must not, the committee concluded, be allowed to deteriorate due to neglect. Meeting the staffing needs of these collections, the committee urged, needed to be separated from the university's teaching mission to ensure continuity, and additional space for research and storage needed to be built.

Space needs for research varied widely across disciplines, committee members noted, but they wrote that "every faculty member and graduate student should have space, adequate in size and free from distraction, in which he can carry on research appropriate to his responsibilities." The committee further recommended that "at a minimum private offices should be provided for all full-time faculty members," providing a hint of just how limited space must have been at the time.[10]

In its concluding section, the committee turned to the administrative organization of the university's research activities. Reflecting the growing importance of research, it recommended the establishment of a standing committee on research to manage allocation of the General Research Fund to support faculty research projects as well as provide advice and recommendations to the administration on research-related matters. The committee also noted the decentralized and potentially confusing arrangements that governed the receipt and disbursement of external research funding and proposed a legally distinct research foundation to consolidate management of sponsored research funds.[11]

Given the general nature of many of the committee's recommendations concerning faculty appointments, support for libraries and research collections, research space, and equipment, it is difficult to identify whether they had much immediate impact. On the other hand, a standing committee on research was created and exists today as a body of the Faculty Senate. Although it took considerably longer, the committee's suggestion to consolidate research support in a separate research foundation was also eventually realized, but the path to achieving it was neither short nor direct.

LAYING THE FOUNDATIONS FOR A MODERN RESEARCH UNIVERSITY: THE 1960S

Around the time that the committee was laboring over its report, KU's leadership was taking steps that would largely define the university's areas of research excellence for the next half century. Consistent with the central importance the committee placed on hiring and cultivating faculty for their engagement with research, each of these measures entailed the recruitment or retention of a few key individuals.

Building a Program in Child Research

In the late 1950s, a small group of KU researchers led by Richard Schiefelbusch was embarking on a trajectory of research that would make KU a leader in the emerging field of applied behavioral science. Their success reflects the confluence of novel ideas with the availability of resources created by an expanding stream of federal funding. This occurred at KU because of the efforts in 1954 of Chancellor Franklin Murphy and George Waggoner, dean of the College of Liberal Arts and Sciences, to dissuade Schiefelbusch from leaving KU to accept a tenured appointment at the University of Illinois.[12]

Seeking to find out what it would take to keep Schiefelbusch in Kansas, Murphy invited him to offer suggestions about what actions the university would need to take to be active in child research. Thinking that

Richard Schiefelbusch reads to a group of children at KU's Bureau of Child Research in 1987.

he was leaving the university, Schiefelbusch offered a candid picture of the changes he believed necessary. Most important, he suggested, KU would need to create a natural environment for child research, such as a child care center that would allow researchers to collaborate in their studies and train their students. Shortly after this, Murphy offered to implement these changes if Schiefelbusch would stay at KU and assume leadership of the Bureau of Child Research, a largely inactive office that had been opened in 1921.[13] Murphy also offered $30,000 in funding (equivalent to about $268,000 in 2013 dollars), an amount that covered the salary of the bureau's director and its administrative staff, but left little to support any actual research.[14]

Murphy had envisioned the Bureau of Child Research primarily as a coordinating body that would bring together disparate units from the Medical School and Lawrence campuses engaged in different aspects of child research. Schiefelbusch soon found, however, that there was little common interest across these units, and he thus embarked on a different path, turning the bureau into a research unit in its own right. To do this, he took an unorthodox path, forging a partnership with Howard Bair, the leader of the Parsons State Hospital and Training Center. Bair was seeking a way to address the needs of profoundly mentally disabled children, and Schiefelbusch and the small team of psychologists he recruited saw in the behavioral theories of B. F. Skinner a potential tool to transform modes of treatment.

By 1958, the team had received its first grant, for $56,000 ($460,000 in 2013 dollars), from the National Institute of Mental Health. Probing "the silence of profound mental retardation . . . [the team] found a possible passage to communication when they proved that these children could learn."[15] When the results of their initial exploration were presented, the news spread quickly and a growing number of visitors found their way to the Parsons facility to learn more. This initial success led to a renewal of their original grant and a 50 percent increase in funding in 1961, as well as the addition in 1962 of a pre-doctoral training grant.

In 1963, Schiefelbusch took the project to a new level by applying for and winning a $2 million grant from the newly established National Institute of Child Health and Human Development (about $15 million in 2013 dollars). These funds supported the establishment of a coordinated research program that engaged scholars on the KUMC and Lawrence campuses as well as at the Parsons Center. Increased funding and greater visibility were accompanied by the recruitment of other researchers.

Despite the success at Parsons, Schiefelbusch recognized that he needed to cultivate a partnership with an academic department if the research program was to be sustained. The department he selected was Home Economics, which with his encouragement would soon be transformed into the Department of Human Development and Family Life (HDFL).

In 1961, Schiefelbusch had recruited Frances Horowitz to join the staff of the Bureau of Child Research. Horowitz had worked at the bureau briefly in 1960 after completing her graduate studies, and Schiefelbusch wanted to bring her back. To do so, he convinced the dean of the College, George Waggoner, to offer her husband, Floyd, a position in the English Department. At the time, KU had a nepotism rule that prevented Frances from being offered a faculty position, but Schiefelbusch was able to offer her an appointment at the Bureau of Child Research, and the couple accepted these positions.

By 1963, the nepotism rule had been changed, and Horowitz moved to a position in the Home Economics Department. Within a few years she had risen to become the chair of the newly reorganized HDFL. In 1965, Horowitz and Schiefelbusch successfully recruited four of the leading researchers in behavioral psychology—R. Vance

A 1970 research project at the KU Bureau of Child Research uses motion picture recording to evaluate and modify behaviors for children with intellectual disabilities.

Hall, Donald Baer, Todd Risley, and Montrose Wolf—all from the University of Washington, solidifying KU's position as the leader in the new field of applied behavioral science. This leadership in turn helped KU to compete successfully in 1967 to become one of the first of a national network of mental retardation (or mental disability as it is described today) research centers funded under federal legislation that had been enacted on October 31, 1963. By the early 1970s, KU researchers had added a fourth location, the Juniper Gardens Children's Project, initially located in the basement of a liquor store in an inner-city neighborhood in Kansas City, Kansas.

The research center funding has been renewed repeatedly since 1967 and continues to the present. During the 1970s and 1980s, the Bureau of Child Research spun off an increasingly diverse array of research groups dealing not only with child research but also with all aspects of the life span. These included, among others, the Gerontology Center, the Beach Center on Disability, the Work Group on Health Promotion and Community Development, the Center for Research

Two children work on writing skills at the Juniper Gardens Children's Project in Kansas City. The project was established in the 1960s by the Bureau of Child Research to study how children from inner-city neighborhoods learn.

Senator Bob Dole (right), Chancellor Gene Budig (second from right), and Dean Frances Horowitz (center) during a tour of the soon-to-be-opened Dole Center for Human Development, 1989.

on Learning, and the Merrill Advanced Studies Center. In the 1980s, the Bureau of Child Research negotiated several difficult transitions, including declining federal funding and the retirement of Richard Schiefelbusch from his position as director. Nonetheless, research activity continued to grow, and with the support of Senator Robert Dole, funding was secured for construction of a new building, the Dole Human Development Center, in 1989.

In 1990, the Schiefelbusch Institute for Life Span Studies (commonly called the Life Span Institute) was established as an umbrella organization, comprising the Bureau of Child Research and many of the offshoots to which it had given rise over the years. At the time, this conglomeration of researchers accounted for approximately one-quarter of the federal research dollars that the University of Kansas received. Since the 1990s, renewed growth in federal funding and astute leadership have helped the Life Span Institute to continue to grow and adapt to the rapid technological and scientific changes that have reshaped behavioral science research.

Putting the School of Pharmacy on the Map

At roughly the same time that Schiefelbusch's research efforts were starting to take off, the university also launched a concerted effort to expand and strengthen the School of Pharmacy. In the early 1960s, the school had just six faculty members and a budget of only a few hundred thousand dollars. In 1966, Chancellor Wescoe hired Howard Mossberg, then a young faculty member at Southwest State University in Oklahoma, to fill the position of dean, which had been left vacant after Duane Wenzel returned to teaching and research. Wescoe, Mossberg, and Ed Smissman, the chair of the Medicinal Chemistry Department, who had been recruited from the University of Wisconsin in 1960, then undertook an ambitious effort to bring Takeru "Tak" Higuchi to Kansas.

Higuchi, the Edward Kremers Professor of Pharmaceutical Chemistry at the University of Wisconsin, where he had taught since 1947, was a prolific scholar who was widely regarded as the "father of physical pharmacy" because of his emphasis on the importance of understanding the basic chemical and physical processes underlying pharmaceutical chemistry. Convincing an established scholar of Higuchi's caliber to leave Wisconsin took a major effort. To get Higuchi, the university offered him what was at the time one of only two Regents professorships at the university.[16] In addition, the university offered Higuchi the resources to develop a nationally recognized program in pharmaceutical chemistry and promised to house him and his students in a new pharmaceutical chemistry building that was already under construction, in what would become the West Campus.

Perhaps the strongest inducement that KU offered, however, was its willingness to support Higuchi's interest in converting scientific discoveries to commercial applications. At Wisconsin, Higuchi was chafing under restrictions that the Wisconsin Alumni Research Foundation imposed on his interactions with the pharmaceutical industry. In contrast, the KUEA was keen to support such efforts, which it hoped would help to promote economic growth in the state.

While Higuchi was only one of several hires made in these years, he was the focal point around which the School of Pharmacy grew. Higuchi was a prolific scholar who published more than 200 articles and acquired more than 50 patents during his career. He was also an influential teacher, who supervised close to 200 graduate students. One colleague estimated that he had "trained more people in upper and middle management in the US pharmaceutical industry than anyone else, and that one-third of the nation's pharmacy school deans and department chairmen [were] former Higuchi students."[17] Beyond these tangible results, however, Higuchi was instrumental in creating, in the words of one former student and colleague, a "culture of cooperation and good citizenship" that helped to nurture new researchers.

Higuchi's example also served to encourage at the school a spirit of entrepreneurship, an engagement in economic development, and a desire to be involved in moving discoveries from the laboratory to the marketplace. In 1968, shortly after Higuchi's arrival at KU, Alejandro Zaffaroni sought Higuchi's participation in a California-based drug research firm. When Higuchi declined to relocate, Zaffaroni, with KUEA's assistance, decided to construct a building on KU's West Campus where Higuchi could carry out his work for the company. In addition to the building, Higuchi extracted 10,000 shares of stock in Zaffaroni's Alza Corporation for the KUEA. The value of these shares appreciated significantly in the next few years, and the KUEA benefited handsomely.

In 1972, Alza chose to relocate its research to California, and its building reverted to the university. Using proceeds from the sale of the shares in Alza, Higuchi and the KUEA established a new corporation, INTERx, capitalized at $5 million, which would occupy the building originally built for Alza. Eight years later, in 1980, the pharmaceutical

Takeru Higuchi in 1977, Distinguished Professor of Pharmacy and Chemistry.

Professor Higuchi inspects new laboratory equipment in the physical pharmacy labs on the university's West Campus.

giant Merck purchased INTERx for $9 million, producing another large return for Higuchi and the KUEA. Higuchi remained in the role of president of INTERx as well as vice president for Merck's research laboratories.

In 1983, Higuchi and the KUEA spun out another private enterprise, Oread Labs, to take advantage of opportunities created by a newly adopted state economic development plan. Drawn up by two KU School of Business professors, Tony Redwood and Chuck Krider, the plan called for funds from the recently established state lottery to be distributed by a newly created entity, the Kansas Technology Enterprise Corporation (KTEC), to fund Centers of Excellence at the Regents institutions. Each center required a corporate partner willing to match state investments dollar for dollar.

Higuchi and the KUEA established Oread Laboratories as a for-profit company to provide the matching funds to establish the KTEC-supported Center for Bioanalytical Research. KUEA invested an initial $750,000 in the venture, and Higuchi rounded up other investors, including the City of Lawrence, which issued industrial revenue bonds to finance its investment. The start-up company ultimately raised $7 million. Thus, Higuchi and the KUEA were pioneers in developing many of the ingredients that would in the next few decades come to characterize university-industry relationships, such as university "incubators" and patent licensing agreements.

Ultimately, the ability to sustain productive relationships with industry depended upon creating and sustaining a first-rate school of pharmacy. In these years, Higuchi, Smissman, and their colleagues were successful in making the KU School of Pharmacy one of the field's leading centers of academic training and research. While recruiting Higuchi was central to the school's rising prominence, its success reflected a collective effort and was ultimately the result of the recruitment of many other talented scholars and the culture of collaboration between the school's Departments of Pharmaceutical Chemistry and Medicinal Chemistry and faculty in the Department of Chemistry in the College. Important in tying these departments together was an emphasis on shared responsibility in the management of expensive research facilities such as mass spectrometry, nuclear magnetic resonance imaging, and x-ray crystallography. Building on these foundations, faculty in the School of Pharmacy have continued the traditions of cutting-edge research and engagement with technology transfer and commercialization established by Higuchi.

Howard Mossberg in 1983.

Developing the Field of Remote Sensing

Another influential addition to the KU faculty in the early 1960s was Richard K. Moore. In 1962, the School of Engineering recruited Moore from the University of New Mexico, where he was the chair of the Electrical Engineering Department. At New Mexico, he had overseen a substantial expansion of the department and led its establishment of a PhD program. Having built the program, however, Moore was ready to move on and was receptive when KU offered him a distinguished professorship.[18]

Moore's work in radar was sufficiently well known that in 1963 he was approached by the National Aeronautics and Space Administration (NASA), which was interested in developing tools for planetary observation to be used in the Apollo program.[19] By 1964, Moore had become a member of the NASA Radar Remote Sensing Advisory Group. This was the beginning of a long-running relationship whereby he played an important part in developing techniques of microwave remote sensing in conjunction with NASA, the US Army, and the Office of Naval Research.

At KU, Moore was instrumental in founding the KU Remote Sensing Lab, in 1964. Recognizing that the value of data generated by

Richard Moore became director of KU's Remote Sensing Laboratory in 1964 as well as director of the Electrical and Computer Engineering Research Laboratory.

remote sensing would be greatest in disciplines outside engineering, Moore was quick to seek partners in other fields, including oceanography and geography. Among the important discoveries that Moore and his partners produced was the demonstration, based on experiments conducted on Skylab, that it is possible to measure from space both the direction and the speed of winds at the surface of the ocean.

Moore was also involved in work supported by the Office of Naval Research to map Arctic sea ice. It was this line of research that brought Prasad Gogineni from India to KU as a graduate student in 1979. After completing his dissertation, Gogineni was obliged to leave the country because of visa requirements, but Moore was instrumental in

*Prasad Gogineni joined the KU faculty
in 1986 and became a leader in research,
teaching, and service in electrical
engineering and computer science.*

connecting him with European researchers working on related topics. A few years later, Gogineni returned to a faculty appointment at KU. At KU, Gogineni continued to pursue novel work in remote sensing. He also spent time at NASA as a program officer, which allowed him to see how complex, multi-institution research projects were built and managed. In 2005, drawing on both his scientific expertise and his experience with large-scale funding, Gogineni secured a grant from the National Science Foundation for an Engineering Science and Technology Center, which established the Center for Remote Sensing of Ice Sheets (CReSIS).

Working in conjunction with colleagues in aeronautical engineering to put sophisticated radar devices on unmanned aerial vehicles, CReSIS has become a major contributor to research documenting the effects of climate change on the polar ice caps. At the same time, CReSIS has stimulated other collaborations within the university, including a multimillion-dollar award from the National Science Foundation to support an interdisciplinary graduate education and research program focusing on the human causes and consequences of global climate change, led by Professor of Sociology Joane Nagel.

CONSOLIDATION AND ADAPTATION:
THE 1970S AND 1980S

In the late 1960s, the conditions that had fostered the growth of significant new research programs at KU came rather abruptly to an end. On the one hand, the external funding environment became considerably less conducive to growth. Federal funding for university research, which had grown much faster than the overall economy after 1957, slowed sharply after 1968. It did not begin to pick up again until the early 1980s (see Fig. 5-1). On the other hand, circumstances internal to the university shifted the focus of leadership from academic matters to other issues. Growing student unrest over US involvement in the Vietnam War coincided with, and to some extent contributed to, turnover in the university's leadership.[20]

During Lawrence Chalmers's tenure as chancellor, his relationship with Francis Heller, who had served as dean of faculties, the chief academic officer for the Lawrence campus, had grown increasingly strained. Shortly before his own resignation, Chalmers asked for Heller's resignation and embarked on a more sweeping administrative reorganization. Then, in 1974, George Waggoner, who had served as dean of the College since the mid-1950s, suffered a stroke and was obliged to resign.

Chalmers's departure ushered in a period of instability at the top for KU. In August 1972, Raymond Nichols, who had served as vice chancellor for administration, was appointed acting chancellor. Nichols's background was largely on the financial and administrative side of the university, and he served primarily as a caretaker while a search was conducted for a permanent replacement. Although Archie Dykes, who succeeded Nichols in 1973, served as chancellor until 1980, his focus during much of this time was on repairing relations with the legislature and the citizens of the state, which had been severely strained by the student activism of the late 1960s and early 1970s.

Turnover at the top coincided with economic difficulties in the state, resulting in tighter budgets for KU. Robert Cobb, who succeeded George Waggoner as dean of the College, described the period from 1975 to 1985 as one of periodic rescissions. "We tried," Cobb recalled, "to recruit the best faculty we could, tried to build the library and maintain infrastructure. . . . [But it] was more a matter of protecting and enhancing the programs we had in place."[21]

Although the focus of the university's leadership may have shifted away from building new areas of research strength, the 1970s and

Jacqueline Heath, KU alumna and medical technologist, at work in 1989 at KUMC in the microbiology section of the clinical laboratories.

1980s were by no means devoid of progress. In 1977, reflecting the growing importance of external research funding to the university and the increased complexity of the requirements attached to these funds, Chancellor Dykes initiated a reorganization of the university's research administration functions. Complementing this administrative reorganization, KU faculty continued to pursue individual research agendas, leading to new initiatives. As such, the work of discovery and dissemination of knowledge continued largely unaffected by the turbulence and turnover in KU's leadership. One of the most important initiatives to emerge in this period was the effort to establish a center for humanistic studies. Meanwhile, the successful research programs that were initiated in the 1950s and 1960s continued to grow and diversify. Even with the slowdown in federal funding, these successful programs of research were able to compete for the support they needed.

Formalizing Research Administration

By the early 1970s, the university was receiving something on the order of $10 million to $14 million annually in federal research support (approximately $50 million to $70 million in 2013 dollars). This was perhaps a six- or seven-fold increase since the early 1960s. As the volume of support increased, the administrative challenges of managing these funds grew as well. More attention had to be given to accounting for the use of resources and ensuring compliance with federal accounting standards. At the same time, as the overall funding environment became more competitive, understanding the priorities and objectives of funding agencies took on greater importance.

Compliance with federal regulations regarding the conduct of research required increased attention as well. By the early 1970s, several well-publicized revelations about abuses of human subjects in government-funded medical studies at other institutions had led to significant tightening of regulations, requiring the university to develop new administrative oversight capabilities and ensure that scholars were complying with the rules.

In the late 1950s, the university had assigned responsibility for research administration to the Graduate School, and William Argersinger, who occupied the position of associate dean, had assumed this responsibility. In 1962, following completion of the committee report on the place of research in the university and reflecting the growing importance of research administration, Argersinger was appointed to a newly created position as associate dean of faculties for research. In 1972, as part of the administrative reorganization undertaken by Chancellor Chalmers, research administration and graduate studies were once again placed within the same organization. In this reorganization, Chalmers named Argersinger vice chancellor for research and graduate studies and dean of the Graduate School. Argersinger in turn appointed Professor of History Henry Snyder as dean of research within this newly established office.[22]

Despite these changes in the location of responsibility for research administration, staff support remained quite limited. Throughout the 1960s and 1970s, Argersinger personally retained responsibility for managing a great many of the necessary tasks. "From about 1968 on,"

William J. Argersinger, in 1979, administrative leader of research activities at KU in the 1960s and 1970s.

he recalled, "my teaching in the department was perforce minimal. . . . I was on continuous call by the chancellor. . . . Most of the active faculty I knew by name, face and interest, including many at KUMC. It was necessary for me to travel frequently to Washington to visit Federal agencies."[23]

The demands of the position and the growing formalization of university administration that followed from the increased scale and complexity of the university in the early 1970s led Argersinger to tender his resignation in the fall of 1977. Following Argersinger's resignation, Chancellor Dykes appointed a committee to consider the future organization of research and graduate studies at KU. After a lengthy review, the committee concluded that these two areas should continue to be part of a combined office and that "public service" should be added to its responsibilities to better promote the university's links with state government, the business community, and the Kansas congressional delegation. In 1978, the university conducted a national search to fill the newly created position of vice chancellor for Research, Graduate Studies and Public Service and dean of the Graduate School.

The result of that search was the selection of Frances Horowitz, an active researcher who had for the past decade served as chair of HDFL.

Frances Horowitz, in 1989. Appointed vice chancellor for Research, Graduate Studies and Public Service in 1978, she was a specialist in the field of child development who began her KU career in 1961 as a research associate with the Bureau of Child Research.

A natural consensus builder, Horowitz purposefully staffed her office with faculty representing the range of disciplines engaged in sponsored research. She also embraced the challenges of research administration and cultivated a staff with the expertise to deal with funding agencies and effectively manage compliance with award conditions. At the same time, she established a "red tape" committee to identify bureaucratic processes that were annoying people and find ways to reduce these aggravations. One early change was her decision to allow non-faculty to serve as the principal investigators on sponsored projects, so long as they had the endorsement of a department or research unit to support the project if funded.

Horowitz also embraced the public service responsibilities of the new office. She cultivated a warm relationship with the Lawrence/ Douglas County Chamber of Commerce and other local business interests and participated actively in their efforts at business recruitment. To increase KU's presence in Washington, DC, she hired a consultant there to work with the Kansas delegation to ensure that KU did not miss opportunities to tap federal funds. These contacts proved important in securing federal funding for construction of the Dole Human Development Center.

Establishing a Home for the Humanities

The idea of creating a center for humanistic studies at KU first surfaced in 1969 when a small group of faculty who formed the Humanistic Studies Group proposed the idea to Chancellor Chalmers. Chalmers took no action, however, and the idea languished until 1975, when Henry Snyder, Richard DeGeorge, University Distinguished Professor of Philosophy, and Hal Orel, University Distinguished Professor of English, raised the idea again with the dean of the College. Describing their motivations, DeGeorge observed that it "was a period of little faculty turnover and we faced the prospect of growing old and stale together."[24] The initial response from the College was lukewarm, however, citing a lack of funds and the likely opposition to the idea from the various departments.

Undeterred, the group drafted a proposal that was sent to the humanities faculty and secured the endorsement of the vice chancellor for Research and Graduate Studies, William Argersinger. With this sponsorship, Chancellor Dykes submitted a proposal to establish a center for humanistic studies to the Board of Regents. The Regents approved it in September 1976, but no funds, space, or administrative support were provided for it. "The future of the center did not look very rosy, and the message we got," DeGeorge recalled, "was that we were on our own."

DeGeorge and Snyder revised their earlier proposal emphasizing faculty development and promotion of humanities on campus and began to approach foundations. In 1977, due in large part to the persistence of Snyder, they were successful in securing a three-year grant from the Andrew W. Mellon Foundation for $315,000 (about $1.2 million in 2013 dollars), only the second grant the foundation had ever given to a public university. Planning a trip to New York, Snyder had sought to contact the foundation to schedule an appointment. Foundation officials, however, rebuffed his initial request, so, as Snyder later explained, "when I arrived in New York, I called the foundation and was again told not to come. . . . I went to their address and rang the doorbell. When they answered, I introduced myself and asked to talk to a program officer. I was ushered in to see one."

"We told you not to come and yet you did," he said. "Why are you here?"

"You did not tell me why you refused me, so I came to find out."

"We do not make grants to public institutions."

"That is a mistake," I said. "Let me tell you why."

Snyder went on to make the case that there were no private institutions of quality between the Mississippi River and California, and that the foundation would need to change its policy if it were to invest in supporting humanities in this region of the country. It took several more visits and a creative approach that emphasized the ways in which supporting the humanities at KU would benefit smaller private institutions in the region before the foundation was convinced, but in the end the grant was secured.[25]

A few weeks after the Mellon Foundation funds were obtained, the College dean appointed Snyder, DeGeorge, and Andrew Debicki, University Distinguished Professor of Spanish, as co-directors of the center. Space for the center was found in two rooms on the main floor of the Spencer Research Library. In August 1978, the center hired its first full-time staff member to serve as assistant to the director; the following spring, the first faculty development seminar was offered. In addition to the seminar, the Mellon Foundation grant provided funding for six visiting fellows from private colleges in the region to spend a semester at KU, engaging in research and interacting with KU faculty. At this time, the center also undertook to manage grant funds for several other projects, including a museum and humanities grant secured by Marilyn Stokstad and a number of NEH-funded seminars. In 1980, the Mellon Foundation renewed its support, providing $200,000 (about $565,000 in 2013 dollars) for another two years.

In 1982, with the end of Mellon support approaching, the center and the libraries submitted a proposal for a National Endowment for the Humanities challenge grant seeking $1.5 million, the maximum amount allowed. To everyone's great surprise, the proposal was successful, and the NEH awarded the university $1 million (about $2.4 million in 2013 dollars), receipt of which required the university to raise a three-to-one match from private funds. Roughly coinciding with receipt of the NEH grant, Ted Wilson replaced Richard DeGeorge as director of the center. Wilson, who had been chair of the History Department and a member of the center's executive committee, had played an active role in preparing the grant proposal to NEH. It now fell to him to raise the $3 million in private donations required to match the NEH award. After considerable effort, Wilson, along with

Andrew P. Debicki, in 1990. A renowned scholar in Spanish and Spanish American poetry, he was named vice chancellor for Research, Graduate Studies and Public Service in 1992.

Vice Chancellor for Academic Affairs Deanell Tacha and KUEA leaders, were successful in convincing the Hall Family Foundation of Kansas City to make a donation of $3.5 million to KU to support the humanities. In recognition of this gift, the center was renamed the Joyce and Elizabeth Hall Center for the Humanities. Funds generated by the $4.5 million endowment were used primarily to support humanities faculty development and enhance library collections.[26] Faculty development funds were used to support faculty travel to visit research collections and participate in scholarly conferences and provide salary supplements for recipients of major grants and fellowships so that they would not suffer a loss of income while on leave. Most important, however, funds were used to endow four Hall distinguished professorships, in American history, American art, American literature, and nineteenth-century studies.[27]

With its expanded activities, the Hall Center was increasingly cramped for space, and in 1984 it found new room in the former Watkins Home, which had recently been vacated by the School of Social Welfare. Coinciding with the move, Wilson lured Janet Crow from her position in the History Department to serve as assistant director. Over the succeeding decades, Crow provided the stability and efficiency that kept the center on course, quickly becoming, in Wilson's words, "the flywheel that made everything run in Watkins Home and in the humanities at KU generally." Reflecting these contributions, her title was changed to executive director in 1993.[28] In the early 1980s, the center was moved administratively from the College to the Office of Research, Graduate Studies and Public Service, reporting to Frances Horowitz, a change that would encourage its support of humanistic research across the university as a whole.

The infusion of funding provided by the 1983 grant helped to invigorate humanities research at KU and made the Hall Center a major presence on campus, with influence extending well beyond faculty in core humanities fields. For example, the center's fall faculty seminar—in which a small group of faculty would engage in extended interdisciplinary dialogue about a timely and provocative theme—involved not just humanists but faculty from the social sciences, arts, professional schools, and the sciences in interdisciplinary dialogue. In 1990, the faculty fellowship program was expanded with the addition of a creative fellowship with the support of the dean of fine arts, Peter Thompson.[29]

Another important step in the Hall Center's development was the establishment of the Humanities Grant Development Office (HGDO).

The Watkins Home for Nurses in 1986. The building became home to the Hall Center for the Humanities until the Hall Center moved to its new location in 2005.

In 1994, the College provided funding to hire a graduate student assistant to help humanities faculty locate grant and fellowship opportunities. This service was highly successful, and with the reorganization of research administration services, orchestrated by Vice Chancellor Barnhill after 1996, it was decided to expand this activity and hire a full-time staff person to support grant development. In early 1998, Kathy Porsch was hired to fill this role. From the outset, she set ambitious goals for the HGDO, lobbying effectively for additional graduate student interns to support her activities and mentoring both new and more established faculty about effective approaches to seeking external funding. The results of these efforts are evident in the sustained stream of grant and fellowship proposals submitted with the HGDO's assistance and in the relatively high success rates of faculty seeking support. Despite a highly competitive funding environment, in most years since 1999, between 20 and 30 percent of KU faculty who worked with the HGDO to submit their applications were successful in obtaining funding.

The Hall Center in 2015.

The infusion of funds provided by the initial NEH challenge grant had established a firm foundation for humanities research, and the Hall Center's subsequent directors, Andrew Debicki (1989–1993) and Hall Distinguished Professor of English William Andrews (1993–1997), built on these foundations, adding new initiatives and expanding a number of the Hall Center's existing programs.[30] By the late 1990s, Professor of Spanish and Portuguese Roberta Johnson had succeeded Andrews as director. In 1997, along with the center's executive director, Janet Crow, and Kathy Porsch, she decided the time was right to make a second challenge grant application to the NEH. This proposal sought almost $600,000 from the NEH (about $890,000 in 2013 dollars), to be matched by close to $2.5 million raised from private donors. While the initial NEH challenge grant had focused on strengthening humanities research at KU, the aims of the second proposal were more expansive, proposing to establish major public outreach and education programs. In 2000, the Hall Center was awarded $500,000, with a four-to-one match contributing an additional $2 million in private funds.[31]

Having led the preparation of the NEH challenge grant, Roberta Johnson stepped down as director in 2000. In 2001, a professor of modern British history, Victor Bailey, replaced Johnson. With characteristic charm and energy, Bailey successfully undertook the task of raising the matching funds that the grant required. Not only did Bailey develop close relations with the Hall Family Foundation and many other supporters of the humanities, he emerged as a visible and highly effective advocate for the humanities on campus and in the state. With the additional support provided by the Hall Center's expanded endowment, he led the expansion of its public engagement, supporting the university's Humanities Lecture Series and the Humanities Weekends in communities across the state and the establishment of a resident fellowship that allowed a prominent nonacademic scholar to spend time at the university.

As its activities grew, it became increasingly evident that the center had outgrown its space in the Watkins Home. In 2005, it moved into a new home in the restored KU Powerhouse Building, providing an exceptional facility in which to host seminars and public events as well as attractive offices to house faculty fellows.[32] By the time of its move, the Hall Center had, under Bailey's leadership, emerged as one of the nation's leading centers for humanities research and an active participant in the international Consortium of Humanities Centers and Institutes. Further strengthening its presence on campus, it had also entered into a partnership with the Spencer Art Museum and the Biodiversity Research Institute to engage faculty from across the university to explore relationships between natural and cultural systems. Building on these accomplishments, in 2011, Bailey, by then the Hall Center's longest-serving director, decided to pursue an unprecedented third NEH challenge grant.[33] Looking to the future, the proposal sought funding to facilitate new approaches to humanistic research, including the development of programs to advance collaborative and interdisciplinary research within the humanities. Once again, the center was successful in securing this funding, reflecting both its past success and the creative vision that it has articulated for its future.

A RENEWED SENSE OF DIRECTION: RESEARCH IN THE 1990S AND BEYOND

After stagnating for more than a decade, federal research and development funding for colleges and universities began to increase again in the early 1980s (see Fig. 5-1). KU was, however, poorly positioned to take advantage of much of the funding that became available in the 1980s and early 1990s. Most of it originated with the National Institutes of Health and was directed toward biomedical research activities. Although some units on the Lawrence campus—such as the School of Pharmacy and the research centers that would become the Life Span

Institute—were able to compete effectively for these funds, the KUMC was dominated by its physician groups, which concentrated mainly on clinical income and devoted relatively little attention to building competitive research programs. As a result, KU did not benefit from the growth in available federal funds in the way that many other universities with academic medical centers did at the time.

Only in the mid-1990s, with the appointment of Robert Hemenway as chancellor, did the university embark once again on a concerted effort to expand its engagement in externally sponsored research. Hemenway's arrival on campus in early 1996 helped to catalyze a set of strategic changes that solidified KU's identity as a research university and created the organizational apparatus to support this commitment.

Creating the KU Center for Research

The idea of establishing a research foundation legally distinct from the university to manage sponsored research funds has had a long history. It dates back at least to the 1962 report on the place of research in the university, which had recommended the establishment of such a foundation. Noting that a number of other public research universities had established similar foundations, the report identified several advantages of the foundation model, including freedom from many of the restrictions on contracting imposed on the university as a state agency; the ability to invest idle funds and to carry funding forward across fiscal years; and the ability to ensure that research funds could not be diverted by the state for other uses. In addition, such an entity could consolidate many of the financial and accounting functions that were dispersed across different university units, reducing the administrative costs and faculty time invested in conducting sponsored research.[34]

Such an entity, the University of Kansas Center for Research, Inc. (CRINC), was in fact chartered in June 1962 as a 501(c)3 nonprofit corporation. For reasons that remain somewhat murky, however, CRINC assumed responsibility only for sponsored research conducted by faculty affiliated with the School of Engineering. In November 1962, all of the assets and liabilities of the Center for Research in Engineering, which had been formed in 1958 by John S. McNown, dean of the School of Engineering, were transferred to CRINC.

The recommendation to establish a research foundation surfaced again in the early 1980s when Vice Chancellor Frances Horowitz charged a committee to look into the organization of research administration.[35] The recommendations of the committee were, however, complicated by the existence of CRINC. The committee struggled, without much success, to envision how the proposed research foundation would relate to CRINC, and, once again, resistance or inertia prevented the implementation of these recommendations.

Not until 1996 was it possible to move forward. The impetus for success at that time was the arrival of Hemenway. Much of the work of making the transition possible was accomplished by Howard Mossberg. Having been recruited in 1966 at age 33 to serve as dean of the School of Pharmacy, Mossberg had presided over the expansion of the school's faculty from 6 to 42 and had seen the school rise to the top ranks in its field. In 1991, after 25 years as dean, Mossberg had been asked to serve as interim vice chancellor for Research, Graduate Studies and Public Service after Frances Horowitz had accepted a position as president of the Graduate School and University Center of the City University of New York.

Although Mossberg chose not to be a candidate for the vice chancellorship, his interim appointment was extended when the candidate selected for the post, Andrew Debicki, professor of Spanish, was awarded a fellowship the following year. After Debicki returned, Mossberg remained in the chancellor's office, where he served as special counselor to the chancellor and picked up responsibilities for technology transfer and commercialization, which Debicki was not inclined to undertake.

Thus, when Hemenway arrived on campus in the spring of 1996, he and Mossberg soon began a lengthy discussion of how to advance the university's research profile.[36] Mossberg was an advocate of the research foundation model, and Hemenway was receptive to this idea, having come from the University of Kentucky, where such a foundation managed all sponsored research. Bringing Mossberg back as vice chancellor for research in 1996–1997, Hemenway charged him with the task of leading an implementation process that would transform CRINC from its role supporting School of Engineering research to a university-wide research foundation.

Over the course of the next year, working with a committee of faculty and administrators, Mossberg addressed the full range of practical issues involved in the transition: developing a policy for the distribution of research overhead, purchasing Youngberg Hall from the KUEA to house the expanded research foundation, and defusing many of the concerns of faculty about the impact that the change would have.

In parallel with these discussions, Hemenway conducted a yearlong study that led to a significant reorganization of university leadership. On the Lawrence campus, the resulting shift to a provost model of organization in which all of the university's academic and nonacademic functions reported to the provost changed the focus of leadership in a way that elevated the importance of the research mission and ensured that university support functions were directed toward academic priorities. David Shulenburger, who had served as vice chancellor for academic affairs and was appointed as provost, recalled that with implementation of the provost model, research performance became an increasingly important consideration, in both individual promotion and tenure decisions and the evaluation of deans.[37]

As part of Hemenway's reorganization, the Office of Research, Graduate Studies and Public Service was dissolved. Andrew Debicki remained dean of the Graduate School and assumed responsibility also for international programs, while a new position, vice chancellor for research, was established. A national search was conducted to fill this new position, and Robert Barnhill, a Kansas native who had earned a BA from KU in 1961 and gone on to earn a PhD in mathematics from the University of Wisconsin, was hired in 1997 to fill the position. Barnhill had spent the past 11 years at Arizona State University, first as chair of the Computer Science Department and then as vice president for research.[38]

Robert Barnhill in 1988.

Perceiving the need for a fresh start with the research foundation, one of Barnhill's first actions was to rename it, changing its identity to the KU Center for Research. At the same time, Barnhill set about the difficult task of creating a unified research administration organization from the staff of CRINC, members of the former Office of Research, Graduate Studies and Public Service, and members of the university's financial services office who had supported sponsored research projects.

Mobilizing Resources to Advance the Research Mission

The administrative reorganization catalyzed by Chancellor Hemenway's arrival raised the stature of research and helped to streamline the research administration functions of the university. Several other strategic changes created the environment in which the potential created by these changes could be realized. The first was Hemenway's decision to change the way in which the university handled the indirect cost payments that were received on federal grants.[39] In the past, these funds had been applied to cover operating costs of the university, but Hemenway chose to transfer these operating costs to the base budget and to use the indirect costs strategically to support research activities.

While a portion of the indirect cost funds were returned directly to the academic units or research centers where research was carried out, the bulk of the funds were received by the KU Center for Research and used to cover research-related expenditures. Rising research volumes, and hence rising indirect cost recovery, thus helped to fund increases in research administration staff, cover the start-up costs for new faculty, purchase research equipment, pay for maintenance of research space, and, eventually, pay the interest costs of bonds issued to pay for the construction of specialized research space on the West Campus.

One of the ways Barnhill utilized these resources was to encourage faculty to pursue larger, multi-investigator projects. Barnhill consciously sought out faculty he thought were well suited to lead such projects and provided encouragement and support needed to pursue these larger-scale projects. These investments resulted in a rapid increase in the number of large grants secured by the university. In addition to the support for the Center for Remote Sensing of Ice Sheets described earlier, among the first of these large awards was a $10 million National Institutes of Health Center for Biomedical Research Excellence award, which was at the time the largest single award received by the university, and an award from the National Science Foundation's Engineering Research Centers program to support the establishment of a Center for Environmentally Beneficial Catalysis, led by Bala Subramanian and Daryl Busch.

As noted in earlier chapters, Hemenway's administration also secured passage of legislation that allowed the state's universities to retain tuition revenues rather than having these payments go into the state general fund. With the passage of "tuition accountability," the university initiated a program of tuition increases, targeting much of the additional funding to support 100 new faculty positions. The additional faculty positions were not to be spread across the university but were to be focused on building and extending existing strengths of the institution. These research "Megathemes," as they came to be called, were identified as part of a campus-wide planning process conducted in 1998.[40]

Research at KUMC

Paralleling the changes on the Lawrence campus, Hemenway also embarked on a set of initiatives intended to revitalize research on the KUMC campus. One of the first steps in this process was to separate the management of the KU Hospital from the Medical School. This separation had first been discussed during the tenure of Chancellor Budig, but it fell to Hemenway to achieve this goal. As with tuition accountability, this change required approval in the legislature, and Hemenway worked closely with Governor Bill Graves to craft legislation that would establish a separate hospital authority. Once management of the hospital was insulated from state oversight, it could begin to make the management changes needed to increase efficiency and raise the revenues needed to modernize. Meanwhile, KUMC administrators were freed to focus on enhancing the research and educational missions of the school.

Early in his tenure, Hemenway committed the university to the goal of achieving comprehensive cancer center designation from the National Institutes of Health, making it the top priority not just for KUMC but for the entire university. The decision to focus on cancer as a priority was important because it cut across departments and units within the Medical School and could thus be a focus for raising research activity across the board. At the same time, it provided a vehicle to strengthen ties between researchers at KUMC and those on the

Lawrence campus, since KU's strengths in drug discovery and development provided a distinctive focus for the cancer center project.

Barbara Atkinson, who had come to KUMC as chair of the Department of Pathology and Laboratory Medicine in 2000, emerged as a leader of the efforts to increase basic science research on the KUMC campus. In 2005, Atkinson replaced Donald Hagen as dean of the Medical School and executive vice chancellor.

At about the same time Atkinson assumed leadership of KUMC, Roy Jensen assumed overall leadership of the National Cancer Center initiative. Although he had grown up in Kansas, Jensen's only connection with KU to that point had been through attending Ted Owens's Basketball Camp as a high school basketball player. But Jensen had been on the faculty at Vanderbilt University Medical School when it was building a comprehensive cancer center and had a good understanding of what was required to build a successful program. Because of his expertise, Jensen emerged as a natural choice to lead the cancer center initiative when Bill Jewel, who had been organizing the effort, announced his plans to retire.

In one sense, the acceleration of KU's efforts to secure cancer center designation and Jensen's appointment could not have come at a worse time. Over the previous five years, the National Institutes of Health had pursued an aggressive expansion, doubling the amount of funding for biomedical research. This expansion came to an end in 2003, triggering a much more competitive national environment for research funds. KU's cancer center initiative, however, coincided with a significant state investment to promote biomedical science. In 2004, the legislature passed the Kansas Economic Growth Act, which established the Kansas Bioscience Authority and dedicated a stream of tax revenue to promote bioscience-based economic development in the state. At the same time, Governor Kathleen Sebelius added a line item for the KU cancer center, providing $5 million in funding annually.

From its establishment in 2004 through 2013, the Kansas Bioscience Authority provided KUMC with close to $50 million in funding to help recruit both established researchers and rising stars to enhance KU's cancer research efforts. In addition to the substantial state investments that the cancer center garnered, the regional benefits that a cancer center designation could be expected to bring helped the KUEA to raise substantial philanthropic contributions from the greater Kansas City community. In all, close to $350 million was invested in the effort by the time the National Cancer Institute announced the National Cancer Center designation in June 2012.

Bold Aspirations for the Future

Expanding the frontiers of knowledge is necessarily a dynamic activity requiring continued adaptation and adjustment. While the basic outlines laid down by Chancellor Hemenway and institutionalized by Vice Chancellor Barnhill have persisted since the late 1990s, one mark of their success has been the ability to accommodate and, indeed, facilitate the changes necessary to keep pace with the changing demands of the university's research mission.

On the Lawrence campus, when Bob Barnhill stepped down as vice chancellor for research in 2003, he was replaced by Jim Roberts. Roberts, professor of electrical engineering, who had been associate vice chancellor under Barnhill, stepped in first in an interim role and then, after the completion of a national search, was appointed in his own right. Under Roberts, KU embarked on a significant expansion of its West Campus research facilities. Major elements in this new research campus included the 106,000-square-foot structure named the Multidisciplinary Research Building, dedicated in 2006, and a Structural Biology Complex built in stages between 2004 and 2008. As was the case with several new research buildings erected on the KUMC campus, the financing of these buildings followed a new model in which the state used its bonding authority to allow the university to issue bonds, but funds to repay the bonds were to be generated from

Professor James A. Roberts in 1996, when he was named associate vice chancellor for Research and Public Service.

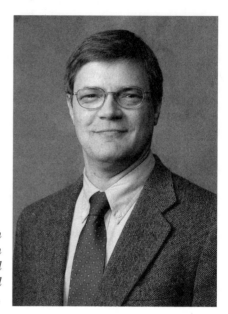

Professor Steven F. Warren, shown in 2010, served as Director of Life Span Studies Institute from 2001 to 2008 and Vice Chancellor for Research and Graduate Studies from 2007 to 2014.

Facilities & Administration payments, often referred to colloquially as "research overhead," on federal grants to researchers using the new facilities.

In 2007, Roberts returned to the faculty, to be replaced by Steven Warren, who had been recruited to KU from Vanderbilt University in 2000 to be the director of the Life Span Institute. One of Warren's major initiatives has been the expansion of the university's technology transfer programs. In 2008, Warren and Paul Terranova, vice chancellor for research on the KUMC campus, established a unified technology transfer program for both campuses. Soon thereafter, the KU Center for Research began construction of a business incubator building, the Bioscience & Technology Business Center, to facilitate commercialization of KU technological innovations and collaboration between KU researchers and industrial partners. Opened in 2010 on the West Campus near the Multidisciplinary Research Building, the 20,000 square feet of office and lab space were quickly filled, and work began on a second phase.

In 2010, following the appointment of Jeff Vitter as provost and executive vice chancellor, the university embarked on a major strategic planning exercise. "Bold Aspirations," as it was titled, encompassed almost all aspects of the university's operations, but a significant theme in the planning process revolved around identifying the university's research strengths and developing a more cohesive strategy of investing in and leveraging those assets to enhance its research profile. As the result of a yearlong process that began with more than 100 research initiatives proposed by individuals and groups of faculty, the university identified four broad, overarching research themes around which faculty recruitment and investments would be focused.[41] It is too soon to judge whether these new interdisciplinary initiatives will significantly reshape KU's research mission in the future, but since their selection in 2011 they have stimulated an ongoing conversation within the university community.

FORGING A RESEARCH MISSION

With the emergence of the information economy over the past half century, research has become an increasingly important contributor to the nation's economic growth. One important consequence of this transformation has been a substantial growth in the volume of university research and development activities. Since 1957, when funding growth began to accelerate, federal research and development funding for colleges and universities increased at four times the rate of growth of national income, rising (in constant 2013 dollars) from $1.7 billion to $42.5 billion by 2011. This increase in the nation's research effort was accomplished by a significant expansion of research capacity beyond the small cadre of elite universities that had dominated scientific research through the 1950s.

The evolution of research at KU is the local reflection of a process that took place nationally as a growing number of the nation's universities became involved in sponsored research. As we have seen, there has always been a strong commitment at KU to advancing the frontiers of knowledge. And over its first century, the university had developed a number of research strengths, especially in areas with importance to the state's population and state government. In addition, individual faculty members carried out programs of scholarship in their individual fields of expertise. The research interests of the faculty continue to be important in the aggregate but are so varied that they cannot be easily summarized or described.

Against this background, however, in the past 50 years the university has seen the expansion of a number of lines of research in which KU can claim leadership nationally and internationally—the most prominent of these being applied behavioral science, drug discovery and development, and remote sensing. These strengths have, in turn, been important in supporting the university's entry into related areas of research, such as special education and cancer treatment. The defining feature of each of these research areas is that they have grown well beyond the scope of a single individual's research and require specialized research space, equipment, and a cadre of personnel to support them. Supporting these research capabilities in turn has required development of the administrative and leadership capabilities to compete for and manage the sponsored research funding that these activities require.

The foundations of these areas of research leadership were laid in the late 1950s and early 1960s through a series of recruitment and retention decisions. At least in retrospect, the decisions to recruit Tak Higuchi and Richard Moore and the effort to retain Richard Schiefelbusch appear remarkably prescient and forward looking. We cannot, of course, know what expectations senior administrators had at the time they made these decisions. Similarly, it is difficult at this distance to know what other recruitment efforts were undertaken but did not turn out to be as effective. What is clear is that at its root the research mission of the university is built on hiring and retaining the right people. Less obvious, but equally true, is that success in research requires providing the resources that these individuals need to do their work. Providing these resources has required continued adaptation in the university's administrative apparatus and the construction of a significant staff of research administrators, research technicians, and other individuals. It has also required large investments in buildings and infrastructure, an effort considerably aided by the substantial fundraising strengths of the KUEA. Private funds have been especially important in supporting the construction of research buildings on the West Campus, making possible the success of the Hall Center for the Humanities and the successful effort to secure National Cancer Center designation for the university.

From the mid-1960s through the mid-1990s, KU's research profile was largely driven by the legacy of the personnel decisions that were made in the late 1950s and early 1960s. New initiatives, such as the Center for Research on Learning, and the School of Education's prominence in special education grew in part from these strengths. Although not a period of major new scientific initiatives, the 1970s and 1980s also saw the formation of what would become the Hall Center for the Humanities. Not until the arrival of Chancellor Robert Hemenway in 1996, however, did KU's senior leadership focus attention on the health of the research mission in a concerted manner. The organizational changes put in place at that time have enabled a second surge of growth in the university's organized research efforts.

Sponsored research expenditures are, of course, just one reflection of the university's research activity and do not adequately capture faculty research in the arts and humanities and in many of the professional schools. Nonetheless, they do serve as a marker of the level and nature of activities in the sciences that have been the focus of much of this history. Figure 5-2 traces the history of KU's research activity by plotting the fraction of all federally funded university research expenditures that is accounted for by KU from 1973 (the first year for which there are data) to 2011.

From the early 1970s, KU's share of federally funded research expenditures dropped sharply, until the late 1970s, when it stabilized. Despite some variation in subsequent years, there was no sustained upward movement until the 1990s, and especially after 1995 one can see a recovery of research funding numbers corresponding to the administrative and strategic changes put in place by Chancellor Hemenway. Although KU's growth in the share of total research expenditures leveled off after 2000, it has continued to climb in rankings relative to other national public research universities. By 2012, it ranked 38th in

Figure 5-2: KU Total Federal R&D as a Percent of
All University-Performed Federal R&D

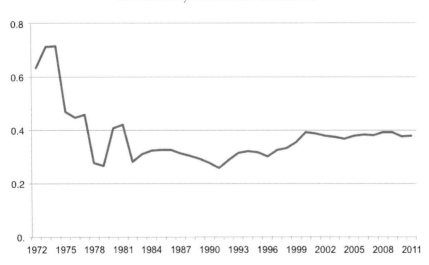

this group, an increase of 17 places in the 17 years since 1996, when it had been 55th. Thus, while KU is not positioned to enter the very top tier of research universities, it has successfully created the infrastructure to sustain a competitive position among the nation's major research institutions.

Part 3

STUDENTS, PROTEST, & SPORTS

CHAPTER 6

KU's Tumultuous Years
Thirty Years of Student Activism, 1965–1995

WILLIAM M. TUTTLE, JR.

THE 1960s was a decade of cultural, political, and social transformation in the United States and at KU. Early in the decade, African American civil rights activists and their white allies used the tactic
of nonviolent civil disobedience in battling for racial equality. In May
1961, for example, the Congress of Racial Equality (CORE) initiated
the Freedom Rides. An integrated group of 13 college-aged people
boarded a bus in Washington, DC, and traveled into the South, where
they braved attacks by white mobs for daring to desegregate interstate
transportation. Within days, scores of additional Freedom Riders had
boarded buses for Alabama, Mississippi, and Louisiana, where they
faced both violence and arrest. The freedom movement was conta-
gious, and by the 1960s and 1970s, the civil rights movement was a
dynamic and motivating force in America society, giving birth to other
freedom struggles, such as the Black Power and antiwar movements,
the New Left, a resurgent feminist movement, and the gay rights
movement, not to mention the environmental movement and equality
movements for ethnic minorities.[1]

No venue was more receptive to the politics of change than America's college and university campuses. "I'm tired of reading history,"
Mario Savio, a graduate student at the University of California at
Berkeley, complained to a friend in 1964. "I want to make it." Within a
few months, Savio had realized his ambition as a leader of the campus

Free Speech Movement, and Berkeley had become synonymous with campus unrest. What began at Berkeley spread to other campuses, especially as the United States escalated its involvement in the Vietnam conflict. Campus unrest gripped literally hundreds of colleges and universities, including major research institutions like the University of Wisconsin in 1967, Columbia University in 1968, Harvard University in 1969, and Cornell University in 1970. The University of Kansas, which some began calling "Berkeley on the Kaw," was among the country's leading universities to be rocked by student activism in the 1960s and early 1970s. During these eventful years, KU students, working with faculty, staff, and people in the community, were passionately engaged with the ideas, politics, and conflicts of the larger world. Moreover, at KU, student activism persisted into the 1980s and 1990s. Indeed, during these later years, KU students grappled not only with long-standing issues of racial, gender, and sexual orientation discrimination, but also with new issues such as divestment from corporations doing business in apartheid South Africa. Since the height of protest on KU's campus occurred from 1965 to 1995, this chapter offers a 30-year window on student activism.[2]

CIVIL RIGHTS AND BLACK POWER AT KU

The five most tumultuous years in the history of the University of Kansas began on the morning of Monday, March 8, 1965, when several hundred students marched to Strong Hall and launched a historic sit-in at the office of Chancellor W. Clarke Wescoe. Many of these protesters had witnessed a horrifying spectacle on television the day before from Selma, Alabama. On "Bloody Sunday," state troopers and sheriff's deputies had brutally assaulted nonviolent freedom marchers with horses, billy clubs, bullwhips, and tear gas. KU's civil rights community was outraged. It was time to act.[3]

The demands presented by KU's Civil Rights Council (CRC) to Chancellor Wescoe that morning were not new. For several years, campus activists had called upon Wescoe's administration to eliminate racial discrimination in student housing, among other issues. On that morning, the CRC announced in a flyer: "WE DEMAND" that the university housing office refuse to list segregated rentals for off-campus dwellings; that the chancellor issue an executive order that fraternities and sororities "immediately abolish racially discriminatory practices"; that the School of Education stop sending student teachers to school

A march for fair housing in 1964. Third from the right is Gale Sayers; other athletes also marched in the protest.

districts with "racially discriminatory hiring practices"; and that the *UDK* "no longer accept advertisements from landlords and/or organizations that practice racial discrimination." Finally, the CRC called for the formation of a committee of students, faculty, and administrators to resolve grievances over racial discrimination on campus.[4]

On March 8, the CRC passed out handbills on Jayhawk Boulevard listing its demands. At 10:00 AM, the protesters entered Strong Hall and marched upstairs to the hallway outside the chancellor's office. The students sat quietly; some did their homework. Among the group were several high-profile black athletes, including All-American football player Gale Sayers and basketball stars Walt Wesley and George Unseld. In fact, it was Unseld who presented Chancellor Wescoe with the group's demands. For his part, Wescoe was visibly upset; according to one of the protesters, he was "very agitated [and] irritated." Dean of Students Laurence C. Woodruff threatened any students who remained at this office beyond closing time at 5:00 PM with arrest, suspension, or expulsion. Faced with such dire consequences, many

Student sit-in protesting for civil rights in the hallway outside the Chancellor's Office in Strong Hall, March 8, 1965.

who had been sitting in left the building. But others stayed, including one CRC member who proclaimed, "We're going to bust this. We'll just have a little civil disobedience to show we aren't going to beg any more. We're going to get what is coming to us." Although the number of demonstrating students had peaked at around 400, there were still 110 left when campus and local police moved in and began making arrests. The majority of those arrested were African American, and one-third were women. "We're all going to jail, all to jail," shouted one of the students as he was loaded onto a bus for the short trip to the Douglas County jail.[5]

That night, more than 500 people, singing the civil rights anthem, "We Shall Overcome," conducted a peaceful candlelight march near the chancellor's residence. The next day, 160 demonstrators returned to Strong Hall. But by that time, Chancellor Wescoe had suspended all of the arrested students. He also had sent the students' parents a telegram to notify them of their children's misdeeds. Wescoe closed his office that day, barring those without appointments from entering. That afternoon, however, he met with representatives of the National Association for the Advancement of Colored People (NAACP) and

CORE, following which two of the CRC leaders were invited to come to Wescoe's residence for a meeting. Wescoe offered not only to reinstate the students but also to appoint a committee to resolve the issues raised by the CRC. In exchange, Wescoe asked the students to stop their protest, and they agreed to do so.[6]

Over the next few weeks, major changes were instituted at KU. The housing office began to reject segregated listings; the School of Education stopped sending student teachers to segregated school districts; and the *UDK* refused to publish discriminatory advertisements. Finally, a University Human Relations Committee was established. The Greek system, however, remained largely unchanged. In fact, not until 1968 did an African American student pledge a previously all-white fraternity.[7]

According to historian Rusty L. Monhollon, "The 1965 demonstration was perhaps the most successful civil rights protest ever in Lawrence." "In part," Monhollon has explained, "the timing was right, and the administration was simply catching up with the tide of civil rights reform sweeping the nation. . . . As well, the students' demands challenged vestiges of racial exclusion that could easily be removed and did not cost the university much financially or administratively."[8]

Not all future campus protests, however, would be resolved so peacefully or so satisfactorily. Indeed, the next five years would be the most violent in the history of the university. The Black Power movement would provoke the next protests, paralleled by growing opposition to the Vietnam War. The movement in Lawrence emerged first not at KU, but at Lawrence High School (LHS). "Black Power," as defined by Kwame Ture (formerly Stokely Carmichael) and Charles V. Hamilton, was "a call for black people to unite, recognize their heritage, . . . build a sense of community, . . . define their own goals, [and] lead their own organizations."[9] Black students at LHS in the 1960s, some of whom had marched earlier in Lawrence for civil rights, believed that the movement had failed to produce meaningful change, and they were becoming increasingly angry and confrontational. According to John Spearman, Jr., a senior at LHS in 1968, the civil rights movement had "failed to get it done," and so he had embraced Black Power. Unlike the nonviolent civil rights movement, which advocated racial integration and Gandhian passive resistance, the Black Power movement advocated black separatism and retaliatory self-defense. The advice of Malcolm X, the chief spokesperson for the Black Muslims and a leading advocate of Black Power, was straightforward: "If someone puts a hand on you, send him to the cemetery." Lawrence first witnessed the public face of Black Power in August 1967 when a group of black teenagers organized on Massachusetts Street and "threatened to burn the town [down]."[10]

When LHS's black students returned for the next school year, they were determined to demand change. Topping their list of demands was a course in African American history. African Americans, observed Carmichael and Hamilton in *Black Power*, "are becoming aware that they have a history which pre-dates their forced introduction to this country. . . . If black people are to know themselves as a vibrant, valiant people, they must know their roots." In May 1968, 50 black students and their parents met with the LHS principal. Led by John Spearman and Beverly Southard, the students eloquently presented their demands. Noting that schools in nearby towns were considering offering African American history courses, one parent asked, "Why does Lawrence always drag its feet, in any field?" One young black woman said that she was told when she asked a teacher for assistance on an assignment, "You niggers can't do anything right." The principal dismissed this complaint, indifferently replying that "teachers sometimes can have a slip of the tongue that doesn't necessarily indicate prejudice."[11]

In September 1968, 50 black LHS students conducted a walk-out to protest inaction on issues they had raised the previous May. As Rick Dowdell, a senior, explained, "You know what they teach us about black history? . . . We know more about the white man's ancestors than we know about our own." "We're serious about these things," added Vanessa Collins, another black student, "and if we don't get them we'll have to use other means." Over the next 18 months, racial tensions rose, and violence, including riots, shootings, physical altercations, and bombings, erupted not only at the high school, but throughout the town and on KU's campus.[12]

Also during the fall semester of 1968, John Spearman enrolled at KU as an articulate advocate of Black Power. Arguing that "not only were universities and colleges unresponsive to the needs of black students and communities, but their mode of education produced exactly the opposite results desired and needed by our communities," he called for the creation of a Black Student Union (BSU), the "primary purpose [of which] was to be totally committed to meeting the needs and desires of black people."[13] In 1970, the BSU presented a five-page list of demands to Chancellor E. Laurence Chalmers: "We, the Black Student Union . . . as the voice of our People and the University component of the black liberation struggle, demand" the hiring of more black faculty and administrators, the recruitment of more black

Black Student Union homecoming queen Lorene Brown and her attendants raise fists in the Black Power salute, Memorial Stadium, 1969.

students ("that each freshman class be at least 10% Black"), and the establishment of a black studies department. "We intend to dedicate ourselves to see that this document becomes a living reality. Our suffering has a limit. We think it is very 'inappropriate' to talk of 'appropriateness,' we want ACTION." And there was action: The BSU's demand for a black studies department eventuated in the establishment in 1971 of the Department of African and African-American Studies (AAAS), in the College of Liberal Arts and Sciences.[14]

The BSU also published its own newspaper, entitled *Harambee* (Kiswahili for "all pull together"). *Harambee*'s fiery rhetoric was as displeasing to whites as it was pleasing to KU's militant black students. In denouncing white students who had ridiculed the BSU, the newspaper stated: "All you young redneck peckerwoods that belong to the 'Keep the Niggers in check organization,' had better take heed. . . . You fools are dealing with Blacks who have said, 'We shall have our manhood

In protest, BSU members dumped 6,000 copies of the UDK *into Potter Lake, February 1970.*

or the Earth shall be leveled in our attempt to get it.'" Another writer explained that blacks had no alternative to violence: "I do what I must out of love for my people. My will is to fight. Resistance is not enough. Aggression is the order of the day."[15]

In February 1970, employees of KU's Printing Service, which published *Harambee*, halted production of the newspaper and conducted a walk-out to protest what they considered its obscene content. Whites at KU and in Lawrence agreed with the Printing Service's action. "I don't think we need to publish this filth," said one outraged Lawrencian. In retaliation, BSU members gathered at Flint, Murphy, Strong, and Summerfield Halls, as well as at various outdoor circulation bins, walked off with 6,000 copies of the *UDK* printed that day, and dumped them into Potter Lake.[16]

Meanwhile, racial violence erupted at LHS, and the reverberations were felt at KU. Shortly after lunch on April 13, 1970, 50 black students burst into the school principal's office and presented him with a list of demands, calling for a black homecoming queen, black cheerleaders, black teachers, a black student union, and additional courses in black history and culture. The students had made many of the same demands in 1968, and now they wanted action. Simultaneously, other black students rampaged throughout the high school, banging on doors, threatening white students, and breaking windows. Members of KU's BSU, including John Spearman and Rick Dowdell, who had joined the LHS students in protest, were arrested. On April 15, racial violence exploded at the school cafeteria; 28 people were injured. On the morning of April 21, violence erupted again when angry black students broke windows in the high school and battled with police officers, who responded with tear gas and mace.[17]

Late on April 20, a multimillion-dollar fire gutted KU's Memorial Union. As the flames shot 30 feet in the air, causing the roof to collapse and destroying the top two floors, 2,000 KU students rushed to the site to gawk. Many, however, also came to help. They cleared the building of furniture and art objects, helped to balance fire hoses, and provided coffee and doughnuts to the firefighters. "The fire could have been a lot worse," said the Lawrence fire chief, "without student help." Law enforcement officials believed that the arsonists were a group of young black men seen leaving the Union shortly after the fire was ignited, but they were never identified, and the case was never solved. The next day, Governor Robert B. Docking placed the city under a three-day dusk-to-dawn curfew. The sale of firearms and explosives was prohibited during the curfew, but arson, firebombings, and sniper fire persisted. Not since the days of "Bleeding Kansas," leading to the American Civil War, had Lawrence and KU been so polarized.[18]

VIETNAM, THE ANTIWAR MOVEMENT, AND DEADLY VIOLENCE IN LAWRENCE

In March 1965, a special visitor came to KU to talk about the war in Indochina. General Maxwell Taylor, former chairman of the Joint Chiefs of Staff and former ambassador to the Republic of Vietnam, was currently serving as special military adviser to President Lyndon B. Johnson. Speaking to a packed audience in Hoch Auditorium, Taylor warned against a communist victory in Vietnam, and he implored students to study the war and support the war effort. "It disturbs me," he said, "to see beatniks carrying signs. This shows they haven't studied the subject." After Taylor's address, the Reverend John Swomley of the St. Paul School of Theology in Kansas City spoke to students, offering

Students assist firefighters in combating the Kansas Union fire, April 20, 1970.

A march on campus protesting the Vietnam War in 1966.

an alternative perspective. "We have been the victims of military propaganda. The military," he added, "is the architect of the war and General Taylor is the chief architect." According to Swomley, the only viable solution to the escalating conflict was a negotiated settlement.[19]

Over the next eight years, the Vietnam War emerged as the major issue of concern among KU students and faculty alike. As the Vietnam War grew, so too did the antiwar movement on the campus. In September 1965, the KU chapter of the Student Peace Union, Students for a Democratic Society (SDS), Student Union Activities, and the KU-Y (YWCA and YMCA) organized a campus teach-in on the war. In addition, a committee of students and faculty established the KU Committee to End the War in Vietnam, which promised to sponsor additional teach-ins. "As a university is supposed to be a center for exchange of ideas," the committee declared, "it is the responsibility of students to inform themselves about a situation [for which] they might have to give their life."[20]

In October 1965, the Student Peace Union picketed the Lawrence draft board, and the next month it sponsored a blood drive for "victims of LBJ's war." George Kimball, an SDS member, and another student were arrested by Lawrence police for protesting with a sign that read, "Fuck the Draft." Still, many KU students supported the war. In November 1966, three Corbin Hall students gathered "bits of Christmas," including a Christmas candle and candy canes wrapped in a *UDK,* to send to American airmen in Vietnam. But antiwar protests increased at KU, many of which were staged at symbols of the American military, such as the ROTC building and ROTC reviews, the draft board, the National Guard armory, and the Sunflower Munitions Plant, located 13 miles east of Lawrence. In February 1969, the Military Science Building was firebombed, and in April, student demonstrators waved toy guns in the faces of ROTC cadets during a review in front of Allen Fieldhouse.[21]

KU students, especially draft-age men (18 to 26 years old), worried as Selective Service increased its monthly quotas. In 1965, draft quotas had tripled from the previous year, from 17,000 to 40,000 per month; and because college students were deferred from the draft, enrollments at KU and elsewhere rose as well. In 1966, when 382,000 draftees were inducted, American troop strength in Vietnam climbed to 385,000. A year later, with the military needing even more troops, such deferments were replaced by the requirement that, to avoid the draft, men needed to have good grades and be working toward a degree. In addition, graduate-school deferments were abolished. In 1969, troop strength in Vietnam peaked at 543,400. In December 1969, the Selective Service System instituted a lottery to determine which men of draft age would be called to service.[22]

In early May 1969, members of the SDS distributed handbills on campus encouraging students to protest—against both the war in Vietnam and the continued presence of ROTC on campus—at the annual Chancellor's Tri-Service Parade and Review in Memorial Stadium. Fearful of violence, Chancellor Wescoe requested that the Kansas National Guard deploy soldiers in Lawrence in case a riot erupted. On May 9, the day of the review, two battalions were positioned on the outskirts of town, and local and state police were on high alert. Later that day, some 175 students and at least one professor marched to the stadium and, nonviolently, disrupted the review. They carried signs that read "ROTC OFF CAMPUS" and "STOP THE WAR." On the field, Rick Atkinson, one of the demonstration's organizers, proclaimed, "If they come to arrest us, do not sit down and let them take you away. Run like hell all over the place." As for the cadets, one stated, "I do not want to shout down the SDS. I want to shoot them down." And another cadet recalled, "I hated the SDS. I thought they were a bunch of liberal, hippie, commies. They were no good rabble rousers that gave KU a bad name . . . even though they were probably right." On the football field,

The National Vietnam Moratorium Day, October 15, 1969, prompted a massive march down Jayhawk Boulevard.

students shouted antiwar slogans; some lay down in front of the cadets to disrupt their line of march, while others danced around the cadets, taunting them. Wescoe, alarmed by what he saw as "anarchism," cancelled the review.[23]

In the wake of the May 1969 protest, conservative politicians demanded that the university harshly discipline the protesters and release their names to the press. KU acquiesced, releasing the names of the 55 students who had chosen to have open hearings with the University Disciplinary Board. Moreover, for participation in the protest, the board suspended 36 students for the fall semester, including the student body vice president, Marilyn Bowman; and the grades of 13 other students who would have graduated after the spring or summer semesters in 1969 were to be withheld until the following January.[24]

In mid-1969, Wescoe left the chancellorship; he was succeeded by E. Laurence Chalmers. Chalmers inherited not only the KU chancellorship, but also a campus and a community in turmoil. In his first week in office, Chalmers, who insisted that he be called "Larry," delivered a speech in Kansas City in which he denounced the Vietnam War.

"There have always been people," he said, "who objected to every war this country fought, but the war in Vietnam is perceived by our students as politically unjustifiable and morally indefensible, and I agree with them on both counts." As heartening as Chalmers's antiwar views were to many KU students, they proved to be alarming to Kansas's rock-ribbed conservatives.[25]

The May 1969 protest, as Rusty Monhollon has written, "marked a turning point in the antiwar movement in Lawrence. Alongside the peaceful protests . . . came confrontational street theater demonstrations led by students and radicals. It also hardened the resistance from the political far Right." The protest also swelled the ranks of the antiwar movement at KU. In October 1969, as part of the National Moratorium against the war, more than 3,000 KU students, faculty, and staff and other Lawrence residents gathered on the campus for an antiwar march down Jayhawk Boulevard. It was a peaceful demonstration; one student waved a sign that read, "Rockchalk, Jaydove, stop war, try love."[26]

Meanwhile, another element of the youth culture was proving disruptive, or at least unsettling, both on campus and in town. Variously known as "hippies," "freaks," or "street people," members of the counterculture frequented the bars and eateries just north of the campus, especially the Rock Chalk Cafe and the Gaslight Tavern. Moreover, as the slogan "Make Love, Not War" suggests, the antiwar movement and the "counterculture" discovered a common cause as the war in Vietnam escalated. Many hippies lived communally in houses near the KU campus or on farms ringing Lawrence. According to one scholar who studied "the young rebels of the 1960s," hippies wore "the most eccentric clothes they could find: military uniforms, cowboy vests, bib overalls, and sack dresses; Indian headbands and felt hats; sandals and motorcycle boots, beads and bells." They proclaimed themselves sexually liberated, and they indulged their taste for illegal drugs, most notably marijuana, but also hallucinogenic mushrooms and LSD. They also cultivated and marketed drugs; one of the best-known dope-harvester groups called itself the Kaw Valley Hemp Pickers. A 1971 poll in the *UDK* found that 69 percent of KU students had smoked marijuana and 92 percent had friends who smoked it. Additionally, hippies from both the East and West Coasts, and various places in between, gravitated to Lawrence and to the bars and street scene atop Mount Oread. "As word about Lawrence spread," a local hippie recalled, "the town became known as a friendly place for wayward freaks. . . . Lawrence was like on the Oregon trail for hippies."[27]

Protesters lined up in front of Strong Hall during the National Vietnam Moratorium Day in 1969.

One local historian has called 1970 "The Year That Rocked River City." That February, students announced the formation of the Lawrence Liberation Front "to serve the people of the Revolutionary Community" by publishing an underground newspaper (*Oread Daily*), starting the Legal Self Defense (LSD) Fund, and operating a G.I. Counseling Service to encourage desertion. In addition to the *Oread Daily*, other radical underground newspapers included *Vortex*, *Screw*, and *Reconstruction*. In March, KU students joined in protests during National Anti-Draft Week; some picketed the Lawrence Selective Service office, while others protested at the Sunflower Munitions Plant, run by subcontractor Hercules, which made rocket propellant for air-to-ground missiles. When a retired army colonel from the John Birch Society spoke on campus, he was pelted with marshmallows during his speech. On Strike Day, April 8, students boycotted classes. That night, Abbie Hoffman spoke before 8,000 people on campus, but he offended both the Right and the Left by wiping his nose on the American flag and proclaiming that Lawrence was "a drag."[28]

As noted above, on April 21, Governor Docking, responding to what was called "a prerevolutionary situation," placed the city under a three-day dusk-to-dawn curfew. The Kansas National Guard patrolled the streets of Lawrence, and the police arrested scores of people for curfew violations and possession of explosives. During the curfew, arson attempts were numerous, including fires at the Military Science Building, Strong and Fraser Halls, LHS, Woods Lumber, and the Lawrence National Bank. Snipers shot at downtown businesses, and "freaks" who gathered at the Rock Chalk Cafe said they were stockpiling bricks for the ensuing conflict, with either "rednecks" or the "Pigs." In the spring of 1970, whites and blacks, straight people and "street people," in Lawrence and on the KU campus, stood on the verge of civil war.[29]

And then, on April 30, the potential for violence escalated further when President Richard M. Nixon appeared on television to announce that the United States had launched an "incursion" into Cambodia, a neutral country bordering Vietnam. Antiwar protests proliferated at KU and across the nation, where 536 campuses were shut down. On May 4, National Guardsmen in Ohio fired into a crowd of fleeing students at Kent State University, killing four young people. Ten days later, police and state highway patrolmen armed with automatic weapons blasted a women's dormitory at Jackson State, an all-black university in Mississippi, killing two students and wounding nine others. The police claimed they had been shot at, but no evidence of sniping could be found.[30]

KU, in the days after the Cambodian invasion, was a powder keg. On May 6, as many as 1,000 KU students rallied in opposition to the continued presence of ROTC on campus. On May 7, some 200 students attacked the Military Science Building with rocks, breaking windows, and five were arrested. For his part, Chancellor Chalmers, on the advice of the Senate Executive Committee, cancelled the annual Chancellor's Tri-Service Parade and Review in Memorial Stadium, scheduled for later that week. He also announced that on Friday, May 8, at 2:00 PM, a university-wide convocation would be held in Memorial Stadium to vote on whether students should have the option of either finishing the semester or ceasing class attendance and taking a grade based on work done to date, so that they could leave KU immediately and engage in political activity of their choice. A rumor spread that student radicals were determined to launch a general strike before the convocation, shutting down the campus altogether. Chalmers heard the rumor but "prayed that it would hold together until 2:00 PM," which it did. Chalmers was greatly relieved when more than 15,000 students, faculty, and staff took their seats in Memorial Stadium. And he was relieved, too, when the alternatives were put to a voice vote, and

An antiwar demonstration on Campanile Hill during the 1972 Kansas Relays.

the overwhelming majority in the stadium stood and shouted "Aye" in favor of ending classes.[31]

Still, racial, political, and cultural tensions remained at fever pitch, especially during the hot summer months of 1970. Rumors spread that local men in pickup trucks, featuring CB radios and loaded gun racks, were patrolling not only "hippie haven" on Mount Oread, but also black neighborhoods in East Lawrence. One vigilante claimed that he had 300 members who, he said, were eager to use "guerilla warfare" to halt the "nigger and hippie militants." For its part, the antiwar movement was more passionate than ever in its commitment to end both the Vietnam War and ROTC at KU. So, too, was the BSU in its dedication to self-determination. On May 12, over 500 students, both black and white, attended a BSU rally at which John Spearman called for Black Power at KU, and he urged blacks to arm themselves. On June 26, Afro House, funded in part by the KU Student Senate, was opened at Tenth and Rhode Island Streets; its goal was to help black people "achieve total liberation in this white society." Like the Black Panther Party elsewhere, Afro House offered breakfast for children in the Lawrence community, a Big Brother–Big Sister Program, and a Liberation School.[32]

On July 16, with the temperature at over 100 degrees, a four-day siege of Lawrence and KU erupted. That evening, vigilantes reportedly fired shots at Afro House, and a black man sitting on the front porch was wounded by buckshot. When police came to investigate, they were fired upon by snipers. Rick Dowdell, the 19-year-old KU student and Lawrence resident who had been a leader of the 1968 LHS black walkout, had just gotten a ride from Afro House to the campus. A police car, with its lights off, followed the car; a chase ensued when the driver tried to return to Afro House. The car struck a curb and stopped. Dowdell jumped from the car, and with a police officer running in pursuit, dashed along an alley toward Afro House; the police officer fired a warning shot. What happened next has been the subject of great controversy and is still hotly contested. What is beyond dispute is that the officer fired four rounds from his .357 magnum, one of which struck Dowdell in the back of the head. He died at the scene. "In Lawrence, Kansas," as Rusty Monhollon has observed, "Black Power and white fear proved a deadly combination."[33]

The killing did not stop, but the next victim, another 19-year-old KU student, Nick Rice, was white. On the evening of July 20, 60 or so militants and hippies on Mount Oread, angered by the killing of Dowdell and cheered on by over 100 spectators, had rebelled, opening fire hydrants, setting small fires, and even tipping over a Volkswagen and

Holding truncheons, Lawrence police officers block a protest near the campus during the summer of 1970.

setting it on fire. Police officers with shotguns and M-1 rifles suddenly shouted, "Shoot 'em," and opened fire into the retreating mob. Nick Rice, like Rick Dowdell, died from a bullet wound to the base of his skull, indicating that rather than charging the police, he was fleeing. Merton Olds, a black graduate student, was also wounded. The next day, Governor Docking issued another emergency proclamation prohibiting the sale of weapons, ammunition, and flammable liquids. He also ordered troopers from the Kansas Highway Patrol to assist local law enforcement, effectively replacing the Lawrence police on Mount Oread, where they were despised.[34]

Journalist Bill Moyers happened to be visiting Lawrence during this fateful week. "The town is large enough," Moyers wrote, "to harbor several communities with their own ways of life. It is small enough for every citizen to feel the impact of colliding values. The people I met," he added, "looked at events through the lens of their own personal experience and defined truth by what they saw: the townspeople who feel threatened, the blacks who feel oppressed, the street people who feel harassed, the students who feel misunderstood, and the police who feel abused."[35] For the rest of the decade, violence did not end—far from it—but it did subside.

As the decade turned, "personal politics" shifted the political agenda. In June 1970, the Lawrence Gay Liberation Front was organized, as was the "Food Conspiracy," which evolved into the Community Mercantile. Earlier that year, KU had celebrated the first Earth Day (actually Earth Week), which featured a speech by KU alumnus Paul Ehrlich, author of *The Population Bomb*. In July, the Women's Coalition was formed to provide abortion counseling, self-defense training against rape, and the operation of a Women's Center in the Wesley Foundation Building. Other organizations formed that year were a Tenants' Union, the KU branch of Zero Population Growth, and KU's Information Center, which was meant to disseminate information and to control rumors. That fall, protesters at American Indian Day gathered at the Natural History Museum to denounce the display of General George Custer's horse, Comanche, which labeled him "the only survivor of the Battle of the Little Big Horn River." "Sitting Bull Lives!" read a sign carried by a protester. In November, CBS's *60 Minutes* televised a segment on the Kaw Valley Hemp Pickers.[36]

Political polarization over the war had increased on the KU campus, where the New Left exemplified by the SDS contended for support with the New Right represented by the Young Americans for Freedom. Most KU students, however, occupied the middle ground. A 1971 poll of 259 candidates for the Student Senate indicated that, on the question, "Would you support student dissent in violation of published and known Board of Regents policies on campus 'order,'" 88 said yes, 88 said no, and 59 were undecided.[37]

In the early 1970s, President Nixon began the process of "Vietnamization," that is, turning primary responsibility for waging the war over to South Vietnam and its army and bringing American troops home. It had already been a long war, particularly for draft-age men. But by 1970, troop strength in Vietnam began to decline. The University of Kansas witnessed its last major antiwar demonstration in May 1972, when Nixon resumed intensive bombing of North Vietnam for the first time since 1968 and ordered the mining of Hai Phong Harbor and other North Vietnamese ports. Scores of students marched down Jayhawk Boulevard chanting antiwar slogans, and the Military Science Building was again attacked by rock-throwing protesters. Dr. Benjamin Spock, America's best-known baby doctor and a leading antiwar activist, spoke on the steps of Strong Hall, calling for peace in Vietnam. The university offered no alternatives this time for students who wished to leave campus to lobby against the war in their hometowns or in Washington, DC. But the Student Senate did issue a resolution

Protesters disrupting the ROTC parade and review in Memorial Stadium, May 1969.

opposing "this major escalation of the Indo-China War" and urging Kansas's congressional delegation to "request the President of the United States to end the bombing of North Vietnam and continue to de-escalate the war."[38]

In 1973, the day after the signing of the Paris peace accords mandating a cease-fire in Vietnam, Nixon ended the draft and inaugurated an all-volunteer military. In 1975, the United States evacuated its last troops and diplomats from Saigon, as the North Vietnamese poured into the city. By then, however, more than 58,000 Americans and 1.5 million Vietnamese had died. Meanwhile, relative calm returned to the KU campus. It had been a stormy ten years for KU, indeed, the stormiest by far in the university's 110-year history.

GAY RIGHTS

Just as KU's civil rights movement was inspired by activism elsewhere, especially "Bloody Sunday" in Selma in 1965, so, too, the gay rights movement at KU was born in the aftermath of events in New York City in 1969. In Greenwich Village, a riot erupted when police raided the Stonewall Inn, a gay bar on Christopher Street; they were greeted with a volley of beer bottles by patrons tired of police harassment. Rioting continued into the night, and graffiti calling for "Gay Power" appeared along Christopher Street. As historian John D'Emilio has written, Stonewall "marked a critical divide in the politics and consciousness of homosexuals and lesbians. A small, thinly spread reform effort suddenly grew into a large, grass-roots movement for liberation . . . as a furtive subculture moved aggressively into the open."[39]

Gay men and lesbians at KU had long feared that disclosing their sexual orientation would mean losing not only their friends but even their families. Nevertheless, in June 1970, students organized the Lawrence Gay Liberation Front (LGLF), determined to be recognized by KU as a legitimate student organization. But the next month, the State of Kansas raised the stakes when Governor Robert Docking signed a bill outlawing "sodomy," which was defined as "oral or anal copulation between persons who are not husband and wife or consenting adult members of the opposite sex." Punishment for the crime was "a term of imprisonment of six months." In August, the LGLF applied for recognition from KU, explaining that its goal was "to secure for homosexuals the rights and liberties established for all people by the word and spirit of the Declaration of Independence and Constitution of this country." Recognition by KU also would convey certain organizational benefits, such as the ability to apply for funds from student activity fees, office space, and rooms in the Union for meetings. But most important, the LGLF argued, recognition would "enable the organization to assume its legitimate role in providing additional perspectives on human experience, it being the function of a university to provide a forum for diverse opinion and thus to insure the richest possible educational environment."[40]

The Student Senate Executive Committee voted in September 1970 to recognize the LGLF, but its recommendation was vetoed by Chancellor Chalmers, who wrote that he did not believe "that student activity funds should be allocated to support or oppose the sexual proclivities of students, particularly when they might lead to violation of state law." Chalmers confessed that he found himself in a "totally impossible situation . . . with reference to Gay Liberation." "As a psychologist and as a human being," he wrote, "I'm of one mind. As an ultimate spokesman for the students and ultimately responsible to the Board of Regents, I'm of a totally different mind. I'm not very adept at mind splitting." In

"Hot to Trot," announces this poster for a gay liberation dance in the Kansas Union in 1973.

his public statements, however, Chalmers seemed to be concerned not about human rights, but about KU's officially condoning an illegal sex act, that of sodomy. The sodomy law became the foundation of KU's refusal to recognize the LGLF as a student organization.[41]

Chalmers's veto gained popular endorsement from KU alumni, politicians in Topeka, and newspapers around the state. John A. Rupf, class of 1961, hailed Chalmers's action, arguing that "it would be a short step from recognition of such a group to a clamor for recognition of the Masochist League, the Satyriasis Club, the Nymphomaniac Association, etc." In March 1971, the LGLF applied again to the Student Senate for recognition, but Chalmers once more vetoed the Senate's recommendation for recognition. In response, the LGLF, with financial support from the Senate to pay legal fees, sued for justice in federal court and hired radical attorney William Kunstler to represent it. Chalmers then vetoed a $600 appropriation that the Student Senate had approved for legal fees. Nevertheless, Kunstler took the case, arriving in Topeka in January 1972. But he was barred from participating by the federal judge, who objected to his "abrasive" public comments regarding the judicial system. The judge also ruled against the LGLF, writing that it was "not difficult to understand the concern of Chancellor Chalmers . . . that the school funds should not be made available for the purpose . . . of supporting the discussion of bizarre sexual activities for which plaintiffs apparently seek . . . public approval." The LGLF, with Kunstler arguing the case, then appealed to the Tenth Circuit Court of Appeals in Denver, which denied the appeal. The LGLF then took its appeal to the US Supreme Court, but the Court voted not to hear the case.[42]

While it took until the early 1980s for the LGLF finally to gain recognition from KU as a legitimate student organization, with the ability to request funds from the Student Senate, KU's gays and lesbians had become an active political and cultural force on campus. Their vibrant community life was exemplified by the proliferation of gay newspapers in Lawrence, including the *Lawrence GLF News*, the *Gay Oread Daily*, the *Yellow Brick Road*, *Up Front*, and *Lavender Luminary*. In the pages of these publications, gays and lesbians expressed pride in their sexual orientation. "We are gay," declared a manifesto by the LGLF, "because we are privileged in the ability to love human beings of the same sex. . . . To all our gay brothers and sisters we ask you to hold up your heads and look the world squarely in the eye as the gay people you are, . . . confident in the goodness of what you do, what you feel, who you are. Gay is beautiful when gay people make it that way."[43]

To raise money for operating expenses such as rent, phone, and advertising and to provide occasions for gay and straight people alike to strut their stuff, the LGLF sponsored dances in the Memorial Union. In the fall of 1971, the Women's Coalition, covering for the LGLF, received approval from KU Events to use the Union Ballroom for a dance. The first dance, with over 400 people in attendance, was a major success, as were all the LGLF dances over the next few years. "When the LGLF had the gay lib dances in the Ballroom," one KU alumnus recalled, "the place would be packed. There were people coming from St. Louis, Chicago and Denver and Dallas." Filling the ballroom at a number of the dances were 800 people. A Union employee remembered that "it was like a mega-event, and people who were not gay would attend, too. . . . It was a big party!"[44]

Ruth Lichtwardt had begun attending the LGLF dances in 1976, and when she became a KU student in 1981, she visited the "gay lib" office in the Kansas Union and became a volunteer. The tiny office, she recalled, was "about 70 square feet, . . . [and it] was, appropriately, a converted closet." In 1981, the organization changed its name to Gay and Lesbian Services of Kansas (GLSOK). Lichtwardt recalled that the GLSOK's "speakers' bureau and peer counseling became more active, and the office was usually overcrowded." In 1982, GLSOK debated whether to apply for Student Senate funding, but it decided that "the dances were doing well and we didn't really need the money." But GLSOK also worried that if it became too politically active, then "the money would be used as a club to keep us in line." In 1983, however, with Lichtwardt as its newly elected director, GLSOK changed its position and applied for funding. Income from the dances had declined, largely because of a change in Kansas liquor laws that forced the Union to stop selling beer at student functions. More important, GLSOK believed that it "deserved the same support as other student organizations." Despite scattered opposition in the Student Senate, GLSOK was funded in the spring of 1983, receiving $493 for rent and telephone.[45]

But that fall semester, a group known as the Freedom Coalition, which was composed of students from the Young Americans for Freedom and a local evangelical church, campaigned to defund GLSOK. In addition, several members of the Freedom Coalition signed up to serve on the Student Senate Finance Committee. As Lichtwardt recalled, when GLSOK testified for renewed funding, hostile students on the Finance Committee "asked questions about sodomy laws, the suicide rate among gay men, the 'great nationwide homosexual conspiracy,' and the like." On the other hand, the GLSOK enjoyed the

Freedom Coalition members march for gay rights in the early 1990s.

fervent support of the governing Costume Party, and especially its leaders, a "pair of self-professed anarchists," student body president Carla Vogel and vice president Dennis "Boog" Highberger. And when the Finance Committee recommended zero funding for GLSOK, the Student Senate ignored the recommendation and voted to restore funding for the organization.[46]

Although the GLSOK had won this battle, the war raged on in 1984 and 1985. Lichtwardt observed that "a new fashion was beginning to appear around campus. People were seen in a new t-shirt. It was white with a ghost in a red circle with a slash through it. It was modeled," she remembered, "on the 'Ghostbusters' logo, only this ghost had long eyelashes and a limp wrist with 'FAGBUSTERS' emblazoned upon it." Also at this time, "open hostility and homophobia were . . . becoming more evident. Physical threats and actual attacks and harassing phone calls against GLSOK . . . increased dramatically." The lug nuts on the car of one member had been loosened. As Lichtwardt recalled, "He and I were driving across campus when a wheel fell off his car. We discovered that two other wheels were loose!" Campus police confirmed that the car had been sabotaged.[47]

In 1984, concerned that the antigay movement was resorting to violence, faculty at KU authored and circulated a petition not only upholding the civil liberties of the GLSOK's members, but also calling upon the KU administration to guarantee their safety on campus. The petition condemned both the harassment and the attitudes underlying the harassment. A history professor, who was one of the originators of the petition, stated that KU administrators "have got to make a specific statement that denounces homophobia." When asked how many faculty members had signed the petition, the professor replied, "It doesn't matter if there is one or 1,000. There is a serious moral issue involved." Two weeks later, the administration finally issued a statement that no one had "the right to coerce, harass, or threaten other individuals," and that any such infraction would be brought "to the attention of law enforcement agencies."[48]

Unfortunately, the administration's admonition did not stop the harassment. A flyer circulated at KU with the heading "FAGS!" It continued: "Now that we have your attention, the C.P.A.F. (Concerned Persons Against Faggotry) would like you to join in 'creative' measures to rid the campus of this menace." Moreover, in the early 1980s, as the AIDS epidemic ravaged America's gay community, including gay men at KU and in Lawrence, antigay violence rose. The National Gay and Lesbian Task Force attributed the increase partly to the "AIDS Backlash." In an article on AIDS in *Rolling Stone*, Ruth Lichtwardt explained that "on this campus, AIDS has given people an excuse to hate gay people. . . . Anti-gay harassment at Kansas has also increased."[49]

Antigay violence nationwide seemed to subside after 1986. Meanwhile, Lawrence and KU were becoming safer and more supportive homes for gay men and women. In 1989, the Douglas County AIDS Project was founded to advocate for AIDS sufferers. As GLSOK evolved, it underwent various name changes, including "LesBiGay Services" in the mid-1990s. But its mission remained the same: to serve the gay community. Moreover, politically, Lawrence's gay community was increasingly a force to be reckoned with in the 1990s. Beginning in 1986, citizens in Lawrence and at KU suggested that it was time to add the words "sexual orientation" to the Human Relations Ordinance of the Code of the City of Lawrence, along with race, gender, and religion, and thereby "prohibit discrimination on the basis of sexual orientation in housing, employment, and public accommodations."[50]

The issue of gay rights reemerged in 1991, when KU and community activists formed the Freedom Coalition to agitate for amending the city code. Members of the coalition included KU LesBiGay Services, the American Civil Liberties Union, and Ecumenical Christian Ministries. The National Organization for Women (NOW) also began to address the issue. Moreover, the Freedom Coalition and NOW joined forces in a new coalition called Simply Equal, the goal of which was to amend the city code. Reaching out to the broader community, Simply Equal emphasized that what was at stake were not only gay rights, but also human rights.[51]

In January 1995, the Lawrence City Commission held a study session on the Simply Equal amendment. At that time, the commission was divided two to two, with one undeclared vote. More than 100 people attended the study session. Six candidates for the City Commission, two of whom supported the amendment, were elected in the February primary, thus earning a place on the ballot for the general election in April; the top three would be elected to the City Commission. The debate over the amendment in Lawrence and on campus was intense, and it was evident that the April election would be a referendum on gay rights. Since only one of the two carry-over commissioners supported the amendment, it was essential that the pro-amendment forces elect their two candidates. Supporters resorted to bullet voting to do so, voting only for their two candidates, and they were successful. On April 25, 1995, the new Lawrence City Commission voted three to two to add the words "sexual orientation" to the city's human relations ordinance. "Sweet victory!" proclaimed Lynne Green, a KU alumna and co-chair of Simply Equal. "It's only taken 10 years, but this is a safer town today."[52]

SOUTH AFRICA, DIVESTMENT, AND CIVIL RIGHTS IN THE 1980S AND 1990S

On May 21, 1979, as students, parents, faculty, and alumni filed into Memorial Stadium for KU's commencement, members of the KU Committee on South Africa (KUSA) handed out flyers that urged the graduates "to express their opposition to KU investments in South Africa by refusing to join the Alumni Association." "Graduation," stated KUSA's flyer, "is a time for speeches about idealism, seeking the truth, and making a contribution to society." "Unfortunately," the flyer continued, "the University of Kansas contradicts these ideals by investing in South Africa, a society structured on the racist principles of apartheid. . . . KU should divest. Let's make the ideals really count for something." And then, during the commencement ceremony itself, two students, Ron Kuby and Laurie Hanley, unrolled a 28-foot banner, which read "KU Out of South Africa." The "S" in "South" resembled

Members of Latin American Solidarity oppose US involvement in Nicaragua and El Salvador during the 1980s.

a swastika. KU police confiscated the banner and arrested Kuby, who himself was graduating with Honors in anthropology, on charges of "interfering with the duties of a police officer" for refusing to take the banner down. Of course, Kuby's arrest violated his First Amendment right to free speech. "Who would care about what went on in South Africa?" Kuby recalled. "If we added the freedom of speech issue to the protest, we'd draw a lot more people. And that's what we did."[53]

In 1980, KUSA continued to agitate for a dialogue with KUEA about divestment. But there was little to talk about, since anti-apartheid protesters advocated total divestment, and KUEA stuck to its policy that although individual donors could declare whether or not their money should be invested in companies doing business in South Africa, KUEA as an entity would not divest. KUSA also suffered setbacks in the Student Senate, which defeated its resolution calling on the KUEA "to carry out its good works by divesting itself of holdings in corporations which support apartheid, and reinvesting the money in Kansas." Following the failure of talks with KUEA and defeats in the Student Senate, KUSA was frustrated by the end of the spring 1980 semester, and its members decided on a final protest before the summer break. Again, the site was Memorial Stadium during commencement.

A dozen protesters unrolled the same banner as in 1979, but as soon as the police arrived, the protesters unfurled a second banner, which read, "Help! We're Being Arrested!" The police arrested 12 of the protesters, but they did not arrest Ron Kuby; instead, they broke his wrist.[54]

Between 1980 and 1983, student interest in divestment flagged. But the issue was revived during Student Senate elections in the fall of 1983. During the campaign, the Costume Party, which ultimately won the election for president and vice president of the student body, asked the KUEA "to divest itself of any investments it may have in companies that do business in South Africa." When it took office in 1984, one of the first bills sponsored by the Costume Party called upon KUEA to divest. Similar versions of this bill had been defeated by the Student Senate in 1979 and 1980, but this time it passed. In March 1985, frustrated by continuing inaction by KU and the KUEA, the Student Senate passed still another resolution "strongly suggest[ing that] the KUEA . . . implement a plan for the divestment of its holdings . . . in the Republic of South Africa by September 30, 1985." Faculty, too, demanded "total divestment." In April, KU's University Council passed this resolution. Still, nothing changed. As one KUSA member told the *UDK*, "I feel like I've been playing the game as fairly as I know how. . . . I don't know what else students of the University can do to get the message across." But Boog Highberger, for one, did know. "Our next step," he recalled, "was disobedience."[55]

On Monday morning, April 29, 1985, and carrying only sleeping bags, toothbrushes, and a few books, Highberger, Carla Vogel, and two comrades walked into the Strong Hall rotunda. Once there, they hung a banner from the second-floor balcony: "KU Get Out of South Africa, South Africa equals Racism equals Apartheid." By late afternoon, the number of demonstrators had grown to 50; that night, 20 slept on the floor of the rotunda. For the next 11 days, the number of protesters ranged from 3 to almost 100. Students, faculty, and people from the community supported the protest by providing food and sleeping bags, and KU professors came to the rotunda to teach seminars on apartheid. On Friday, May 3, the demonstrators participated in an hour-long anti-apartheid rally in front of Strong Hall, featuring street theater, music, and speakers.[56]

At the conclusion of the rally at Strong Hall, some 45 people marched to the Youngberg Hall offices of the KUEA on West Campus. Two representatives were allowed inside the building, while the others waited outside. The two articulated the demonstrators' position to a KUEA vice president, and when they refused to leave, he conde-scendingly said, "Oh, come on kids." An hour passed before several other people entered the building. According to the police, "some of them burst inside and created quite a disturbance," and 16 protesters were handcuffed and arrested for criminal trespass. The students were frustrated, but on May 8, a letter arrived from former KUSA member Ron Kuby and the radical attorney William Kunstler, for whom Kuby worked in New York City. "It is gratifying to see," they wrote, "that once again, Kansans are living up to their long anti-racist history by plac-ing their liberty on the line to fight for the freedom of others." The letter "picked us up," Highberger recalled. And the next day, with re-newed enthusiasm, 150 demonstrators marched to Youngberg Hall to conduct a sit-in. At the hall, they were met by the police; 45 students were arrested, and 4 more were arrested at Strong Hall for briefly oc-cupying Chancellor Gene Budig's office. Nonviolence, on both sides, prevailed. "The march was fantastic!," one student wrote. "I was at the front of the line and it was so great just looking back and seeing all those people united for a cause and marching and chanting."[57]

During the sit-in at Strong Hall, Highberger started a "log book," in which he urged the demonstrators "to suggest ideas, discuss feelings & frustrations, draw pictures, write poetry." One wrote: "It is impossible for me to describe how my life has changed [because of the sit-in]. This is the feeling I've been waiting for all my life. . . . I feel so much love and kinship within this group of people." Still, despite the pro-testers' devoted feelings of community, the KUSA had accomplished little. The KUEA had made it clear that it would neither budge from its position opposing divestment nor open a dialogue with the students. For his part, Budig did not take the initiative in facilitating such a di-alogue, and his inaction added to the protesters' distrust of the KU administration. Perhaps most important, the academic year was almost over; and students and faculty alike soon would be dispersing in all directions.[58]

In August 1985, the anti-apartheid movement returned in full force. The KUSA issued three demands to the KUEA: to create "a representa-tive committee . . . to make recommendations on the social responsi-bility a university should have" in relation to the brutality of apartheid; to ask Chancellor Budig to clarify his position on divestment given the state of emergency declared in South Africa on July 21, 1985; and to demand that the KUEA Board of Trustees participate "in a public forum regarding its position where it can be analyzed, defended, and challenged." In August, the KUEA did invite one representative from

During the 1979 commencement, students Ron Kuby and Laurie Hanley unfurl a banner protesting KU's investments in South Africa.

KUSA to attend a meeting on divestiture. Jane Ungermann, the KUSA representative who attended the meeting, was displeased with the KUEA's total inflexibility. "Their purpose is to make money, and they don't care where it comes from. . . . They're not willing to give on this issue. We'll have to go back to the streets." The next day, the KUSA did just that, conducting a silent demonstration outside Hoch Auditorium during convocation. The demonstrators set up a box to represent a coffin and placed a bucket of 600 rocks next to it and a sign that read: "Join us. Place a pebble in the coffin in memory of another human being who has been killed in South Africa."[59]

In November, the KUSA reached out to new allies, Blacks Against Apartheid and KU Democrats, to stage an anti-apartheid rally in front of Stauffer-Flint Hall. Speakers denounced apartheid and demanded that the KUEA divest. Some were upset that Chancellor Budig had refused an invitation to speak to the rally. At one point, Aaron Lucas of Blacks Against Apartheid urged the protesters to "march over to Strong Hall. If the administration doesn't hear us over here, they'll hear us over there." Frustrated after months of protests and perhaps gripped by the passion of the moment, some 150 protesters stormed into Strong Hall; 50 squeezed into Chancellor Budig's suite and demanded to speak with him but were told that he was at the Med Center. Five demonstrators who refused to leave his suite were arrested. "We lost control," Lucas later acknowledged.[60]

The final KUSA protest began on March 17, 1986, when KUSA activist Chris Bunker pitched a pup tent outside Youngberg Hall and announced that he would remain there "indefinitely." Over the next 26 days, Bunker and other protesters camped outside Youngberg Hall. They erected a shanty as a symbol of the impoverished conditions in which black South Africans lived. "Camping at Youngberg is inconvenient," wrote one protester, "and sometimes wet and cold, but we have no choice." In addition, several times people harassed the protesters, including "a man wearing camouflage, a black beret and boots and with his face blackened [who] tried to kick down the shanty." The man ran away shouting, "Long live South Africa. Die Negroes." On the other hand, Nana L. Ngobse, a graduate student from South Africa, wrote the *UDK* urging students to enlist in the cause: "We shall appreciate all the help we can get. And remember, South Africa has a dream, too."[61]

On April 6, the KUSA held what was to be its final rally at Strong Hall; it then marched to Youngberg Hall, chanting, "KKK, UEA." Four days later, the KUEA announced that it had adopted a selective divestment policy. Campers at Youngberg ended their protest and, with it, KUSA itself. Despite the high ideals and courage of its members, the anti-apartheid movement had achieved limited success. But had it been worthwhile? Boog Highberger thought it had been. "The problem," he said, "was that we had an abstract goal coupled with a long chain of events. . . . Whatever the case, the university should be a laboratory for democracy. It must teach students about democracy."[62]

RACE AND RACISM ON CAMPUS:
THE CONTINUING STRUGGLE

In the late 1980s, the civil rights of African Americans and other minorities was a frequent issue on campus. In February 1988, for example, a journalism instructor arranged for an in-class interview with members of the Ku Klux Klan, and a journalism student arranged a radio interview with the same two Klansmen on KJHK. In response, black ministers from Lawrence and Kansas City, explaining that people of all races knew full well the hatred that the Klan would espouse, demanded that the visit and the radio show be cancelled. They were cancelled, but when the Klan threatened to sue the university, KU offered Hoch Auditorium for "a free speech forum with the Klan." On the evening of March 8, as 2,000 people entered Hoch for the forum,

Opponents of the Ku Klux Klan urge people to boycott the KKK Forum held at Hoch Auditorium in 1988.

another 2,500 people, including civil rights activists and black ministers and their parishioners, gathered outside Hoch. "Don't go in," they implored. Moreover, several months later, when the Klan announced plans to organize a "klavern" in Lawrence, a KU organization known as the Academic Freedom Action Coalition sponsored an anti-Klan rally outside of Stauffer-Flint. Several professors spoke. Two of the anti-Klan speakers later received death threats, and the office door of a third speaker was defaced with a swastika. But the Klan changed its plans and did not return to KU.[63]

And then, on March 30, 1990, Ann Dean, a KU student working for a local pizzeria, arrived at the Sigma Alpha Epsilon (SAE) fraternity house to deliver pizzas. It was 2 AM, when Dean, an African American, was confronted on the second floor of the house by an inebriated white man, who was an SAE pledge. He struck Dean's hand and knocked the pizzas to the floor; then he yelled a racial slur at her, using the "N" word, and threw one of the pizzas at her. Moreover, while she was leaving the SAE house, another fraternity member called her a "bitch" and said, "You deserved it." In the meantime, her car had been burglarized, and two pizzas, a soft drink, and a cassette tape had been stolen. Dean reported the assault to the police and met with detectives, but the drunken man was not arrested. As she explained later, "My rights as a human being were invaded, as well as my rights as a woman and a Black person, and I was just trying to do my job."[64]

Racial tensions on campus mounted as rumors of the assault spread. On Sunday morning, about 30 black students gathered in the front yard of the SAE house to protest not only Friday's incident but also the lack of an arrest. "White people get hurt, Black people go to jail," complained Mark McCormick, a junior. "Black people get hurt, nobody goes to jail." On Thursday evening, a forum in the Kansas Union, sponsored by the Black Men of Today, addressed the incident and KU's limited response to it. The implicated pledge still lived in the SAE house, and KU, arguing that this was an "off-campus incident," had not brought disciplinary charges against him or the fraternity. Ann Dean filed a nonacademic misconduct complaint with the Office of Student Life, but it produced no immediate results. And the Black Men of Today and their major ally, a group calling itself Students Concerned about Discrimination, were not satisfied when David Ambler, the vice chancellor for student affairs, explained the lack of an official response by stating, "There are no magic wands that will make people love each other, or respect each other. The only wand we have in the University is education." It appeared that, in the absence of disciplinary action, a major protest was in the offing.[65]

At noon on April 11, 70 students marched from Strong Hall to the SAE house. Once there, a get-well card stating that racism was "a social disease" was delivered to the chapter president. At 12:20, a slightly larger group marched into Strong Hall, chanting, "We want action" and demanding to see Chancellor Budig. Mark McCormick led 80 protesters to the second-floor administrative offices. "The reason for the protest is that we have no avenue for communication," McCormick said. "This is what we have to do to get an audience of administrators." Added Andrea Katzman, the organizer of Students Concerned about Discrimination, "We wouldn't be here if they had listened to our concerns." When the students were told that Chancellor Budig was at the KU Medical Center but would return to campus by 4:00, they said they would wait.[66]

When Budig returned, some 500 protesters awaited him. Eager to hear what he had to say, they filled the rotunda and lined the second-floor railing for what proved to be a nonviolent and productive rally. "Today," the chancellor said, "I offer the institution's apology to Ann Dean. I have asked the executive vice chancellor to take appropriate action." Under the glare of television lights, he apologized to students for the lack of communication about KU's plans to improve race relations on campus, including improving "the reception of the campus to minority recruitment, both faculty and student minority recruitment." The protesters were uplifted as they left Strong Hall. "The crowd was extremely cordial," stated Lawrence's chief of police, "and just wanted to exercise their right of free speech. It was a very, very good crowd."[67]

A LEGACY OF STUDENT ACTIVISM

From the demonstrations for African American civil rights, Black Power, and peace in Vietnam, to the demonstrations for women's and gay rights and divestment from South Africa, and from the mass 1965 and 1990 protests in Strong Hall to the passage of the Simply Equal amendment in 1995, the KU campus was the site of 30 years of political passion and activism. Observers are still surprised that such tumult roiled a university in Kansas, considered by many to be a staunchly conservative state. But the University of Kansas was—and is—a unique institution. During these years, political dreamers and freedom fighters alike came to Lawrence to live, study, and agitate for change. As a result, both KU and Lawrence became centers of new ideas and liberal and radical sentiments; and these were vital assets to KU's reputation as a university for students who want to learn about the larger world.

And what about the student activists themselves, those young women and men who became passionately engaged with the ideas, politics, and conflicts of the world in which they lived? Even today, many of these people are similarly engaged in bringing social and economic justice and political change to their communities and their nation. "The spirit of the sixties did not die as its bearers got older," two scholars have observed, "nor did they betray that spirit. Perhaps the spirit waits for a new opportunity that will permit the tide of collective action once more to rise."[68]

CHAPTER 7

A Seat at the Table

Student Leadership, Student Services, and the New Empowerment

KATHRYN NEMETH TUTTLE

R ISING costs are a primary issue in American higher education, yet in 2002 and the decade that followed, KU student leaders backed tuition increases and voted, several times, to raise student fees. In doing so, they upheld the legacy of having a student voice in university affairs and the decisions that affected them; they made a difference for their fellow students with important services; and they showed a willingness to pay more for the benefits accrued. Dallas Rakestraw, a political science major, co-chaired, with a KU faculty member, the Ad Hoc Committee on University Funding, which approved a substantial tuition increase in 2002. "In a lot of respects now they are getting a seat at the table," said Rakestraw, explaining students' acceptance of the tuition increases. "I'm a firm believer that whenever you empower someone, they become a lot more interested in the process and see the benefits."[1]

Student empowerment leading to university benefit through improved services and policies and a healthier and safer campus is a key theme of the last 50 years at the University of Kansas. Generations of student activists took action, and as Baby Boomers, Gen Xers, and Millennials, they have left a mark on the quality of student experiences and the campus as a whole. First, KU women students, although initially hesitant to challenge restrictions placed on their behavior, dramatically transformed opportunities for the entire campus. Next, the creation of the Student Senate empowered students and allowed them to not only shape university governance but also strategically use student fees to improve campus life. Beginning in the 1960s, KU students stepped forward countless times to create and fund needed services, and students played a unique and crucial role in tuition decisions. Although in general less likely to hold demonstrations than were other student activists, their actions were equally successful in improving student life. Student services also grew dramatically during this era, evolving to support students with their everyday concerns as well as their futures in times of rapid change. As such, today's students exemplify a new activism reflective of their ongoing passion to improve the campus, the community, and the world beyond.

"PRODUCE AS MANY AUTONOMOUS ADULTS AS WE CAN": THE WOMEN WHO CHANGED KU

Unlike Strong Hall protesters in 1965, discussed in the previous chapter, few KU women students publicly opposed the parietal restrictions that controlled where they lived, when they could leave and return to their residence halls, scholarship halls, and sororities, and when, and if, they could fraternize with men. Parents and the Kansas public expected the university to act in loco parentis. Traditional regulations, which controlled student behavior through rules imposed on women, arose during an era when sexuality was supposed to be constrained and women's virtue upheld. Such constraints were thought to lead to self-regulation. At KU, the Associated Women Students (AWS), founded in 1947, established "rules and regulations to govern the lives of young women that will help them to govern themselves."[2]

But the goal of Emily Taylor, KU's forward-thinking dean of women, was to move beyond self-governance to self-determination, and, according to biographer Kelly Sartorius, it was "Dean Emily" who pushed women students to challenge restrictions on their freedom. Taylor championed equal rights for women students not only at KU but nationally as well; in 1958, she established the first Commission on the Status of Women on a university campus. In 1960, KU was the first university in the nation to adopt a house-key policy, which gave senior women the right to come and go freely to their residences. AWS cautiously approved the Senior Privilege Plan but required parental approval, attendance at an orientation session, and

Dr. Emily Taylor, who served as dean of women at KU from 1956 until 1975, and Associated Women Students president Anne Peterson Hyde.

obedience to a detailed set of regulations. The rules were shrouded in concerns about women's safety but motivated by fears about damage to reputations.[3]

At the same time, some KU women flaunted these regulations by staying out whenever it suited them. Anne Ritter, AWS Senate president when the Senior Plan was adopted, recalled late-night trips with Dean Taylor to residences where they found half the women absent, despite records indicating they were in their rooms. But the senior house-key plan was successful, and in 1962 Taylor recommended ending closing hours for all women except freshmen. This was a step too

Associated Women Students officer candidates, spring 1969.

far, however, for the self-regulating AWS, a cautious KU administration, and parents who were not ready for the university to stop representing their interests.[4]

However, by 1966 some women students, chafing under existing
restrictions, took a strong stand to expand their autonomy. "Liberaliza-
tion of rules to allow coeds to become responsible women is a national
trend and if KU is to continue to attract intelligent, mature women, we
cannot continue to cloister them as damsels potentially in distress," declared Jacke Thayer, *UDK* editorial page editor, openly chastising her
less-progressive sisters prior to the biennial AWS Rules Convention.
"If sweeping changes are not made, the blame will rest solely with the
apathy of campus coeds and the 19th century mentality of AWS house
members and convention delegates."[5] Other groups joined the fight;
the Civil Rights Council, Students for a Democratic Society (SDS), and
other groups met with Provost James Surface to challenge the university's in loco parentis role controlling students', especially women
students', private lives. While the national SDS focused on the Vietnam War, the KU chapter, formed in the fall of 1965, initially took on

university control of students' nonacademic lives, including social and personal control of KU women students.[6]

The AWS Rules Convention of March 1966 featured a debate among three factions: a progressive group, primarily of scholarship hall students; a more conservative group of sorority women concerned about standards and reputations; and a third group that focused on the safety of women students. For the first time, women students living off campus, as well as married women students, participated in the conversation and added a broader perspective. The contentious debate continued into a second weekend, when the women finally voted to end hours for seniors, juniors, and second-semester sophomores. As parental letters of protest arguing for restraint rather than indulgence flooded into Chancellor W. Clarke Wescoe's office, a behind-the-scenes compromise quietly removed the new freedoms for sophomore women. After a semester-long debate, Wescoe ended restrictions only for seniors (who already had keys) and juniors; freshmen and sophomore women still had closing hours of 11:30 PM during the week and 1:00 AM on weekends.[7]

Although the struggle continued over the next two years, the limited changes of 1966 altered the battle for women's freedom. Author Sara Paretsky voted as a KU undergraduate at the AWS convention and challenged the group to become more relevant to contemporary women by focusing on their work rather than their social lives. She accused the university of maintaining the gender restrictions that women students had at home rather than encouraging their development as mature equals. And in 1968, a *UDK* editorial title proclaimed, "Women Still Chained."[8]

Freshman women heard the chains rattling. While AWS surveys reported only a small percentage of freshman women in favor of extending open hours to entering students, an informal survey of first-year women at Ellsworth Hall found otherwise: 75 percent favored ending restrictions. In 1968, the rules caught up with reality when sophomore closing hours were ended and juniors earned the right to live off campus. McCollum Hall women successfully petitioned to wear casual clothes to dinner and to expand visiting hours to members of the opposite sex.[9]

By the next year, KU women students challenged the authority of the AWS to set standards of any kind for them. All Student Council (soon to become the Student Senate) vice presidential candidate Marilyn Bowman championed a proposal to have some "open" and some "closed" halls, which the university would adopt for incoming freshmen. "The history of past attempts to help women," Bowman stated, "has taught us that protectionism is not satisfying, doesn't lead to intellectual or emotional maturity, and, in fact, is too often a thinly veiled excuse for paternalism and control." Finally freshman women were liberated from closing hours in the fall of 1969, apparently making KU one of the first universities in the country to extend these rights to all women students. Compared to the tumult in 1966, the final barrier falling made hardly a sound.

Emily Taylor's leadership was key to this process, and her view prevailed in the end: "Relaxing parental rules removed a windmill to fight. We could pay attention to the larger issue—sex discrimination. I believe in equality and our sole function is to produce as many autonomous adults as we can."[10] She created AWS committees that focused on equity and academics, and she challenged women students to develop their confidence and intellectual capabilities.[11] In 1970, Taylor founded a resource and career-planning center, which became the Emily Taylor Women's Resource Center in 1977 and is now the Emily Taylor Center for Women and Gender Equity.[12]

The end of parietal restraints and the growing women's movement challenged the sexual order in many ways. In a 1964 AWS survey, 91 percent of senior women had agreed that sexual intercourse for couples that were not engaged was unacceptable, and 83 percent said it was wrong even for engaged couples. By the end of the decade, most students deemed these judgments obsolete. For this transformation to occur, battles were fought on many fronts, starting with the basic issue of reproductive freedom. In 1960, the Food and Drug Administration approved oral contraceptives, the "Pill." In 1963, the Kansas legislature authorized distribution of contraceptive information and services to married women over 18 and to any woman referred by a physician. In 1965, the federal government initiated funding for family planning services. But Dr. Raymond Schwegler, director of KU's student health services at Watkins Memorial Hospital, would have none of it. In a 1966 forum, Schwegler announced that Watkins would not provide contraceptives to unmarried KU students "under any circumstances" nor "contribute to the recreational activities of the campus." Following this, many negative letters, primarily from men and a few married women, appeared in the *UDK* challenging Schwegler's and the university's right to control student morality and decision making. Finally, in 1967, in a letter to the *UDK*, an unmarried woman student declared her own sexual freedom and her right to take the Pill, but she was allowed to remain anonymous, despite paper policy. She was a symbol

Daisy Hill residence halls on the western edge of the main campus, built in the early 1960s.

of both the continuing protection of a female student's reputation and the recognition that an increasing number of unmarried students were having sex and using the Pill.[13]

But where were KU women getting their contraceptives? Dr. Dale Clinton, director of the Lawrence–Douglas County Health Department, was an early proponent of birth control due to concerns about the population explosion. Clinton set up a birth control clinic at the health department in 1966, where he freely distributed the Pill to KU students without a physical exam. Although controversial, Clinton's impact on students' access to birth control was substantial. By 1971, the health department reported serving over 8,500 birth control clients, and it is likely that most were KU students. In addition, the Dean of Women's Office expanded birth control information, and Taylor declared that contraception was an issue of "personal control over reproduction." When another major provider, the Douglas County Family Planning Association, closed in 1970, KU women students became increasingly frustrated that birth control and gynecological services were unavailable at Watkins, the campus health center funded by student fees. It would take dramatic action by women, including the takeover of a university building in 1972, for KU and Schwegler to change the policy on the distribution of birth control to unmarried women students.[14]

When Robin Morgan, a poet and noted feminist activist, spoke at the Kansas Union Ballroom on February 2, 1972, few knew her talk would galvanize a group of KU women, who came to be known as the February Sisters, to occupy a campus building. Even more remarkable, the demands of the February Sisters and resulting KU policy changes transformed rights, education, services, and leadership for women, as well as for the university as a whole. And just as in the 1965 Strong Hall sit-in, the demands made were well-reasoned arguments grounded in the facts of injustice and the university's failure to take action despite federal mandates.

Concerns about women's rights at KU had been growing for some time. Among female faculty and staff members, Committee W (for Women) of the American Association of University Professors was a focal point for discussion of key issues. Its May 1971 report found that the top salary of a female full professor at KU was $17,999 while the top male professor earned $31,999 ($100,000 and $178,300, respectively, in 2013 dollars). It also pointed to significant discrepancies in salaries, with the average salary for women faculty members $2,000 ($11,000 in 2013 dollars) less than that for men. In addition, a study by the Commission on the Status of Women on employment and salary issues found that only 10.8 percent of all faculty members were women and that there were no female academic deans, directors, vice chancellors, or members of the Board of Regents.[15]

The Women's Coalition, formed in the spring of 1970, formulated a more radical approach. By that fall, the group's office in the Wesley Foundation building, across from the Kansas Union, was functioning as a de facto women's center, providing information on birth control and abortion, rape counseling, self-defense, and issues for gay students. While the Women's Coalition and Commission on the Status of Women often disagreed on strategy and tactics, they agreed that equity issues for KU women had reached a critical stage. Moreover, student funding for the Women's Coalition was funneled through the more mainstream Commission on the Status of Women.[16]

Robin Morgan's talk did not call for a building takeover, but it did bring together a large number of women with similar concerns—not only over reproductive rights but also over affirmative action related to hiring practices, demands for a women's studies department, and discrepancies in scholarships for and recruitment of women students. At the end of her talk, Morgan asked the 100 men in the audience of 350 to leave, and she then held a closed-door meeting with the remaining women. Many of the women shared their anger about the lack of child care and women's health services and pay disparities. Committee W met the next day and expressed its dissatisfaction with the lack of an affirmative action program and characterized the university's attitude as one of "delay" and "indifference." Later that day, as many as 100 women staff and faculty, faculty wives, and graduate and undergraduate students met in the Wesley building to discuss a plan of action.[17]

On the evening of February 4, twenty women and four of their children took over the East Asian Studies building at 1332 Louisiana Street. The women arrived with food and sleeping bags and chained the doors shut. The building was chosen both because of its "potential suitability" as a day care center and because one of the women involved had a key. They called themselves the "February Sisters," and flyers with demands were posted around campus. They called for an affirmative action program; a day care center; a woman to fill the vacant vice chancellor of academic affairs position; the end of unfair employment practices; a women's studies department; and a women's health program that would include ready access to birth control.[18]

Chancellor Chalmers, notified of the takeover at his bridge party, initially ignored the news. Chalmers had spent most of his first two years in office dealing with public reaction to campus demonstrations, the Union burning, and the killing of two KU students. He later called in Dean Emily Taylor for assistance. She added five women, including Marilyn Stokstad, professor and chair of art history, and Elizabeth Banks, associate professor of classics, to her negotiation team and sent Professor Banks to the East Asian Studies building. Meetings between five of the February Sisters and the chancellor, with a group that included the Senate Executive Committee, the dean of women, and the university attorney, lasted throughout the night, as did consultations with the rest of the occupiers. Finally, the Senate Executive Committee issued a resolution supporting a day care center and women's health program. The women left the East Asian Studies building before 9:00 in the morning and mingled with 60 women who had rallied at the entrance, thus preventing identification of the occupiers and possible expulsion from the university or loss of jobs. A press release issued that day described the February Sisters' actions as "non-violent, non-destructive and carried out with the specific intention of showing

Children at Hilltop Child Care Center in 1973, one of the key demands of the February Sisters.

our strength and solidarity, and of drawing public attention to our pressing needs."[19]

In both public pronouncements and private discussions, Chalmers's reaction to the February Sisters takeover and demands was less enlightened than his response to the 1970 antiwar demonstrations. He called the seizure of the building "irregular and counterproductive," and some of the negotiators characterized him as angry and unwilling to compromise. He ordered that electricity and water to the building be shut off, and he implied that some of the demands, such as a child care center, were already being addressed. In fact, KU had delayed responding to federal requirements to create a written affirmative action plan for the extension of Title VII to employees of educational institutions. Throughout the previous year, Chalmers's response to the federal mandate had been to ask male administrators in Student Affairs, Minority Affairs, and his office to develop the plan, with virtually no input from women faculty, students, or administrators, including Dean Taylor. "Universities throughout the U.S. are and always have been male dominated, and the University of Kansas is no exception," stated Taylor in her support of the February Sisters' actions. "All concerned women are asking for is concrete evidence of good faith intentions on the part of the university to correct the inequities that so glaringly exist."[20]

KU did respond to most of the February Sisters' demands. Watkins started to prescribe birth control pills for unmarried women students and to provide gynecological services, although complaints about moralistic attitudes from the health center administration and providers continued until Dr. Schwegler retired. Hilltop Child Care (now Development) Center opened in August 1972 in the old Wesley Foundation building, site of the de facto women's center, with spots for 50 children. The Women's Studies Program and the first special major in Women's Studies started in the fall of 1972, with Professor Janet Sharistanian of the English Department serving as the first program director. On February 16, Chalmers appointed an Affirmative Action Board with a woman as chair and a February Sister as a member, but the final plan was not issued until over a year later. Marilyn Stokstad became the first female associate dean in the College, and Shirley Gilham Domer was hired as the first affirmative action officer in 1972. In 1978, Frances Horowitz was named vice chancellor for research and graduate studies, and in 1981, Deanell Tacha became vice chancellor for academic affairs. Robin Morgan was invited back to speak at the 20-year celebration of the February Sisters' actions. Angela Davis spoke at the 40th anniversary in 2012, as did some of the original February Sisters, who reminisced about the occupation and reflected on a KU where the chancellor is a woman, as are several academic deans.[21]

The support for the February Sisters' actions was widespread among KU women. Joan Handley, the chair of the Commission on the Status of Women, bemoaned the administration's failure to respond and applauded "the courage of the women who . . . achieved something others were not able to achieve by working within the system." And in their own 1973 progress report, the February Sisters affirmed: "We have made the unacceptability of our situation . . . known. We have identified problems and suggested directions toward solutions. . . . The laws are, in general, on our side and anyone of us or two or five or fifty can, if we are willing to make the effort, force the university community to treat us as human beings."[22]

The women's movement also changed the way the campus viewed other gender issues related to safety and health, including sexual assault and abortion. Women's safety was a longtime KU concern and for years had been used as a common justification for restricting women students' freedom. But the women's movement opened frank discussion of a harsh reality—sexual assault. As early as 1965, the *UDK* expressed concern about lighting on campus; a student request for lighting made in 1968 was turned down by the administration allegedly due to higher priorities, such as putting in new sidewalks and landscaping.[23]

Dark streets and walkways provided a haven for rapists, and, alarmingly, the number of reported rapes in Lawrence surged from 4 in 1970 to 26 in 1972. That fall, a group of women founded Rape Victim Support Services (RVSS, later called Douglas County Rape Victim/Survivor Services and today known as GaDuGi SafeCenter) for both the Lawrence and the KU communities. The initial purpose was not only to provide support to victims/survivors of sexual violence, but also to change the way law enforcement, medical providers, and the courts responded. The Dean of Women's Office played a role in education and advocacy as well, by providing rape kit workshops for police officers and medical personnel.[24]

Women took action to remind the entire campus about sexual assault with the Whistlestop campaign in 1974, which provided women students with a handy tool for protection. The yellow plastic whistles would serve not only "as obvious distress signals," said Casey Eike, assistant to the dean of women, but also "as a symbol of women standing together against assaults and as a reminder that there is a danger in walking alone. We want to show that women are tired of assaults and are willing to take action together in some program to stop them." It did not please some in the university community that 5,000 whistles, as well as bumper stickers and posters, would so publicly sound the alarm about sexual assault on campus. A *UDK* editorial decried the "rape hysteria," and the director of admissions expressed concerns about loss of enrollment. Kala Stroup, then the assistant dean of women and KU's last dean of women, recalled that this advocacy nearly cost Dean Emily Taylor and her their jobs: "The whistle campaign was a three-year affair, and it was building awareness around rape, first for women, then to campus, and then the faculty . . . [that] there's such a thing as date rape . . . and women getting attacked on campus." Many, including some from the Alumni Association, thought this was, according to Stroup, "giving KU a bad name, but we were encouraging everyone, especially women, to be concerned." The Student Senate created a Rape Prevention Task Force that recommended improved lighting, campus patrols, and security phones. The concern about security led to the

A women's rights demonstration with an anti-abortion protester, 1980s.

establishment of the blue emergency phone system that connects directly to the KU Office of Public Safety.[25]

Other demands for women's rights made the news at KU: the *UDK* ran a front-page story on the nightmare of illegal abortions in 1967, and two years later the newspaper described a raid on an abortion provider in Kansas City that involved two women believed to be KU students. California and Colorado legalized abortion that year, and in 1970 Kansas authorized abortions, with three licensed physicians approving, to prevent damage to the mother's physical or mental health.

Conversely, anti-abortion vigils, which were first held on campus in September 1971, would continue for the next 40 years. A *UDK* article in 1972 reported that Watkins Health Center was treating fewer illegal abortions. With the 1973 Supreme Court decision in *Roe v. Wade* legalizing abortion, the nature of concerns about abortion changed and the anti-abortion protests intensified. Whether abortions were to be performed at the KU Medical Center was a frequent topic during political debates in the 1980s and 1990s. Graphic abortion displays on the lawn in front of Strong and Stauffer-Flint Halls became annual points of contention and distress from the 1990s to the present. Anti-abortion and pro-choice student groups continue to make their voices heard on campus.[26]

Concerns about sexual assault grew in the 1990s with passage of the federal Cleary Act, which required reporting of sexual assaults on campus and in the nearby community, as well as the Supreme Court confirmation hearings for Clarence Thomas, featuring Anita Hill's dramatic charges of sexual harassment. In 1991, KU charged a Law School professor with demanding sex for grades from a female student; the details came out in public hearings and he was dismissed for moral turpitude a year later. At the same time, women students, echoing the Whistlestop campaign from 20 years earlier, blew their whistles in front of Wescoe Hall every 15 seconds to mark the frequency of sexual assault in the United States. Yet again, direct action by KU women students forced a change in university policy: by the spring of 1993, KU had a new sexual harassment policy, as well as one on consenting relationships, which focused on the power differential between faculty and student and supervisor and employee.[27]

Students, persistent in addressing safety concerns, funded expanded campus lighting in 1997 with a new student Campus Safety fee that continues to this day. Elise Higgins, community affairs director for Student Senate, championed the creation of a lighted pedestrian pathway between campus and downtown Lawrence in 2009. The next year, the Campus Safety Advisory Board allocated $100,000 of student fees toward the project, which was completed along Twelfth Street. In 2011, the US Office of Civil Rights, responding to student charges of failure to enforce Title IX at campuses across the country, issued new guidelines for handling sexual assault. These guidelines became components of KU's sexual harassment policies, administered by the Office of Institutional Opportunity and Access, in conjunction with Public Safety, the Emily Taylor Center for Women and Gender Equity, and, in the case of students, Student Affairs. New students, as well as faculty and staff, are required to complete online training on sexual harassment and sexual violence. New sanctions for noncompliance were added in the fall of 2014. But nationwide and at KU, outrage was widespread; students rallied at the US Department of Education in 2013 to demand stricter enforcement of federal laws on sexual violence on campuses. In 2014, the US Department of Education's Office of Civil Rights made public its Title IX investigation of 76 higher education institutions, including KU, for sexual violence and harassment complaints. KU student anger grew in the fall of 2014 over the university's handling of an alleged rape case and the lenient punishment of the perpetrator. A group called the September Siblings formed, proclaiming their link to the February Sisters and their historic fight for equal rights for women. Like their predecessors, the September Siblings issued a list of demands, including providing victim advocates, revising sexual assault policies and punishments, and creating an investigative committee with a majority student membership. The name of the group signaled the activism of both male and female students on this issue. The group's use of social media and a digital protest, including an "anti-recruitment" video and website, demonstrated advanced communication capabilities and results. "I fully believe that's the one thing we are doing right," said Angela Murphy, the KU graduate student designated by Chancellor Gray-Little to co-chair a new sexual assault task force, that is, "students mobilizing to affect positive change at the University."[28]

"A RADICAL THING EVEN BERKELEY AND COLUMBIA DON'T HAVE": KU'S STUDENT SENATE

The civil rights and antiwar protests of the 1960s and 1970s radically changed campuses across the nation, specifically by expanding students' legal rights. Student demands for free speech, including free press rights; due process; the rights to protest, demonstrate, and organize; access to their own educational records; and taking an active role in institutional governance, led to a rights revolution at KU and across the country. The civil rights movement provided the pivotal Supreme Court cases that established students' rights to protest on campus. Responding to these legal changes, the American Association of University Professors, the National Association of Student Personnel Administrators, and other groups issued a "Joint Statement on Student Rights and Freedoms" in 1967. The statement recognized student rights to "free inquiry and free expression" as members of a "community of scholars." KU's current Code of Student Rights and Responsibilities, the Senate Code, and the Student Senate's existence and authority extend directly from these Supreme Court decisions and the Student Rights and Freedoms declaration.[29]

The struggle for KU students' role in institutional governance has a long history. In 1943, KU students voted to unite the Men's Student Council and the Women's Student Government Association into the All Student Council (ASC). This action was, in part, a rejoinder to Chancellor Deane W. Malott's decrees on holiday breaks, student press rights, and, most important, the student activity fee, without seeking input from students. For years, students involved with campus leadership complained that ASC bills were vulnerable to rejection by the Council on Student Affairs, made up of administrators, faculty, and nonelected students, and to veto by the chancellor. By the spring of 1967, student demands to have a say in the university decisions affecting them produced a demonstration of 400 in front of Strong Hall; the following year, the number in a similar protest almost quadrupled, to 1,500. A student organization calling itself Voice (later named Student Voice and then Peoples Voice) organized the 1968 protest. "It is clear that students do not have and are not intended to have an effective voice on all those matters affecting their lives," wrote the members of Voice in a letter to the chancellor. Acting provost Francis Heller riled students at a forum that spring by describing students as "transients" and stating that it was "exceedingly difficult to fit into the University decisions the contributions of individuals whose commitment is of a passing nature."[30]

Heller's comments ignited a firestorm of response from Voice and other students. Voice demanded that Wescoe "publically repudiate" Heller's comments, end his veto power over ASC decisions, and support 50 percent student representation on committees dealing with student affairs. Within two days, over 1,700 students had signed the letter with these demands. Wescoe responded with a refusal to repudiate Heller's remarks, a downplaying of his veto power, and an assertion that the university did in fact value student opinions. Not appeased, Voice threatened a Strong Hall sit-in for Monday, May 6, 1968. On Sunday, student body president Clif Conrad, who had expressed modest support of Voice demands, and leaders of the University Senate gathered for an emergency meeting to forestall the protest. Out of these meetings came the ASC-recommended proposal for a Student

Voice leader Hamilton Salsich, KU graduate student, addresses a crowd on campus during debates about student rights and university governance in 1968.

Faculty Committee on Governance—composed of six students, four from ASC and two from Voice, and six faculty members—to create a way to give students voting membership in the University Senate and more input on university affairs and issues that affected their lives.[31]

The joint committee met diligently throughout the summer of 1968. Ambrose Saricks, professor of history and Senate Executive Committee chair, and Conrad co-chaired the group; Charles Oldfather, professor of law and university attorney, took primary responsibility for crafting the new Senate Code. The Student Faculty Governance Committee final report made sweeping recommendations that led to profound and long-lasting reform of the governance structure at the University of Kansas. The committee stated the premise of its work clearly: "Students should have an effective voice in all decisions of the university which directly and substantially affect them." They called for abolition of the ASC and the creation of a Student Senate with representation based on the academic units of the College and Schools, as opposed to living groups. A new University Senate included all members of the Faculty Senate and the Student Senate, and the University Council, which functioned as the governing and policy-making unit, included 13 students. The Senate Executive Committee added three students, with a student to be named as vice chair. Importantly, students were added to most University Senate committees, including Academic Policies and Procedures. Shared governance was born at the University of Kansas, and in 1968 KU students wielded greater authority than at any other university in the United States. "This is a very radical thing—something which even Berkeley and Columbia don't have," explained student body vice president Joe Goering.[32]

Despite a dissenting report from Voice members who wanted more student representation, the *UDK* spoke out in favor of the majority proposal, and by February 1969 both the University Senate and the ASC had approved the new Senate Code, readying it for a student referendum. A whopping 94 percent of the 2,444 students voting favored the new Senate Code, which soon won the approval of Chancellor Wescoe and the Board of Regents. The effect of the code was seen immediately when a student was named to the chancellor's search committee for the first time and schools and departments added students to their committees, based on the code's policy of 20 percent student representation. The Senate Code laid the foundation for KU student activism for decades to come and even in the short term may have forestalled a more turbulent future for KU. "In my opinion, the reason K.U. 'weathered' the Vietnam era as well as it did was the opportunity

Ballot boxes for a Student Senate election, 1987.

for students, faculty, and staff to participate in the decision-making process," wrote Chancellor E. Laurence Chalmers more than a decade after he left KU. And a university press release extolled "the most progressive University governmental innovation in the nation." As the 1969 *Jayhawker* yearbook described it, "The new Senate Code is . . . symbolic of a quiet revolution. . . . [It] provides the mechanisms by which students may participate in deciding the goals, operations, and purposes of the university."[33]

With the new Student Senate meeting for the first time in the fall of 1969, the race for student body president and vice president was hotly contested that spring. Coalitions formed and reformed, and candidates stepped forward and withdrew at a dizzying pace. The *UDK* endorsed the Independent Student Party and candidates David Awbrey and Marilyn Bowman because they exhibited the "energy" to "make the Senate Code work" and were the best option to make the new Student Senate a "force" in the university. There was a record turnout of 30 percent of the student body for the April 1969 elections, and Awbrey and Bowman won by a slim margin of 106 votes. The Independent Student Party, which had taken on the progressive concerns of Voice, won a total of 26 seats of the 67 in the Student Senate, double the number of any other party.[34]

Chancellor Chalmers (center) with the newly elected Student Senate president and vice president, David Awbrey and Marilyn Bowman, in 1969.

When the Student Senate met on September 18, 1969, its first order of business was to elect a new vice president, as the university had suspended Bowman for her participation in the ROTC Review protest. An attempt to impeach her in May had failed, and it was only the beginning for the Senate's turbulent first year. Nevertheless, the initial year was a resounding success on two fronts: the Student Senate gained financial control over the entire student fee (previously it had control over about 40 percent of the total), and it passed the Code of Student Rights, Responsibilities, and Conduct. This code, which was largely a response to treatment of students in the ROTC protest, focused on confidentiality of student records and disciplining of students, especially related to nonacademic conduct.[35]

The control of student fees and the Code of Student Rights, Responsibilities, and Conduct continue to be the basis for a strong student voice at KU. But some observers are questioning whether the student voice at KU today is heard in the same way as when the Senate Code was enacted; the 20 percent student representation on university committees is still in effect, although recent administrative decisions have weakened student input, especially on search committees.

A Student Senate meeting in 1981.

Senate elections frequently faced challenges as well, including the removal of Darren Fulcher, the first African American elected Senate president, in 1991. The Senate voted to impeach Fulcher due to a charge of misdemeanor battery against his then-girlfriend. Fulcher had entered a diversion agreement that required him to remain silent about the incident before he was elected. The Judicial Board upheld the Student Senate's action, and Vice President Alan Lowden took office in December. Vice Chancellor David Ambler understood the complexities of the issue and had a good relationship with Fulcher, so it was difficult for him to stay neutral. Fulcher's removal received attention by the national media, but the administration let the Student Senate have the final say. Today, Fulcher is an attorney in Kansas City. KU students elected two more African Americans in the next decade—Justin Mills in 2001 and Michael Wade Smith in 2010.[36]

Campaign infractions rocked the 2014 campaigns with the disqualification of the Jayhawkers coalition, due to campaign finance violations, and the University Judicial Board Appeals Panel requirement of a second election. A challenging year of governing followed; nevertheless, for the first time since the World War II era, two women led the Student Senate—Morgan Said and Miranda Wagner. They presided in recently renovated chambers in the Kansas Union that feature a plaque affirming the Student Senate's unique legacy.[37]

"BINDING US TOGETHER":
STUDENT AFFAIRS AND STUDENT SERVICES

Student protests and the death of in loco parentis led to dramatic changes in the functioning of student affairs and the organization of student services. But it was another 1960s explosion, in college student enrollment, that expanded the bureaucracy of the university and student services. Prior to 1965, KU organized student services through the Dean of Men and Dean of Women's Offices, as well as Admissions and Records, Housing, Health Services, Aids and Awards, and the Union. Laurence C. Woodruff, dean of students from 1953 to 1967, coordinated the various offices and programs through the Student Personnel Council. Created in the enrollment surge, Aids and Awards became the Office of Student Financial Aid in 1965, and total aid grew from $750,000 in 1962 to $4 million by 1970. This increase reflected not only skyrocketing enrollment but also federal financial aid programs launched by the Higher Education Act of 1965.[38]

Enrollment growth necessitated more student housing at KU. The most significant increase, spurred on by the availability of financing through the federal Housing Act of 1950, occurred from 1955 through 1966 with the addition of nine residence halls. By 1966, almost one-third (4,818 of 14,892) of all KU students lived in residence and scholarship halls, and fraternities and sororities added another 17 percent. In 2012, by comparison, 20 percent of KU students lived in university housing while 80 percent lived off-campus.[39]

Coeducational residence halls were a symbol of the 1960s surge and, some argued, signs of the sexual revolution and push for gender equity. McCollum opened as a coed hall in 1964 and separated sexes by wings and floors; various controversies ensued, including complaints about "hanky panky" in public areas and the calling for crackdowns on "public displays of affection." But the move to more coed halls was inevitable: by 1966, with Ellsworth, Hashinger, and Oliver joining the list, half of the students living in university housing were in coed residence halls. A 1972 survey of American Association of Universities institutions found that 90 percent had coed halls. Many students and student affairs professionals argued that coeducational living created greater gender equity and more friendships based on individuals, not on gender roles based on conventional expectations. McCollum Hall was a "successful experiment . . . [and the] intermingling of sexes has resulted in building of spirit and hall unity," declared an assistant dean of men. By the fall of 2012, only one hall, Corbin, remained single-sex (for women), while all other residence halls were coed.[40]

The Greek system was another form of housing, although not all students could participate. The 1965 Strong Hall protest highlighted discrimination by fraternities and sororities through exclusionary clauses in their charters that kept Greek houses white and largely Christian. But by the fall of 1965, the Kansas Board of Regents had passed a new policy meeting Civil Rights Council demands, which required all student organizations to confirm that they did not select or reject members on the basis of race, religious faith, or national origin and that there were no local or national restrictions on membership. All KU fraternities and sororities had to sign the document, but Civil Rights Council surveys done with fraternity members that fall described an attitude of resentment against the idea of forced integration.[41]

In 1978, a report on fraternity discrimination, precipitated by the rejection of an African American honors student from Junction City during sorority rush, showed painfully slow progress; from 1969 to 1977, only 5 of the 23 white fraternities had offered bids to African Americans. With new initiatives, which included outreach to students and working with individual fraternities, the number doubled to 10 the following year. The report also discussed black fraternities increasing their recruitment of white men. "After the first prestigious fraternity pledges a Black student, the issue will be all but dead," the report optimistically noted. At that time, Beta Theta Pi, one of KU's top fraternities, had no minority membership, which for purposes of the study included Jewish students as well as students of color. Slow progress in diversifying the system has characterized the last several decades. In 1993, Greeks for Responsible Education Enhancing Cultural Sensitivity brought together Black Panhellenic, Black Student Union, Panhellenic, and Interfraternity Council representatives to create better communication, and a KUnity leadership retreat continued this effort.[42]

Still, contributions by members of the Greek community are evident. Since 1990, Rock Chalk Revue, which pairs fraternities and sororities in original musical productions, has raised over $1 million and contributed over 25,000 hours of community service. The Greek system typically produces many of KU's student leaders, and members of fraternities and sororities maintain higher grade-point averages and

A chorus line during the Rock Chalk Revue in 1977.

retention rates than the average for KU undergraduates as a whole. Membership in the Greek system has remained stable in recent years: including black fraternities and sororities and other multicultural Greek organizations, KU has 45 Greek organizations with over 3,000 members, about a sixth of the undergraduate population. Student Affairs administrators and the Greek community initiated a Community Standards program in 2007; chapters are required to educate all members in key areas of concern, including diversity, hazing, sexism and sexual assault, and alcohol and drug use. These continue to be major issues for both the Greek community and the university as a whole. In 2014, KU dedicated a Divine Nine Room in the Kansas Union that honors historically black Greek letter organizations. Fraternities and sororities have been a continuing presence in student life, presenting ongoing challenges with equity and inclusion, as well as the individual difficulties and accomplishments of maturing undergraduates.[43]

In the 1990s, the Department of Student Housing, responding to changing student expectations, began the renovation of Templin and Lewis residence halls on Daisy Hill to two- and four-person suites. New academic resource centers were added, and students praised the halls as being more comfortable and homelike. Similar renovations of Ellsworth, Hashinger, and Gertrude S. Pearson followed from 2004 to 2012.[44] Four new scholarship halls—KK Amini, Margaret Amini, Rieger, and Krehbiel—added 200 spots for high-ability students, including those with financial need, from 1997 to 2008. The decision to build Rieger Hall on historic Ohio Street and tear down existing homes angered the community, and KU realized it had to work directly with the Oread neighborhood in the design of the new hall. "It is a beautiful building. It looks like, in some sense, it's been there forever," said Jeffrey Weinberg, assistant to the chancellor, about the Queen Anne–style residence hall. He quoted one formerly angry protester as saying, "This is a stunning building, and I think it's going to enhance the neighborhood."[45]

Two student services offices were created directly in response to the changed environment created by student protests. The University Information Center, or KU Info as it is known today, started as a rumor control center in the turbulent spring of 1970, functioning out of the Dean of Women's Office. Students approached the office about a rumor control number; an office phone line, 864-3506, was offered and continues as KU's most-remembered phone number. Student volunteers immediately answered questions such as, "Is the National Guard coming?" It became a separate office in July 1970, just as the campus and the community had experienced the killings of two students and a citywide curfew. KU Info evolved into a more general information service by the end of the decade but remains a unique student service nationally.[46]

When African American students formed the Black Student Union (BSU) in 1970 and presented a list of demands to Chancellor Chalmers, they called for a new office to promote the recruitment and retention of minority and low-income students. The university's initial response was to fund tutoring and remedial courses and to hire an assistant to the chancellor for urban affairs. The BSU submitted additional demands that eventually resulted in the hiring of 17 African American faculty members, as well as staff members in the Dean of Men and Dean of Women's Offices, Admissions, and Financial Aid. The office changed its name to Office of Minority Affairs in 1972 with expanded cultural programming and advising and counseling services.

The Multicultural Resource Center, charged with promoting cultural awareness among all groups on campus, was added in 1995, albeit in a war surplus building lacking visibility. A shift from programming to supporting students academically started in 2000 with the creation

Students Mike Mader and Zena Monsour answer phones for KU Info, 1989.

of the Hawk Link program, and the name change to Multicultural
Affairs reflected a broader focus. Student body president Jonathan Ng
led efforts to build the new Sabatini Multicultural Resource Center in
2003, and operations moved to this highly visible location adjoining
the Kansas Union, with more space for academic resources and tutoring, in 2009. The office now reports to the Office of Diversity and
Equity.[47]

Student unrest, enrollment growth in numbers and diversity, and
the proliferation of new student services led to demands for more
accountability and a new layer of administrative oversight, nationally

Students line up to use KU on Wheels, 1975.

and at KU. William Balfour, named dean of student affairs in 1968, became KU's first vice chancellor for student affairs two years later. In this regard, KU followed national trends; by 1978 over 75 percent of large public universities had a similar position. KU followed yet another trend: the elimination of the positions of dean of men and dean of women. By 1976, fewer than 4 percent of women administrators reported that they held the title of dean of women. Kala Mays Stroup served as KU's final dean of women from 1975 to 1978 and Donald K. Alderson was the last dean of men. This change was not without controversy. Women faculty members, staff, and alumnae, especially those serving on the newly formed Emily Taylor Women's Resource Center Advisory Board, protested the elimination of the dean of women's position and feared the loss of the only position that guaranteed a woman in the higher levels of KU's administration. They did get a guarantee that the center would remain a freestanding unit, and it continues today as the Emily Taylor Center for Women and Gender Equity.[48]

David Ambler became vice chancellor in 1977 and transformed student services and student affairs administration during his 25 years in that office. Because of his experience with the tragedy at Kent State University, he was well aware of the impact of student protest on a campus. Compared to Kent State, given the atmosphere and attitudes on the KU campus, he was more optimistic about the future. Ambler attributes this to KU's strong history and traditions and a "more

David Ambler speaks to the Presidents' Council Meeting while Jennifer Papenek of Gay and Lesbian Services of Kansas and Jamie Cutburth of the Association of University Residence Halls look on, 1993.

sophisticated student body." He used his first year to study the current organization and services. Ambler said that his reorganization plan had been intended to focus on "those things which bind us together as human beings . . . [and] to serve as a model to defeat those forces in our society that would rank us differently by our sex, the color of our skin, our religious beliefs or our ethnic and national heritage." Ambler created the Student Assistance Center (SAC) to fill some of the individual guidance and support roles traditionally played by the dean of men's and dean of women's offices. The SAC grew to include services for students with disabilities, tutoring, and study skills workshops.

Also new was the Student Organizations and Activities Center, now known as the Student Involvement and Leadership Center, which included an adviser for fraternities and sororities. The new student affairs structure and Ambler's expertise and graduate study in higher education led to new levels of professionalization and specialization in student services. Perhaps more important, the vice chancellor for student affairs reported directly to the executive vice chancellor, as did the vice chancellors for academic affairs and research and graduate studies. Ambler remarked that it was important to see his role as an "executive officer" who could make "policy decisions at the institutional level," and he was encouraged to seek this voice by the KU student affairs staff. And as occurred on a national level, with the transformation of student legal rights, including women's rights, student activism, and changed cultural and parental expectations leading to the end of in loco parentis, student affairs administrators could focus their attention on student development and academic support.[49]

One of the most important new services benefited students with disabilities. KU was known as a place unfriendly to disabled students, in both services and the physical challenges of a campus on a hill. Section 504 of the 1973 federal Rehabilitation Act forced needed changes at KU and other institutions, and disability advocate Roger B. Williams used the power of a lawsuit to suspend construction of Wescoe Hall to ensure the inclusion of ramps for wheelchair users like him.[50] Williams met with Mary Lou Reece, student body vice president, in 1975 to urge the Student Senate to work with the Lawrence Bus Company to buy lift-equipped buses, and they discussed the plight of wheelchair users in Wescoe Hall, where elevator doors were kept locked. "Mr. Williams informed me that KU is known as a school that wheelchair handicapped people cannot attend," a disturbed Reece wrote to Chancellor Archie Dykes. "I think we should do all we can to give those people the same choice as anyone else to come to a great school like KU." Dykes agreed to open the Wescoe elevators for public use as a trial during the summer, and that fall the University Committee for the Architecturally Handicapped worked with Executive Vice Chancellor Del Shankel to open similar key-operated elevators in other buildings. The elevators opened and one more barrier fell.[51]

Even then, too little had been done by the time Ambler arrived at KU in 1977. That year, new federal regulations were published and a Lawrence Campus 504 Taskforce developed transition plans for compliance. The task force found serious problems, especially in the area of transportation. The only staff members assisting KU students with disabilities were two part-time graduate assistants in the Dean of Men's Office. Ambler designated full-time administrators in SAC to develop services, and they focused on improving transportation and providing accommodations in the classroom. It was clear that modifying the student-run KU on Wheels buses was too expensive, so the SAC worked with Student Senate, KU on Wheels, and the Executive Vice Chancellor's Office to fund and staff vans with lifts for wheelchairs. The Bus 63 system, featuring door-to-door service, started in the spring of 1979

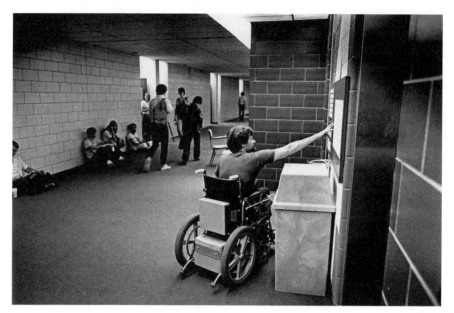

Tom Davis-Bissing looks at a bulletin board in Wescoe Hall, 1979.

with 3 passengers and quickly grew to serve 20. Roger Williams's advocacy and the SAC's implementation and focus on access as a right and
not a privilege made a significant difference for students with disabilities at KU.[52]

Programs and services grew, not just for mobility-impaired students
but also for those with hearing, vision, and learning disabilities. The
Americans with Disabilities Acts (ADA) of 1990 and 2008 required
equal access to educational and co-curricular programs and facilities,
reasonable and effective classroom accommodations, and the ability
to receive information in accessible formats. Student Access Services,
part of the Academic Achievement and Access Center, the successor of
the SAC, has staff to assist students who are deaf or hard of hearing or
who have physical, psychiatric, vision, autism spectrum, or learning or
attention deficit hyperactivity disorders. And since 2012 the university
has focused more broadly on access and education through the new
Office of Institutional Opportunity and Access and its Accessibility and
ADA Education program. All faculty members and selected staff members are required to take online training on the ADA and academic accommodations, and there are new Accessibility Ambassadors, students
with disabilities who serve on campus-wide committees to expand
accessibility and inclusion. Moreover, the Student Senate challenged

KU graduate student Nivene Young listens to lectures at Rainbow House, 1989.

the university to make the site of administrative power—Strong Hall—truly user-friendly with an accessible front entrance, more than a century after the building opened. And a new student group—AbleHawks and Allies—has stepped forward as a visible force for advocacy and promotes disability as a multicultural issue.[53]

The creation of Counseling and Psychological Services as a separate entity provided another valuable service for students. Initially, the University Counseling Center provided services through faculty members and graduate students in the Counseling Psychology Department, as did the Student Mental Health Center, operating out of Watkins Student Health Center. In 1991, these entities merged, along with career counseling and testing services, into Counseling and Psychological Services. The University Placement Center, later Career and Employment Services, continued to offer job search and employer interview services until 2004, when it was renamed the University Career Center and added career counseling and internship programs.

Improving academic support for students was another key concern. When Robert Hemenway became chancellor in 1995, he restructured the university to become more student-centered and pushed for the creation of centers to improve undergraduate academic advising and writing. The Freshman-Sophomore Advising Center, now the

Undergraduate Advising Center, and the KU Writing Center continue to provide crucial student academic support and work to improve student persistence. In another move to improve recruitment and retention, the restructuring shifted the reporting of several key offices, including Admissions and Scholarships, University Registrar, and New Student Orientation, to the Provost's Office through Associate Provost for Academic Services Kathleen McCluskey-Fawcett, instead of Student Affairs. Student Affairs added Recreation Services to its portfolio and reorganized the Department of Student Life.[54]

After 25 years of service, David Ambler retired in 2002, and a task force recommended yet another reorganization, which brought together various units that supported student success to better integrate them with academic programs. The next year, Marlesa Roney became the new vice provost for student success with responsibilities for 20 different student support units, from Academic Technology Services to the University Career Center. Roney created new administrative clusters and priorities to improve recruitment and retention, initiated a new student information system, integrated food services, and oversaw the opening of the $17 million Student Recreation Fitness Center. In addition, to reflect changing relationships between KU students and their parents, her office created the KU Parents Association, offered a parent assistance phone line, and started regular communication with parents via an e-newsletter. "Because of the level of involvement we've had from parents, students are not quite sure how to be engaged in the process," commented Tammara Durham, current vice provost for student affairs. "They don't know how to act on their own, in their own best interest. I'm not sure they know how to advocate for themselves."[55]

In 2011, following strategic planning led by new provost Jeffrey Vitter, another reorganization followed that had a major impact on student services. The new model was reminiscent of the 1997 changes, but with a renewed focus on enrollment management, first-year experiences, and experiential learning. Bold Aspirations, the university's five-year strategic plan, called for enhancement of first-year intellectual and experiential learning experiences, as well as improved recruitment and retention of undergraduates. A new unit titled Undergraduate Studies was created to include academic support for students, as well as a new Office of First-Year Experience and Centers for Civic and Social Responsibility and Undergraduate Research, led by Vice Provost and Dean Ann Cudd. First-year students now start their academic lives at KU with a Common Book and the opportunity to take small, faculty-led seminars and participate in a learning community in their

Tammara Durham advises a student in the Freshman-Sophomore (now Undergraduate) Advising Center, 1999.

residence hall. All undergraduates can be certified, through a combination of coursework and real-life experience, in Service Learning,
Research, Leadership Studies, or Global Awareness.[56]

"REGARDLESS OF THE PURPOSE OR POLITICS": DIFFERENT FORMS OF STUDENT ACTIVISM

As campus protests diminished, KU students turned to different forms
of activism—more focused on campus concerns, student needs, and
the environment. Furthermore, the Student Senate demanded and,
in some cases, created new student services. In the 1970s and 1980s,
the Student Senate created and funded KU on Wheels, Whomper, the
original campus recycling center, and Legal Services for Students. In
addition, student fees funded Hilltop Child Development Center, the
new $3.6 million Watkins Memorial Health Center, renovations to the
Kansas Union, and the building of the $2.5 million Burge Union. And
Student Senate and KU law students pushed for the creation of an
Ombudsman's Office to mediate conflicts among members of the university community. KU on Wheels, the campus bus system, was, for a
time, the only student-run bus program in the country. The Lawrence
Bus Company had provided bus services on campus for decades, until
the fall of 1971, when it ceased operations due to lack of funds. The
Student Senate used student fees to continue operating the system,
and after a slow start, ridership grew 35 percent in the first year. The
Student Senate Transportation Board expanded routes and ridership,
but, sadly, increased resources led to a significant misuse of funds for
almost a decade and an embezzlement conviction. Nevertheless, KU
on Wheels survived the problem and ran effectively for the next 25
years. As the need for better connections with the Lawrence bus system and accessible buses grew, the administration of KU on Wheels
moved from the Student Senate to the KU Parking and Transit Department in 2007. Students remained involved through the Transportation Board, and the Student Senate approved a $20 fee increase to
purchase new buses. New crimson and blue buses, some using alternative fuels, replaced the old lime-green ones, a familiar sight on campus
for decades. By 2008, a Student Senate and KU Parking and Transit
decision eliminated KU student bus passes for both campus and Lawrence buses, which resulted in a doubling of ridership numbers. In
addition to the regular bus service, student fees funded Saferide, to
provide free, late-night rides from Lawrence community locations to a

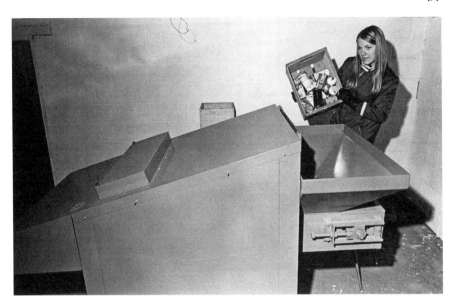

Feeding the "Whomper" in 1971.

student's residence, and SafeBus, a late-night bus system on weekends. Both programs are models for other universities across the nation.[57]

From transportation to the environment, KU students continued their activism; they joined 20 million Americans across the country to celebrate the first Earth Day on April 20, 1970. It was the start of the modern environmental movement, and the array of events at KU was impressive: Paul Ehrlich, noted environmentalist who had earned graduate degrees at KU, spoke; an environmental teach-in was held throughout the week; and Ecology Action held a canoe float down the Kansas River to survey the ever-present water pollution.[58]

Recycling emerged as the next significant environmental issue. The Student Senate swung into action with the Whomper, Inc., or officially the University of Kansas Reclamation Center, a nonprofit entity that recycled aluminum, tin cans, glass, bottles, and newspapers for the entire community. From its start in January 1971, it operated in the Memorial Union and later moved to locations on New Hampshire Street. Adequate funding was a constant issue, and by the end of 1973, with Student Senate subsidies ending, control of the operation passed on to an informal community board. With declining options for glass and can recycling, the operation focused on newspaper recycling and then ended altogether in 1976. Still, at a time when the city offered no recycling options, KU student leaders had provided Lawrence with its first organized recycling efforts.[59]

From the 1980s to the present, KU students have continued to lead with the campus environmental effort; Environs, a student organization started in 1985, played the key role initially. Environs pushed the Kansas Union to end the use of Styrofoam products in 1989 and, with the Student Senate, initiated aluminum can recycling throughout the campus. The program was so successful that the university took it over and created the Environmental Ombudsman Office, staffed by student "recycling technicians," in 1990. Students initiated and researched projects such as more efficient library lighting and low-flow shower-heads in residence halls. The Student Senate approved a $1 student fee to support recycling in 1997, which was matched by the university, and also provided a grant to hire more recycling technicians. The office changed names over the decade, but student input through an advisory board continued, and today it is called the Sustainability Leadership Board. The Student Senate approved the Sustainable Campus fee in 2002, which continues today to support recycling and renewable energy and sustainability. Impelled by over 1,000 student signatures advocating a broader effort, KU initiated the Center for Sustainability in 2007. Chancellor Bernadette Gray-Little signed an Earth Day proclamation recognizing KU students for this effort and as one of the earliest creators nationally of green fees that support the environment, renewable energy, and energy efficiency. She lauded students' efforts in initiating and implementing the Student Rain Garden, featuring 2,500 native plants, and the Potter Lake cleanup project.[60]

Legal issues were another student concern. Steve Leban, student body president in 1977–1978, surveyed students and found that 60 percent indicated they would pay a fee to fund a legal services program. Primary areas of need were tenant rights, including rental contracts, consumer rights, insurance, car accidents, and traffic violations. The Student Senate approved funding, and Legal Services for Students opened its doors in the spring of 1978. After 35 years, this service continues to advise KU students on most legal matters, including providing landlord-tenant court representation. Tax workshops and income tax assistance have been added, with assistance from an IRS grant. Four attorneys, as well as legal interns from the KU School of Law, served 3,057 clients in 2013.[61]

Moreover, KU student leaders, such as student body president Lisa Ashner, in 1983, have sought to heal some of the wounds of the Vietnam conflict by promoting an on-campus Vietnam Memorial, along

A student stands in front of the Vietnam Memorial.

with Vietnam veterans Thomas Berger and John Musgrave. "The Vietnam Memorial for the University of Kansas is not a towering statue commemorating lofty ideals or glorious victories," said John Onken, a junior and winner of the design competition, "but a humble gift in recognition of those who fought and died in Vietnam, regardless of the purpose or politics that sent them there." Onken's sentiments echoed the spirit of the KU students who created the memorial to honor fellow students who were killed in an unpopular war. A site was selected at the west entrance to Memorial Drive, and KU student Doran Abel and Professor Stephen Grabow redesigned the monument into an L-shaped wall of native Kansas limestone etched with the names of the 57 honored veterans who lost their lives or were missing in action. It was dedicated on May 25, 1986, and was the first freestanding Vietnam memorial on a college campus in the country.[62]

"SOMETHING WE ALL SHARED": STUDENT LIFE CONTINUES

"To some of us KU is frats, functions and football and to others it's shyness, scholarship, and slide rules," observed John Hill, Jayhawker yearbook editor. "To some people, KU is long hair, love-ins, and LSD and to others it is a simple matter of readin,' writin' and Red Dog." Hill pointed to the continuity of college student life, even in turbulent 1968, and described the "parental, social, and economic pressures for a good degree." For some, by the mid-1970s and into the 1980s, the campus saw a return to "normalcy." The 1974 Jayhawker reported the increased popularity of fraternities and sororities and featured a two-page spread on streaking, with students attempting to break a University of Missouri record of 600 streakers at a time. Demonstrating a measure of refinement compared to their bitter rival, only 30 naked KU students showed up. Still, two students threw off their black robes to streak at Commencement. The following year, Chancellor Archie Dykes described a "return to more traditional values. . . . The general recession of our economy has moved students to be more cautious. . . . They are more eager to gain security and job opportunities and less optimistic about their future." Students expressed practical concerns as well: the Student Senate passed a resolution demanding computerized enrollment and a central advising system; these reasonable expectations would take a decade and two decades, respectively, to fulfill, but no protests occurred. "Sit-ins, marches, and mass meetings are passé. Now is the time of the individual answer," the 1976 Jayhawker declared, adding that "the concerned student of the sixties has become the disenchanted recluse of the seventies." Nevertheless, the impact of the February Sisters and the women's movement could be seen that year in the election of Tedde Tasheff as KU's first female student body president since the male-diminished campus of World War II.[63]

By 1980, concerns about student ennui arose anew: "Students today are quiet, almost submissive," said N. Ray Hiner, professor of history and education. "It's like they're just putting in time; they're missing a genuine intellectual excitement—the idea of learning simply for the sake of learning. Students have goals but they're specific; they're limited by economic fears," he added. Historian Helen Lefkowitz Horowitz described the same student worries and focus on grades, job skills, and financial security and the lack of "sparks of intellectual life" in her book *Campus Life*. KU students were not unique in this respect, although the anti-apartheid and gay rights protests of the 1980s showed a strong strain of activism continuing on Mount Oread.[64]

At least some advancements were made in technology in the 1980s; enrollment in Allen Fieldhouse, a rite of passage, ended in 1982. Pre-enrollment for the spring semester of 1983, via what was termed an "on-line system," signaled the end of IBM punch cards, long lines in Allen Fieldhouse, and jostling with fellow students for space in quickly closing classes. Students were of divided minds about the changes; computerized enrollment did not turn out to be the panacea some expected, with computer crashes and long lines at the new Enrollment

An adult student studies in the library at the Edwards Campus with her child. With jobs and families, adult students have less time for campus organizations and politics than traditional undergraduates.

Center in Strong Hall. "We used to gripe about the fieldhouse but it was a true love-hate relationship," lamented one student. "It was the initiation that everyone—Greeks and GDIs, jocks and hipsters, intellectuals and radicals alike—had to go through to become a full-fledged KU student. It was something we all shared, sort of like the Nuclear Threat and Ronald Reagan."[65]

Drinking alcohol was another shared experience for most KU students. While the 1960s and 1970s saw an increase in drug use, especially marijuana, alcohol consumption, as evidenced in the bars near campus, continued to be a major diversion. The biggest change came in 1985 when Kansas outlawed the sale of 3.2 beer to 18 year olds and established 21 as the legal age to purchase and possess alcohol. KU changed many of its related policies, including restricting alcohol in university housing for the first time since 1971. With the continued misuse of alcohol by some college students and a rise in binge drinking, many have questioned the efficacy of the law. For example, the Amethyst Initiative, signed by 135 college presidents, calls for a rethinking of the alcohol age limit. Nevertheless, alcohol and drug misuse are a continuing concern at KU and reached a new height in

2009 with the death of a freshman at a fraternity after a heavy night of drinking. This incident led to a new alcohol policy, which requires the notification of parents of students under 21 who violate the alcohol or drug policy on campus and also requires all new students to take an online alcohol education course. Student Affairs instituted an amnesty policy, as well, to encourage students to seek help in alcohol-related emergencies without the fear of repercussions. Recent educational approaches, such as the Jayhawk Buddy System and Bystander Education, focus on peers watching out for each other to prevent risky behaviors.[66]

From Baby Boomers to Gen Xers to Millennials, generations of KU students have experienced other perils and violence—at home and abroad. Student protests against the Vietnam War and apartheid in South Africa were organized and passionate; student responses to the 9/11 attacks and the Gulf War were more muted, with some focusing on improving the treatment of returning veterans. "Peace Rally Condemns Leaders, Not Soldiers," a *UDK* headline ran in 1991, reflecting the mood of the era, as did a rally of 200 students for the troops in the Gulf that concluded at the KU Vietnam Memorial. Yellow ribbons supporting the troops appeared everywhere, and as one student commented, "Just because we support the troops, it does not mean we support the policies that got them there." War collided with basketball in March 2003 when KU's first-round NCAA game was interrupted by an announcement of the first US casualties in the war in Iraq. Since then KU students have always lived with their nation at war—in Afghanistan or Iraq—and the number of veterans on campus has grown, as have the programs to support them—such as the Wounded Warrior program and a special veterans' lounge established at the Burge Union. A new tradition started at the 2014 commencement when graduating veterans wore red, white, and blue honor cords.[67]

Moreover, a series of tragic events, including the Oklahoma City bombing, the Columbine massacre, 9/11, the Virginia Tech massacre, and the Sandy Hook school shootings, frame 20 years of violence within the United States experienced by successive groups of KU students. "I think our generation has become so accustomed to violence . . . we really have become a little bit numb to it all," observed Hannah Bolton, 2012–2013 student body president. "Violence is happening constantly . . . another shooting, another bombing." While Bolton was president, the Student Senate passed a resolution opposed to the concealed carry of weapons on campus. "We look at this decade of violence. . . . It's the Columbines. It's the Sandy Hooks," said former Vice Provost Roney. "It's everything that these students have experienced in terms of violence domestically but then there's this background of war that says, 'Well, we live in a violent world anyway.' And then there's this infusion of violence in technology and video games. . . . My sense is there's this kind of desensitization to what violence really means in our world."[68]

Technology is certainly another key to understanding KU students in the last 20 years: students in the 1990s had been playing video games for years when they arrived at KU. The 1994 *Jayhawker* heralded the arrival of electronic mail. That same year KJHK became the first radio station in the world to provide a continuous live signal over the Internet, and the *UDK* appeared on the World Wide Web in 1996. Students and faculty went online in 2000 with the Blackboard course management system. The next year, everyone could play iTunes on their iPods, and the isolation began. "The trick, I guess, is to know when to slip into your own bubble and crank the soundtrack that will help you get through the day," Matt Bechtold said in his "iPod Isolation" article, "and when to take off the 'do not disturb' sign and start a conversation with a fellow Jayhawk." Hannah Bolton commented that her fellow students communicated with everyone except those they sat with: "We are constantly connected to everything except for what's happening right around us." Finally, KU went online for enrollment in 2003, and the next year everyone was on Facebook and then Twitter, Instagram, and a quickly evolving list of other social media. In 2011, KU was ranked the number eight university for social-media savvy, based on the use of Facebook, Twitter, and YouTube. The Student Senate furthered students' connectivity by providing half of the $2.6 million funding for a 2008 initiative to greatly expand wireless access on campus. This access creates better virtual connections, but questions remain about students' real relationships with each other, with faculty, and with learning.[69]

"WHEN STUDENTS GET BEHIND SOMETHING": THE NEW ACTIVISM

Jaden Gragg learned about the Alta Gracia living-wage apparel factory on a study abroad trip to the Dominican Republic in 2013, where she lived with one of the factory workers. Impressed with what the factory provided for its workers and the community, she returned to KU on a mission to stock Alta Gracia clothing at the Kansas Union Bookstore and started a chapter of the United Students Against Sweatshops. Her demand was bold: a switch to 50 percent Alta Gracia apparel. The Bookstore, with no one company providing more than 15 percent of its stock, resisted, and Gragg and her group staged a protest on Valentine's Day, holding signs decorated with hearts. Her approach, while lighter in spirit than that of earlier protesters, was effective, and by March the Bookstore had ordered Alta Gracia Jayhawk apparel, in a smaller proportion. Both sides had learned something. The Union Bookstore's approach was to engage and find a way for the students to achieve success; Gragg translated her international experience into action on campus.[70]

Jaden Gragg is symbolic of the new KU student activism, as are the students involved with the Center for Community Outreach. Every spring, students from this organization go "Into the Streets" to demonstrate about community issues such as homelessness and hunger. They may not rival the civil rights and antiwar protests of the 1960s in fervor, but their commitment to change is steadfast. Student body president Michael Schreiner started the Center for Community Outreach in 1990, and today it includes 14 different programs, from the Jubilee Café, which serves breakfast to the needy in a restaurant-like setting, to the Music Mentors, for elementary and middle school students, to Earth, which grows organic food for local food pantries. As many as 5,000 KU students volunteer annually in their efforts to engage with the local community and beyond. Alternative Spring Breaks extends the volunteer experience to semester and weekend immersions that can include course credit. Spring 2014 programs included serving at the Cincinnati Homeless Coalition, Alzheimer's Services in Memphis, and preservation efforts at Zion National Park in Utah.

The Student Senate committed $27,000 to create an Office of Service Learning staffed by students in 2001, and finally, four years later, the university used tuition enhancement money to initiate a Center for Service Learning with a part-time director. Within two years, the director became full time, and additional staff followed, and in 2012 it was renamed the Center for Civic and Social Responsibility with a new office in Strong Hall. Once again, students led the way in establishing a university program. Their focus in the Lawrence community took on added meaning when student body president Michael Wade Smith initiated The Big Event in 2011, a community-wide service project that matches KU students with Lawrence residents to complete a variety of jobs. In 2014, 3,000 student volunteers fanned out to 350 job sites across Lawrence. "I think it is an incredible testament to how much

Working with the Center for Community Outreach, KU students went homeless for 24 hours. Pictured here are Deidre Backs, Matt Caldwell, Jama DeFever, Chris Hess, and Kate Turnbull.

KU students care about the Lawrence community and about this university," remarked Hannah Bolton, who organized it.[71]

The list of Student Senate–initiated and –funded projects from 1990 to 2015 reinforces its claim to authoritative leadership: the Watkins Student Health Center $5.6 million expansion; the new $3.3 million building and expansion of Hilltop Child Development Center; the Sabatini Multicultural Resource Center; and the Ambler Student Recreation Fitness Center (a $17 million project approved by a student referendum in 1998 that opened in 2003, with a $6.1 million expansion in 2007). Student body president Kevin Yoder led the successful initial project with a better location and smaller fee increase than a proposal that had been soundly defeated two years earlier. President Andy Knopp used a creative, and questionable, funding approach by offering coveted student basketball seating to the KU Athletics Department to build the addition. In 2014, the Student Senate voted to end a $25 per semester athletics fee, which the chancellor upheld, but then she imposed a $12 per semester student recreation fee to cover the bond payments created by the deal.[72]

Inside the Ambler Student Recreation Fitness Center.

It was not only buildings and programs that concerned KU student leaders but also rising tuition. When KU, and the other Regents institutions, gained tuition ownership in 2001, Provost David Shulenburger developed a five-year Tuition Enhancement Plan, vetted through dozens of campus meetings and affirmed by the Ad Hoc Committee on University Funding. Student leaders played a crucial role throughout, and, according to some experts, KU students were unique among students at public universities in their influence on tuition decisions and how tuition monies would be spent. A Student Senate resolution called for the creation of the Ad Hoc Committee, which not only had equal numbers of student and faculty members but was co-chaired by a student. The process resulted in significant tuition increases, of $16.50 per credit hour. While the Student Senate opposed the increase, the Ad Hoc Committee and the *UDK* endorsed the plan because of promised improvements for students, including expanded course offerings, more funds for advising, grants for needy students, and increased wages for student employees. Despite mixed student support, student leaders had significant input into how new tuition dollars would be spent during the next five years, through a newly created Student Tuition Committee recommended by student body president Jonathan Ng. Through communication and consultation, students and the administration both achieved key goals, and students got the all-important seat at the table.[73]

Student leaders were not finished with the question of tuition changes, however. Over five years, the plan raised $43 million for educational enhancements, with $8.6 million earmarked for tuition grants for students with unmet financial need. But the impact on students and their families was profound: in 2001, average tuition and fees for an in-state undergraduate was $2,884 per year; in one year it jumped 20.8 percent, to $3,484; and by 2006 it was at $6,153, a 113 percent rise in five years. During this time of rapid increases, student body president Steve Munch and vice president Jeff Dunlap proposed fixed tuition rates, to provide more predictability and better planning for students and families. The proposal was part of their campaign platform, and as Vice Provost Marlesa Roney commented, "What an amazing initiative for student leaders to take on . . . thinking about how can the University of Kansas be affordable." The administration bought into Munch and Dunlap's reasoning, and the Four-Year Tuition Compact started in the fall of 2007, keeping tuition rates for an entering undergraduate stable for four years. It continues today, even as resident undergraduates paid $10,107 in 2013–2014, three-and-a-half times as much as students in 2001.[74]

Tuition increases, changes in federal financial aid, and the economic crisis, especially in 2008, led to the most significant issues for current KU students, according to former student body president Bolton—concerns about graduating with high loan indebtedness and the inability to secure good-paying jobs after graduation. At KU, the average debt for graduating seniors with loans increased from $17,347 in 2002 to $27,219 in 2013; in those same years, the percentage of students graduating with such debt increased from 37 percent to 53.8 percent. While these figures are sobering, average loan debt across the United States in 2012 was $29,400. And in 2014, the KUEA provided $27.2 million in scholarships to 6,000 KU students. In response to these financial challenges, Student Senate leaders pushed for a financial literacy program. With Student Senate, Student Success, Memorial Unions, and School of Business support, Student Money Management Services opened in 2010. It provides financial literacy education on budgets, savings, credit cards, and the managing of debt.[75]

Student Senate support of student services continued in 2014 when it assumed more than half of the funding of KU Info and renewed its assistance to the financially strapped and community-based Headquarters Counseling Center, started and staffed by many KU students, which provides suicide prevention for the community, as well as funding for the Willow Domestic Violence Center and the GaDuGi SafeCenter, which serves rape survivors. Also in 2014, the Student Senate voted to fund a full-time coordinator, for the Lesbian, Gay, Bisexual, Transgender, and Queer Resource Center, previously staffed only by a half-time graduate assistant position. "Students decided that it's a priority that the University is not currently seeking," said Mitchell Coda, Queers and Allies media coordinator. "Typically when students get behind something, the University will make a change." This was true in 1965, and it is true in 2015. KU students have left a real legacy of activism and have fought against injustice. They have made a lasting difference for fellow students and the university and had a say in decisions that affect them. They are true Jayhawkers.[76]

CHAPTER 8

"Crimson and the Blue"
An Era of Athletic Achievement

FRANCIS B. "BERNIE" KISH

THE past 50 years for Kansas Athletics have been marked by a tradition of excellence in sports competition and also changes in the
gender equity and racial makeup of its student-athletes and teams. In
addition, its athletics program has become a big business, in line with
other major universities. It has also been characterized by a loyal and
enthusiastic legion of fans, both locally and across the country. KU
athletics stands today as one of the great institutions in collegiate competition, proudly looking forward to the future.

The story of KU's athletic tradition begins with men's basketball
and football, the university's principal revenue sports, but it has assumed many other dimensions in this period. Beginning in the early
1970s, with the implementation of Title IX, women's athletics have
become a vital, respected, and highly visible aspect of the KU athletics program. The Jayhawks now have ten women's sports, and these
teams have represented the university with distinction nationally and
in conference play. Many female athletes have earned All-American
and All-Conference honors, and one track and field athlete won an
Olympic gold medal.[1]

A notable change also occurred in the racial makeup of athletics
at KU. In the 1960s, very few student-athletes or coaches were African
American. That has changed over the years, with African American
athletes playing a vital role in almost every sport at KU, both men's
and women's. During this period, Kansas also hired African American
head coaches for its football, women's basketball, and track and field

teams. There has been a marked increase in black assistant coaches, particularly in football, men's basketball, and track and field. This has been a very positive development, for both KU athletics and the institution as a whole.

Since 1965, the athletics program at KU has steadily progressed toward becoming a big business, with the budget growing from about $9 million in the early 1990s to almost $80 million in 2014. The salaries of coaches, particularly in the two revenue sports, basketball and football, have been major contributors to the escalating budget, along with a facilities arms race.[2] Beginning in the early 2000s, KU built a new football complex and practice fields, a rowing boathouse, and a state-of-the-art facility for its track and field, soccer, and softball programs.

In the early 1990s, changes began to take place in the composition of athletics conferences nationwide. Several schools bolted conferences, lured mostly by the financial gain from television contracts. KU stayed true to its roots. In 1965, Kansas was a member of the Big Eight, and since 1996, when that conference expanded, it has been in the Big 12 Conference. Its loyalty has paid off, with enhanced conference revenues being instrumental in funding its athletics programs.

Ten men have served as athletics director since 1960, and there were also five acting or interim athletics directors. Four earned degrees on Mount Oread. All of them enjoyed success, some greater than

Fans in Allen Fieldhouse with the "Beware of the Phog" banner, 1995.

others, and all faced challenges associated with managing a big-time athletics program.[3] As a matter of comparison, from 1911, when the position of athletics manager/athletics director was instituted at Kansas, until 1950, there were only four athletics directors and one interim director. This difference clearly reflects how the responsibilities of the job have expanded, especially with regard to balancing the athletics budget, maintaining winning programs, and negotiating public scrutiny.[4]

The major focus of this chapter is on the coaches and student-athletes in each of the sports and the exemplary reputation they have collectively earned for KU athletics. Kansas is known, and rightfully so, as a "basketball school." In this chapter, however, readers will note that every KU sport has enjoyed its day in the sun. National and conference championships, NCAA postseason play, All-American and All-Conference honors, Olympic athletes, and coaches of the year in many different sports are all part of the Crimson and Blue, Rock Chalk Jayhawk, history of athletic distinction.

KANSAS BASKETBALL: A TRADITION OF EXCELLENCE

The University of Kansas has a long heritage of basketball excellence. It is arguably the most storied program in America. The inventor of the game, Dr. James Naismith, taught physical education at KU from 1898 until 1937 and was the Jayhawks' first basketball coach. Dr. Forrest C. "Phog" Allen, often called the "Father of Basketball Coaching," coached at KU for 39 years and is its winningest coach. Historic Allen Fieldhouse, opened in 1955, is generally considered to be among the most iconic venues in college basketball.[5]

KU's list of basketball accomplishments is undeniably impressive. Among them are the second-most wins in the history of the game (2,126 through the 2013–2014 season); 5 national championships and 14 Final Four appearances; 17 players and coaches selected for the Naismith Memorial Basketball Hall of Fame; and 21 players selected as first-team consensus All-Americans.[6]

Since 1964, Kansas basketball has continued to maintain its place of honor in college basketball lore. There has been head coaching stability: only five men have occupied the position, two of whom are Naismith Hall of Fame inductees. The Jayhawks have won 26 Big Eight and Big 12 Conference titles, including ten straight from 2004 until 2014. There have been nine Final Four appearances and three NCAA championships. At Allen Fieldhouse, the site of 212 consecutive sell-out crowds through the 2013–2014 season, the Jayhawks have won over 95 percent of their games since 2003.[7] Finally, in 2014, Kansas was selected by the International University Sports Federation to represent the United States in the 2015 World University Games in Korea, the first time that a university team rather than all-stars would represent the country.[8]

This remarkable period began with a coaching change. In the summer of 1964, following the resignation of Dick Harp, 34-year-old Oklahoman Ted Owens, who had been Harp's assistant since 1960, became the Jayhawks' head basketball coach. Harp had led the Jayhawks for eight seasons, posting a record of 121–82, winning two conference titles, and advancing to the NCAA tournament twice.[9]

Owens, who came to Mount Oread following a highly productive coaching stint at Cameron College in Oklahoma and a stellar playing career for the Oklahoma Sooners, was an instant success at KU. His first squad posted a 17–8 record and a second-place finish in the Big Eight. During the remainder of the decade, his teams had four 20-win seasons and won two conference titles and four Big Eight Holiday tournament championships. Center Walter Wesley from Fort Myers, Florida, and Jo Jo White of St. Louis, Missouri, were named first-team All-Americans. The 1965–1966 and 1966–1967 teams advanced to the NCAA tournament.[10]

The 1966 NCAA tournament is forever etched in the memory of the Jayhawk faithful. KU was optimistic going into the tournament, having a talented team led by a solid group of stalwart performers: White, Wesley, Al Lopes, Riney Lochmann, Delvey Lewis, and Rod Franz. The regionals were played in Lubbock, Texas. After defeating Southern Methodist in the regional semifinal, 76–70, Owen's squad faced Texas Western in the regional final. It was an epic clash. Jo Jo White hit a 35-foot jump shot at the buzzer of the first overtime that seemingly won the game, but an official ruled that he had stepped out of bounds. Texas Western prevailed in the second overtime, 81–80, and went on to defeat Kentucky for the national title.[11]

The 1966–1967 squad also enjoyed a banner year, finishing with a 23–4 record and capturing the Big Eight title with a 13–1 record before losing to Houston in a first-round NCAA tournament game in Allen Fieldhouse. Owens's 1967–1968 and 1968–1969 teams were selected to play in the National Invitational Tournament in New York City. The 1967–1968 team advanced to the championship game, losing to Dayton. Outstanding performers on these teams, in addition to

Bud Stallworth retrieves the ball at Allen Fieldhouse, 1971.

White, were forwards Franz and Rodger Bohnenstiel, plus sophomore center Dave Robisch.[12]

The success Ted Owens and his Jayhawks experienced in the 1960s continued in the next decade. During the 1970s, Kansas earned four berths in the NCAA tournament, reached two Final Fours, won four Big Eight titles, and had three players named first-team All-Americans.[13]

KU's 1971 and 1974 Final Four teams were both outstanding. The 1971 edition was led by All-American Robisch, along with Isaac "Bud" Stallworth, Roger Brown, Pierre Russell, and Aubrey Nash. The Jayhawks lost to Coach John Wooden's UCLA Bruins in the NCAA semifinal game in Houston. The 1974 team posted a 23–7 record and tied for first place in the Big Eight. The Jayhawks were led by five juniors, Danny Knight, Roger Morningstar, Dale Greenlee, Rick Suttle, and freshman Norm Cook. KU was defeated by Al McGuire's Marquette Warriors in the NCAA semifinal game in Greensboro, North Carolina.[14]

KU also made it to the Big Dance in 1975 and 1978, when both teams won Big Eight championships. The 1978 men's team was sparked by freshman guard Darnell Valentine, who had a spectacular career at

Kansas and earned first-team All-American honors as a senior. Owen's other All-American in the 1970s was Stallworth. The Hartselle, Alabama, native was also an Academic All-American and set a KU scoring record for a conference game, with 50 points against Missouri in 1972 in Allen Fieldhouse.[15]

Ted Owens's career at KU came to a close following the 1982–1983 season. He had a sparkling 348–182 record and is KU's third-winningest coach, behind Phog Allen and Roy Williams. Owens was the Big Eight Coach of the Year five times and Basketball Weekly's National Coach of the Year in 1978.[16]

Owens's successor, Larry Brown, also had a remarkable run in his five years at KU. His teams posted a 135–44 (.754) record, appeared in five NCAA tournaments, made it to the Final Four in 1986, and won the national championship in 1988.[17]

The 1985–1986 edition of the Jayhawks is considered one of the very best teams not to win a national title. Paced by brilliant sophomore Danny Manning, sensational shooters Ron Kellogg and Calvin Thompson, center Greg Dreiling, and point guard Cedric Hunter, the Jayhawks posted a 35–4 record and won the Big Eight regular season and tournament titles. The Hawks suffered a heartbreaking 71–67 loss to Duke in the NCAA semifinal in Dallas.[18]

In the spring of 1988, Larry Brown and his Jayhawks, a team eventually dubbed "Danny and the Miracles," were crowned national champions. "The Miracles" were a talented group who epitomized teamwork. The team also included Kevin Pritchard, Milt Newton, Chris Piper, Jeff Gueldner, Scooter Barry, Clint Normore, Keith Harris, Lincoln Minor, and Mike Maddox. KU had an up-and-down season, finishing the campaign 21–11, and were considered a "bubble" team for the NCAA Tournament. Kansas received an at-large bid and proceeded to make a dramatic run to the title game with wins over Xavier, Murray State (a 61–58 nail-biter), Vanderbilt, and, in the regional final, Kansas State.[19]

The 1988 Final Four, the 50th, was played at Kemper Arena in Kansas City. The Jayhawks prevailed in the semifinal game, defeating Duke, 66–59. In the championship game against Big Eight rival Oklahoma, KU defeated the Sooners, 83–79, with Danny Manning scoring 31 points, snagging 18 rebounds, and icing the win with four clutch free throws.[20]

Kansas became the first unranked team and the first with double-digit losses to win a national championship. Manning, not surprisingly, was named the tournament's Most Valuable Player. A few months after

Danny Manning pumps in 42 points against SMSU in 1987.

winning the national title, Larry Brown resigned to become the head coach of the NBA's San Antonio Spurs. He had a spectacular career in the NBA and was inducted into the Naismith Memorial Basketball Hall of Fame in 2002.[21]

In early November 1988, the NCAA informed the university that it was being placed on probation for violations that had occurred in 1986.[22] Penalties included "loss of three scholarships; being banned from the NCAA tournament in 1989; and not being able to bring recruits on campus for a year."[23]

In July 1988, Roy Williams, an unheralded assistant for Dean Smith at North Carolina, became the seventh head coach in the storied history of Kansas basketball. Williams led the Jayhawks to an extraordinary 418–101 record (.805) in 15 years and won more games in this time than any other coach in Division I history. Kansas made it to four Final Fours under Williams, playing in championship games in 1991 and 2003. He also won nine conference titles; his 2002 squad became the only team in Big 12 history with a perfect conference slate, 16–0.[24]

Williams produced a bevy of outstanding players, four of whom were selected as first-team consensus All-Americans: Nick Collison, Drew Gooden, Raef LaFrentz, and Paul Pierce. Ten of his players were first-round NBA draft selections. Williams's record of excellence was recognized with several coaching awards, including the Naismith Coach of the Year three times and the 2003 John R. Wooden Legends Coaching Award. In 2007, he was enshrined in the Naismith Memorial Hall of Fame.[25]

All of Williams's Final Four teams (1991, 1993, 2002, and 2003) were sources of great pride for Jayhawk fans. The 1991 KU team, sparked by Mark Randall, Terry Brown, Adonis Jordan, Richard Scott, Alonzo Jamison, and Mike Maddox, went all the way to the championship game in Indianapolis, where it was edged by Duke. Two years later, KU advanced to the NCAA semifinal game in New Orleans before coming up short against North Carolina. One of Williams's best Kansas teams was the 1996–1997 Jayhawks. Sparked by a superb cast that included guards Jacque Vaughn and Jerod Haase, forwards Paul Pierce and Raef LaFrentz, and center Scott Pollard, KU finished the campaign 34–2. Kansas's only two losses came at the hands of Missouri in Big 12 play and of Arizona in the NCAA Sweet 16.[26]

The 2002 and 2003 teams were true powerhouses. The 2002 team, led by Nick Collison, Drew Gooden, and Kirk Hinrich, finished the season with a 33–4 record, and the 2003 squad completed the campaign with a 30–8 record and another Big 12 title before falling to Syracuse in the NCAA championship game. In addition to Collison, Gooden, and Hinrich, sharpshooting Jeff Boschee and Wayne Simien were key members of the 2002 team; and Simien, Keith Langford, and Aaron Miles were valuable contributors in 2003.[27] In early April 2003, Williams returned to his alma mater, the University of North Carolina, to become the Tar Heels' head coach.

Coach Roy Williams presides over Midnight Madness, on October 14, 1989, a yearly tradition at which fans can observe the Jayhawks' first practice of the season.

Within a week of Williams's departure, Drue Jennings, KU's interim athletics director, hired Coach Bill Self away from the University of Illinois. Over the last 11 years, Self has clearly established himself as one of the elite coaches in college basketball with a splendid overall record of 325–69 (.825). His Jayhawks have captured one national championship, ten straight Big 12 Conference titles, and six league tournament championships and have reached two Final Fours, five Elite Eights, and seven Sweet 16s. He has been selected the Big 12 Coach of the Year on three occasions, and in 2008 he won eight National Coach of the Year honors.[28]

Several of Self's players have achieved recognition as well. Wayne Simien, Marcus Morris, and Thomas Robinson were Big 12 Players of the Year. Mario Chalmers, Cole Aldrich, and Jeff Withey were Big 12 Defensive Players of the Year, and Sherron Collins earned the Big 12 Sixth Man Award in 2008. Sixteen Jayhawks were All–Big 12 first-team selections, and 16 student-athletes were also NBA draft selections.[29]

All 11 of Self's KU teams have been a competitive force nationally. Six of his teams have won 30 or more games. In addition to the 2008 national champions, the 2011–2012 Jayhawks also were spectacular, finishing the season at 32–7 and making a run all the way to the NCAA championship game against Kentucky. Tyshawn Taylor, Elijah Johnson, Jeff Withey, and Thomas Robinson were standouts on this team.[30]

Bill Self's 2007–2008 Jayhawks had arguably the best season in KU's storied basketball history, culminating with a dramatic victory over Memphis in the NCAA championship game. KU set a school record for wins in a season with a 37–3 record. They won both the Big 12 regular season and tournament titles and earned a number-one seed in the NCAA tournament for the second consecutive year.[31]

KU's road to the Final Four at the Alamodome in San Antonio included victories over Portland State, UNLV, Villanova, and Davidson. The Davidson game in the regional final went down to the wire, with the Jayhawks holding on for a 59–57 win. In the national semifinal, KU defeated Roy Williams's North Carolina Tar Heels, 84–66. This victory set up a meeting with Memphis, the number-one team in the tournament, coached by former Kansas assistant John Calipari.[32]

In one of the most memorable comebacks in NCAA tournament history, the Jayhawks rallied from a 60–51 deficit with 2:12 remaining in regulation. Kansas tied the game in the final seconds and won it in overtime, 75–68, for its third NCAA title and fifth national championship. KU was paced by the gritty play of Brandon Rush, Darrell Arthur, Mario Chalmers, Sasha Kahn, Sherron Collins, and Darnell

Bill Self speaks with his team before a game in 2007.

Jackson. Chalmers hit the biggest shot of the game (known as "Mario's Miracle"), a contested three-point shot that tied the score at 63 and sent the game into overtime. Mario was named the Final Four's Most Outstanding Player.[33]

Self has continued to recruit top players and win conference titles, going to the NCAA tournament annually. The KU tradition of excellence in basketball, reflecting the genius of Dr. Naismith and Phog Allen, continues to flourish in the twenty-first century.

KANSAS FOOTBALL

If basketball has been KU's athletic calling card, football has offered Jayhawk fans a heritage with moments of pride also. Football at KU since 1960 has been marked by occasional periods of success and noteworthy accomplishments by outstanding student-athletes. There have been 11 head coaches during the past 53 years, with teams posting a record of 251 wins, 349 losses, and 14 ties for a .408 winning percentage. The Jayhawks have participated in 11 bowl games, winning six. KU's dramatic victory over Virginia Tech in the 2008 Orange Bowl was a special highlight. KU won one conference title, sharing the Big Eight championship with Oklahoma in 1968. Stellar players like John Hadl, Gale Sayers, Bobby Douglass, John Zook, David Jaynes, Bruce Kallmeyer, Aqib Talib, and Anthony Collins earned first-team All-American honors.[34]

The 1960s began with the successful teams of Coach Jack Mitchell, led by such stars as All-Americans John Hadl and Gale Sayers, posting winning seasons for four of the first five years of the decade. Two subsequent disappointing seasons, however, led to Mitchell's departure and the arrival of Pepper Rodgers, who came to KU from UCLA. His four years at KU were highlighted by a Big Eight championship, a trip to the Orange Bowl, and All-American honors for Bobby Douglass and John Zook.[35]

Led by quarterback Bobby Douglass of El Dorado, Kansas, the first edition of Rodgers's Jayhawks finished in a tie for second in the Big Eight with a 5–2 record and defeated Border War rival Missouri, 17–6. Rodgers's second year at KU proved to be even more magical. The Jayhawks posted a 9–1 regular season record with the only loss coming to Oklahoma in Norman, 27–23. KU finished the season with wins over its archrivals, a 39–29 defeat of Kansas State and a 21–19 victory over Missouri in Columbia. KU lost to undefeated Penn State in the Orange

Gale Sayers, the "Kansas Comet," played for seven seasons for the NFL's Chicago Bears after leaving KU.

Bobby Douglas runs against Penn State in the 1969 Orange Bowl.

Bowl, 15–14, after a penalty for 12 men on the field permitted the Joe Paterno–led Nittany Lions to succeed on a two-point conversion attempt. Rodgers was named the Big Eight Co-Coach of the Year.[36]

Rodgers's final two seasons were disappointing, with a combined 6–15 record. Highlights were John Riggins rushing for 1,131 yards in 1970 and becoming the KU career rushing leader with 2,706 yards. Pepper resigned to take the head coaching job at UCLA and was replaced by longtime KU assistant coach and former KU player Don Fambrough.[37]

At this time, the Big Eight was one of the strongest and most competitive conferences in the country. Fambrough would serve two stints as the KU head coach, 1971–1974 and 1979–1982. The first edition of his Jayhawks won 19 games, and his 1973 Liberty Bowl team, led by All-American quarterback David Jaynes, was one of KU's finest. He also defeated KU rivals Kansas State and Missouri in three out of four games. Fourteen players from the Liberty Bowl team, which lost to North Carolina State, 31–18, went on to NFL careers. The 1981 edition of Fambrough's Jayhawks posted an 8–3 regular season record and earned an invitation to play Mississippi State in the Hall of Fame Bowl in Birmingham. They lost 10–0, playing without injured quarterback Frank Seurer. The Jayhawks were led throughout the season by Seurer and several All-Conference players: offensive guard and co-captain David Lawrence, wide receiver Wayne Capers, linebacker Kyle McNorton, and kicker Bucky Scribner.[38]

Bud Moore, an assistant coach and former player for the legendary Paul "Bear" Bryant at Alabama, replaced Fambrough in 1975. He installed a wishbone offense and found the perfect quarterback to direct it, Nolan Cromwell, from Ransom, Kansas (a defensive back originally). That first season was a huge success, and Moore was named Big Eight Conference Coach of the Year. Cromwell came out as a wishbone quarterback in the third game of the season. The Jayhawks defeated Oregon State, 20–0, as Cromwell set an NCAA record for quarterbacks by rushing for 294 yards, including a 79-yard touchdown scamper. One of the most notable victories in KU football history came against the undefeated Oklahoma Sooners in Norman. KU dominated, 23–3, as Cromwell sparked the offense, while the Jayhawk defense completely shut down the Sooners, ending their 28-game winning streak and 37-game unbeaten string. Oklahoma did not lose another game in 1975 and eventually was crowned national champion. The Jayhawks won seven games and were selected to meet the Pitt Panthers in the

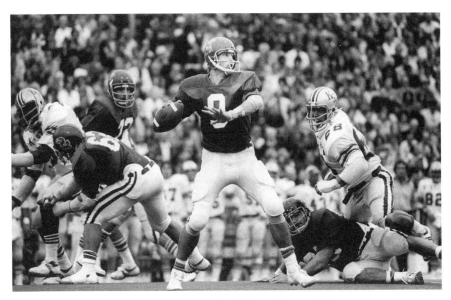

Nolan Cromwell sets to throw a pass against Kansas State, 1975.

Sun Bowl in El Paso, coming up short, 33–19, against a team led by All-American Tony Dorsett.[39]

Moore's 1976 team won six games, despite a season-ending knee injury to Nolan Cromwell. His Jayhawks won just three games in 1977, including victories over Kansas State and Missouri, and only one game in 1978. After a terrific start, Bud Moore's Jayhawks slipped conspicuously. He posted a 17–27–1 career record and Fambrough stepped in again.[40]

In October 1983, the NCAA announced the results of an inquiry into football recruiting irregularities that had occurred at KU in 1980 and 1981.[41] Also during this period, 1983–1985, 26 players were declared academically ineligible, a situation that prompted considerable consternation on campus.[42]

Fambrough was replaced after his second tour with KU by Mike Gottfried, the 38-year-old head coach at the University of Cincinnati. His tenure as the Jayhawks coach lasted for three seasons, during which his teams won 15 games. In addition to a victory over nationally prominent Southern California, Gottfried's Jayhawks also upset highly ranked Oklahoma and won five of six games against Missouri and Kansas State. Two of his outstanding players were All-American placekicker Bruce Kallmeyer and linebacker Willie Pless. Following the 1985 season, Gottfried resigned to become head coach at the University of Pittsburgh.[43]

Following two disappointing seasons with former KU assistant Bob Valesente at the helm, Jayhawk fans were ready for another change. In December 1987, KU hired Glen Mason, the energetic 37-year-old head coach from Kent State, who had played for Woody Hayes at Ohio State. Mason remained on the Jayhawks sidelines for nine seasons, posting a 47–54–1 record.[44]

In 1991, Kansas had its first winning football season in ten years, with a 6–5 record. That year also saw Mason's gritty running back, Tony Sands, gain nationwide attention by rushing for 396 yards against Missouri in Memorial Stadium, ranking second all-time in NCAA single-game history. Sands finished his career with 3,788 rushing yards, second only at KU to June Henley's (Henley played for Mason from 1993 to 1996) 3,841 yards.[45]

Mason led KU to two bowl games, the 1992 and 1995 Aloha Bowls, played in Hawaii. Surprising the prognosticators in 1992, KU posted an 8–4 record and finished third in the Big Eight Conference. KU's standout players were defensive linemen Dana Stubblefield and Gilbert Brown (both of whom went on to long NFL careers), quarterback Chip Hilleary, and placekicker Dan Eichloff. Mason's Jayhawks capped the season with a dramatic 23–20 victory over Brigham Young in Hawaii. Stubblefield was chosen the game's Most Valuable Player.[46]

In 1995, KU was a surprise team in college football. Picked to finish in the bottom half of the Big Eight, the Jayhawks finished the season with a 10–2 record and road wins over strong Colorado and Oklahoma teams. They then thrashed UCLA in the Aloha Bowl, 51–30. Quarterback Mark Williams passed for three touchdowns and was picked as the bowl's Most Valuable Player, and KU career rushing leader June Henley led the ground attack. Following the season, Mason was honored as the Big Eight Coach of the Year.[47]

Prior to the Aloha Bowl, Mason announced that he would be leaving for the University of Georgia, but he changed his mind and stayed at KU another year before departing for the University of Minnesota. He was replaced by Terry Allen, the highly successful coach of the University of Northern Iowa, who would lead the Jayhawks through five straight losing seasons, compiling a 20–33 record. That record included, however, three wins over Missouri and ten victories against Big 12 Conference competition. Chuck Woodling, sports editor of the *LJW*, noted that Allen was likeable, commenting that "Terry Allen is a good man who never had anything good happen to him at Kansas."[48]

Coach Mark Mangino celebrates with the 2008 Orange Bowl team.

KU moved quickly to replace Allen. In early December, Mark Mangino, the offensive coordinator at Oklahoma, was named the Jayhawks' head coach. His first season resulted in a 2–10 record, but the general feeling among fans was that KU was playing hard and becoming more competitive; football season ticket sales climbed to their highest point since 1969.[49]

In his eight seasons at KU, Mangino's teams posted a 50–48 record and played in the Tangerine, Fort Worth, Orange, and Insight Bowl games, winning three of those and producing several outstanding players. The 50 wins is the second-highest total of any coach in KU football history, behind only A. R. Kennedy (1904–1910). His 2007 season was arguably the best in KU football history, with a 12–1 record, a tie for first place in the Big 12 North, and the defeat of Virginia Tech, 24–21, in the Orange Bowl. Following that season, Mangino won all the National Coach of the Year Awards.[50]

The Orange Bowl victory, among the greatest in KU history, was sparked by the play of KU's dynamic quarterback, Todd Reesing, and the game's Most Valuable Player, Aqib Talib. Reesing threw for one touchdown and ran for another, while Talib's 60-yard interception for a touchdown set the tone for an inspired Kansas defense that had two more interceptions and three quarterback sacks. Following the season, two of Mangino's players received first-team All-American honors, Talib and offensive tackle Anthony Collins.[51]

Mangino's final year at KU, 2009, was full of promise. The Jayhawks won their first five games, but Reesing was injured in the Colorado game in Boulder and was hampered the remainder of the season. The

Jayhawks lost the rest of their games and finished with a 5–7 record. Late in the season, the Kansas Athletics Department conducted an internal investigation of allegations that Mangino had physically and mentally abused players, which led to his resignation in December 2009.[52]

Mangino was replaced by former Nebraska great and University of Buffalo coach Turner Gill. The first African American head football coach at KU, he was given a five-year contract. Gill's teams struggled, however, and posted a two-year 5–19 record. The day after a season-ending loss to Missouri, KU announced that Gill had been fired. Athletics Director Sheahon Zenger commented that "new leadership was necessary to place us on the path to championships in the Big 12 Conference" and that he had "the utmost respect for Turner Gill as an individual."[53] Less than two weeks later, Charlie Weis was introduced as KU's new coach. A protégé of legendary NFL coaches Bill Parcells and Bill Belichick, Weis had been the Notre Dame head coach from 2005 to 2009 and more recently offensive coordinator for the Kansas City Chiefs and the University of Florida Gators.[54]

Weis immediately began to mold a new football culture at KU. He stressed to his players the non-negotiable values of accountability, academic responsibility, discipline, and conditioning. Weis's team competed hard and won four games in his first two years, including the Jayhawks' first victory over a Big 12 Conference opponent since 2010.[55] However, following the fourth game of the 2014 season, a 23–0 loss to Texas, Athletics Director Zenger dismissed Weis, commenting: "I normally do not favor changing coaches in mid-season. But, I believe we have talented coaches and players in the program and I think this decision gives our players the best chance to begin making progress right away."[56] Clint Bowen, Weis's defensive coordinator, a former KU player, and longtime assistant coach, was named interim head coach.[57]

In early December, Zenger introduced David Beaty, an assistant coach and recruiting coordinator from Texas A&M, as the 38th head coach of the KU football team. Beaty received a five-year contract at a base salary of $800,000 annually plus incentives, which could total $1.5 million. The Texas native had previously served as an assistant at Kansas under Mark Mangino and Turner Gill.[58]

THE RISE OF WOMEN'S ATHLETICS

Women's athletics has a long and rich history at the University of Kansas in both intramural and extramural competition. In the late 1960s,

Women's sports rapidly expanded with the passage of Title IX in 1972. Softball is pictured here during the 1987 season.

Marlene Mawson, an associate professor in Health and Physical Education, became KU's first advocate for women's extramural sports, organizing and coaching sports such as field hockey, basketball, softball, and volleyball. This began to change, however, in 1972 with the passage of Title IX of the Education Amendments Act, which prohibited the exclusion of women from any educational activities at institutions that received federal funding. This included intercollegiate athletics. One of the objectives of the statute was to give women an equal opportunity to develop their skills and apply them competitively.[59]

In June 1974, Marian Washington was hired as assistant director of intercollegiate athletics/women's sports. She had dual responsibilities as an administrator and women's basketball coach. Washington, a graduate of West Chester State College in Pennsylvania, was a highly acclaimed basketball and track and field athlete. At the time of her appointment, she was a graduate student and physical education instructor at KU.[60]

In July 1974, the women's intercollegiate athletics program began with ten sports: field hockey, gymnastics, basketball, golf, tennis, swimming, volleyball, track and field, cross-country, and softball. The

Marian Washington coaches a game in 1999. She is credited with contributing to the growth in varsity women's sports after Title IX.

budget for the program grew steadily over the next several years, with funds coming from both the Kansas legislature and the KU Student Senate. In the spring of 1976, KU began providing scholarships for female student-athletes.[61]

During the first ten years following the passage of Title IX, KU women's student-athletes represented their school admirably. Washington's basketball team was consistently ranked nationally, the swimming and diving team won eight consecutive Big Eight championships, and several other sports were competitive in conference play. However, field hockey and gymnastics were dropped for financial reasons.[62]

Women's Basketball

For 31 seasons, Marian Washington was the face of Kansas women's basketball. She became KU's head coach in 1973 and served the university with distinction until her resignation in January 2004. During that span, her teams won or earned a share of seven Big Eight and Big 12 titles and advanced to NCAA postseason play 11 times, including two runs to the Sweet 16. She was named the Big Eight Conference Coach of the Year in 1992 and 1996 and the Big 12 Coach of the Year in 1997. Highly regarded nationally, Washington served as an assistant coach on the 1996 gold medal US women's Olympic basketball team. Among her many honors were selection for the Women's Basketball Hall of Fame and recognition by the Black Coaches Association with its Lifetime Achievement Award. In 1996, she received the William I. Koch Outstanding Kansas Woman of the Year award.[63]

Washington also mentored three Kodak All-Americans, Tameka Dixon, Angela Aycock, and Lynette Woodard. Dixon was a 1997 honoree and the Big Eight Conference Player of the Year in 1996 and snagged the same accolade from the Big 12 Conference the following year. Aycock, who was recognized in 1995, was a three-time All–Big Eight Conference first-team selection. Woodard, a Wichita native, who played at KU from 1978 to 1981, is perhaps the most outstanding student-athlete in the history of women's college basketball. She was a four-time Kodak All-American, a two-time Academic All-American, and the all-time leading scorer in women's collegiate basketball history, with 3,649 points. Woodard was co-captain of the 1984 US Olympics gold medal women's basketball team and the first woman to play for the Harlem Globetrotters. She has been enshrined in the Naismith Memorial Basketball Hall of Fame and the Women's College Basketball Hall of Fame.[64]

Washington's teams struggled in the twilight of her career; her last three teams won only five games in the rugged Big 12 Conference. Following her resignation, Athletics Director Lew Perkins saluted her achievements at KU, noting, "Marian Washington has been a pioneer—a leader—a mentor and a terrific basketball coach. It's not a business for her—it's a passion."[65]

The hiring of the highly regarded 40-year-old head coach Bonnie Henrickson in 2004 signaled a commitment to put Kansas women's basketball in the top echelon of the sport. Henrickson came to KU from Virginia Tech, where she had led the Hokies for seven years, to a 158–62 record, 7 postseason appearances, and 20 or more wins every season. In her ten years with KU, the Jayhawks have posted four 20-win seasons, advanced to postseason play seven times, and produced four first-team All–Big 12 selections and 29 Academic All–Big 12 honorees. Her overall record is 173–154.[66]

In the 2012 NCAA tournament, Henrickson's Jayhawks defeated Nebraska and number eight–ranked Delaware, before falling to perennial powerhouse Tennessee in the Sweet 16. A year later, they beat

Lynette Woodard in 1979.

Angela Goodrich pull-up jumper.

Colorado and South Carolina prior to coming up short in the Sweet 16 against the eventual NCAA tournament runner-up, Notre Dame. Center Carolyn Davis and guard Angel Goodrich were the standouts for the Jayhawks' first Sweet 16 team, and Goodrich was a key player again the following year.[67]

Both Davis and Goodrich will be remembered as two of the finest players in KU women's basketball history. Davis earned first-team All–Big 12 Conference honors in 2011 and 2012 and was a second-team selection in 2013, when her season was cut short with a knee injury. Goodrich, whose electrifying point guard play thrilled Jayhawk fans for four years, was a first-team All–Big 12 selection in 2013. She became the second Henrickson player selected in the WNBA draft when picked by the Tulsa Shock. In addition to Davis and Goodrich, Crystal Kemp and Danielle McCray also were first-team All–Big 12 selections in 2006 and 2009, respectively. McCray was drafted by the WNBA Connecticut Sun in 2009.[68]

TRACK AND FIELD

By the 1960s, the University of Kansas was very well known for the excellence of its track and field teams under legendary coach Bill Easton, whose Jayhawks won NCAA Outdoor championships in 1959 and 1960. He had coached 54 All-Americans and 22 national champions, as well as seven Olympic gold medal winners. The outstanding performers on those championship teams were distance runner and future Olympic gold medal winner Billy Mills, four-time All-American sprinter Charlie Tidwell, NCAA champion and javelin record holder Bill Alley, and hurdler and future Olympic silver medal winner Cliff Cushman.[69]

In 1965, Bob Timmons replaced Easton, and his reign as the Kansas head track coach from 1965 to 1988 was equally as impressive. Coach Timmons's KU teams won 13 Big Eight Indoor and 14 conference Outdoor titles. Even more significant, his Jayhawks captured NCAA Indoor championships in 1966, 1967, and 1970. His 1970 Outdoor squad shared the NCAA title with Oregon, Brigham Young, and Drake, a remarkable fourth NCAA title in five years.[70]

Timmons's most notable protégé was Jim Ryun, a standout for the coach at Wichita East, who followed him to KU. However, several other of Timmons's Jayhawks were noteworthy performers in the late 1960s. John Lawson was the NCAA cross-country champion in 1965; Gary

Billy Mills earned All-American cross-country honors three times in the 1960s and won an individual title in the Big Eight cross-country championship. He represented the United States in the 1964 Tokyo Olympics, winning a gold medal.

Ard won three All-American awards in the long jump in 1966 and 1967, and Ron Jessie won the NCAA long jump in 1969.[71]

Ryun arrived at KU in 1965 and began perhaps the most storied career in Jayhawk track history. From 1965 to 1969, he set world records in 880 yards, 1,500 meters, the mile, two- and three-mile runs, plus the 5,000 meters. He also snagged five NCAA titles (four Indoor and one Outdoor). In 1966, *Sports Illustrated* named him its Sportsman of the Year, and he also earned the prestigious Sullivan Award as the top amateur athlete in America. A three-time Olympian, he captured the silver medal in the 1,500 meters at the 1968 Olympic Games in Mexico City. In 1982, Ryun was inducted into the National Track and Field Hall of Fame.[72]

To close out the decade, KU won the 1969 NCAA Indoor championship and finished second in the NCAA Outdoor championship. A year later, the Jayhawks were even better, sweeping the Big Eight and NCAA Indoor and Outdoor championships. The 1970 NCAA champions were led by a splendid trio of shot-putters. Known as the "Pachyderms," Karl Salb, Steve Williams, and Doug Knop finished first, second, and third in the 1969 and 1970 championships, earning All-American honors. The following year, KU swept the Big Eight shot put event for the fifth consecutive time.[73]

During the 1970s, under the leadership of Coach Bob Timmons, KU continued as a dominant force in track and field, winning eight of nine Big Eight Outdoor conference titles and four Indoor championships. Individual Indoor national champions were Terry Porter in the pole vault and Theo Hamilton in the long jump. The two-mile and one-mile relay teams also captured national Indoor honors. Outdoor national champions were Sam Colson in the javelin and Randy Smith in the high jump. The 440-yard relay team also earned national honors.[74]

The KU women's track program began in 1973 with Marian Washington as its first coach. Teri Anderson took over the program in the late 1970s and led the Jayhawks to second-place finishes in the Big Eight Conference Indoor and Outdoor championships, as well as a third-place finish in the Indoor national meet in 1979. Sheila Calmese, a sprinter, was an outstanding performer for KU. She was the first three-time All-American in KU women's track history and still ranks second all-time in the 100-meter dash in the KU women's Outdoor record book. Calmese won the Indoor national championship in the 300-yard dash in 1978. Two other performers, Charmane Kuhlman in the long jump and high jumper Shawn Corwin, earned All-American honors.[75]

Jim Ryun was one of the most celebrated runners in college history.

Carla Coffey, Kansas's second African American head coach, re-placed Teri Anderson as the women's track and field coach in 1981 and took KU to seven national championship meets during the decade of the 1980s. Under Coffey, Kansas achieved national recognition in the throwing events. Anne Grethe Baeraas and Denise Buchanan earned All-American honors in the javelin and shot put, respectively. A particularly noteworthy performer, Halcyon "Tudie" McKnight, earned All-American recognition in the long jump three times. In 1995, the Kansas Relays women's long jump event was named in her honor.[76]

Beginning in 1979 and through the 1990s, Kansas gained a national reputation for excellence in the jumping events. KU had 31 All-Americans in the pole vault, high jump, long jump, triple jump, heptathlon, and decathlon events. The chief architect of these accomplishments was Rick Attig, the vertical jumps coach from 1985 to 2000. The Jayhawks' notable All-American pole-vaulters during this period were Jeff Buckingham, Chris Bohanan, Scott Huffman, Pat Manson, Cam Miller, and John Bazzoni. Huffman participated in the 1996 Olympic Games, and Manson's vault of 18'8" in the 1989 Big Eight Indoor championships remains a KU record. Rounding out those with All-American honors for KU men were Sanya Owolabi, the 1980 NCAA Indoor triple jump champion, Warren Wilhoite in the long jump, and high jumper Nick Johannsen.[77]

When the legendary Bob Timmons resigned in 1988, he was replaced by his former pupil Gary Schwartz, who assumed responsibility for both the men's and the women's programs. As a student-athlete, Schwartz had won a Big Eight championship in the discus throw and was team captain as a senior. In 12 years, Schwartz produced 41 All-Americans (men and women) and led the KU men to a fourth-place tie in the 1989 NCAA Indoor championships.[78]

Several KU women achieved national recognition with Schwartz as coach. All-Americans included Mary Beth Labosky in the high jump, Heather Berlin in the javelin, Cathy Palacios in the mile, Kristi Kloster in the 800 meters, Andrea Branson in the pole vault, and Candace Mason in multiple events. Kloster was the 1996 NCAA Indoor champion in the 800 meters. Mason, who earned five All-American honors in the pole vault, pentathlon, and decathlon, also was an Academic All-American.[79]

In May 2000, KU hired a head coach destined to restore the Jayhawks' track and field program to its glory days. Stanley Redwine, a former All-American middle-distance runner at Arkansas, came to Mount Oread after six years as the successful head coach at the University of Tulsa. Over the next 14 years, Redwine produced and mentored 145 All-Americans, 15 individual national champions, and four Olympians, earned three Big 12 Conference team titles, and captured the 2013 NCAA women's Outdoor championship.[80]

Four of Redwine's male athletes won gold medals in the Indoor and Outdoor NCAA championships. The Indoor champions were

Coach Bob Timmons.

Scott Russell and Egor Agafonov in the weight throw and sprinter Leo Bookman in the 200-meter dash. Bookman was also an Outdoor champion in 200 meters, as was Jordan Scott in the pole vault. On the women's side, the Indoor champions were Amy Linnen and Natalia Bartnovskaya in the pole vault, Diamond Dixon in the 400-meter dash, and Andrea Geubelle in the triple jump and the long jump. Lindsey Vollmer captured an Outdoor title in the heptathlon.[81]

Andrea Geubelle, NCAA champion in two events.

Olympic gold medal winner Diamond Dixon.

Redwine also mentored four Olympians: Charles Gruber (1,500 meters, USA, Atlanta-2004); Scott Russell (javelin, Canada, Beijing-2008); Nickesha Anderson (4x100 meter relay, Jamaica, Beijing-2008); and Diamond Dixon (4x400 meter relay, USA, London-2012). Dixon, who won four Big 12 Conference titles and four more All-American honors in 2012, brought home a gold medal from London.[82]

The 2012–2013 seasons marked the most successful stretch in Redwine's illustrious coaching career, capped by his women's team winning the NCAA national Outdoor championship. It was the first women's national championship in any sport at KU and also the first national Outdoor title for Kansas since 1970, when Bob Timmons's men's team was victorious.[83]

The 2013 Jayhawk women's national championship track team.

Of Coach Redwine's 13 entries in the meet, 11 picked up points for the Jayhawks. Superstar and multiple All-American Andrea Geubelle earned 16 points with second-place finishes in the long jump and triple jump. Lindsay Vollmer captured KU's first-ever individual gold medal for the women's program in the national championships by winning the grueling seven-event heptathlon. Natalia Bartnovskaya won silver in the pole vault, and Jessica Maroszek finished fourth in the discus throw. Kansas totaled 60 points, well ahead of runner-up Texas A&M's 48 points. Following this landmark season, Redwine was named the NCAA Women's Head Coach of the Year.[84]

CROSS-COUNTRY

Kansas has a rich and proud cross-country heritage. Legendary KU runners like Wes Santee, Al Frame, Herb Semper, Billy Mills, and Jim Ryun helped to shape this tradition of excellence. In 1965, John Lawson won the NCAA cross-country championship, and since Lawson's notable accomplishment, seven Jayhawk men and one woman have earned cross-country All-American honors. The men include Brent Steiner (1984), Michael Cox and David Johnston (1994), Benson Chesang (2004), Paul Hefferon (2006), and Colby Wissel (2006 and 2007). Chesang, a native of Kenya, was the Big 12 Conference champion in 2004 and 2005, KU's first back-to-back conference champion since John Lawson in the mid-1960s. Julia Saul, perhaps the greatest female cross-country runner in Kansas history, captured All-American recognition in 1992. And the KU women were crowned NCAA Midwest regional champions in 1993 and 1994. Kansas also boasts one of the nation's premier cross-country courses, Rim Rock Farm. Located north of Lawrence, it was purchased in 1970 by Coach Bob Timmons and his wife, Pat. They gifted the property to the university in 2006.[85]

SWIMMING AND DIVING

Kansas swimming and diving established a tradition of excellence that began in the 1960s and has continued to the present. Coaches like Dick Reamon, Bill Spahn, Gary Kempf, and Clark Campbell produced teams and individuals who were highly regarded within the Big Eight and Big 12 Conferences and nationally. Following his graduation from KU in 1962, Dick Reamon, a six-time Big Eight champion in the butterfly and individual medley, became the head coach of the Jayhawk men's swimming and diving team. Over the next 15 years, Reamon would set a standard for excellence, winning eight straight conference championships from 1968 to 1975 and compiling a sterling 90–36 dual meet record. Additionally, he produced 218 All–Big Eight swimmers, 107 conference gold medalists, six All–Big Eight Swimmers of the Year, and 15 All-Americans.[86]

At the conclusion of the 1977 season, Reamon stepped down as head coach to go into business. His individual event All-Americans included Kim Bolton (50-yard freestyle), Tom Kempf (1,650-yard freestyle), and Don Pennington (500-yard freestyle).[87] It was during Reamon's tenure, in 1967, that the new Robinson Center Natatorium opened, and it remains the home of the Kansas swimming and diving program.

Following Dick Reamon's resignation, Bill Spahn, the highly regarded mentor of the powerful Wichita Swim Club, became the KU head coach. Spahn served in this position until 1981 and won Big Eight championships in 1977 and 1979.[88]

In 1981, Gary Kempf, the highly successful KU women's swimming coach since 1976, became responsible for both the men's and the women's programs. Kempf, a former Big Eight Conference Swimmer of the Year, led both the men's and the women's programs, for 18

All-American and national champion swimmer Tammy Thomas.

and 24 years, respectively. Kempf's head coaching record was exemplary. His women's teams won 13 Big Eight titles, including a remarkable nine straight titles from 1976 to 1983, and he posted a dual meet record of 124–33, winning 79 percent. He was named Big Eight Women's Coach of the Year five times, Men's Coach of the Year four times, and the NCAA Women's Coach of the Year in 1983. His women's teams finished in the top 25 of the national championships ten times.[89]

During Kempf's tenure, two KU women won NCAA titles, Tammy Thomas and Michelle Rojohn. Thomas, competing from 1980 to 1983, set American records in the 50- and 100-yard freestyle, finished first in the 1983 NCAA championships in those events, and earned All-American honors 17 times in individual events and relays. She was the Big Eight Co-athlete of the Year in 1983. Rojohn was the 1996 NCAA champion in three-meter diving.[90]

One of Kempf's outstanding male swimmers was Ron Neugent, a Wichita native who transferred from Southern Methodist. He earned All-American honors in 1983 by finishing 11th in the NCAA 1,650-yard freestyle and set five KU and two Big Eight individual records.[91]

In 2002, Clark Campbell became KU's swimming and diving team head coach. Campbell, a Kansas graduate and former swimmer, returned to Mount Oread after serving as the head coach at the University of Evansville, in Indiana. During his 12 years at KU, he has posted an impressive 83–49 meet record and his swimmers and divers have been recognized with All-American, Big 12 Conference, and academic honors. In 2014, the team had its best year ever under Campbell, finishing second in the Big 12 championship. Campbell was honored as the Big 12 Coach of the Year.[92]

Two swimmers and one diver have earned All-American honors over the past 12 years: Julia Kuzhil in the 100-yard backstroke, Chelsie Miller in the 400-yard individual medley, and Erin Mertz in three-meter diving. Campbell's swimmers hold almost half of the 21 pool records at the Robinson Natatorium. They include Maria Mayrovich in the 50- and 100-yard freestyle, Miller in the 1,000-yard freestyle and the 400-yard individual medley, Kuzhil in the 100- and 200-yard backstroke, and Danielle Hermann in the 200-yard individual medley plus the 200-yard freestyle relay and 200-yard medley relay teams.[93]

BASEBALL AND SOFTBALL

Baseball traces its roots at KU back to 1880 and enjoys a rich history of varsity competition. In the 1960s, it was headed by Floyd Temple, an icon whose name would become synonymous with the sport for the next 28 years on Mount Oread. Temple lettered in football and baseball and became the Jayhawks' baseball coach in 1954. While serving as the coach, he recorded a .500 or better record in 14 of those 28 years and won the Big Eight Conference tournament in 1976. Hampered in the early years by having only four scholarships, he fared much better in his last six seasons. When the number of grants in aid was increased to 13, Temple won 171 games, for a .629 winning percentage. He coached four All-Americans and seven future major leaguers, including Steve Renko, Bob Allison, and Chuck Dobson.[94]

A highlight of the 1990s was the performance of the KU baseball team under the tutelage of Coach Dave Bingham. Bingham, who had enjoyed success at Emporia State, was hired in 1988. Over the next eight years, he posted 249 wins, including 30- and 40-win seasons. In 1993 and 1994, Bingham's Jayhawks registered the best back-to-back seasons in KU history. The 1993 edition won 45 games, a KU record, and advanced to the College World Series in Omaha.[95]

The journey to Omaha was spectacular. After being eliminated by Oklahoma State in the Big Eight tournament, KU played in its first-ever

Chancellor Gene Budig gives a good-luck handshake to catcher Kent Shelley before a Jayhawks home opener in 1982. Budig was an avid fan and became commissioner of the American League of baseball upon leaving KU. Shelley became a highly successful coach at Johnson County Community College.

NCAA regional tournament in Knoxville, Tennessee. The Jayhawks lost the first game to Fresno State and then defeated Tennessee, Rutgers, Clemson, and Fresno State in 10 innings to dramatically capture the championship and earn a trip to the Series. Although coming up short against Texas A&M and Long Beach State, the team had earned the respect of the college baseball community. It was paced by five

All-Americans: pitchers Jim Walker and Jamie Splittorff (a freshman and 1994 selection), second baseman Jeff Berblinger, catcher Jeff Niemier, and outfielder Darryl Monroe.[96]

The 1994 season saw KU win 40 games, post a 17–9 Big Eight record, and once again move on to NCAA regional tournament play. This time, after defeating number four–ranked Ohio State, the team was eliminated after losses to Jacksonville and Brigham Young. In addition to the All-Americans on the 1993 and 1994 teams, pitcher Curtis Shaw also earned All-American recognition in 1990. Two other noteworthy baseball players in the 1990s were All-Americans Josh Kliner and Isaac Byrd. Kliner and Byrd both played in KU's final Big Eight season in 1996. Kliner, a second baseman, led the Big Eight with a .438 batting average and was named a first-team All-American by the American Baseball Coaches Association. Byrd, an outfielder, who also starred for the football Jayhawks, batted .393 and was named a third-team All-American.[97]

In July 2002, Ritch Price was hired as KU's new baseball coach, replacing Bobby Randall. Price a native of Oregon, came to Lawrence from Cal Poly in San Louis Obispo, California. Known as a player's coach and an excellent recruiter, he has had six 30-win seasons and three especially magical seasons, 2006, 2009, and 2014.[98]

His 2006 team posted 43 victories, the second-best total in KU history. Although seeded sixth in the Big 12 tournament, the Jayhawks won four straight games to capture the conference championship and advance to the NCAA tournament. It was KU's first conference baseball title since winning the Big Seven championship in 1949. The Most Valuable Player in the tournament was Jayhawks centerfielder Matt Baty. After defeating Hawaii, 9–6, in the NCAA regional opener, they were eliminated by losses to Oregon State and Hawaii.[99]

The 2009 season was one of the most memorable in the long tradition of Kansas baseball. The Jayhawks won 39 games, posted a sparkling 25–3 home record, and finished fourth in the Big 12 Conference standings. Sophomore third baseman Tony Thompson had a spectacular season for KU, winning the Big 12 Conference Triple Crown with a .389 batting average, 21 home runs, and 82 runs batted in. He received All-American recognition from four different publications. As in 2006, KU advanced to the NCAA regionals. Following an opening loss to Coastal Carolina, the Jayhawks defeated Dartmouth and Coastal Carolina before being eliminated by North Carolina.[100] In 2014, KU won 35 games, finished a best-ever third in the Big 12 race, and advanced to the NCAA tournament. The Jayhawks opened tournament play with a win over Kentucky before losing to Louisville and Kentucky.[101]

Price has coached 44 players who were drafted or signed by professional organizations and four players who went on to play major league baseball. Two of his players, Thompson and relief pitcher Don Czyz, earned All-American honors. He has also had the unique distinction of mentoring his three sons, Ritchie, Ryne, and Robby, as Kansas baseball players.[102]

KU softball began competition in the late 1960s with Marlene Mawson and Linda Dollar coaching the first teams. Following the passage of Title IX, Sharon Drysdale, a professor in Health, Physical Education, and Recreation, took over the reins of the Jayhawks and guided them through five successful seasons, which all included appearances in the Association for Intercollegiate Athletics for Women (AIAW) World Series. In 1977, Bob Stanclift, from Lawrence, became the KU head coach for the next 11 years. Stanclift's teams won over 68 percent of their games, claimed three Big Eight Conference titles, and advanced to the AIAW World Series twice and the NCAA tournament on two occasions.[103]

Three Jayhawks, Jill Larson, Tracy Bunge, and Sheila Connolly, earned All-American honors in the Stanclift era. Larson, a third baseman and KU's first softball All-American, led the Jayhawks in 1981 with a .341 batting average. Bunge, who later in her career served as the KU coach for 13 years, was a standout pitcher and an All-American in 1986. Sheila Connolly earned All-American honors in 1986 and 1987. An outstanding all-around athlete who played shortstop and centerfield, Connolly batted a blistering .391 in her senior year and also led KU in hits, runs scored, triples, and stolen bases. She also was a star in the classroom, earning first-team Academic All-American recognition. KU retired her number 11 jersey.[104]

In 1988, Kalum Haack was hired to replace Stanclift. Coach Haack's teams won 283 games during his highly successful eight-year stint with the Jayhawks. They were ranked in the national polls for four straight seasons, 1991–1994, won the NCAA Midwest regional title in 1992, and advanced to the College World Series that same year. They also played in the Midwest regionals again in 1993 and 1994. Haack's premier athlete during his tenure as KU coach was Camille Spitaleri, arguably the greatest player in KU softball history. A third baseman, she became KU's only three-time All-American (1990, 1991, and 1992). She was also a two-time All–Big Eight first-team selection, ranks second on the KU career hits list, had her number 10 jersey retired, and is a member

Students line up for tickets at Allen Fieldhouse, a long-standing KU tradition.

of the KU Athletics Hall of Fame. Pitcher Stephani Williams and short-stop Christy Arterburn, both second-team All-Americans, also played vital roles in the success of Haack's great teams of the early 1990s.[105]

Former KU All-American pitcher Tracy Bunge served as the Jay-hawks head coach from 1997 to 2009. Her squads won over 53 percent of their games and advanced to the NCAA regionals four times. Bunge's 2006 team had a storybook ending to its season. Despite posting an 8–10 conference record and finishing sixth in the Big 12 Conference, the Jayhawks won the conference tournament and thus qualified for the NCAA tournament. In the NCAA regionals, they defeated Brigham Young twice prior to being eliminated by Washing-ton. Outfielder Christi Musser and pitcher Serena Settlemeier earned All-American and Academic All-American recognition for Bunge's teams. Settlemeier is KU's all-time home run leader.[106]

In June 2009, Megan Smith, an assistant coach at Louisiana State University, was named the coach of the Jayhawks, replacing Bunge. Under Smith's guidance, the softball team showed steady progress, culminating with a 34–23 record in 2014 and KU's first NCAA tour-nament bid since 2006. In 2013, Kansas defeated the country's top-ranked team, the Oklahoma Sooners, in Lawrence on Senior Day and finished fourth in the Big 12 Conference race. It was the softball program's first-ever win over a number one–ranked team. Smith's standout player was outfielder Maggie Hull, who completed her four years on Mount Oread in 2013 and was named a first-team Academic All-American.[107]

ROWING AND SOCCER AS VARSITY SPORTS

In 1995, KU added rowing and soccer as women's varsity sports. With an average of 75 women participating annually, rowing was a big boost for the university's compliance with Title IX regulations. Its first and only coach has been Kansas graduate Rob Catloth. During his 19-year tenure, Catloth has built a strong foundation for the program and achieved many noteworthy results. KU demonstrated its full commitment to the program in 2009 with the construction of the KU Boathouse in Lawrence's Burcham Park. This $6 million facility was a major enhancement for Catloth's program, permitting the team to work out indoors during the winter months and providing a huge assist in recruiting.[108]

KU rowers participate in both the Big 12 Conference and Conference USA. Some of their accomplishments include an Intercollegiate Rowing Association championship in 1999, winning the Kansas Cup competition over Kansas State for five straight years, and 10 first-place finishes in 2005. In 2012, the Varsity Four won the Conference USA and Big 12 championship. In 2012–2013, KU rowers had 31 first-place finishes against the rugged Big 12 and Conference USA competition.[109]

Catloth's women athletes have excelled not only in the water but in the classroom as well. Lindsey Miles and Kara Boston were named recipients of the prestigious Big 12 Prentice Gautt Postgraduate Scholarship in 2007 and 2008, respectively. And in 2013, Elizabeth Scherer was honored as the Big 12 Scholar-Athlete of the Year.[110]

KU's first soccer coach was Lori Walker, a University of North Carolina graduate and former Tar Heels player. Walker stayed on Mount Oread for two years and was replaced by Dan Magner, who also coached KU for two seasons. In February 1999, KU hired Mark Francis, who has been leading the KU soccer program for 16 years.[111]

During his career at KU, the native of London, England, and three-time All-American at Southern Methodist has brought Kansas the stability necessary for a winning program. His accomplishments include a Big 12 Conference championship, six NCAA postseason appearances, including a Sweet 16, and eleven seasons with ten or more victories. Francis has also coached six All-Americans and four Academic All-Americans.[112]

Francis's 2014 Jayhawk squad, led by first-team All–Big 12 selections Liana Salazar, Caroline Van Slambrock, and Ashley Williams, posted a 15–6 record that included a best-ever 8–0 record to start the season. The Jayhawks finished third in the Big 12 Conference and advanced to the NCAA tournament.[113]

His teams had an outstanding run in the early 2000s, earning spots in the NCAA tournament in 2001, 2003, and 2004. The 2004 edition of the Jayhawks was arguably the finest team in KU soccer history. Led by forward Caroline Smith and goalkeeper Meghan Miller, Kansas won the Big 12 Conference with an 8–2 record and also defeated Creighton in the NCAA tournament before falling to Nebraska. Francis was honored as the Big 12 Conference and Central Region Coach of the Year.[114]

In 2008 and 2011, Kansas again returned to the NCAA tournament. The 2008 Jayhawks picked up 13 wins and defeated Denver in the tournament. Several players received recognition for their efforts during the year. Emily Cressy was selected as a Freshman All-American and the Big 12 Rookie of the Year. Cressy, Monica Dolinsky, and Estelle Johnson made the All–Central Region Team. Dolinsky was also a first-team All–Big 12 selection. In 2011, Kansas's success was sparked by junior Whitney Berry and freshmen Liana Salazar and Ingrid Vidal. All three snagged All–Big 12 Conference and All-Central Region honors. Both Berry and Vidal repeated as All–Big 12 first-team selections in 2012.[115]

As indicated earlier, six of Francis's players have earned All-American honors. Four were members of the 2004 team: defenders Holly Gault and Afton Sauer; goalkeeper Meghan Miller; and forward Caroline Smith. Forward Emily Cressy was honored in 2008. Smith, a three-time All-American, is a KU soccer legend, holding career records in points, goals, shots, shots on goal, and game-winning goals. She starred in the classroom as well, being named an Academic All-American twice.[116] Liana Salazar was an All-American selection in 2014, and Caroline Van Slambrouck earned Academic All-American recognition in the same year.[117]

VOLLEYBALL

Like most other women's sports at KU, volleyball had its start in the late 1960s under the direction of Marlene Mawson. During the early 1970s, two women who coached other women's sports on Mount

Oread, Linda Dollar and Ann Laptad, helped to mold the volleyball squad. Laptad was the coach of the 1971–1972 Jayhawks, recognized as "the first Kansas Volleyball team."[118] From 1975 until 1998, KU had limited success competing in the rugged Big Eight and Big 12 Conferences. Coach Bob Stanclift's teams posted three winning seasons in the mid-1970s, winning over 60 percent of their matches. Frankie Albitz, who coached the Jayhawks for nine years (1985–1993), had her most noteworthy campaign in 1986 when the Jayhawks finished with a splendid 26–9 mark and broke even in Big Eight play.[119]

In 1998, Ray Bechard, the highly successful coach at Barton Community College, was hired as KU's new head volleyball coach. He replaced Karen Schoenweis, who had been the Jayhawks' coach for four years. Over the next 17 seasons, Bechard became KU's winningest volleyball coach, compiling 295 victories and guiding the Crimson and Blue to six NCAA tournament appearances. At KU and Barton, through the 2014 season, he has logged a noteworthy 1,011–286 (.779) career record.[120]

In 2014, Bechard recorded his 1,000th career victory against Cleveland State, and KU—for the third straight year—earned an NCAA tournament bid. The young and highly competitive Jayhawks finished the Big 12 conference season in a second-place tie with Oklahoma and Iowa State.[121]

In 2012 and 2013, Kansas had its best-ever back-to-back seasons. The Jayhawks were 26–7 in 2012 and 25–8 in 2013 and hosted NCAA tournament games in Allen Fieldhouse both years. The 2013 edition of the Jayhawks advanced to the NCAA Sweet 16, defeating Wichita State and Creighton before losing to the University of Washington. Bechard was named Big 12 and American Volleyball Coaches Association (AVCA) Midwest Region Coach of the Year for both years. Following the 2012 season, middle blocker Caroline Jarmoc became KU's first-ever volleyball All-American as a second-team selection, and she became a third-team pick in 2013. The 2013 Jayhawks earned numerous honors. Erin McNorton was the Big 12 Setter of the Year, and Chelsea Albers, Sara McClinton, McNorton, and Jarmoc were named to the All–Big 12 first team. Taylor Soucie was selected the AVCA Midwest Region Freshman of the Year.[122]

Under Bechard, the Horejsi Center opened in 1999 and became one of America's most raucous and intimidating volleyball venues. With its loyal fan base, KU volleyball consistently ranks in the Top 50 attendance leaders.[123]

Coach Ray Bechard huddles with his team in 2013.

Bechard had several other outstanding student-athletes take the court for him over the years. A few of those were Josi Lima, an All–Big 12 first-team selection for four years; Jill Dorsey and Brianne Riley, KU's career digs leaders; Katie Martincich, the Big 12 Sportsperson of the Year in 2007–2008; and Taylor Tolefree, the Big 12 Scholar-Athlete of the Year in 2012.[124]

TENNIS

Kansas women's tennis began competition as a varsity sport in 1976, with former KU basketball player Tom Kivisto as its first head coach. Over the next 20 years, until Kansas became a member of the Big 12, the Jayhawks won six Big Eight team titles. Included in this number were a remarkable five straight championships from 1992 to 1996, with Chuck Merzbacher as the head coach for the last four.[125]

The Jayhawks had several outstanding individual performances during this period. Most notable among them was Eveline Hamers, who captured three straight Big Eight singles titles from 1989 to 1991 and was a four-time All-American selection for four years. Nora Koves, Tracy Treps, and Kylie Hunt also won Big Eight singles titles, while Christie Sim won the Big 12 championship in 1997. In addition to Hamers, other KU standouts to earn All-American honors in singles were Koves, Hunt, and Mindy Weiner.[126]

A spectacular accomplishment for the women's program came in 1994 when Nora Koves and Rebecca Jensen captured the NCAA doubles championship. It has been the only national title in KU tennis history, men or women. Koves and Jensen were two-time All-Americans in doubles competition, and Christie Sim and Kylie Hunt were also All-Americans in doubles.[127]

Kansas had twelve men's tennis coaches from the mid-1960s until 2001, when the men's sport was discontinued by the Athletics Department for budgetary reasons. The most stable and successful period for the program was from 1983 to 1996 when Scott Perelman and Michael Center were the head coaches. Perelman had a career record of 153–106, while Center logged a spectacular 83–28 record. Under Perelman's leadership, the Jayhawks captured three straight Big Eight titles (1987–1989) and were Region V champions in 1987, 1988, and 1992. John Falbo was the Big Eight singles champion in 1988 and also earned All-American honors in doubles, with Craig Wildey in 1988 and Jim Secrest in 1989.[128]

Michael Center's Crimson and Blue netters won three consecutive Big Eight championships, as well as Region V championships in 1994, 1995, and 1996. Kansas had several Big Eight champions and All-Americans during the 1980s and 1990s. The Big Eight singles champions were Mike Wolf and Enrique Abaroa (also a Big 12 champion). Doubles champions included Wolf and Wildey, Falbo and Wildey, Paul Garvin and Carlos Fleming, and Abaroa and Xavier Avila. All-Americans in addition to Falbo, Wildey, and Secrest were Avila and Abaroa in singles and Abaroa and Luis Uribe and Chris Walker and Wildey in doubles.[129]

GOLF

The Kansas women's golf program had its beginning in 1973 with Nancy Boozer as its first coach. Since its establishment, the program has had several dedicated coaches, as well as many outstanding golfers. Two noteworthy team accomplishments came in 1990 when Coach Brad Demo's Jayhawks captured the Big Eight championship and in 2014 when Coach Erin O'Neil's squad had the best year in the history of the program. Both teams advanced to the NCAA tournament.[130]

Over the years, several Jayhawk golfers have earned individual honors. Holly Reynolds had the best performance by a Jayhawk in an NCAA championship, finishing in a tie for 15th in 1993. Reynolds also leads KU women in Top Ten career finishes with 21. Amanda Costner was another Jayhawk superstar on the course and in the classroom. She finished first in the 2007 Big 12 tournament, earned All–Big 12 first-team honors in 2006 and 2007, as well as Academic All–Big 12 selections for three years, and she won the prestigious Big 12 Sportsperson of the Year in 2007. Emily Powers was also a first-team All–Big 12 selection in 2008 and an Academic first-team Big 12 honoree for two years.[131]

The 2014 Kansas women's golf season was one for the ages. O'Neil's team tied for fourth in the Big 12 tournament, qualified for the NCAA tournament by tying for fifth in Central Region play, finished in the Top Ten in every tournament throughout the year, had ten top-five tournament finishes, and placed 23rd in the NCAA tournament. The team was paced by seniors Thanuttra "Fhong" Boonraksasat and Megan Potee, junior Minami Levonowich, sophomore Yupaporn "Mook" Kawinpakorn, and freshman Pornvipa "Faii" Sakdee.[132]

KU men's golf traces its roots back to the 1930s and has had several notable coaches; however, the face of the men's golf team for almost three decades was legendary coach Ross Randall. He headed the program from 1980 to 2007. His Jayhawks won a conference championship and produced a bevy of outstanding golfers. Kansas captured the Big 12 Conference title in 1999, and Randall was named the Conference Coach of the Year. He also produced four runners-up in the Big Eight and Big 12 Conferences.[133]

Several KU golfers have excelled under Randall's leadership and knowledge of the game. Five of his student-athletes, John Sinovic, Matt Gogel, Chris Thompson, Ryan Vermeer, and Kris Marshall, were honored as All-Americans. Thompson, Vermeer, and Marshall, as well as Travis Hurst, Kevin Ward, and Gary Woodland, were All–Big 12 Conference selections. Gogel and Slade Adams were Big Eight Conference championship medalists. And Gogel, Thompson, and Woodland represented KU at various times on the PGA tour.[134]

WRESTLING AND GYMNASTICS

During the 1960s, Bob Lockwood, a 1961 KU physical education graduate, was instrumental in introducing wrestling and gymnastics as varsity sports at KU. They were discontinued, however, due to budgetary concerns. [135]

THE KU MARCHING BAND

Although the fortunes of Kansas football have been mixed over the past 50 years, one area of continued excellence on fall days at Memorial Stadium has been the performance of the Marching Jayhawks. During this period, the band has had outstanding directors, such as Russell Wiley, Kenneth Bloomquist, and Robert Foster. Foster, who led the organization from 1971 until 2001, saw it double in size, from 120 to 250 musicians. In 1972, women were added to its ranks. Since the late 1940s, the KU Marching Band has hosted an annual Band Day in Lawrence for high school bands in Kansas and Missouri, typically in conjunction with a football game in the fall. The excellence of the KU Marching Band was recognized in 1989 when it received the prestigious Louis Sudler National Intercollegiate Marching Band Trophy. The band is currently under the direction of Paul Popiel and has grown to 285 members. Adding to the performance of the band is the Spirit Squad, consisting of cheerleaders and the Rock Chalk Dancers. Pep bands also enliven the atmosphere for games at Allen Fieldhouse and the Horejsi Center.[136]

The period from 1960 to 2014 was a remarkable one for Kansas Athletics. As the foregoing suggests, the array of wonderful athletes and teams over the past five decades has been truly extraordinary. Successes on and off the fields and courts, enhancements to facilities, increases in important revenue streams, commitment to an enriched student-athlete experience, and the stability of the Big 12 Conference are sources of pride that need to be built upon and strengthened for the future. Also, lessons learned from a few unpleasant incidents should be remembered to prevent similar occurrences.

Since 2000, there has been a significant upgrade of athletics facilities at KU. The construction of the Anderson Football Complex, the

Band Day in 1986. High school bands from across the region visit KU for this event each year.

Burcham Park Rowing Boathouse, the Booth Family Hall of Athletics, and Rock Chalk Park, along with enhancements to venerable Allen Fieldhouse and Hoglund Ballpark, provided Jayhawk student-athletes and fans with some of the finest athletics facilities in the nation. The completion of state-of-the-art Rock Chalk Park signals a major step forward for Kansas. KU is now able to host national and conference track and field events at this premier venue, as well as soccer and softball tournaments. The next facility on the agenda for major renovation is historic Memorial Stadium, which hosted its first game in 1921.

Funding for KU's athletics program remains an ongoing challenge. Fortunately, Kansas has a generous core of committed and loyal Jayhawk donors. As of 2014, the Williams Education Fund was raising about $18 million annually. These funds are vital, because in all likelihood, costs related to support of student-athletes, tuition and fees for scholarships, salaries for coaches, and construction and enhancement of facilities will continue to grow.[137]

The importance of Big 12 Conference revenues will continue to be a vital element for the financial viability of Kansas Athletics. The primary sources of these revenues are television contracts, bowl games, and the NCAA basketball tournament. As Blair Kerkhoff of the *Kansas City Star* noted in the spring of 2014, for the first time in history at KU, conference revenues exceeded revenue from men's basketball and football ticket sales.[138]

Conference realignment issues had a huge impact on KU in the summer and fall of 2011, with four schools leaving the Big 12.[139] However, with former Big Eight commissioner Chuck Neinas serving as interim commissioner, two schools were added, Texas Christian University and West Virginia University, creating a stable ten-member conference. Throughout this unsettling time, Chancellor Bernadette Gray-Little and Athletics Director Dr. Sheahon Zenger were strong and consistent supporters of the Big 12.

Over the past 50 years, there were also troubling episodes for Jayhawk fans and alumni. Two major probations were levied by the NCAA in the 1980s against the football and basketball programs. Then, in the early summer of 2010, the university was rocked by improprieties committed by employees in the athletics ticket office and the Williams Educational Fund.[140]

A commitment to student-athletes remains a high priority for the Athletics Department. The Academic Support Program, which was begun in the late 1980s by Chancellor Gene Budig and Athletics Director Bob Frederick, has had only one director, Paul Buskirk. The operating budget for the program has grown by leaps and bounds over the years. A new program, KU Leads, instituted by Zenger in 2011, focuses on providing student-athletes with the training and resources for a meaningful and fulfilling personal and professional life following their graduation.[141]

The future looks bright for Kansas Athletics. The university is a member of a stable, viable, and highly respected conference, the Big 12. Revenues and donations to support the athletics program are on the rise; its student-athletes are excelling in the classroom and in competition; several KU coaches are regarded among the finest in the nation; facilities are first rate, with plans to make additional improvements; and caring and committed leadership is in place. A sense of optimism, trust, and confidence permeates the Jayhawk faithful as they wave the wheat and chant: "Rock Chalk Jayhawk—KU."

Notes

INTRODUCTION. DECADES OF TRANSFORMATION

1. Clifford S. Griffin, *The University of Kansas: A History* (Lawrence: University Press of Kansas, 1974), chap. 33. Information for the tables in the Introduction was drawn from University of Kansas Profiles, produced by OIRP since 1978. Earlier figures were taken from the university's annual budgets and reports of the University Registrar and the KUEA, all located in the University Archives. Inflation adjustments in these tables and throughout the text are based on the Consumer Price Index utilized by the US Department of Labor.

2. The liberalism and radicalism of many KU students that shocked traditional Kansans may have been reflective of student origins, which were largely metropolitan. Nearly a third were from out of state, a high number for the Midwest. Many were from Missouri, especially Kansas City, but others were from Illinois and points east. Even within Kansas, KU students were more likely to be from the state's major urban areas than from the rural west, where most Kansas wheat was harvested each year. In 1969, for instance, nearly a third of KU's Kansas-born freshmen were from Johnson County in suburban Kansas City, and another 15 percent were from the Topeka and Wichita areas. Altogether, just six predominantly urban counties—three in metropolitan Kansas City—sent two-thirds of native Kansan freshmen to KU. The university's student body, in that case, hardly represented the state's population. If Kansas was becoming somewhat less rural, KU was drawing its students disproportionately from its most urbanized areas. This may account for some of the openness to new ideas and political change that the university's students exhibited. Even if it was associated with a rural past, KU in the 1960s and beyond was a largely urban and cosmopolitan institution.

3. Rusty L. Monhollon, *"This Is America?" The Sixties in Lawrence, Kansas* (New York: Palgrave Macmillan, 2004), chap. 7.

4. Report of a Review Visit to the University of Kansas, Lawrence, March 2–6, 1969, for the Commission on Colleges and Universities of the North Central Association of Colleges and Secondary Schools, RG 0/20, Box 1, University Archives, KU, 1–2, 8, 11, 15. The student protest era may have caused public relations problems for the university, but it also helped it gain

a reputation for freedom of expression and alternative living arrangements and as a force in the struggle against racism and other forms of discrimination. As William Tuttle shows in Chapter 6, early chapters of Students for a Democratic Society (SDS) and the Congress on Racial Equality (CORE), along with other groups, led civil rights protests and gave voice to the growing antiwar movement. Small but regular demonstrations, sit-ins, and other forms of protest characterized these years, keeping Lawrence and KU in the news and helping to make the city a destination for those in search of independence from traditional values and conventions. While the youthful political scene in Lawrence may have frustrated and enraged some conservative Kansans, it proved attractive to a new generation of Americans interested in doing things differently. See Monhollon, *This Is America?* chap. 9.

5. John R. Thelin, *A History of American Higher Education* (Baltimore: Johns Hopkins University Press, 2004), chap. 7; Dongbin Kim and John L. Rury, "The Changing Profile of College Access: The Truman Commission and Enrollment Trends in the Postwar Era," *History of Education Quarterly* (August 2007): 47, 3, 302–327.

6. "Report of a Review Visit to the University of Kansas, Lawrence, February 16–19, 1975," Commission on Colleges and Universities of the North Central Association of Colleges and Secondary Schools, RG 0/20, Box 2, University Archives, KU, 36–37, 40–41.

7. Ibid., 36; Letter from Chancellor Dykes to Richard DeGeorge, May 1, 1974, Accreditation File, RG 0/20, Box 2, University Archives, KU. Lack of consistency in leadership also had hampered planning, a problem noted prominently in North Central Association visitors' reports in both 1969 and 1975.

8. Planning for this campaign began in 1962, and in 1965 some $35 million in needs were identified by a committee of administrators and faculty members. A consulting firm's report in the middle of the decade noted the unusually high level of support among nearly 400 KU alums interviewed around the country and their strong loyalty to the institution, with more citing its "academic excellence" than any other single factor. See Ketchum, Inc., *The University of Kansas: A Study and Analysis*, n.d., KUEA Records, RG 65, Box 6, University Archives, KU. For a summary of the evolution and outcomes of the Program for Progress, see KU News Bureau, "April 30 Endowment Totaled $32,740,119," KUEA Records, RG 65, Box 7, University Archives, KU.

9. David C. Miller, *The University of Kansas in Transition: Dean David R. Waggoner and the College of Liberal Arts and Sciences from the Second World War through the 1970s*, unpublished manuscript, University of Kansas, author's personal copy, 74–80.

10. See Chapter 8 below.

11. Report of a Review Visit to the University of Kansas, Lawrence, October 15–17, 1984, for the Commission on Colleges and Universities of the

North Central Association of Colleges and Secondary Schools, Accreditation File, RG 0/20, Box 2, University Archives, KU, 1–4. Between 1980 and 1985, the number of students increased by only a few hundred.

12. Letter from Dykes to DeGeorge, May 1, 1974. He expressed concern, for instance, about a sizable public university in the state's largest city and believed that KU should build stronger ties to nearby Topeka and Kansas City.

13. 1984 KU Self Study, 20.

14. "Goin' to Johnson County," KU History, December 3, 1992, http://kuhistory.com/articles/goin-to-johnson-county/, accessed June 26, 2014. As the name suggests, the Regents Center was initially intended to serve all the state's public institutions, but KU programs predominated from the start.

15. Report of a Review Visit to the University of Kansas, 1984, 8–11. See also "KU's Endowment Program," LJW, May 20, 1980, 4, an editorial noting the continuing rapid growth of KUEA under Chancellor Dykes, KUEA president Todd Seymour, and board chair Olin Petefish. KUEA's failure to undertake a campaign in this era may have been due to the transition from Irvin Youngberg, KUEA's executive secretary from 1949 to 1975, to Seymour's presidency, which ran until 1991. See Tim Carpenter, "President of KU Endowment to Leave His Post in October," LJW, September 25, 1991, 1.

16. "Gays on Campus," Jayhawker Yearbook, 1980, 92; "Living the Dream," Jayhawker Yearbook, 1986, 64.

17. Report of a Review Visit to the University of Kansas, 1984, 20–21.

18. KUEA, A Window to the Future, Annual Report, 1991–1992.

19. Report of a Review Visit to the University of Kansas, 1984, 16, 21, 46, 71–80; "Academic Excellence Lures Students," Jayhawker Yearbook, 1981–1982, 50. One sign of faculty excellence in the humanities was the many awards won by KU professors, including scores of highly competitive fellowships from the National Endowment for the Humanities, the American Council of Learned Societies, the National Humanities Center, and the John Guggenheim Memorial Foundation, along with more than 230 Fulbright fellowships for study and teaching abroad since 1965. For an accounting of these and other awards, see the "Faculty Awards" webpage compiled by KU's OIRP at http://www2.ku.edu/~oirp/profiles/FY2014/6a-010_to_6a-385.pdf. See also Chapter 5 below.

20. "Only One More Field House Enrollment," Jayhawker Yearbook, 1981–1982, 47; "The End of Joe's Run," KU History, May 16, 1980, http://kuhistory.com/articles/the-end-of-joes-run/, accessed June 29, 2014; "Joes Bakery Is a Sweet KU Tradition," LJW, August 25, 1997.

21. See Chapter 8 below.

22. "University Students Protest KUEA Investments," LJW, March 19, 1986.

23. Report of a Review Visit to the University of Kansas, 1984, 98.

24. 1994 KU Self Study, Accreditation File, RG 0/20, Box 1, University Archives, KU, 25–27, 65.

25. "Email Brings KU to the Information Highway as Students Plug In and Log On," *Jayhawker Yearbook*, 1994, 50–51.

26. 1994 KU Self Study, 64.

27. Tony Coast, "Matters of Status," *Jayhawker Yearbook*, 1995, 380–383.

28. 1994 KU Self Study, 63–64.

29. Henry Steck, "Corporatization of the University: Seeking Conceptual Clarity," *Annals of the American Academy of Political and Social Science* 585 (January 2003): 66–83.

30. 1994 KU Self Study, 92, 147–149; Scherry Sweeny, "Gene A. Budig," *Jayhawker Yearbook*, 1992, 142–144.

31. OIRP, *University of Kansas Profiles*, 2012, Table 7-125.

32. Ibid.; 1994 KU Self Study, 79–80.

33. 1994 KU Self Study, 107.

34. Anna Kostick, "Chancellor Gene Budig," *Jayhawker Yearbook*, 1990, 124–125.

35. Jennifer Hughes, "From the KC Royals Board of Directors to the Kansas Board of Regents, Gene Budig Makes a Difference," *Jayhawker Yearbook*, 1994, 42–43; 1994 KU Self Study, 65–68.

36. "KU Arranges for $1 Million Fund for Minority Students," *Jayhawker Yearbook*, 1991, 23.

37. Report of a Review Visit to the University of Kansas, Lawrence, October 9–12, 1994, for the Commission on Colleges and Universities of the North Central Association of Colleges and Secondary Schools, Accreditation File, RG 0/20, Box 1, University Archives, KU, 77.

38. "Celebrating Heritage," *Jayhawker Yearbook*, 1992, 184; "Minority Support," *Jayhawker Yearbook*, 1993, 236; Denise Neil, "AASU: Breaking Stereotypes," *Jayhawker Yearbook*, 1994, 66–67; "HALO: Supporting Hispanic Heritage," *Jayhawker Yearbook*, 1994, 74–75.

39. "Hilltoppers: Scott Rutherford," *Jayhawker Yearbook*, 1992, 156.

40. Shelly Salon, "Sexual Harassment," *Jayhawker Yearbook*, 1993, 62.

41. "Women's Issues: The 'Year of the Woman' Extends to Campus," *Jayhawker Yearbook*, 1993, 54–55.

42. Shelly Heffron, "NOW/WSU: Promoting Awareness," *Jayhawker Yearbook*, 1994, 92–93.

43. Cindy Marin, "LESBIGAYSOK: Namely, a New Philosophy," *Jayhawker Yearbook*, 1994, 64–65.

44. See Chapter 9.

45. See Chapter 5.

46. Sara Chadwick, "Chancellor's Decision Kick Starts Goal to Make the University More Student Friendly," *Jayhawker Yearbook*, 1997, 261.

47. Kay Albright, "Outcome of Legislative Session Is Positive," *Oread*, June 6, 1997, 1; "University Differential Tuition Report FY2003–FY2010, University of Kansas," November 2010, OIRP, passim. While tuition-raising authority was granted to the Board of Regents, KU took the lead in advocating for this

change in policy. John Rury interview with former Board of Regents president Reggie Robinson, October 17, 2014.

48. 2004 KU Self Study, 51.

49. Ibid., 43.

50. "Up to the Moment," *Jayhawker Yearbook*, 1999, 180; "Our History," The University of Kansas Hospital, http://www.kumed.com/about-us/our-history, accessed June 26, 2014.

51. "Sources Say KU's National Cancer Institute Application Was Successful, Formal Announcement Expected in July," *LJW*, June 28, 2012; "The University of Kansas Cancer Center Earns National Cancer Institute Designation," *KUMC News*, July 12, 2012.

52. 2004 KU Self Study, RG 0/20, Box 2, University Archives, KU, 8–9.

53. Ibid., 9; Project DEEP, Final Report: University of Kansas, March 2004, http://www2.ku.edu/~oirp/DEEP/FinalReport_033104.pdf, accessed June 26, 2014.

54. 2004 KU Self Study, 70–71; "Politics as Usual," *Jayhawker Yearbook*, 2004, 17.

55. Lauren Airey, "Money Talks," *Jayhawker Yearbook*, 2002, 66.

56. Jessica Fergen, "For Your Info," *Jayhawker Yearbook*, 2003, 45.

57. 2004 KU Self Study, 34–35; Jana Caffrey, "Tools for Success," *Jayhawker Yearbook*, 2001, 60.

58. 2004 KU Self Study, 40.

59. "Just Read the Articles," *Jayhawker Yearbook*, 2003, 36; "Survey Says KU Students Party on National Scale," *Jayhawker Yearbook*, 1998, 52.

60. "Calendar Wars," *Jayhawker Yearbook*, 2004, 34–35.

61. Jacinta Carter, "Restoring Black Pride," *Jayhawker Yearbook*, 1996, 56; Corey Peck, "Diverse," *Jayhawker Yearbook*, 1999, 58.

62. "Gender Bender," *Jayhawker Yearbook*, 2002, 136; "Queen for a Day," *Jayhawker Yearbook*, 2003, 46–47.

63. "Joe Is Back," *LJW*, August 8, 2009; "Neon Sign, Donut Recipes from Joe's Bakery Sold to KU Unions," *LJW*, May 3, 2001.

64. University of Kansas Athletics, https://search.yahoo.com/search?fr=chr-greentree_sf&ei=utf-8&ilc=12&type=216107&p=athletics%20ku.edu, accessed June 26, 2014.

65. 2004 KU Self Study, "Integrity Challenges," 106–108; Jenny Schierbaum, "Sex and the Campus," *Jayhawker Yearbook*, 2000, 28–41; "Controversy 101," *Jayhawker Yearbook*, 2003, 71. When a legislative intern took the course in 2003, a state senator denounced it as obscene and offered a bill to defund the School of Social Welfare if it continued to be offered. The measure ultimately was vetoed by Governor Kathleen Sebelius, and the university conducted an investigation that found charges of obscenity and other improprieties against Professor Daily "without merit."

66. 2004 KU Self Study, 108. This group led the board to adopt new science standards that allowed students "choice" between evolution and other,

religiously inspired, explanations of the origins of life. This controversy drew national attention, but it had little direct impact on KU.

67. "Change for the School of Fine Arts," *Jayhawker Yearbook*, 2008–2009, 111; KU Info, http://www.kuinfo.ku.edu, accessed June 26, 2014.

68. Bernadette Gray-Little, "KU and the AAU," Office of the Chancellor, May 2, 2011, http://www.chancellor.ku.edu/messages/2011/may02, accessed June 26, 2014.

69. Bernadette Gray-Little, "Chancellor Discusses KU's Bold Aspirations with State Representatives," Office of the Chancellor, February 7, 2012, http://www.chancellor.ku.edu/speeches/2012/feb07, accessed June 26, 2014.

70. KUEA, *Momentum*, Annual Report, 2013; KUEA, *We Will Never Stop Learning*, Annual Report, 2005.

71. According to data provided by the National Association of College and University Business Officers, in 2013 KU ranked 63rd among all institutions in the size of its endowment and 20th among public institutions. Retrieved at http://www.nacubo.org/Documents/EndowmentFiles/2013NCSEEndow mentMarket%20ValuesRevisedFeb142014.pdf.

72. Bernadette Gray-Little, "KU Cancer Center Earns NCI Designation," Office of the Chancellor, July 12, 2012, http://www.chancellor.ku.edu /messages/2012/ju112, accessed June 26, 2014.

73. KU Office of the Provost, University Core Curriculum Committee, Procedures and Criteria for Appointment, May 14, 2012, http://policy.ku.edu /provost/university-core-curriculum-committee, accessed June 26, 2014.

74. Molly Martin, "Far from Home: International Students Discuss the Adaptations to KU Life," *Jayhawker Yearbook*, 2011, 48–49.

75. "The ABCs of Balancing a Family, Work, and School," *Jayhawker Yearbook*, 2008–2009, 49–50.

76. "Excessive and Accepted: A Sobering Conversation," *Jayhawker Yearbook*, 2008–2009, 95–96.

77. Calculated from KU Profiles, 2012, Student Origin by County, 2009.

78. See Chapter 8 below. The success of KU's various teams, however, was marred by a scandal regarding the illicit sale of tickets by Athletics Department employees, numbering more than 17,000 for basketball and 2,000 for football. This episode was soon overshadowed by the acquisition of James Naismith's basketball rules manuscript for display in the newly opened Booth Hall of Athletics adjacent to Allen Fieldhouse, highlighting the long history of athletic accomplishment that lay behind the success of today's teams.

79. Brandon Sayers, "Debating Their Way to Tradition," *Jayhawker Yearbook*, 2010, 56–57.

80. These issues are discussed in Chapter 3.

81. Peter Hancock, "'I'm a Kansas Guy': Thousands Greet Obama during KU visit," *LJW*, January 22, 2015.

82. KUEA, http://www.kuendowment.org/s/1312/endowment/index .aspx?sid=1312&gid=1&pgid=588, accessed June 26, 2014.

1. "LIFT THE CHORUS EVER ONWARD":
LEADING THE UNIVERSITY

1. W. Clarke Wescoe, Opening Convocation Address, September 20, 1965, 2/12, Box 1, Artificial Records, University Archives, KU. The author thanks the University of Kansas Alumni Association for its contributions to this chapter. At least since Archie Dykes, various Alumni Association publications have included comprehensive, insightful, and balanced accounts of each KU chancellor, typically at the beginning, at ten years, and then at retirement. "Lift the Chorus Ever Onward" is a line from the KU Alma Mater.

2. Wescoe, "Opening Convocation Address, September 20, 1965"; Office of the Chancellor, www.chancellor.ku.edu/previous-chancellors, accessed March 18, 2013. One—Del Shankel—served twice as acting chancellor; the second time he was officially designated as KU's 15th chancellor.

3. Eliot Hughes, "Notre Dame Provost Speaks on Role of Flagship Universities," *LJW*, http://www2.1jworld.com/news/2014/mar/06/notre-dame-provost-speaks-role-flagship-universiti/?print, accessed March 10, 2014.

4. Robert Birnbaum, *How Colleges Work* (San Francisco: Jossey-Bass, 1988); Michael Cohen and James March, *Leadership and Ambiguity: The American College President*, 2nd ed. (Boston: Harvard Business School Press, 1974); Gene A. Budig, in Roger Martin and Jennifer Sanner, "A Decade with Chancellor Budig," *Kansas Alumni Magazine* (September/October 1991): 20–21.

5. Birnbaum, *How Colleges Work*, 27.

6. Ibid.; Cohen and March, *Leadership and Ambiguity.*

7. Individuals such as Kay Clawson, Don Hagen, and Barbara Atkinson at the Medical Center and Emily Taylor, George Waggoner, Frances Horowitz, Ed Meyen, Deanell Tacha, Robert Cobb, and David Ambler, among others, will not get their due here. Other influential executive vice chancellors and provosts such as Judith Ramaley, David Shulenburger, and Jeff Vitter will get some attention in this chapter.

8. Guide to the Records of the University of Kansas, Chancellor's Office Records, 1865–, W. Clarke Wescoe, 2/12, University Archives, KU. A Pennsylvanian by birth, Clarke Wescoe earned his undergraduate degree at Muhlenberg College and his medical degree from Cornell University. Following a stint as professor of pharmacology at Cornell, Wescoe accepted a professorship at the University of Kansas Medical School in 1951 and was named dean a year later, a position he held until 1960.

9. J. H. Nelson to Mr. Ray Evans, W. Clarke Wescoe, March 20, 1960, Series No. 2/12/6, Personal Correspondence, 1960–1975, Box 1, University Archives, KU; W. Clarke Wescoe interviewed by Deborah Hickle, October 16, 1990, University of Kansas Medical Center Oral History Program, University Archives, KU.

10. Ninety-Fifth Annual Convocation and Installation of W. Clarke Wescoe, September 19, 1960, W. Clarke Wescoe, 2/12, Artificial Records, University Archives, KU.

11. Ray Morgan, "Education Today May Spell Survival Tomorrow," *Kansas City Star*, September 10, 1961, W. Clarke Wescoe, Series No. 2/12, Artificial Records, University Archives, KU.

12. University of Kansas Forty-Ninth Biennial Report, W. Clarke Wescoe, Series No. 2/12, Artificial Records, University Archives, KU. These changes are too numerous to track in this chapter. Only major changes will be noted.

13. This new governance structure replaced what Clifford Griffin describes as a lazy, moribund faculty senate. Several changes have been made to this system since 1968, but the structure remains essentially intact. Students and faculty, and now staff, collectively participate in decision making on policy matters pertaining to the entire university through the University Senate and its executive committee. See "Recap of University Senate/University Council/SenEx Committee Membership," n.d., Office of University Governance.

14. W. Clarke Wescoe, State of the University Address, June 2, 1968, Series No. 2/12, Artificial Records, University Archives, KU.

15. W. Clarke Wescoe, State of the University Address, June 1, 1969, 20–21, Series No. 2/12, Artificial Records, University Archives, KU.

16. "Recap of University Senate/University Council/SenEx Committee Membership."

17. W. Clarke Wescoe, Letter of Resignation to Board, September 11, 1968, Series No. 2/12/6, Personal Correspondence, Box 1, University Archives, KU; W. Clarke Wescoe, fall 1968 Convocation Speech, Series No. 2/12, Artificial Records, University Archives, KU; *Kansas City Kansan*, editorial, September 18, 1968, Series No. 2/12/0, Artificial Records, University Archives, KU; W. Clarke Wescoe, "Reminiscences on Educational Administration," *Cornell University Medical College Alumni Quarterly* (Summer 1970): 11, Series No. 2/12/8, University Archives, KU.

18. Francis Heller, "K.U. Notes, 1948–1972," n.d., document submitted to Endacott Society Oral History Project, University Archives, KU. Reportedly, the names were supplied, but to the attorney general, who never released them.

19. W. Clarke Wescoe, "Farewell to Graduates," June 2, 1967, pp. 5–7, Series No. 2/12, Artificial Records, University Archives, KU. Wescoe went on to work for Sterling Drug Company, from which he retired in 1985. The new humanities building was named for Wescoe upon its opening in 1974; Wescoe Pavilion at the Medical Center was also named in his honor. Wescoe died in 2004.

20. W. Clarke Wescoe, "State of the University Report, 1969," p. 10, Series No. 2/12, Artificial Records, University Archives, KU.

21. Ibid.; Spencer Research Library History, http://spencer.lib.ku.edu /about/history, accessed April 3, 2014.

22. Wescoe, "Opening Convocation Address, 1965"; Charles R. Higginson, "Major Fundraising Campaigns in Behalf of the University of Kansas," personal communication, December 3, 2013. By the end of Wescoe's term, the endowment was worth $38,322,487 ($243,255,902 in 2013 dollars).

23. Wescoe, State of the University Report, 1969, 16-17, Series No. 2/12, Artificial Records, University Archives, KU.

24. Unlike Wescoe, Chalmers's selection as chancellor was the result of a formal search and interview process conducted by an advisory committee of students, faculty, and Regents, a process that has continued in some form to this day.

25. "Super Cop Makes Arrests," Kuhistory.com, Timeline, May 12, 1972, kuhistory.com/#/timeline/1970, accessed February 28, 2014.

26. E. Laurence Chalmers, Jr., "19 Days and Nights," Correspondence: General, 1969–1970, Spring Disruptions, Series No. 2/13/1, Box 3, University Archives, KU.

27. Judy Corcoran, Editorial, *Topeka Capital Journal*, n.d., Chalmers, Series No. 2/13/9, Morgue File, Box 1, University Archives, KU. University of Kansas Board of Regents, "E. Laurence Chalmers: KU's Eleventh Chancellor,"; E. L. Chalmers, Vita, University Relations, Series No. 2/13/9, Box 1, University Archives, KU. Chalmers was an easterner, born in New Jersey, who earned his bachelor's degree, master's degree, and PhD in psychology from Princeton.

28. Michael Gaughan, n.d., untitled paper, E. Laurence Chalmers Morgue File, Series No. 2/13/9, Box 1, University Archives, KU; Michael Fisher, "The Turbulent Years: The University of Kansas, 1960–1975, a History" (PhD diss., University of Kansas, 1979), University Archives, KU.

29. Judy Corcoran, "Involvement Pleases New K.U. Chancellor," *Topeka Capital Journal*, February 11, 1969; Fred Kiewit, "Eager for Challenge of K.U.," *Kansas City Star*, February 16, 1969; Diane Wengler, "Dissent Is Healthy If Orderly," *Topeka Capital Journal*, March 13, 1969; *Wichita Eagle*, "New K.U. Head Airs Views on Leadership," March 14, 1969, all in Series No. 2/13/9, Morgue File, Box 1, University Archives, KU.

30. Francis Heller, "K.U. Notes, 1948–1972," n.d., document submitted to Endacott Society Oral History Project, University Archives, KU; Raymond Nichols interviewed by J. Thissen, n.d., Endacott Society Oral History Project, University Archives, KU. In 2015, the Regents voted to name the Art and Design building after Chalmers.

31. Fisher, "The Turbulent Years."

32. "Chalmers Speaks to a Small Group of Kansas City Community Leaders," *Kansas City Times*, September 30, 1969, Series No. 2/13/9, Morgue File, Box 1, University Archives, KU.

33. See Fisher, "The Turbulent Years," for one such argument; Cohen and March, *Leadership and Ambiguity*.

34. Corcoran, "Involvement Pleases New KU Chancellor," *Topeka Capital Journal*, February 11, 1969.

35. University of Kansas Biennial Report, 1970, LD 2671.U55, University Archives, KU; Fisher, "The Turbulent Years"; E. L. Chalmers, 1971, "The Changing Role of the President," n.d., Series No. 2/13/8, Box 3, University Archives, KU.

36. E. L. Chalmers, Opening Convocation Address, fall 1971, Series No. 2/13/8, Box 4, University Archives, KU.

37. Heller, "K.U. Notes."

38. Chalmers, Opening Convocation Address, fall 1971.

39. E. L. Chalmers to Henry Bubb, May 24, 1971, Correspondence, Series No. 2/13/3, Box 1, State Board of Regents, 1970–1971, University Archives, KU.

40. University of Kansas, 1972 Biennial Report, LD2671.U55, 1/0, Serial C.1, University Archives, KU; E. L. Chalmers, letter to Regents protesting attempts to cut the Graduate Research Fund in half, Correspondence with Regents, Series No. 2/13/3, Box 1, Folder 2, University Archives, KU.

41. Fisher, "The Turbulent Years"; University of Kansas Biennial Report, 1970, 486.

42. Heller, "K.U. Notes," 101; Raymond Nichols interviewed by J. Thissen, n.d., Oral History Project, KU Retiree's Club, 72–75, University Archives, KU.

43. Nichols interviewed by J. Thissen.

44. These decisions proved to be somewhat controversial because they involved displacing Frances Heller, the longtime, well-connected, dean of faculties.

45. Guide to the Records of the University of Kansas, Chancellor's Office Records, E. Laurence Chalmers, Series No. 2/13/9, Box 1, University Archives, KU; Jane Allen and Derek Guthrie, "Chalmers Appointed Director of Chicago Art Institute," *LJW*, October 10, 1972, Series No. 12/13/9, Box 1, 1972, University Archives, KU; "Keeper of the Peace: Chancellor Who Led KU in Turbulent Vietnam War Dead at 81," *Kansas Alumni Magazine* 1 (2010); Office of the Chancellor, E. Laurence Chalmers Morgue Files, Series No. 2/13/9, Box 1, University Archives, KU; "He Was the Right Man," *Wichita Eagle*, editorial, August 22, 1972, Series No. 2/13/9, Box 1, 1972, University Archives, KU. Shortly after his departure from KU, Chalmers was appointed director of the Chicago Art Institute, where he served until 1987. He died in 2009.

46. Raymond Nichols Morgue Files, Series No. 2/14/9, Box 1, University Archives, KU; D. Bartel, "Raymond Nichols: Five Chancellors and Half a Century Later," *Kansas Alumni Magazine* (November 1972).

47. Nichols interviewed by J. Thissen. He earned money from selling wheat during World War I and paid half of his way through KU, where he earned a bachelor's degree and a master's degree, the latter in journalism.

48. Raymond Nichols Biography and Curriculum Vitae, Raymond Nichols Morgue Files, Series No. 2/14/9, Box 1, University Archives, KU; Bartel, "Raymond Nichols."

49. Raymond Nichols, State of the University Remarks, April 19, 1973, Raymond Nichols Speeches, 1972–1974, Series No. 2/14/8, Box 1, University Archives, KU.

50. Ibid., 41; Deborah Teeter, personal communication, February 21, 2014.

51. Nichols, State of the University Remarks, April 19, 1973. He also continued Chalmers's plan for expansion of the Medical Center, which was "designed to increase the production of doctors and specialists in related health fields who are much needed in various sections of the State." He announced that KU would be asking the 1973 legislature for funds for the visual arts building and for a new building for "our grossly overcrowded School of Law."

52. Nichols interviewed by J. Thissen, 75–76.

53. P. Hancock, "Tributes for Former Chancellor Pour in after Death of 'Mr. KU,'" *LJW*, October 14, 1999; Megan Maciejowski, "Remembering Ray," *Kansas Alumni Magazine* 6 (1999); Raymond Nichols Morgue Files, Series No. 2/14/9, Box 1, University Archives, KU. Nichols died in October 1999 at the age of 95, 27 years after serving as KU's 12th chancellor and as right-hand man to five previous chancellors and adviser to his four successors—Dykes, Shankel, Budig, and Hemenway.

54. Board of Regents News Release, April 13, 1973, Archie Dykes Morgue Files, 1973–, Series No. 2/15/9, Box 1, University Archives, KU.

55. Vance Hiner, "Dykes Resigns, Surprises KU," *University Daily Kansan*, June 9, 1980, Vol. 90 (144), p. 1.

56. "Predecessors," *Kansas Alumni Magazine* 92, no. 4 (August/September 1994): 45. He earned bachelor's and master's degrees from East Tennessee State and a doctorate in educational administration from the University of Tennessee at Knoxville in 1959. Dykes's administrative portfolio was varied (high school principal and superintendent), and his rise in administration was rapid. He served as chancellor of the University of Tennessee at Martin and in 1971 was named chancellor of the University of Tennessee at Knoxville, a job he held for two years before being named to the KU chancellorship; Jack McNeely, "Dykes Enters Third Year of Solid Leadership," *UDK*, 1975, Archie Dykes Morgue Files, 1973–, Series No. 2/15/9, Box 1, University Archives, KU.

57. "Predecessors," 45.

58. "Predecessors"; Delbert Shankel, personal communication with author, November 2013; Daniel Reeder, "The 13th Chancellor," *Kansas Alumni Magazine* (September 1978): 2.

59. Archie R. Dykes, Installation Address, August 27, 1973, Archie Dykes Morgue Files, 1973–, Series No. 2/15/9, Box 1, University Archives, KU.

60. "Inflation Hits State Universities Hard," *Kansas Alumni Magazine* (October 1975).

61. Dykes, Installation Address; "Inflation Hits State Universities Hard"; "Dykes Outlines Goals for Higher Education," *Kansas Alumni Magazine* (May 1973).

62. Bob Womack, "Reflections on Archie Dykes," *Kansas Alumni Magazine* (June 1974): 2–5.

63. "Dykes Is Synonym," *UDK*, August 23, 1978, 6; Womack, "Reflections on Archie Dykes."

64. Womack, "Reflections on Archie Dykes."

65. "Inflation Hits."

66. Ibid.

67. "Administration Restructured: Shankel, Rieke Picked for Executive Posts," Archie Dykes Morgue Files, 1973–, Series No. 2/15/9, Box 1, University Archives, KU.

68. Delbert Shankel interviewed by Calder Pickett, Endacott Society Oral History Project, University Archives, KU.

69. Vance Hiner, "Dykes Resigns, Surprises KU"; Logan, *UDK*, April 25, 1979.

70. "Predecessors"; Phil Goldberg, "Dykes Gets High Marks as an Administrator," *LJW*, June 5, 1980; "Ice Cream Social Honors Hospital Centennial," www2.kumc.edu/publications/centerexpress/070606.pdf, accessed February 21, 2014; Anne Marvin, "Goin' to Johnson County," KUHistory.com, December 3, 1992, accessed March 14, 2014; "KU Growth Highlighted Dykes' Years," *LJW*, June 5, 1980.

71. "Predecessors."

72. Ibid.

73. Diane Swanson, "Strong Hall Shuffle Brings Challenge, Controversy," *UDK*, August 21, 1980, 5; Kathy Russell, "U.S. to Investigate KU on Title IX," *UDK*, August 21, 1980, 1.

74. Goldberg, "Dykes Gets High Marks."

75. Dykes left KU to become CEO of Security Benefits Insurance Company, a job he held until 1987. Chancellor Gene Budig announced in 1981 that the library at the KU Medical Center would be named the A.R. Dykes Library. Budig cited Dykes's major contributions to the growth of the Med Center, including being responsible in large part for construction of the library that bears his name. In 1982, Dykes was named to the Kansas State Board of Regents, the only former administrator to be so named. He held that position until 1986. Dykes was awarded the University of Kansas Distinguished Service Citation, and the alumni awarded him the Fred Ellsworth Medallion. In 2015, he continues his involvement in both the University of Tennessee and the University of Kansas. See "Dr. Archie R. Dykes, 2002 Distinguished Alumni Award," www.etsu.edu/alumni/awards/02award_dykes.aspx, accessed June 24, 2013.

76. "Chancellor Shankel," *UDK*, April 29, 1981, 4. Del Shankel was born in Plainview, Nebraska, to Canadian parents. He earned a bachelor's degree in English at Walla Walla College in 1950. He came to KU as an assistant professor of microbiology in 1959 after earning a PhD in microbiology from the University of Texas at Austin. He worked his way up the academic ranks and was promoted to full professor in 1968.

77. Swanson, "Strong Hall Shuffle Brings Challenges."

78. Hurst Lavinia, "New Administrators Plan to Support Status Quo," *UDK*, August 21, 1980; "Shankel Takes KU Reins," Report from the University of Kansas, summer 1980, Delbert M. Shankel, Series No. 2/16, Artificial Records, Box 1, University Archives, KU.

79. Del Shankel, interview by author.

80. See Kathy Brussell and Ray Formanek, "Banners Fly at Convocation," *UDK*, August 26, 1980. At commencement the previous May, a group of protesters unfurled banners in protest over a Regents policy prohibiting "the display of banners at non-political events." See Cindi Currie, "Shankel Requests Views on Banners," *UDK*, September 9, 1980. They were arrested and charged with criminal trespassing, disorderly conduct, or both. Goldberg, "Shankel Opens KU School Year at Convocation," *LJW*, August 25, 1980, 1, 3; Goldberg, "Banner Protest Charges Dropped," *LJW*, August 29, 1980, 1, 3; Kathryn Kase, "Committee Sends Free Speech Report to Shankel for Policy Final Approval," *UDK*, February 20, 1981, 1, 11.

81. Dan Bowers, "Shankel Gets Faculty Support," *UDK*, March 13, 1981, 3.

82. Ibid.; Kathryn Kase, "Shankel Discusses Problems, Solutions," *UDK*, March 27, 1981, 1.

83. Kansas Board of Regents, News Release, March 20, 1981, Gene A. Budig Morgue Files, Series No. 2/17/9, Box 1, University Archives, KU.

84. Gene A. Budig, Curriculum Vitae, Gene A. Budig Morgue Files, Series No. 2/17/9, Box 1, University Archives, KU; Gene A. Budig, Short Biography, Gene A. Budig Morgue Files, Series No. 2/17/9, Box 1, University Archives, KU. One of three adopted children, Budig credited his family's hardships for much of his success. Two family influences seemed especially strong: religion and baseball. He joked to Roger Martin and Jennifer Sanner in the *Kansas Alumni Magazine*: "My mother wanted me to be a Catholic priest. I wanted to be 2nd baseman for the New York Yankees. We were both disappointed." Roger Martin and Jennifer Sanner, "A Decade with Chancellor Budig," *Kansas Alumni Magazine* (September/October 1991): 18–25. He earned his bachelor's, master's, and doctoral degrees from the University of Nebraska, the latter degree in higher education administration.

85. Gene A. Budig, Installation Address, August 24, 1981, Gene A. Budig Speeches, 1977–1989, Series No. 2/17/8, Box 1, University Archives, KU; "The Chancellor Settles In," *Kansas Alumni Magazine* (September 1981), Gene A. Budig Morgue Files, Series No. 2/17/9, University Archives, KU.

86. Gene A. Budig, State of the University, All University Supper, 1982, Gene A. Budig Speeches, 1977/89–1990/95, Series No. 2/17/8, Box 1, University Archives, KU; Gene A. Budig, Opening Convocation Address, 1992, Gene A. Budig Morgue Files, Series No. 2/17/9, University Archives, KU.

87. Budig, Opening Convocation Address.

88. Jerri Niebaum Clark, Jennifer Jackson Sanner, and Bill Woodard, "Budig Makes His Move: KU's 15th Chancellor Leaves the Hill for His Dream Job," *Kansas Alumni Magazine* (August/September 1994): 20.

89. Martin and Sanner, "A Decade with Chancellor Budig"; Clark, Sanner, and Woodard, "Budig Makes His Move."

90. Martin and Sanner, "A Decade with Chancellor Budig."

91. Clark, Sanner, and Woodard, "Budig Makes His Move."

92. See Report of a Review Visit, 1969, 1974, 1984, Institutional Self-Study, Artificial Records, Series No. 0/20, Box 1, University Archives, KU.

93. Report of a Visit, 1995, Institutional Self-Study, Artificial Records, Series No. 0/20, Box 1, University Archives, KU, 9.

94. Gene A. Budig, State of the University, All University Supper, 1982; Clark, Sanner, and Woodard, "Budig Makes His Move." Throughout the 1980s, KU's average salaries had dropped from 96.5 percent of peer average to 88.6 percent by 1988. The legislature followed with the second year of Margin of Excellence in 1990, bringing KU's salaries up to 92.1 percent of its peers. The third year was not funded, however. In 1994, KU received its best budget in five years, although KU salaries were still only about 87.9 percent of those of its peers.

95. Clark, Sanner, and Woodard, "Budig Makes His Move."

96. Ibid.; Higginson, unpublished document from KU Endowment Association.

97. Clark, Sanner, and Woodard, "Budig Makes His Move."

98. Lisa Maloney, "Low-Key Approach Effective for Budig," *UDK*, February 19, 1987, 1, 10.

99. Deanell Tacha quoted in Clark, Sanner, and Woodard, "Budig Makes His Move," 19.

100. Clark, Sanner, and Woodard, "Budig Makes His Move."

101. Tim Carpenter, "KU Again Calls on Shankel," *LJW*, August 1994; "Shankel Pinch Hits Again," *Kansas Alumni Magazine* (August/September 1994). Delbert Shankel interviewed by Calder Pickett, Endacott Society Oral History Project, University Archives, KU.

102. Carpenter, "KU Again Calls on Shankel."

103. Memo from Meyen, July 22, 1994, Delbert M. Shankel Morgue Files, University Archives, KU; Delbert M. Shankel, Faculty Convocation, August 22, 1994, Delbert M. Shankel Morgue Files, University Archives, KU.

104. Delbert M. Shankel, State of the University Address, April 21, 1995, Delbert M. Shankel, Series No. 2/16/8, Box 1, University Archives, KU; Coleen McCain, "KU Bids Farewell to Shankel," *UDK*, May 1, 1996.

105. Chris Lazarrino, "With Class and Dignity," *Kansas Alumni Magazine*, No. 3, 2009, p. 28; Clark, Sanner, and Woodard, "Budig Makes His Move"; Tim Carpenter, "Regents Pick Typical Leader, Survey Shows," *LJW*, January 15, 1995; Chris Lazarrino, "The Hemenway Decade," *Kansas Alumni Magazine*, No. 5, 2005, p. 23. He earned a bachelor's degree from the University of Nebraska at Omaha, majoring in English, and a PhD in English from Kent State University at the age of 24; Jennifer Jackson Sanner, "Hemenway's Outlook," *Kansas Alumni Magazine*, 93, No. 1 (February/March 1995).

106. Jennifer Jackson Sanner, "Hemenway's Outlook," 20.

107. Lazarrino, "The Hemenway Decade."

108. Carpenter, "Regents Pick Typical Leader"; Lazarrino, "The Hemenway Decade"; University of Kansas, "2005 NCA Self-Study Report," University Archives, LD2671.U55, 2005, www2.ku.edu/~oirp/NCA/report_pdf/Self Study_volume1.pdf, accessed March 29, 2014.

109. "Hemenway Shares Views and Ideas at Press Conference," *Oread*, January 20, 1995, Robert E. Hemenway, Artificial Records, 1995–, Series No. 2/19, Box 1, University Archives, KU.

110. "Robert E. Hemenway, 130th Convocation Address, 1995," *Oread*, www.oread.ku.edu/Oread95/OreadAug25/page1/hemenwayconv.html, accessed April 4, 2014; "Chancellor Robert E. Hemenway's Characteristics of a Great University," Appendix 2, Initiative 2015, University of Kansas Strategic Planning for 2008–2015, http://www2.ku.edu/~oirp/planning/docs/Task ForceCharges_012408.pdf, accessed March 28, 2014; Kay Albright, "Freshman Chancellor Sets Goals for KU's Future," *Oread*, Robert Hemenway, Series No. 2/19, Artificial Records, 1995–, Box 1, University Archives, KU.

111. Lazarrino, "The Hemenway Decade," 24.

112. "Chancellor OK's Reorganization," February 1, 2001, *Oread*, http://www.oread.ku.edu/Oread02/Feb1/staff.html, accessed April 4, 2014.

113. Lazarrino, "The Hemenway Decade," 24.

114. Robert E. Hemenway memorandum, March 7, 1996; University of Kansas, "2005 NCA Self-Study Report."

115. University of Kansas, "2005 NCA Self-Study Report."

116. Ibid., 28.

117. Ibid., 32.

118. Susan Twombly and Christopher Morphew, "Voting with More Than Their Feet: Tuition Rising and Student Power in the Academy," paper presented at the annual meeting of the Association for the Study of Higher Education, November 2005.

119. University of Kansas, "2005 NCA Self-Study Report."

120. See www.oread.ku.edu/Oread03/Nov21/goal.html, accessed December 3, 2013; and Higginson, "Major Fundraising Campaigns in Behalf of the University of Kansas."

121. Lazarrino, "The Hemenway Decade."

122. Ibid.

123. University of Kansas, "2005 Self-Study Report"; Lazarrino, "The Hemenway Decade."

124. Robert E. Hemenway, CEO Assessments 2005, 2006, 2007, 2008; Mary Burg, personal communication.

125. Hemenway, CEO Assessments.

126. Hemenway, CEO Self-Assessment, 2008.

127. Press Conference Statement by Chancellor Robert Hemenway, KU news release, archive.news.ku.edu/2008/December/8/statement.shtml, retrieved November 27, 2013. The men's basketball team won the NCAA championship, and the debate team was ranked first in the nation.

128. See https://www.chancellor.ku.edu/speeches/2011/jan27, for Bold Aspirations quote.

129. Chris Lazarrino, "Kansas on Her Mind," *Kansas Alumni Magazine* 4 (2009); Bernadette Gray-Little, Opening Convocation Address, August 19,

2009, www.chancellor.ku.edu/speeches/2009/aug19, accessed March 29, 2014; Caitlin Doornbos, "Chancellor Shares Insights into Life, Leadership," *LJW*, March 25, 2014, 3; A. Ross Stewart, "Next Chancellor Brings New Era for Jayhawks," *UDK*, July 22, 2009. The fourth of eight children and a self-described ornery child, she credits her mother with instilling a sense of high expectations and a love of reading in her daughter and the nuns at her Catholic high school for helping her obtain a scholarship to Marywood College in Scranton, Pennsylvania, where she earned a bachelor's degree in psychology. From there, she went on to earn a master's degree and PhD in psychology from St. Louis University.

130. Gray-Little, Opening Convocation Address, 2009. Bernadette Gray-Little, "Toward the Horizon," Inauguration Address, April 11, 2010, www.chancellor.ku.edu/speeches/2010/apr11, accessed March 29, 2014; Gray-Little, "Toward the Horizon"; Bold Aspirations website, boldaspirations.ku.edu, accessed March 29, 2014; Bernadette Gray-Little, "Presentation to Regents," December 14, 2011.

131. Bold Aspirations, www.provost.ku.edu/sites/provost.drupal.ku.edu/files/docs/strategic-plan-20110914.pdf, accessed January 30, 2014.

132. "KU Core," kucore.ku.edu, accessed January 30, 2014.

133. See www.chancellor.ku.edu/messages/2012/apr30, accessed October 1, 2013.

134. University of Kansas Profiles, 2008, 2009, 2010, 2012, 2013, Table 1-140, OIRP.

135. Kansas Board of Regents Minutes, June 20–21, 2012, http://www.kansasregents.org/resources/PDF/2068-FJune20–21,2012Minutes.pdf, accessed April 29, 2014.

136. J. Selingo and J. Stripling, "Nebraska's Ouster Opens a Painful Debate with AAU," *Chronicle of Higher Education*, Chronicle.com, May 2, 2011, accessed October 25, 2013; KU and the AAU, Office of the Chancellor, May 2, 2011, www.chancellor.ku.edu/messages/2011/may02, accessed March 29, 2014.

137. "University of Kansas Cancer Center Awarded National Cancer Institute Designation," psf.cobre.ku.edu/news/7–12–12, accessed January 30, 2014.

138. See http://www.chancellor.ku.edu, accessed April 18, 2014.

139. See http://www.kuendowment.org/s/1312/endowment/index.aspx?sid=1312&gid=1&pgid=540, accessed September 11, 2014.

140. Arthur Cohen, Florence Brawer, and Carrie Kisker, *The American Community College*, 6th ed. (San Francisco: Jossey-Bass, 2014).

2. THE UNIVERSITY AND GOVERNMENT:
MANAGING POLITICS

1. Docking's specific phrasing came from his 1969 budget message: "This budget was designed to be austere but it was also designed to be adequate." See

http://www.kslib.info/Documents/messages/budget_message_1969.pdf, accessed April 10, 2014.

2. Bob Beatty, "You Have to Like People: A Conversation with Former Kansas Governor William H. Avery," *Kansas History* 30 (2008): 65.

3. In Kansas, aside from the Supreme Court, the most important actor in pressing for reapportionment reform was the *Hutchinson News*, which ran a series of articles for which it won a Pulitzer Prize. See Burdett Loomis and Dennis Chanay, "Legislative Change under the Gun: The 19th Century Kansas House Enters the 20th Century, 1966," paper given at the Midwest Political Science Association meeting, 2011.

4. Personal communication from James Pottorf, June 3, 2014.

5. Governor's Budget, Schedule 4; Volume 1, Schedule 3, "Expenditures from State General Fund by Agency" (FY1986–FY2003); Schedule 2.2 (FY2004–FY2013).

6. *LJW*, February 8, 2014, http://rangeless3.rssing.com/browser.php ?indx=3393860&item=83.

7. "25 Years of Declining State Support for Public Colleges," *Chronicle of Higher Education*, March 3, 2014, http://chronicle.com/article/25 -Years-of-Declining-State/144973?cid=megamenu.

8. Clifford S. Griffin, *The University of Kansas: A History* (Lawrence: University Press of Kansas, 1974), chap. 27, provides an excellent overview of the mission that Chancellor Franklin Murphy took on as he sought to convey the great need for the university to expand and modernize itself in the 1950s. His battles with Governor Docking and many members of the state legislature were remarkably strident and public. This brief account relies heavily on Griffin's account.

9. This account relies on Clarke Wescoe's oral history interview, Endacott Society Oral History Project, RG 67/745, Box 71, University Archives, KU.

10. KU press release, December 14, 1963, W. Clarke Wescoe Morgue File, RG 2/12/9, Box 1, University Archives, KU.

11. "Interview with Chancellor Clarke Wescoe," *Kansas Alumni Magazine*, February 1968; "Education: Academe's Exhausted Executives," *Time*, September 27, 1968, http://content.time.com/time/magazine/article/0,9171 ,902330,00.html, accessed February 11, 2015.

12. The *Parsons Sun* editorialized, "It is not because he has failed to master the heavy duties and trials of the chancellorship that Dr. Wescoe is leaving Mt. Oread. It is precisely the opposite. He has mastered and perfected them." In so doing, Wescoe became a popular and influential leader across the state, in an era when the KU chancellor was a considerably more important public figure than would be the case in later years. The *Independence Daily News* observed, "Besides being extremely intelligent, a marvelous public speaker, and a tremendously interesting speaker, Clarke Wescoe is blessed with a rare sense of humor. This has made him extremely popular with the vast majority of the student body, faculty, alumni and citizens of Kansas and elsewhere." Although the *LJW* did praise the chancellor, ironically it took the *Manhattan*

Mercury to give him his full due: "This highly intelligent and sensitive man has made a profound impression on KU in particular and higher education in general in the course of having headed the medical school and as chancellor of the University. . . . There needs to be a resounding chorus of appreciation for the many contributions of this man who adopted Kansas, which in turn so enthusiastically adopted him." These quotations appeared in the September 17, 1968, editions of these publications and can be found in Newspaper Clippings, August 1968–September 1968, Box 10, University Archives, KU.

13. Although originally named as "interim" chancellor, that qualifier was dropped and Nichols retired at the end of his tenure as chancellor. See the discussion of this in Chapter 1.

14. Delbert Shankel interview, April 9, 2014.

15. Ibid.

16. Richard Von Ende interview, May 3, 2014.

17. Ibid.; Wint Winter, Jr., interview, April 9, 2014.

18. Von Ende interview.

19. Interview, 2014, anonymity requested.

20. Marlin Rein interview, April 22, 2014.

21. Ibid.

22. See, for example, Thomas G. Mortenson, "State Funding: A Race to the Bottom," *Presidency* (Winter 2012), American Council for Higher Education, accessed May 12, 2014, at http://www.acenet.edu/the-presidency/columns-and-features/Pages/state-funding-a-race-to-the-bottom.aspx.

23. Rein interview.

24. Mike Hayden interview, April 2, 2014. Of course, Budig would leave KU in 1994 to become president of the American League.

25. Rein interview.

26. Ibid.

27. Winter interview.

28. See Chapter 1 on Del Shankel's 1994–1995 tenure as chancellor during adverse fiscal conditions.

29. Tim Carpenter, "Challenges Keep Budig Optimistic, Enthusiastic," *LJW*, August 19, 1999. The third year eventually was not funded, but the success of winning the commitment was significant in shifting the debate over education in Kansas.

30. Jon Josserand interview, April 12, 2014.

31. "Budig at Bat," KU History, August 1, 1994, accessed at http://kuhistory.com/articles/budig-at-the-bat/.

32. Bill Graves interview, April 23, 2014.

33. Rein interview.

34. Ibid.

35. David Shulenburger interview, April 24, 2014.

36. "Hemenway Leaving Mark on KU Campus," *LJW*, July 4, 1999.

37. Rein interview.

38. Shulenburger interview.

39. See section 76-719 of the Kansas Statutes, which empowers the Board of Regents to approve tuition levels, with funds returning to the institutions, found at http://kansasstatutes.lesterama.org/Chapter_76/Article _7/#76–719. For an overview of the process for allocating these funds, see "Tuition Enhancement Allocations, University of Kansas, Lawrence and Edwards Campuses, Updated January 2005," at http://www2.ku.edu/~oirp /Tuition/Tuition_Allocation_Rpt_2005.pdf.

40. On this point, see the discussion of Hemenway's planning efforts in Chapter 1.

41. David Twiddy, "University of Kansas Cancer Center gets National Cancer Institute designation," *Kansas City Star*, July 12, 2012, accessed at http:// www.bizjournals.com/kansascity/news/2012/07/12/ku-cancer-center-is -expected-to.html?page=all.

42. Shulenburger interview.

43. Information in this section draws upon the KUMC's narrative, accessed at http://www.kucancercenter.org/about-us/nci-designation/nci-2008.

44. Stephen Wolgast, "A Dangerous Challenge to Free Speech in Kansas," *Kansas City Star*, May 13, 2014, accessed at http://www.kansascity.com /2014/05/13/5021742/a-dangerous-vote-for-free-speech.html.

45. Ben Unglesbee, "KU School of Business Celebrates Groundbreaking," *LJW*, October 18, 2013, accessed at http://www2.1jworld.com/news /2013/oct/18/ku-school-business-celebrates-groundbreaking/, May 3, 2014. The story reports that in the wake of the governor's statement, "the crowd groaned."

CHAPTER 3. THE IDEA OF A LIBERAL EDUCATION:
CONTINUITY AND CHANGE

1. The epigraph quote comes from "Friend on the Court," *Kansas Alumni Magazine* 2 (2001): 31.

2. The Association of American Colleges and Universities' "Liberal and Liberal Arts Education: A Guide to Terminology" offers these definitions: "Liberal education" is "an approach to college learning that . . . emphasizes broad knowledge of the wider world (e.g., science, culture, and society) as well as in-depth achievement in a specific field of interest." *Liberal arts and sciences* are "disciplines spanning the humanities, arts, sciences, and social sciences." *Liberal arts* typically refers "only to the disciplines in the humanities, arts, and social sciences." *General education* is "the part of a liberal education curriculum that is shared by all students. . . . [It] provides broad exposure to multiple disciplines and forms the basis for developing essential intellectual, civic, and practical capacities." Debra Humphreys and Patrick Kelly, *How Liberal Arts and Sciences Majors Fare in Employment: A Report on Earnings and*

Long-Term Career Paths (Washington, DC: Association of American Colleges and Universities, 2014), 2.

3. Clifford S. Griffin, *The University of Kansas: A History* (Lawrence: University Press of Kansas, 1974), 544–593.

4. *University of Kansas General Information Catalogue, 1965–66*, University Archives, KU, C-5. Catalog statements of general education course and credit hour requirements are always "maximal," indicating what the student with no previous course credit or exemption must fulfill. There are of course a variety of ways in which students may enter the university having already fulfilled certain of the requirements: for example, credit for Advanced Placement (AP) high school courses, passing competency exams in areas such as foreign language, attaining high scores in English or math on the ACT or SAT tests, and exemption from, say, first-semester English by being in the Honors Program.

5. *Annual Catalogue of the University of Kansas, 1959–1960*, University Archives, KU.

6. Ibid.

7. When Social Welfare, still a department in the College in 1965, became an independent school in 1969, it joined the list of undergraduate professional schools that admitted students only after two years in the College.

8. *University of Kansas Catalogues of the Schools, 1973–74*, University Archives, KU, A-5.

9. *University of Kansas General Information Catalogue, 1969–70*, University Archives, KU, 40.

10. Ibid., E-4.

11. Ibid., L-6.

12. John Willingham, *A Review of Fifty Public University Honors Programs* (Portland, OR: Public University Press, 2012).

13. A 1936 KU graduate and 1947 Wisconsin PhD in English, Waggoner became dean of the College in 1954 and remained in that position for 21 years. In rapid succession, he inaugurated the Honors Program in 1955, led the major reform of the general education requirements that went into effect in 1959, and completely restructured freshman-sophomore education into the Colleges-within-the-College experiment that began in 1966.

14. Francis H. Heller, "Undergraduate Honors Work at the University of Kansas: A Retrospect," in *Notes: The College of Liberal Arts and Sciences* (Summer 1990): 4; College Honors Program, Artificial Records, Series No. 17/5, Box 2, University Archives, KU.

15. Griffin, *The University of Kansas*, 310.

16. Heller, "Undergraduate Honors Work," 5.

17. A native of Vienna, Austria, Heller came to the United States in 1937 as a refugee from Nazism and studied law at the University of Virginia. From 1942 to 1947, he served in the US Army. He earned a PhD in political science from the University of Virginia in 1947, and in 1948 he joined the KU faculty.

Heller quickly earned a reputation as an excellent teacher and a person with a talent for administration. From 1957 to 1962, he directed the Honors Program, and from 1967 to 1972, he was chief academic officer and acting provost for the Lawrence campus. Heller was the Roy A. Roberts Distinguished Professor of Law and Political Science from 1988 until his retirement in 2003.

18. Heller, "Undergraduate Honors Work," 5.

19. Ibid.; *University of Kansas General Information Catalogue, 1970–71*, University Archives, KU, B-7–8.

20. Heller, "Undergraduate Honors Work," 5.

21. Appointed a chief judge of the U.S. Court of Appeals for the Tenth Circuit in 1985, she retired in 2008 and in 2011 was named dean of the Pepperdine University School of Law.

22. University of Kansas Office of Academic Affairs, Deanell Tacha, Core Curriculum Material, "Report on the Commission on the Improvement of Undergraduate Education," n.d., RG 10/0/5, Box 5, 21, University Archives, KU.

23. Ibid., 23.

24. *Notes: College of Liberal Arts and Sciences* (Summer 1990): 1.

25. E. Jackson Baur, "Recommendation to the College Administrative Committee for Improving the Classroom as a Learning Situation," November 5, 1965, RG 17/0, Box 1, University Archives, KU.

26. University of Kansas Colleges-within-the-College, Records, "Reorganization of the Lower Division, College of Liberal Arts and Sciences, University of Kansas: Colleges-within-the-College Project," grant proposal to Carnegie Corporation, 1966, RG 63/0, Box 1, University Archives, KU.

27. *Time*, September 9, 1966.

28. KU News Bureau, July 1966, University of Kansas Colleges-within-the-College, Records, RG 63/0, Box 1, University Archives, KU.

29. In an interview in the *UDK* for March 4, 1966, Jerry Lewis noted that all freshmen had to take English as freshmen, that 80 percent took speech, and that a substantial percentage were taking introductory courses in areas such as biology, history, psychology, and sociology. He estimated that there were about 20 courses in which a large number of freshmen enrolled.

30. The Nunemaker Tutorial Plan: Report to the Educational Policies Committee by Thomas Gale, Director, Nunemaker College, RG 63/3, Colleges-within-the-College, Nunemaker College. See also "Nunemaker College Starts Tutorial Program," *LJW*, October 7, 1970. The Tutorial Program was designed to accommodate 20 top honors students. It covered the four semesters of the freshman and sophomore years, with students spending one semester each in the humanities, the social sciences, and the natural sciences and a fourth semester of concentrated study in one of the three areas. Working closely with a faculty member and a senior honors student, the students took classes entirely on an audit basis, were supposed to read substantially in each area of study, and wrote a comprehensive paper on the semester's work.

31. The Honor for Outstanding Progressive Educator (HOPE) award is KU's oldest teaching award (1959) and the only one decided and awarded entirely by students—each year's senior class. As for the PIHP curriculum, the Pearson faculty had a very well-known (and also very controversial) predecessor in the Great Books Program at the University of Chicago, created in the 1930s by University of Chicago president Robert Hutchins and the highly energetic Aristotelian philosopher Mortimer Adler. Pearson faculty members became notable for their unusual pedagogy and for their enriching of the Pearson experience through a variety of extracurricular activities. Students were not allowed to take notes in class, in order to focus their attention on the lectures and discussion, and they were required to memorize a good deal of poetry. The extracurricular instructional and social activities ranged from medieval calligraphy to formal ballroom dances to study abroad trips.

32. "Report of the Committee on Evaluation and Advancement of Instruction on the Pearson Integrated Humanities Program," March 20, 1972, Colleges-within-the-College, Records, 1967–1976, RG 63/0, Box 2, University Archives, KU. See especially pp. 8–10. One of the main concerns of the committee, and also of some humanities chairs in letters to the committee, was the complete autonomy and lack of accountability of the PIHP.

33. See, for example, Professor Quinn's response to the chair of the committee in a letter of October 27, 1972, Colleges-within-the-College, Records, Box 2, University Archives, KU. This was one example of what seemed to many to be an aggressiveness and defiance with which the PIHP faculty members— typically with considerable eloquence—argued their case and defended the program against its critics.

34. In its flourishing years, the PIHP faculty regularly taught classes of around 200 Pearson College students. Although some PIHP students inevitably became critical of what they considered the "condescension" and "dogmatism" of the teachers or of the content, structure, and rather singular demands of the program, and in some cases dropped out, there were others who, while remaining skeptical or rejecting the "party line," looked back on the program as a highly valuable and indeed "defining" experience and were proud of having been part of it. Then there were the "true believers," those who became persuaded not only that PIHP was an exceptional educational experience but that the worldview and the pedagogy of the three faculty represented the genuine path to discovering truth, beauty, and goodness in an objective and universal sense. And through the years, the devotees of the program have continued to sing its praises to others and to deplore its demise. Advocates and those they have influenced have written books and articles down to the very recent past. Ironically, PIHP outlived the demise of the Colleges-within-the-College, albeit in severely attenuated form, as the Integrated Humanities Program. The four courses, now reduced to three credit hours each, continued to be taught and to appear until 2011 in the College portion of the university catalog under the course listings for Humanities, a

long-established (1947) interdisciplinary degree program that united with Western Civilization in 1997.

35. In 1964, Frances Degen Horowitz was charged by Dean Waggoner with converting KU's Department of Home Economics into the Department of Human Development and Family Life (now the Department of Applied Behavioral Science). From 1978 to 1991, she served as KU's vice chancellor for Research, Graduate Studies, and Public Service, and from 1991 to 2005 as president of the CUNY Graduate Center.

36. "Report of the Ad Hoc Committee on the Future of the Colleges within the College Program, March 1972," Colleges-within-the-College Records, 1967–1976, RG 63/0, Box 2, University Archives, KU, 21–22.

37. Ibid., 26.

38. For a detailed account of this period at KU, see Chapters 6 and 7. See also, in Chapter 1, the sections on Chancellors Wescoe and Chalmers.

39. Amy Fitzmaurice, "The Development of the Department of African, African American and Caribbean Studies at the University of Kansas," unpublished manuscript, 1992, 4. Fitzmaurice was a student historian of the creation and growth of KU's African and African-American Studies Department.

40. Ibid., 6–7.

41. Information provided by Bill Tuttle in an e-mail to author dated April 22, 2014. Tuttle was a faculty member in American Studies as well as History. American Studies and African and African-American Studies faculty have cooperated closely through the years on course offerings, research, special events, and recruitment. See also two *UDK* articles about the course: "Negro History to Be Taught at KU in the Fall Semester," May 17, 1968; and "'Negro History' Limited to 26 after Big Demand," September 20, 1968. See also University of Kansas Artificial Records, African Studies, "History," 1992, RG 17/16, Box 1, University Archives, KU.

42. Gordon was educated at Bethune-Cookman College (Florida), Howard University, Michigan State University, and Union Theological Seminary. He chaired African and African-American Studies from 1970 to 1980 and has had a long association with KU's Life Span Institute. Gordon was a recipient of KU's Steeples Faculty Award for Outstanding Service to the People of Kansas. He is the author, co-author, and editor of several books, among them *African Leadership in the Twentieth Century* (2002) and *The African Presence in Black America* (2004).

43. *University of Kansas Catalogues of the Schools, 1973–74*, University Archives, KU, A-12–15. This era witnessed a complete restructuring of KU's Senate Code, approved in March 1969, to include student representation of 20 percent on all committees, from the new University Senate down to school and department governing structures and curricular committees.

44. Ibid., A-14. The courses could be principal courses, courses for which principal courses were a prerequisite, and junior-senior courses.

45. Report of the Commission on the Improvement of Undergraduate Education (1981), University of Kansas Office of Academic Affairs, Deanell

Tacha, Core Curriculum Material, RG 10/0/5, Box 5a, University Archives, KU, 5.

46. Ibid., 6.

47. Ibid., 10.

48. Ibid., 11. The six recommendations were: developing ways to create a more intellectually stimulating undergraduate environment; creating a university-wide core curriculum; establishing clearly defined, university-wide academic standards and procedures; encouraging and rewarding undergraduate teaching; implementing regular evaluation of the quality of undergraduate education; and communicating to prospective students and to the state KU's commitment to excellence in undergraduate education. My focus here will be on the proposal to create an all-university core curriculum. I want at this point, however, simply to mention other important commission proposals, some of which were implemented either at the time or eventually, by way of indicating the report's impact and influence: for example, freshman library orientation, undergraduate research grants, review and consolidation of honors programs, more effective targeting of scholarship funds, creation of a university-wide freshman-sophomore advising system, early enrollment, and specific proposals to encourage and reward undergraduate teaching.

49. Ibid., 31.

50. University Committee on the Core Curriculum, "A Brief History of Deliberations on the Theme of Common Academic Experience for All KU Students" (n.d., but sent in early 1984), University of Kansas Office of Academic Affairs, Deanell Tacha, Core Curriculum Material, RG 10/0/5, Box 5a, University Archives, KU, 2. Tacha of course strongly supported and promoted the idea of a university-wide core curriculum.

51. Ibid., 3.

52 Ibid., 5.

53. Remarks of the Dean, College Assembly Meeting, September 14, 1982, University of Kansas Office of Academic Affairs, Deanell Tacha, Core Curriculum Material, RG 10/0/5, Box 5a, University Archives, KU, 3.

54. Proposals of the Dean's Task Force on General Education, working draft, October 2, 1983, ibid., 1–3. In the spring of 1984, the task force sent a formal proposal to the dean and vice chancellor on developing a writing-across-the-curriculum program, requesting the formation of a university-wide committee to examine desirability, resource needs, and faculty participation and to make recommendations.

55. Proposals from the Committee on Undergraduate Studies and Advising, April 26, 1985, ibid., 2–7. The divisional areas' topical subgroups were as follows: natural sciences and mathematics: physical sciences, biological sciences, earth sciences, and mathematical sciences; social sciences: individual behavior, culture and society, and public affairs; humanities: historical studies, literature and the arts, and philosophy and religion. Students were required to take one principal course under each topical subdivision.

56. Proposals of the Dean's Task Force on General Education, working draft, 7–8. These included the same requirements in English, math, and oral communication-logic as for BA students: six principal courses, two in each of the major divisions and no more than one in any topical group; a minor concentration requirement consisting of nine hours of junior-senior level coursework in a single department outside the major; and both the Western Civilization and the non–Western culture requirements. The Committee on Undergraduate Studies and Advising added, "A principal reason for retention of the B.G.S. degree is that it serves the needs of transfer and non-traditional students who enter the College having done university-level work already. The proposal would reduce the amount of freshman-sophomore level work . . . while preserving—through the added Minor Concentration Requirement— the breadth that is implied in a General Studies degree." The total general education credit hours required for the BA were 72; for the BGS, 54.

57. See Humphreys and Kelly, *How Liberal Arts and Sciences Majors Fare.*

58. Between 1999 and 2009, the average rate of students leaving KU after the first year was 20 percent. During the same period, the average rate of those who graduated in four years was a little over 33 percent, with the percentage rising to only 49 percent after six years. Statistics from OIRP, 2014.

59. "Assessment of General Education," September 2002, OIRP, RG 4, Box 406, University Archives, KU.

60. *Guide to the KU Core*, University of Kansas, 2012.

61. The BGS has also been revised into two options. Option A is the BGS with a major, which requires a secondary field (second major or minor). Option B is the BGS in Liberal Arts and Sciences, requiring one course each in fifteen College departments, World Language and Culture (two courses in a foreign language, or three in world or non-Western culture), and two additional natural science and/or mathematics courses.

62. This model of a "core" curriculum is not new with KU. The influential Harvard Core Curriculum, which has been through many revisions, consists of a set of goals that students can fulfill by taking a wide range of courses. A number of other universities have similar general education curricula.

63. For example, in fulfilling Goal 1, Outcome 1, Critical Thinking, a student may take a course in finance, atmospheric science, Danish, dance, or any of a number of other courses among the 157 listed. The almost 300 courses listed under Goal 3, Breadth of Knowledge, which requires one course each in arts and humanities, social sciences, and natural sciences, likewise permit a very wide range of choices.

4. THE GLOBAL DIMENSION

1. Francis H. Heller, "Per Aspera ad Mundum: The University of Kansas Faces the World," for the Office of International Programs of the University

of Kansas, 2003, International Programs Records, Artificial Records, 1879–2000, Series No. 12/0/1, Box 1, University Archives, KU, 18.

2. "International Education at the University of Kansas: A Prospectus for Future Development, September 1962," International Programs Records, Artificial Records, 1879–2000, Series No. 12/0/1, Box 1, University Archives, KU, 1.

3. Ibid., i–ii.

4. Ibid., 1.

5. "Report on the First Year of the Ford Foundation Grant in Support of International Programs," International Programs Records, Artificial Records, 1879–2000, Series No. 12/0/1, Box 1, University Archives, KU.

6. Ibid., 2.

7. J. A. Burzle, "Foreign Study Opportunities," 1960, Study Abroad Records, Artificial Records, 1959/60–1991/92, ibid.

8. "Interview with J. A. (Toni) Burzle," by Calder Picket, July 9, 1991.

9. Charles L. Stansifer and Maria Eugenia Bozzoli, "The University of Kansas and the Universidad de Costa Rica: Origins of an Exchange Relationship," International Programs Records, Artificial Records, 1879–2000, Series No. 12/0/1, Box 1, University Archives, KU, 13–20.

10. Ibid., 28–33.

11. Ibid., 42.

12. "The International Campus," *Newsletter for International Students, Research Scholars, and Staff* 5, no. 2 (November 1965): 7.

13. Rostow, as quoted in ibid., 4.

14. Appendix A, "A Program of Foreign Aid in Engineering Education," International Programs Records, Artificial Records, 1879–2000, Series No. 12/0/1, Box 1, University Archives, KU, 2.

15. Ibid.

16. "Clark Coan Retires after 33 Years," *Horizons* (February/March 1990): 3.

17. An Interview with Clark Coan, by Calder Pickett, December 10, 1990, 25–26.

18. "The International Campus," 1.

19. Padma Jayaraman, "Foreign Students at the University of Kansas," in *Newsletter for International Students, Research Scholars, and Staff* 5, no. 2 (November 1965): 7–8.

20. "Clark Coan Retires after 33 Years," 4.

21. An Interview with Mary-Elizabeth Debicki, by Jewell Willhite, September 15, 1998, 23.

22. An Interview with George Woodyard, by Jewell Willhite, July 26, 2005, 28–29.

23. Ibid., 30–31.

24. Mary-Elizabeth Debicki, Annual Report (Spring 1994–Spring 1995), KU Office of Study Abroad, 5.

25. "Horizons' Interview with Clark Coan: Part II," *Horizons* (Spring 1990): 2.

26. "Directing International Student Services into the Next Millennium," *Horizons* 13, no. 2 (Spring 1999): 6.

27. "Horizons' Interview with Clark Coan: Part II," 2.

28. "Directing International Student Services into the Next Millennium," 6.

29. Debicki interview, 6.

30. "Participation Table, KU–Non KU, 1959–present," Table provided by Angela Perryman, director, Office of Study Abroad.

31. Jane Irungu, as quoted in NAFSA, "Internationalizing the Campus 2005: Profiles of Success at Colleges and Universities," 37. She had followed her husband to the United States.

32. Ibid., 34–43.

33. KU Mission Statement, http://www.ku.edu/about/mission/, accessed May 24, 2014.

34. "New Academic Accelerator Program Will Provide Enriched Option for International Students," http://news.ku.edu/2014/02/20/new-ku-academic-accelerator-program-will-provide-enriched-option-international-students, accessed February 6, 2015; Academic Accelerator Program Guidebook, 2015–2016, Lawrence.

5. FORGING A UNIVERSITY RESEARCH MISSION

1. I would like to express my appreciation to the following individuals who spoke with me about their roles in the history of research at KU: Barbara Armbrister, Robert Barnhill, Richard DeGeorge, Jay Darnell, Don Deshler, William Duellman, Prasad Gogineni, Frances Horowitz, Roy Jensen, Kim Moreland, Howard Mossberg, Kathy Porsch, Del Shankel, David Shulenburger, Val Stella, Deb Teeter, Paul Terranova, and Linda Trueb. I would also like to thank George Wilson, Kevin Boatright, and Steve Warren, as well as the editors and the authors of the other chapters of this volume for their perceptive comments on earlier drafts of this chapter.

2. "The Place of Research in the University," June 1962, RG 3/0, Box 2, Artificial Records, 1952/53–1965/66, University Archives, KU, 3. Much of the material in this chapter was gleaned from interviews I conducted with a number of participants about the events described here. In 2015, faculty at KU are expected to devote 40 percent of their working time to scholarship, as much as they devote to their educational responsibilities. The remaining 20 percent is allocated to service to the university and profession.

3. Clifford S. Griffin, *The University of Kansas: A History* (Lawrence: University Press of Kansas, 1974), 3, 72, 80, 398, 481–482.

4. See Hugh Davis Graham and Nancy Diamond, *The Rise of American Research Universities: Elites and Challengers in the Postwar Era* (Baltimore: Johns Hopkins University Press, 1997), especially chap. 2.

5. Rising rates of college attendance and increased federal financial aid contributed to a massive increase in the number of undergraduates arriving on campus in the 1960s. See Introduction.

6. William J. Argersinger, Jr., to W. Clarke Wescoe, September 9, 1960, File 31, Box 3, Chancellor's Office Records, W. Clarke Wescoe, RG 2/12/5, Correspondence—Departmental, 1960/1961, University Archives, KU.

7. Griffin, *The University of Kansas*, 511, 521, 539. This amount is equivalent to about $2.6 million in 2013 dollars.

8. Ibid., 678–679, 680–682.

9. "The Place of Research in the University," 37.

10. Ibid., 42, 45.

11. Ibid., 52–62.

12. This and the following paragraphs draw heavily on Karen Salisbury Henry, "Just What We Needed," http://kuhistory.com/articles/just-what-we-need/, accessed March 5, 2013; and Richard L. Schiefelbusch and Stephen R. Schroeder, eds., *Doing Science and Doing Good: A History of the Bureau of Child Research and the Schiefelbusch Institute for Life Span Studies at the University of Kansas* (Baltimore: Paul H. Brookes, 2006), chaps. 2, 5, 9.

13. It had been opened by Florence Sherbon of the Home Economics Department, who persuaded the state legislature to fund it. See http://kuhistory.com/articles/just-what-we-need/.

14. The comparison to today's price is based on the change in the Consumer Price Index between 1955 and 2013 using the calculator available at http://www.measuringworth.com.

15. Henry, "Just What We Needed."

16. Funded by the Kansas Board of Regents, these positions are reserved for distinguished scholars who can contribute to the state's economic development as well as the university's academic distinction. The other Regents Professor at this time was Charles Michener, an entomologist specializing in bees.

17. Mark Hersey, "It's All in the Delivery," http://kuhistory.com/articles/its-all-in-the-delivery/, accessed July 14, 2013.

18. Richard K. Moore interview, Endacott Society Oral History Project, University Archives, KU, 15.

19. Ibid., 20.

20. In 1969, W. Clarke Wescoe resigned his post as chancellor and was replaced by Laurence Chalmers. Chalmers's brief tenure in the chancellorship, 1969–1972, was largely taken up with responding to student demands and protests, leaving little opportunity to set direction for the research enterprise.

21. Robert Cobb interview, Endacott Society Oral History Project, University Archives, KU, 34.

22. William J. Argersinger, Jr., "Reminiscences of William J. Argersinger, Jr.," June 16, 1989, University Archives, KU, 22–23.

23. Ibid., 25.

24. This quotation and much of the account in the next several paragraphs is from Richard DeGeorge's reminiscences about the early years of the Hall Center, in Victor Bailey and Janet Crow, eds., *In Retrospect: 25th Anniversary,*

1976–2001 (Lawrence: University of Kansas and Hall Center for the Humanities, 2001), 11–14.

25. Ibid., 8–9.

26. Ibid., 15–20.

27. An account of how the challenge grant funds were used is provided in the 2000 challenge grant application (Photocopy, Hall Center, 2000), 11–15.

28. Bailey and Crow, *In Retrospect,* 19.

29. Ibid., 31.

30. Ibid., 28.

31. Ibid., 29–30.

32. For the renovation of the Powerhouse Building, see John H. McCool, "Back in Power," http://kuhistory.com/articles/back-in-power/, accessed March 29, 2014.

33. As of 2014, having held the position of director since 2001, Bailey has been director for close to one-third of the Hall Center's 38-year history.

34. "The Place of Research in the University," 60–62.

35. "Report of the Research Foundation Committee," August 1981, Governance, Research: Correspondence, Memoranda, Minutes, and Artificial Records, Series No. 3/7/12, University Archives, KU.

36. Hemenway's appointment officially began on July 1, 1996, but when he accepted the KU position the University of Kentucky terminated his appointment, leaving him free to spend much of the spring at KU planning for his transition.

37. David Shulenburger, interview by author, January 27, 2013.

38. During his time in the latter office, Arizona State had doubled the amount of its external research funding.

39. Formally these payments are referred to as Facilities & Administration costs. For federal grants, they are calculated as a percentage of the direct costs of conducting the research. The rate used for these calculations is determined through a lengthy process of negotiation with accountants from the federal government based on university costs and research expenditures.

40. The four areas identified in 1998 were information technology, human biosciences, the human condition, and environmental science and engineering. Robert E. Barnhill, "The Research 1 University: Strategies and Public Agenda," MASC Report no. 104, Merrill Advanced Studies Center, June 2000, 31. See also the discussion of the emergence of KU research investment themes in "KU Research Directions," Provost's Council, September 13, 2005, http://www2.ku.edu/~oirp/planning/docs/2005_KUResearch Directions.pdf, accessed March 1, 2014.

41. These themes are the following: sustaining the planet, powering the world; promoting well-being, finding cures; building communities, expanding opportunities; and harnessing information, multiplying knowledge. See http://www.provost.ku.edu/strategic-plan, accessed January 17, 2014.

6. KU'S TUMULTUOUS YEARS:
THIRTY YEARS OF STUDENT ACTIVISM, 1965–1995

1. In my 40-year career teaching American history at KU, I required my students to write original papers based on research in primary sources. Many chose KU topics, and their papers have richly informed my chapter in this volume. In my endnotes, I have gratefully acknowledged their contributions. William M. Tuttle, Jr., "Reform and Conflict at Home: A Turbulent Era, 1961–1974," in Mary Beth Norton et al., *A People and a Nation: A History of the United States,* 6th ed. (Boston: Houghton Mifflin, 2001), 853–881; Terry H. Anderson, *The Movement and the Sixties* (New York: Oxford University Press, 1995); Raymond Arsenault, *Freedom Riders: 1961 and the Struggle for Racial Justice* (New York: Oxford University Press, 2006); Taylor Branch, *Parting the Waters: America in the King Years, 1954–1963* (New York: Macmillan, 1989); David Chalmers, *And the Crooked Places Made Straight: The Struggle for Social Change in the 1960s* (Baltimore: Johns Hopkins University Press, 1996); Charles DeBenedetti, *An American Ordeal: The Antiwar Movement of the Vietnam Era* (Syracuse: Syracuse University Press, 1990); John D'Emilio, *Sexual Politics, Sexual Communities: The Making of a Homosexual Community in the United States* (Chicago: University of Chicago Press, 1983); Sara Evans, *Personal Politics: The Roots of Women's Liberation in the Civil Rights Movement and the New Left* (New York: Knopf, 1979); David Farber, *The Age of Great Dreams* (New York: Hill and Wang, 1994); Allen J. Matusow, *The Unraveling of America: A History of Liberalism in the 1960s* (New York: Harper & Row, 1984); James T. Patterson, *Grand Expectations: The United States, 1945–1974* (New York: Oxford University Press, 1996); Kirkpatrick Sale, *The Green Revolution: The American Environmental Movement, 1962–1992* (New York: Hill and Wang, 1993).

2. Tom Engelhardt, *The End of Victory Culture: Cold War America and the Disillusioning of a Generation* (Amherst: University of Massachusetts Press, 2007); Todd Gitlin, *The Sixties* (New York: Bantam Books, 1987); David Maraniss, *They Marched into Sunlight: War and Peace, Vietnam and America, October 1967* (New York: Simon & Schuster, 2003); James Miller, *"Democracy Is in the Streets": From Port Huron to the Siege of Chicago* (New York: Simon & Schuster, 1987); Seth Rosenfeld, *Subversives: The FBI's War on Student Radicals and Reagan's Rise to Power* (New York: Farrar, Straus & Giroux, 2012); Tom Wells, *The War Within: America's Battle over Vietnam* (Berkeley: University of California Press, 1994).

3. Rusty L. Monhollon, *"This Is America?" The Sixties in Lawrence, Kansas* (New York: Palgrave, 2002), 71–73. For the history of the civil rights movement at KU and in Lawrence prior to 1965, see William M. Tuttle, Jr., "Separate but Not Equal: African Americans and the 100-Year Struggle for Equality in Lawrence and at the University of Kansas," in *Embattled Lawrence: Conflict and Community,* edited by Dennis Domer and Barbara Watkins (Lawrence: KU Division of Continuing Education, 2001), 139–151; Kristine M. McCusker, "'The Forgotten Years' of America's Civil Rights Movement: Wartime Protests at the University of Kansas, 1939–1945," *Kansas History* 17 (Spring 1994):

26–34; Kristine M. McCusker, "Interracial Communities and Civil Rights Activism in Lawrence, Kansas, 1945–1948," *Historian* 61 (Summer 1999): 786–801; Rusty L. Monhollon, "Taking the Plunge: Race, Rights, and the Politics of Desegregation in Lawrence, Kansas, 1960," *Kansas History* 20 (Autumn 1997): 138–159.

4. W. Clarke Wescoe, "Report to the Board of Regents," March 14, 1965, in Chancellor's Office, Executive Secretary Case Files, 1959–1965, RG 2/0/1/1, Box 9, "Civil Rights Demonstration" #1, University Archives, KU; "Sit-In at Wescoe's Office," *LJW*, March 8, 1965; Marian Warden, "Today's Protest Follows Arrest of 110 Monday," *LJW*, March 9, 1965; Bill Mayer, "Tone of KU Incident a Source of Pride," *LJW*, March 9, 1965; Marian Warden, "Normal Pace at KU Today—Strong Hall Sit-In Ends," *LJW*, March 10, 1965; Noah Briles, "Pursuit and Practice of Civil Rights at the University of Kansas, 1960–1969," paper written for W. Tuttle's History 496.

5. Wescoe, "Report to the Board of Regents," March 14, 1965; "150 Sit-In Stand-Out by Wescoe's Office," *UDK*, March 8, 1965; "Arrests No Curb on Demonstration," *UDK*, March 9, 1965; "Special Meeting Called," *UDK*, March 9, 1965; James J. Fisher, "Object at KU," *Kansas City Times*, March 9, 1965; John Petterson, "Wescoe Acts to End Demonstration," *Topeka Daily Capital*, March 10, 1965; "Wescoe Takes Stand for KU Sit-In Trial," *Topeka Daily Capital*, May 18, 1965; "Lawrence and Alabama," *Iola Register*, March 9, 1965; John Cathcart-Rake, "The Strong Hall Sit-In: Protest and Backlash in the Free State," paper written for W. Tuttle's American Studies 451.

6. Wescoe, "Report to the Board of Regents," March 14, 1965; "150 Sit-In Stand-Out by Wescoe's Office"; "Arrests No Curb on Demonstration"; "Special Meeting Called"; Fisher, "Object at KU"; Petterson, "Wescoe Acts to End Demonstration."

7. Monhollon, *This Is America?* 73, 75; Wescoe, "Report to the Board of Regents," March 14, 1965; Petterson, "Wescoe Acts to End Demonstration"; "CRC Explains Activities, Future Plans for Civil Rights," *UDK*, March 19, 1965; Rusty L. Monhollon, "Black Power, White Fear: The 'Negro Problem' in Lawrence, Kansas, 1960–1970," in *Race Consciousness: African-American Studies for the New Century*, edited by Judith Jackson Fossett and Jeffrey A. Tucker (New York: New York University Press, 1997), 253–254; "First Negro Pledge Would 'Do It Again,'" *UDK*, October 9, 1968.

8. Monhollon, *This Is America?* 73–75. This is a definitive history of Lawrence in the 1960s.

9. Stokely Carmichael and Charles V. Hamilton, *Black Power: The Politics of Liberation in America* (New York: Vintage Books, 1967), 44.

10. Rusty L. Monhollon, "Reconstructing the Sixties: Culture, Race, and Identity in Lawrence, Kansas, 1945–1975" (PhD diss., University of Kansas, 1999), 220–222; Monhollon, "Black Power, White Fear," 254; Tuttle, "Reform and Conflict at Home," 866.

11. Carmichael and Hamilton, *Black Power*, 38–39; Monhollon, "Black Power, White Fear," 254–256; Jack Zimmerman, "Negroes at LHS Air

Grievances," *LJW*, May 22, 1968; Valerie A. Schrag, "Pride, Determination, and Awareness: The Role of African American Parents in the Racial Conflicts at Lawrence High School, 1968–1970," paper written for W. Tuttle's History 974; John L. Rury and Shirley Hill, "An End of Innocence: African-American High School Protest in the 1960s and 1970s," *History of Education* 42 (2013): 486–508; Beryl Ann New, "A Fire in the Sky: Student Activism in Topeka, Kansas, and Lawrence, Kansas, High Schools in 1969 and 1970" (EdD diss., University of Kansas, 2007).

12. *LJW*, September 25, 1968.

13. John H. Spearman, Jr., "The BSU: The Necessity for a Base," *Jayhawker Yearbook* 82 (1970): 408–409.

14. Harold R. Nye, Kansas Bureau of Investigation, to Kent Frizzell, Attorney General, June 10, 1970, in Box 7, Folder 410:7:24, "Kansas Board of Regents 1970 Disturbance," Elmer Jackson Papers, University Archives, KU; BSU demands and related letters, in Black Student Union Records, RG 67/13, Box 1, University Archives, KU; "BSU Presents 'Demands,'" *UDK*, February 27, 1970; "LHSU Presents Demands," *UDK*, March 6, 1970; Anne Ferraro, "The Rise and Impact of Black Power in Lawrence," paper written for W. Tuttle's American Studies 450.

15. *Harambee* 1, nos. 1–2 (1970).

16. "Printers Hold Walkout," *UDK*, February 18, 1970; "BSU Confiscates *UDK*'s," *UDK*, February 24, 1970; "Harambee Status Uncertain," *UDK*, February 25, 1970; "Attorney General Rules on Harambee: Paper Not Obscene," *UDK*, February 26, 1970; Nye, Kansas Bureau of Investigation, to Frizzell, Attorney General, June 10, 1970.

17. Hub Meyer, "LHS Disruption Results in Charges, Suspensions," *LJW*, April 14, 1970; "High School Fights Erupt, Students Hurt," *LJW*, April 15, 1970; "LHS Is Tense but Quiet," *LJW*, April 16, 1970; "Classes on Monday, Knox Asks Normalcy," *LJW*, April 18, 1970; "Proposal at LHS Beaten by Students," *LJW*, April 20, 1970; Hub Meyer, "Violence at School Center," *LJW*, April 21, 1970; Anita Strecker, "18 Arrests on Thursday for Breaking of Curfew," *LJW*, April 24, 1970; "Violence Erupts at LHS," *UDK*, April 16, 1970; "Police Disperse Blacks at LHS," *UDK*, April 17, 1970; Brian Hack, "'The Time Has Come for Liberation': Lawrence High School and the Black Student Movement, 1960–1970," paper written for W. Tuttle's History 617.

18. Monhollon, *This Is America?* 151.

19. Robert J. Rollins, "Gen. Taylor Explains War Issues," *Kansas City Times*, March 27, 1965.

20. "Viet Nam Teach-In Possible," *UDK*, September 22, 1965; "New Committee Seeks Peace in Viet Nam," *UDK*, September 23, 1965; Monhollon, *This Is America?* 77. See also Michael P. Fisher, "The Turbulent Years: The University of Kansas, 1960–75: A History" (PhD diss., University of Kansas, 1975).

21. Lee Byrd, "Student Left Will Demonstrate Saturday for Viet Nam Peace," *UDK*, October 12, 1965; Lee Byrd, "SPU Joins Viet Nam Protest," *UDK*, October 18, 1965; Walt Jayroe, "Letter Planned Backing War," *UDK*,

October 26, 1965; "SDS Proposes Blood Drive for Viet Nam," *UDK*, November 1, 1965; "KU Students Display Patriotism," *UDK*, November 16, 1965; M. Warden, "Jeers, Laughter Greet KU's Anti-War Antics," *UDK*, April 30, 1965; Monhollon, *This Is America?* 78–79.

22. US Department of Commerce, *Bicentennial Edition: Historical Statistics of the United States, Colonial Times to 1970* (Washington, DC: GPO, 1975), 1143; Spencer C. Tucker, *The Encyclopedia of the Vietnam War: A Political, Social, and Military History* (New York: Oxford University Press, 1998), 107; Christian G. Appy, *Patriots: The Vietnam War Remembered from All Sides* (New York: Viking Penguin, 2003), 162–163; Christian G. Appy, *Working-Class War: American Combat Soldiers and Vietnam* (Chapel Hill: University of North Carolina Press, 1993); Lawrence M. Baskir and William A. Strauss, *Chance and Circumstance: The Draft, the War, and the Vietnam Generation* (New York: Random House, 1978), 6–7, 28–29, 36; "Numbers Decide Draft Fate," *UDK*, December 2, 1969.

23. "Radicals Might Appear at the ROTC Review," *UDK*, May 8, 1969; "'Peace' Demonstration, Demonstrators Disrupt Review," *UDK*, May 12, 1969; Audrey Curtis, "The Disruption of the 1969 Chancellor's Annual Review of the ROTC," paper written for W. Tuttle's History 616; Jay Sexton, "Divided Loyalty: ROTC Cadets at the University of Kansas, 1966–1970," paper written for W. Tuttle's History 616.

24. "VP Bowman Says UDB Too Harsh," *UDK*, September 17, 1969; Dick Wintermote, supplement to *Kansas Alumni Magazine* 67 (June 1969): 1–2.

25. "Statement by Chancellor Chalmers," May 11, 1972, in Student Senate, President's Correspondence, Box 1, Dillon 71–72, Vietnam War, University Archives, KU.

26. Rusty L. Monhollon, "Lawrence, Kansas, and the Making of the Sixties," in *Embattled Lawrence: Conflict and Community*, 211; Sexton, "Divided Loyalty"; Monhollon, *This Is America?* 79–80, 128–133; Douglas Scheffner, "ROTC Controversy Nothing New to KU," *UDK*, October 7, 1969; "War Protest Round-Up," *UDK*, October 16, 1969; "ROTC Week Proclaimed by Council; Moratorium Communists Backed?" *UDK*, November 5, 1969.

27. Edward K. Spann, *Democracy's Children: The Young Rebels of the 1960s and the Power of Ideals* (Wilmington, DE: Scholarly Resources, 2003), 101–118; John Kifner, "Marijuana: Random Harvest in the U.S.," *New York Times*, November 7, 1969; Marijuana Poll, *UDK*, October 8, 1971; David Ohle et al., eds., *Cows Are Freaky When They Look at You: An Oral History of the Kaw Valley Hemp Pickers* (Wichita: Watermark Press, 1991), unpaginated preface; Timothy Miller, *The Hippies and American Values* (Knoxville: University of Tennessee Press, 1991), 25–50; Louie Louis, "Picking Hemp in Douglas County," in *Embattled Lawrence: Conflict and Community*, 243–248; Matthew C. Clark, "The Gaslight Tavern: A Lawrence Legacy," paper written for W. Tuttle's American Studies 450.

28. Clark Coan, "1970: The Year That Rocked River City" (copy in author's possession); Nye, Kansas Bureau of Investigation, to Frizzell, Attorney General, June 10, 1970; Rachael Augustyn, "The Times They Are A-Changin',"

paper written for W. Tuttle's History 131; Jenni Carlson, "With Different Eyes: Differences in Coverage of Student Protest and Violence at the University of Kansas in the *Lawrence Journal-World* and *University Daily Kansan*," paper written for W. Tuttle's History 131.

29. Coan, "1970: The Year That Rocked River City"; Barbara Downing, "Lawrence, Kansas, Spring, 1970," paper written for W. Tuttle's History 616; Monhollon, *This Is America?* 151, 157–159; "Third Night Curfew Calmer," *UDK*, April 24, 1970.

30. Tuttle, "Reform and Conflict at Home," 873; Brenna Hawley, "A Generation Ablaze," *UDK*, April 20, 2010.

31. E. Laurence Chalmers, "19 Days and Nights," *Kansas Alumni Magazine* 69 (May 30, 1970): 2–5; Statement of the Senate Executive Committee, May 8, 1970, in Steve Clark, "Chalmers Fields Alumni Questions," *Kansas Alumni Magazine* 69 (May 30, 1970): 3; Bill Mayer, "KU Mob Breaks Windows," *LJW*, May 7, 1970; "Docking Angry over KU Action," *LJW*, May 7, 1970; "Docking Hails Action at KU," *LJW*, May 9, 1970; Bob Womack, "Thousands Back Chalmers," *UDK*, May 11, 1970; Ralph Gage, "Chalmers Reflects as KU Tension Eases," *LJW*, May 11, 1970; Leticia Bryant, "Perceptions of Disorder," paper written for W. Tuttle's American Studies 450.

32. Monhollon, "Lawrence, Kansas, and the Making of the Sixties," 214; Coan, "1970: The Year That Rocked River City"; Monhollon, *This Is America?* 109.

33. "In Memory of Rick 'Tiger' Dowdell: The Truth Prevails," *Harambee* (July 1970): 1; Monhollon, "Lawrence, Kansas, and the Making of the Sixties," 216–217; Monhollon, *This Is America?* 165–168; Monhollon, "Black Power, White Fear," 248–249, 259; Jerry Schwartz, "Patrolman Shot Answering Call," *LJW*, July 18, 1970; Jerry Schwartz, "Seven Arrested in Local Unrest," *LJW*, July 20, 1970; "Garret Relieved of Police Duties," *LJW*, July 20, 1970.

34. Monhollon, "Lawrence, Kansas, and the Making of the Sixties," 216–217; Monhollon, *This Is America?* 168–169; Coan, "1970: The Year That Rocked River City"; Jerry Schwartz, "Leawood Youth Killed in Monday Flare-Up," *LJW*, July 21, 1970; "City Declares Emergency," *LJW*, July 21, 1970; "Wounded Student: 'I Was Blessed,'" *LJW*, July 21, 1970.

35. Bill Moyers, *Listening to America: A Traveler Rediscovers His Country* (New York: Harper & Row, 1971), 122.

36. Coan, "1970: The Year That Rocked River City."

37. Rebecca E. Klatch, *A Generation Divided: The New Left, the New Right, and the 1960s* (Berkeley: University of California Press, 1999), 66, 215–217, 277; Robbie Lieberman, *Prairie Power: Voices of 1960s Midwestern Student Protest* (Columbia: University of Missouri Press, 2004), 108–117, 143–160, 210–223, 247–257; KU News Bureau, News Release, March 2, 1971, in Student Senate News Releases, RG 3/11/3, Box 1, University Archives, KU.

38. Tucker, *Encyclopedia of the Vietnam War*, 112–113; David B. Dillon, resolution of Student Executive Committee, April 20, 1972, in Student Senate,

President's Correspondence, Dillon 71–72, RG 3/11, Box 1, Vietnam War, University Archives, KU.

39. D'Emilio, *Sexual Politics, Sexual Communities*, 239.

40. Kansas Penal Code, Section 21-3505 (July 1, 1970); Patrick Dilley, *Queer Man on Campus: A History of Non-Heterosexual College Men, 1945–2000* (New York: Routledge Falmer, 2002), 168–169; Beth Bailey, *Sex in the Heartland* (Cambridge: Harvard University Press, 1999), 178, 180; Jason Gordon, "Back to the Front: The Lawrence Gay Liberation Front and the Struggle for Recognition," paper written for W. Tuttle's American Studies 450.

41. Stacey Reding, "Paving Gayhawk Lane: The Lawrence Gay Liberation Front and Chancellor Chalmers' Veto," paper written for W. Tuttle's History 666; KU News Bureau, Press Release, September 5, 1970, in University Relations, News Releases, September 1970, RG 881, University Archives, KU; E. Laurence Chalmers to Jim Winkler, October 4, 1971, in E. Laurence Chalmers, Correspondence, General O–Z, 1971–1972, RG 2/13/1, Box 6, University Archives, KU; Bailey, *Sex in the Heartland*, 179.

42. Reding, "Paving Gayhawk Lane"; Dilley, *Queer Man on Campus*, 169–173; Bailey, *Sex in the Heartland*, 180–183; Gordon, "Back to the Front"; Jamie Tilma, "The Lawrence Gay Liberation Front, 1970–1973," paper written for W. Tuttle's History 496; "Gay Lib Hires Kunstler," *LJW*, July 22, 1971; "$600 for Gay Libs Wouldn't Be Fees," *UDK*, September 23, 1971; "Gay Lib Party under Review by KU Group," *LJW*, September 30, 1971; "KU's Gay Libbers File Federal Suit," *Topeka Capital*, December 14, 1971; Robert H. Clark, "Kunstler Barred from U.S. Court," *Kansas City Star*, January 27, 1972; "Kunstler Incurs a Judge's Wrath," *New York Times*, January 28, 1972; "Gay Liberation Request Denied," *Topeka Capital*, February 12, 1972; "Gay Liberation Seeks Reversal," *LJW*, February 23, 1972; "Kunstler Requests Court Order KU Gay Lib Okay," *LJW*, November 17, 1972.

43. The Women and Men of the Lawrence Gay Liberation Front, "On Our Own," *Vortex* 4, no. 2 (1971). For copious information about the Lawrence Gay Liberation Front dances, the legal cases, and Lawrence's gay newspapers, see the anthology compiled by David Drake Barney, *Gay and Lesbian History at the University of Kansas* (Lawrence: University of Kansas, Student Assistance Center, 1992).

44. Dilley, *Queer Man on Campus*, 175–179; Bailey, *Sex in the Heartland*, 184–185; Gordon, "Back to the Front"; "Gay Lib Party under Review by KU Group," *LJW*, September 30, 1971. In 1972, in one of the most successful protests in KU history, the February Sisters occupied a KU building and demanded the establishment of a women's studies program, a women's health program, and a day care center for the children of KU students, staff, and faculty. See Chapter 7.

45. Ruth Lichtwardt, "A Stroll Down Gayhawk Lane," part 1, "1976–1986: The Dance & Go to Sambo's Years," and Ruth Lichtwardt, "A Stroll Down Gayhawk Lane," part 2, "Private Activities, Habits, or Proclivities," both in Barney,

Gay and Lesbian History at the University of Kansas; Stacey Reding, "Fighting 'Fagbusters': Gay and Lesbian Services of Kansas' Struggle for Recognition," honors thesis written for W. Tuttle's History 498; Sara Kempin, "Senate Bill to Finance Gays Angers Some," *UDK*, April 14, 1983; Sara Kempin, "GLSOK Allocation Draws Fire from Some Senators," *UDK*, April 26, 1983.

46. Lichtwardt, "A Stroll Down Gayhawk Lane," part 2; Reding, "Fighting 'Fagbusters.'"

47. Lichtwardt, "A Stroll Down Gayhawk Lane," part 2; Reding, "Fighting 'Fagbusters.'"

48. Professor Bill Tuttle quoted in David Lassiter, "Faculty Petition Favors Rights of GLSOK Group," *UDK*, October 25, 1984. See also Mary Carter, "KU Officials Issue Harassment Policy," *UDK*, November 9, 1984; Lichtwardt, "A Stroll Down Gayhawk Lane," part 2; Reding, "Fighting 'Fagbusters.'"

49. Reding, "Fighting 'Fagbusters'"; "FAGS" flyer in author's possession; Lindsy Van Gelder and Pam Brandt, "AIDS on Campus," *Rolling Stone* (September 25, 1986): 89.

50. Reding, "Fighting 'Fagbusters'"; Jarrod Cruz, "Life Styles: Les-BiGaysOk, a 25-Year-Old Story," *Jayhawker Yearbook*, 1996, 276; Jennifer Presley, "A History of the Simply Equal Amendment: A Human Rights Initiative," paper written for W. Tuttle's American Studies 450.

51. Jennifer Benjamin, "Gay-Rights Law Loses on Vote," *Wichita Eagle-Beacon*, January 21, 1988; Presley, "A History of the Simply Equal Amendment"; "Portrait of an Activist [Ben Zimmerman]," *UDK*, February 16, 2000. This "Freedom Coalition" should not be confused with the earlier conservative organization by that name.

52. David Toplikar, "City Mulls Gay Rights Law," *LJW*, January 19, 1995; Mark Fagan, "Human Rights Seen as Key City Issue," *LJW*, March 1, 1995; Mark Fagan, "Bullet Voters Hit Target in Election," *LJW*, April 7, 1995; Mark Fagan, "Simply Equal Hails Victory," *LJW*, April 26, 1995; Presley, "A History of the Simply Equal Amendment." An excellent film on the Simply Equal movement is *Shades of Gray* (2000), by filmmaker Tim DePaepe.

53. Jason Schreiner, "Will to Protest: The Anti-Apartheid Movement at the University of Kansas, 1978–1986," paper written for W. Tuttle's American Studies 450; Umut Bayramoglu, "Liberty and the Law," *UDK*, April 23, 1997; "Group Seeks Stock Divestiture at KU," *LJW*, February 27, 1979; Laurie Wolkey, "New S. African Investment Policy Criticized," *UDK*, February 28, 1979; "Endowment Group Firm on South African Policy," *LJW*, March 8, 1979; "Endowment President Meets with Protesters," *UDK*, March 8, 1979; "Black Students Join Anti-Apartheid Cause," *UDK*, April 2, 1979.

54. Schreiner, "Will to Protest"; Dennis "Boog" Highberger, "A Portrait of the Lawyer as a Young Maniac," *Disorientation* 4 (1989): 9–10; Tony Fitts, "Protest Goes On amid Orientation," *UDK*, June 21, 1979; Tony Fitts, "Trustees Refuse to Meet with S. Africa Committee," *UDK*, July 12, 1979.

55. Schreiner, "Will to Protest"; Nancy Stoetzer, "25 Gather to Protest Ties to South Africa," *UDK*, March 26, 1985; J. Strohmaier, "KU Forum Urges Swift

Divestment," *UDK*, March 29, 1985; "Chancellor Opposes Divestiture Measure," *UDK*, April 26, 1985; "Statement by Budig Gets Mixed Reviews," *UDK*, April 29, 1985.

56. Schreiner, "Will to Protest"; Cindy McCurry, "Sit-In Adopts Festive Atmosphere," *UDK*, April 30, 1985; Cindy McCurry, "Sit-In Delegates Talk with Cobb, Ambler," *UDK*, May 2, 1985; "Students Protesting Policy to Continue Sit-In at KU," *LJW*, May 3, 1985.

57. Schreiner, "Will to Protest"; Katharine Weickert, "16 Arrested in KU Protest on South Africa," *LJW*, May 4, 1985; Jim Snell, "Arrests Don't Deter Protest at Strong Hall," *LJW*, May 5, 1985; Doug Hitchcock, "Protesters Awaiting Response from KUEA," *LJW*, May 7, 1985; Doug Hitchcock, "Endowment Association Refuses to Cut South Africa Investments," *LJW*, May 8, 1985; Doug Hitchcock, "Anti-Apartheid Activists Plan Protests," *LJW*, May 9, 1985; Doug Hitchcock, "Protesters Arrested at KU," *LJW*, May 10, 1985.

58. Schreiner, "Will to Protest"; "Log Book," copy in personal files of W. Tuttle.

59. Jennifer Benjamin, "Divestment Battle to Persist," *UDK*, August 26, 1985; Jennifer Benjamin, "KU Group Vows Fight to Endure," *UDK*, August 27, 1985; Schreiner, "Will to Protest."

60. Jennifer Benjamin, "Blacks Say They'll Join in Protests," *UDK*, October 11, 1985; Jennifer Benjamin, "Protesters Ask to Meet Budig: 5 Are Arrested," *UDK*, November 5, 1985; Jennifer Benjamin, "Action Urged at Anti-Apartheid Rally," *UDK*, November 5, 1985; Schreiner, "Will to Protest."

61. Letters to the editor in "Mailbox," *UDK*, April 3, 1986; Russell Gray, "Campers Continue Protest Despite Recent Harassment," *UDK*, April 7, 1986.

62. Schreiner, "Will to Protest."

63. See timeline for the anti-Klan rally, in Eric Gorski and Buck Taylor, "Student to File Complaint in SAE Incident," *UDK*, April 30, 1990.

64. Interview with Ann Dean, May 12, 2014; Eric Gorski, "Fraternity Group Argue at Hoch," *UDK*, April 2, 1990; Eric Gorski, "Student Turns in Complaint," *UDK*, April 9, 1990.

65. Gorski, "Fraternity, Group Argue at Hoch"; Eric Gorski, "Racism Debated at Forum," *UDK*, April 6, 1990; "Pizza Incident Spurs Complaint," *LJW*, April 7, 1990; Carol B. Shiney, "SCAD Criticizes Forum, Report," *UDK*, April 9, 1990; Gorski, "Student Turns in Complaint."

66. Bill Tuttle, notes for his morning meeting with Chancellor Budig, Executive Vice Chancellor Ramaley, and Vice Chancellor Ambler, April 11, 1990, and Gene A. Budig to Bill Tuttle, April 12, 1990, copies of both in W. Tuttle's personal files; Eric Gorski and Jonathan Plummer, "Protesters Descend on Strong," *UDK*, April 12, 1990.

67. Gorski and Plummer, "Protesters Descend on Strong"; Deb Gruver, "Protest Leaders Say They'll Keep Pressing KU for Action," *LJW*, April 12, 1990; Pam Sollner and Jonathan Plummer, "Officials Meet with Minority Leaders," *UDK*, April 13, 1990. Not until April 25, 1990, almost a month after the incident, was an arrest made, charging the man with disorderly conduct

and battery. In the interim, the man, while again inebriated, had been arrested for a separate reported battery at a Lawrence apartment complex. See Eric Gorski, "Two Members Willfully Leave SAE Fraternity," *UDK*, April 25, 1990; Eric Gorski, "KU Student Charged in Racial Case," *UDK*, April 26, 1990; Ric Anderson, "Student Is Charged in KU Pizza Incident," *LJW*, April 26, 1990; Gorski and Taylor, "Student to File Complaint in SAE Incident."

68. Jack Whalen and Richard Flacks, *Beyond the Barricades: The Sixties Generation Grows Up* (Philadelphia: Temple University Press, 1989), 283.

7. A SEAT AT THE TABLE: STUDENT LEADERSHIP, STUDENT SERVICES, AND THE NEW EMPOWERMENT

1. Susan B. Twombly and Christopher C. Morphew, "Tuition Rising and Student Power in the Academy: A New Student-Centeredness?" Paper presented at the annual conference of the Association for the Study of Higher Education, Philadelphia, 2005, 22. At KU, students demanded the creation of, and served equally on, the Ad Hoc Committee and as a result saw an added $8.6 million in tuition grants, increased wages for student employees, and improvements in advising and other services. In addition, a new Student Tuition Committee oversaw usage of millions of dollars of new programming funds over the next five years.

2. Beth Bailey, *From Front Porch to Back Seat: Courtship in Twentieth-Century America* (Baltimore: Johns Hopkins University Press, 1988), 84–88; John Rury and Glenn Harper, "The Trouble with Coeducation: Mann and Women at Antioch, 1853–1860," *History of Education Quarterly* 26 (Winter 1986): 486–489; Kathryn Nemeth Tuttle, "What Became of the Dean of Women? Changing Roles for Women Administrators in American Higher Education, 1940–1980" (PhD diss., University of Kansas, 1996), 320; "A.W.S. Regulations for University of Kansas Women," Dean of Women's Papers, Box 1, RG 53/0, University Archives, KU.

3. Kelly C. Sartorius, "Experimental Autonomy: Dean Emily Taylor and the Women's Movement at the University of Kansas," *Kansas History: A Journal of the Central Plains* 33 (Spring 2010): 6, 17. See also Kelly C. Sartorius, *Deans of Women and the Feminist Movement: Emily Taylor's Activism* (New York: Palgrave Macmillan, 2014).

4. Sartorius, "Experimental Autonomy," 15–16.

5. Jacke Thayer, "Closing—Question of the Hour," *UDK*, March 11, 1966, 2.

6. Eric Morgenthaler, "Surface Defends University Rules," *UDK*, March 14, 1966, 1, 4; Beth Bailey, *Sex in the Heartland* (Cambridge: Harvard University Press, 1999), 91.

7. Bailey, *Sex in the Heartland*, 97–104; Sartorius, "Experimental Autonomy," 18–20.

8. Sara Paretsky and Nancy Gallup, "Associated Women Sycophants or Frailty, Thy Name Is the Women's Program," *University Review* 3 (March 1967), in AWS Chronological Records, 1965/66–1969/70, Box 2, RG 67/12, University Archives, KU; Betsy Wright, "Women Still Chained," *UDK*, January 10, 1968.

9. "A.W.S. Regulations Questionnaire," Spring 1968, AWS Records, 1967/68 folder, RG 67/12, University Archives, KU.

10. "WLF, ISP Ask AWS to Quit," *UDK*, April 17, 1969, 13; Sartorius, "Experimental Autonomy, 3; Sid Moody, "K.U.'s Class of '73 Matured in Troubled Years," *Kansas City Star*, May 13, 1973, 51.

11. Sartorius, "Experimental Autonomy," 9; Tuttle, "What Became of the Dean of Women?" 351. Taylor, who was hired by KU in 1956, made her presence known immediately when she announced she would report directly to Chancellor Franklin Murphy rather than to newly promoted Dean of Students Laurence Woodruff. Both Taylor and Murphy recognized the importance of having a top-level female administrator. As Taylor recalled, "I made it perfectly clear when I came here that nobody spoke for me but me. I don't play the game of going through someone else. If you want me it's going to have to be a direct relationship." Until her resignation in 1975 to become director of the Office of Women in Higher Education of the American Council on Education, Dean Taylor reported directly to five chancellors.

12. Ann Gardner, "KU 'Legend' Emily Taylor Dies: Former Dean Mentored Generations of Women," *LJW*, May 2, 2004, 1.

13. Bailey, *Sex in the Heartland*, 116, 119–121; Lee Stone, "Senior, Freshmen Women Vote Same on Sex," *UDK*, May 4, 1964, 1; "Survey of Women's Morals Grew from Study at Michigan State," *UDK*, May 4, 1964, 10.

14. Bailey, *Sex in the Heartland*, 123–124; Julie Thatcher, "Dean Taylor Discusses Sex, the Pill, and the New Morality," *UDK*, January 9, 1970. The Douglas County Family Planning Association, an affiliate of Planned Parenthood, which required physical exams, closed due to overwhelming demand, primarily from KU students.

15. Phyllis Agins, "Female Faculty Members Are Left Behind at KU," *UDK*, October 12, 1971; Marsha Libeer, "Research Group Checks Sex Discrimination Cases," *UDK*, November 11, 1971.

16. Marsha Libeer, "Women's Group Expands in Membership, Scope," *UDK*, October 13, 1971, 6; Kate Manske, "Women's Lib Workshops Cover Variety of Topics," *UDK*, March 3, 1971, 2; Rusty Monhollon, *"This Is America?" The Sixties in Lawrence, Kansas* (New York: Palgrave, 2002), 196–197.

17. "A Statement of Action," February 4, 1972, February Sisters, Position Papers & Statements Folder, and "A History of the Seizure and Occupation of the East Asian Studies Building by the February Sisters or What It Takes to Make Men Move," February 2, 1972, 2–4, February Sisters, History Folder, both in RG 67/126, University Archives, KU. Ibid. states that 20 women occupied the building, while some later accounts put the number at 30.

18. "A Statement of Action"; "A History of the Seizure and Occupation"; Bailey, *Sex in the Heartland*, 127–129.

19. "A History of the Seizure and Occupation"; "A Statement of Action"; "Press Release," February 6, 1972, February Sisters, History Folder, RG 67/126, University Archives, KU.

20. Bob Womack, "Chalmers Concerned over Women's Lib Assertions," *LJW*, February 16, 1972; Ann Eversole, interview by author, digital recording, Lawrence, May 7, 2013; "Larry," Letter to the Editor, *UDK*, March 7, 1972; "Statements of Women Faculty Released to February Sisters," February 6, 1972, February Sisters, Faculty Women Folder, RG 67/126, University Archives, KU.

21. Judy Henry, "Watkins Staffs Clinic for Women," *UDK*, February 22, 1972; Gail Pfeiffer, "Hilltop Director Selected," *UDK*, April 19, 1972, 10; "The February Sisters' Demands: A Progress Report" [1973], February Sisters, 1973 Folder, RG 67/126, University Archives, KU.

22. Joan Handley, Letter to the Editor, *UDK*, February 12, 1972; "The February Sisters' Demands: A Progress Report"; "February Sisters," printout of February 2012 website on 40th anniversary, February Sisters, Box 2, 2011–2012 Folder, RG 67/126, University Archives, KU.

23. [Christine Leonard], "Women's Decade of History," 1, 3, 1972, February Sisters, History Folder, RG 67/126, University Archives, KU; "Coeds Want More Hill Lights," *UDK*, February 15, 1968; "Little Money Is Available for Lighting," *UDK*, March 6, 1968.

24. Bailey, *Sex in the Heartland*, 197–198; GaDuGI SafeCenter, http://www.gadugisafecenter.org, accessed December 26, 2013; Kala Stroup, interview by author, digital recording, Lawrence, July 17, 2013.

25. "Whistlestop Whistles on the Way," *UDK*, April 2, 1974; "Whistlestop Won't Help," *UDK*, April 9, 1974; "Whistlestop May Hurt Enrollment," *UDK*, April 19, 1974; "Unified Effort Sought to Stop Rape," *UDK*, April 11, 1974; Kala Stroup, interview by author.

26. "Abortion: A High-Priced Nightmare" and "How Many Choose Abortions at KU?" *UDK*, May 16, 1967; "Abortion Raid in KC Involves 2 Local Women," *UDK*, April 23, 1969; "For 2 Coeds; Over Painful Memory," *UDK*, October 14, 1970; "Anti-abortion Vigil Held," *UDK*, July 9, 1971; "Watkins Treating Fewer Illegal Abortions," *UDK*, February 28, 1972; "Anti-abortion Display Creates Unrest at KU," *UDK*, September 22, 1998.

27. *Jayhawker Yearbook*, 1993, 2, 91.

28. Adam Strunk, "12th Street to Be Brought to Life," *UDK*, January 25, 2011; Rebekka Schlichting, "New Lights on Mt. Oread Make Path Safer at Night," *UDK*, February 6, 2012; Sara Lipka, "Protesters Call for Stricter Sanctions on Colleges That Mishandle Sexual Assault," *Chronicle of Higher Education*, July 16, 2013, http://chronicle.com/article/Protesters-Call-for-Stricter/140375, accessed June 4, 2014; McKenna Harford, "Breaking the Silence," *UDK*, September 10, 2014, 1.

29. William A. Kaplin, *The Law of Higher Education: A Comprehensive Guide*

to Legal Implications of Administrative Decision Making, 2nd ed. (San Francisco: Jossey-Bass, 1986), 303–322; Tuttle, "What Became of the Dean of Women?" 324–325. Many student affairs leaders, including David Ambler, think that the student legal rights movement had as profound an effect on students and administrators as the antiwar movement and the counterculture. David Ambler, interview by author, tape recording, Lawrence, December 20, 1994.

30. John H. McCool, "Of the Students, by the Students, for the Students," KU History, http://kuhistory.com/articles/of-the-students-for-the-students/, accessed December 26, 2013; Tony Arnold, "Student Participation at the University of Kansas, 1966–1969: Changes in Policy Formulation," paper written for W. Tuttle's History 496; Bailey, *Sex in the Heartland,* 95–96; "Group Sends Demands to Chancellor," *UDK,* April 29, 1968, 1, 7; "KU Military Debated," *UDK,* April 24, 1968, 1.

31. "Activist Leaders Discourage Sit-In" and "Students Ask for 'More Effective Voice,'" *UDK,* May 6, 1968, 1, 5, 8; Jason Fizell, "Voice: Students and Their Efforts for Representation at the University of Kansas, 1968–1969," paper written for W. Tuttle's American Studies 696.

32. "Report of Student Faculty Committee on University Governance," September 1968, 1–2, Student Faculty Committee on University Governance, Governance Records, 1968, Box 1, RG 3/0, University Archives, KU; Arnold, "Student Participation at the University of Kansas, 1966–1969"; "Voice Explains Position," *UDK,* May 7, 1968, 1. At this time, university governance at KU consisted of the University Senate, made up of all tenured faculty and most administrators, and the Senate Council, elected from the Senate members, which was the smaller, policy-making group and met more frequently.

33. Richard Louv, "Code In, ASC Out," *UDK,* February 21, 1968, 1; Arnold, "Student Participation at the University of Kansas, 1966–1969"; KU News Bureau, "The University of Kansas Creates a New Student-Faculty Government," March 20, 1969, Student Senate, Governance Records, News Releases Folder, 1968–1969, RG 3/11/3, University Archives, KU; Rick Von Ende, "Sounds of Silence," *Jayhawker Yearbook,* 1969, 290–291.

34. Angela Reilly, "The Origins, Struggles, Accomplishments, and Effects of the Independent Student Party," paper written for W. Tuttle's History 131; "Reform-Loving ISP Backs the Pill, Pass-Fail Western Civ in Platform," *UDK,* November 15, 1967, 1, 5; "Kansan Endorsement," *UDK,* April 21, 1969; "ISP Wins by Slim Margin"; McCool, "Of the Students."

35. Reilly, "The Origins of the Independent Study Party," *UDK,* April 5, 1970. Poor senator attendance was part of the problem, and frustrations grew about the lack of communication with the student body as well as the slow pace of the faculty-dominated legislative process.

36. Bretton Zinger, "The Great KU Controversy," *Jayhawker Yearbook,* 1992, 56–61; David Ambler, interview by author, digital recording, Lawrence, May 1, 2013.

37. Ben Unglesbee, "Student Senate Attempts to Reform Elections," *LJW,* November 9, 2013, 3A–4A. In 2013, the Ad Astra coalition won on a platform

of accessibility and transparency, beating out the long-standing KUnited coalition for only the second time in 19 years. It promoted, and the Senate passed, stricter campaign rules, which led to new disputes. Amelia Arvesen, "Elections Commission Certifies, Releases Full Results of 2014 Elections," *UDK*, April 29, 2014, 1. Even though the Jayhawkers, heirs to the KUnited, garnered 61.4 percent of the vote for the presidency and vice presidency, the Elections Commission certified Grow KU, with 31.6 percent, as the winners. In the fall of 2014, the University Judicial Board Appeals Panel ruled that a new election be held to avoid a distorted voting process. Said and Wagner were reelected. Scott Rothschild, "2014 Student Senate Election Nullified," *LJW*, August 26, 2014, 3A; Miranda Davis, "Grow KU Wins Re-election," *UDK*, September 11, 2014, 2A.

38. Gwen G. (Barstow) Bohling, "Forty Years of Growth: Student Affairs at the University of Kansas," paper written for D. Katzman's History 666; Tuttle, "What Became of the Dean of Women?" 326–329. Nationally, college attendance more than doubled during the 1960s, and enrollment boomed at KU, from 10,320 students in 1960 to over 19,000 students a decade later. Across the country, student affairs administrators had to provide services and housing for 4.4 million more students in 1970 than they had in 1960; another 3.6 million students would be added by 1980.

39. Clifford S. Griffin, *The University of Kansas: A History* (Lawrence: University Press of Kansas, 1974), 635; University of Kansas, OIRP, *KU Profiles*, "Housing Patterns of Students," Table 9-201, fall 2012, http://www2.ku .edu/~oirp/profiles/current/9–201.pdf, accessed January 10, 2014.

40. "Hanky-Panky in McCollum Causes Embarrassment for the Residents," *UDK*, December 6, 1967; "Hall, Parents React to McCollum PDA Claim," *UDK*, December 8, 1967; Bailey, *Sex in the Heartland*, 207–208; Tuttle, "What Became of the Dean of Women?" 352–353; "Residence Hall Policies among Institutions in the Association of American Universities," *Journal of the National Association of Women Deans and Counselors* 35 (Spring 1972): 136–138; *Jayhawker Yearbook*, 1967, 170.

41. "Policy on Organizational Membership," University of Kansas Student Organization Records, AWS, Box 1, RG 67/12, University Archives, KU; Monhollon, *This Is America?* 71–75.

42. "Report on Discrimination in Fraternities," May 1, 1978, Office of Student Affairs, Correspondence Subject Files, Interfraternity Council, 1978–1979, Box 17, RG 76/0/6, University Archives, KU. The report discussed Greek Endeavor, a new program focusing on cultural diversity and Greek image; in later years its focus expanded to include sexual orientation, alcohol, and AIDS, which grew out of earlier efforts to diversify the Greek system.

43. Student Involvement and Leadership Center, "Greek Life Annual Report: 2012–13 Year in Review," 2013, http://www.silc.ku.edu/greeklife, accessed April 28, 2014; "Divine Nine Room Dedicated at the University of Kansas," Press Release, Student Involvement and Leadership Center, KU, March 26, 2014.

44. The transformation of Daisy Hill residence halls progressed with the 2014 ground-breaking for the construction of two first-year–focused halls on a residential quadrangle. The halls will house 350 residents each and continue the trend of offering suites as well as single-occupancy rooms and a connecting commons building featuring a classroom and advising, tutoring, and group study rooms, as well as a kitchen and media and game rooms. KU will raze McCollum Hall, the three-winged giant, with many components recycled for other uses, to provide room for a parking lot. New students in 2015 will occupy luxurious accommodations, as compared to the 1965 KU freshmen, who had to trudge down a long hallway in McCollum to use a shared restroom. Ben Unglesbee, "KU Celebrates Groundbreaking of New Daisy Hill Residence Halls," *LJW*, March 5, 2014.

45. Jeffrey Weinberg, interview by author, digital recording, Lawrence, September 18, 2013.

46. Reilly, "From Rumor Control to Information Center." The Information Center provided a 24-hour telephone service for students to get accurate information in times of turmoil.

47. Office of Multicultural Affairs, "Our Story," http://www.oma.ku /history, accessed November 4, 2013. Office of Multicultural Affairs reporting changed from the executive vice chancellor to the vice chancellor for student affairs in 1987, and to some this signaled a move away from central diversity concerns and toward programming.

48. It took the naming of Ambler as vice chancellor in 1977, as well as the departure of Emily Taylor to the American Council on Education in 1975, for this transformation to come to KU. Tuttle, "What Became of the Dean of Women?" 329–331.

49. Ambler, interview by author, 2013; Bohling, "Forty Years of Growth," 7–9; David A. Ambler, "Rock Chalk, Jay Hawk! Student Life on Mount Oread, 1866–1990," a lecture in celebration of the 125th anniversary of the University of Kansas, Lawrence, November 13, 1990, General Records, 125th Anniversary, RG 0/8, University Archives, KU; Tuttle, "What Became of the Dean of Women?" 323–324. This reorganization centered on the areas of student service, student environment, and student enrollment and retention, with new deans of student life and student services (later educational services); the reorganization continued the dean of admissions and records.

50. Ray Pence, "Teaching the Able Majority: Roger B. Williams and the Rehabilitation Act of 1973 at the University of Kansas," paper written for W. Tuttle's American Studies 998. Williams, journal editor and illustrator for the paleontology program, chaired the University Committee for the Architecturally Handicapped, started by Vice Chancellor William Balfour to bring KU into compliance with Section 504.

51. Mary Lou Reece to Archie Dykes, June 11, 1975, John A. Myers to Delbert Shankel, September 15, 1975, and W. Max Lucas to Mary Lou Reece, June 19, 1975, all in Governance Records, Student Senate,

Presidents' Correspondence, Box 1, File 1975–1976, RG 3/11, University Archives, KU. Retrieving a key to Wescoe elevators required a trip across the street and then entrance into Strong Hall by the back door. Why there had been such a resistance to student use of elevators is unclear. Assistant to the Chancellor W. Max Lucas mentioned to Reece that he had to "ascertain how many people actually do use the elevators for vertical transportation."

52. Pence, "Teaching the Able Majority." Williams left KU, but he went on to play a larger role in Lawrence with the formation of Independence, Inc., an advocacy, training, and transportation service for individuals with disabilities in Lawrence and northeast Kansas.

53. Student Access Services, http://disability.ku.edu, accessed March 4, 2014; Accessibility & ADA Education, http://ioa.ku.edu/accessibility-ada -education, accessed March 4, 2014; "Class Credit," *Kansas Alumni Magazine* 111, no. 6 (November 2013): 11; Robert Pyatt, "Student Senate Passes Accessibility Resolution," *UDK*, October 17, 2013.

54. "Chancellor Fills in More of the Organization Chart," *Oread*, March 15, 1996, 1, 8.

55. Tammara Durham, interview by author, digital recording, Lawrence, July 1, 2013.

56. *Bold Aspirations: The Strategic Plan for the University of Kansas, 2012–2017,* 2012, 16, 19, 22, http://www.provost.ku.edu/sites/provost.drupal.ku.edu /files/docs/strategic-plan-20110914.pdf, accessed April 23, 2014. In this new structure, Enrollment Management, including Admissions, Financial Aid and Scholarships, University Registrar, and Student Information Systems, became a separate unit under the direction of Matt Melvin. Student Affairs, led by Durham, retained traditional units such as Student Housing, Unions, Student Health Services, Student Involvement and Leadership Center, Legal Services for Students, Recreation Services, CAPS, and Hilltop; added Student Money Management Services; and expanded the purview of Student Conduct and Community Standards.

57. KU News Bureau, "KU on Wheels Successful: New System Begun," January 24, 1974, Student Senate, News Releases Folder, 1974–1975, RG 3/11/3, University Archives, KU; "Douglas County Victims of White-Collar Crimes Receive Little, If Any, Restitution," *LJW*, April 2, 2007; "KU on Wheels in Red $320K," *LJW*, February 28, 2008; "Better Safe Than Sorry," *UDK*, December 2, 2009. Ambler emphasized that the autonomy and authority wielded by KU's Student Senate was exceptional compared to universities across the country, especially in making decisions about the use of student fees, and that the Senate took this authority seriously.

58. Clark Coan, "1970: The Year That Rocked River City," in author's possession.

59. "Whomper to Close Doors," *LJW*, November 29, 1976, 2, 7; Whomper, Inc., Collection, RH 3/MS 1053, Kansas Collection, KU.

60. "Recycling Plan Promoted," *UDK*, January 26, 1990, 8; "Campus Recycling to Become More Efficient," *UDK*, February 2, 1998, 1; "Center for

Sustainability Points Eye to Future," *Oread*, February 7, 2007, 1, 6; "Chancellor Signs Earth Day Proclamation; KU Takes Steps to Improve Sustainability," KU News Release, April 16, 2010, http://archive.news.ku.edu/2010/Apr./16/earthday.shtml, accessed January 15, 2014.

61. Jeffrey Cameron Arnold, "Legal Services Outline for the University of Kansas," August 16, 1978, Student Organization Records, Legal Services for Students, Box 1, RG 67/316, University Archives, KU; Legal Services for Students, http://www.legalservices.ku.edu, accessed January 22, 2014.

62. "Vietnam Memorial Makes Progress," *Jayhawker Yearbook*, 1986, 54–55; John Onken, "The Hard Facts of the Vietnam Memorial," February 6, 1984, General Records, Vietnam Memorial, Artificial Records, RG 0/22/178, Box 1, University Archives, KU. A major contributor for the project was K. K. Amini, benefactor of two KU scholarship halls.

63. John Hill, "Perspective 68," *Jayhawker Yearbook*, 1968, 3; *Jayhawker Yearbook*, 1974, 29, 32–33; *Jayhawker Yearbook*, 1975, 27, 70; *Jayhawker Yearbook*, 1976, 71, 88.

64. *Jayhawker Yearbook*, 1980, 85; *Jayhawker Yearbook*, 1983, 19. College had become a place where "individuals acted out their private dramas of personal fulfillment and ambition." See Helen Lefkowitz Horowitz, *Campus Life* (Chicago: University of Chicago Press, 1987), 261–268.

65. *Jayhawker Yearbook*, 1983, 19.

66. "Alcohol and KU," http://www.alcohol.ku.edu, accessed May 29, 2014. The law was in response to the National Minimum Drinking Act, which punished states that failed to raise the drinking age with a reduction in federal highway funding. Local politicians and businesses opposed the change, citing enforcement and economic challenges.

67. "Peace Rally Condemns Leaders, Not Soldiers," *UDK*, January 22, 1991, 1; "Rally Shows Support for Troops in Gulf," *UDK*, January 28, 1991, 3; *Jayhawker Yearbook*, 1991, 65.

68. Hannah Bolton, interview by author, digital recording, Lawrence, May 9, 2013; Marlesa Roney, interview by author, digital recording, Lawrence, May 8, 2013.

69. Matt Bechtold, "iPod Isolation," *Jayhawker Yearbook*, 2008–2009, 48; Bolton, interview by author.

70. Matt Erickson, "Student Activists Lead Charge to Change Clothing at KU," *LJW*, March 26, 2013, 1A, 5A; David Mucci, interview by author, digital recording, Lawrence, July 8, 2013.

71. The Center for Civic and Social Responsibility, http://ccsr.ku.edu/history, accessed April 22, 2014; Bolton, interview by author.

72. "KU Chancellor Upholds Students' Elimination of Athletics Fee but Creates New Fee in Its Place," *LJW*, March 27, 2014, 1.

73. Twombly and Morphew, "Tuition Rising and Student Power in the Academy," 8–12, 21–23, 30.

74. OIRP, *KU Profiles*, "Tuition and Fees for Two Semesters," Table 9-303, 1969–1970 to 2010–2011, http://www2.ku.edu/~oirp/profiles/old/9-303.pdf, and "Four-Year Tuition Compact," http://www2.ku.edu/~oirp/Tuition

/CompactTOC.shtml, both accessed April 25, 2014; Roney, interview by author. She also noted that it was a mature way to view college costs.

75. OIRP, "Common Data Set," 2002–2003 and 2013–2014, http://www2.ku.edu/~oirp/Common/index.shtml, accessed April 25, 2014.

76. McKenna Harford, "Senate Approved Full-Time LGBTQ Coordinator," *UDK*, April 9, 2014, 1, 3; Ben Unglesbee, "Student Senate Opens Line of Funding for Headquarters," *LJW*, February 1, 2014, 4A.

8. "CRIMSON AND THE BLUE":
AN ERA OF ATHLETIC ACHIEVEMENT

1. In the early 1990s, KU established the position of senior woman administrator in athletics, emphasizing even more the importance of women's sports.

2. By 2014, the KU football coach's salary was about $2.5 million a year and the basketball coach was paid just under $5 million annually. Both of these salaries were within the range of salaries of top coaches in these sports around the country. See Steve Berkowitz, "Paying Big to Keep Bill Self Employed," *USA Today*, April 13, 2013, http://www.usatoday.com/story/sports/ncaab/big12/2013/04/03/kansas-coach-bill-self-contract-compensation-package/2048027/, accessed June 24, 2014; "Charlie Weis to Earn $2.5 Million a Year," *ESPN College Football*, December 14, 2011, http://espn.go.com/college-football/story/_/id/7353310/charlie-weis-contract-kansas-jayhawks-guarantees-25m-year, accessed June 24, 2014; Pat Kaufman, interview by author, KU Athletics CFO, June 17, 2014.

3. Of the ten athletics directors, one retired, three resigned to take jobs elsewhere in intercollegiate athletics, four resigned and worked outside of athletics, one was dismissed, and one continues to serve as athletics director.

4. "Personal History Fact Sheet, KU Athletics: Administrators and Coaches, 1890–2014," prepared by Spencer Research Library. KU athletics directors since 1960 (not including interims): Arthur "Dutch" Lonborg (1950–1963); Wade Stinson (1964–1972); Clyde Walker (1973–1977); Bob Marcum (1978–1981); Jim Lessig and Del Shankel (1982); Monte Johnson (1983–1986); Bob Frederick (1987–2001); Al Bohl (2001–2003); Lew Perkins (2003–2010); and Sheahon Zenger (2011–present).

5. Kansas Men's Basketball Media Guide, 2013–2014, 126–147. Naismith's original rules of basketball will soon be on display at the university. All Kansas Media Guides referenced in this chapter are written and produced by the staff of the Communications Department of Kansas Athletics.

6. Ibid.

7. Ibid.; Brad Gilbert, "Fact Sheet: KU Basketball," Kansas Athletics Communications, May 2014.

8. Matt Tait, "KU Tradition Touted as 'Great Fit' for Games," *LJW*, June 18, 2014, C1.

9. Kansas Men's Basketball Media Guide, 2013–2014, 136. Harp's 1956–1957 team, led by the legendary Wilt Chamberlain, lost to North Carolina, 54–53, in the now-historic triple overtime national championship game at Municipal Auditorium in Kansas City.

10. Ibid., 136, 193–197.

11. Bob Hurt, *Topeka Capital Journal*, March 13, 1966; Kansas Men's Basketball Media Guide, 2013–2014, 194; Ted Owens with Jim Krause and Jesse Tuel, *At the Hang Up* (Olathe, KS: Ascend Books, 2013), 145–148.

12. Kansas Men's Basketball Media Guide, 2013–2014, 194.

13. Ibid., 194–196.

14. Ibid.

15. Ibid., 147, 166, 196.

16. Ibid., 136.

17. Ibid., 137, 197, 198.

18. Ibid., 197.

19. Ibid., 198.

20. Ibid., 134.

21. Ibid., 134, 137.

22. Francis B. Kish, "The Role of the University President in the Governance of Intercollegiate Athletics" (PhD diss., University of Kansas, 1998), 131–132.

23. Roy Williams with Tim Crothers, *Hard Work* (Chapel Hill, NC: Algonquin Books, 2009), 96.

24. Kansas Men's Basketball Media Guide, 2013–2014, 137.

25. Ibid.

26. Ibid., 200.

27. Ibid., 201–202.

28. Ibid., 137.

29. Ibid.

30. Ibid., 202–204.

31. Ibid., 203.

32. Ibid., 135.

33. Ibid. Arthur led KU in scoring, with 20 points, followed by Chalmers with 18.

34. Kansas Football Media Guide, 2013, 190–195, 158–159.

35. Max Falkenstien with Matt Fulks and Doug Vance, *A Good Place to Stop* (Overland Park, KS: Power House Books, 2007), 61–72, 73–84; Kansas Football Media Guide, 2013, 159, 184, 191. The assistants on Rodgers's staff who eventually became head coaches were John Cooper (Tulsa, Arizona State, Ohio State); Terry Donahue (UCLA); Dick Tomey (Arizona); Dave McClain (Wisconsin); and Don Fambrough (Kansas).

36. Falkenstien, *A Good Place to Stop*, 74–82; Kansas Football Media Guide, 2013, 159, 172, 191.

37. Falkenstien, *A Good Place to Stop*, 83–84.

38. Ibid., 118–120; Kansas Football Media Guide, 2013, 162, 169, 173, 191.

39. Falkenstien, *A Good Place to Stop*, 111–115.

40. Ibid., 115–116; Kansas Football Media Guide, 2013, 191–192.

41. Kish, "The Role of the University President," 130. The inquiry cited ten violations, the most serious being references to "money and other benefits that would reasonably lead a prospective student-athlete to . . . enroll at the University of Kansas." The football program was placed on probation for two years and prohibited from playing on television during 1984 and 1985 and in postseason games following the 1985 season.

42. Ibid., 164.

43. *Kansas Alumni Magazine* (February 1983): 8; Kansas Football Media Guide, 2013, 192; Kish, "The Role of the University President," 149.

44. Kish, "The Role of the University President," 154; Kansas Football Media Guide, 2013, 192–193.

45. Kansas Football Media Guide, 2013, 130, 184.

46. Ibid., 174, 193.

47. Ibid.

48. Ibid., 193; Chuck Woodling, "Allen Deserves Better Than to Be Left Twisting in the Wind," *LJW*, November 4, 2001, C1; Chuck Woodling, "Allen Bows Out with Class," *LJW*, November 5, 2001.

49. KU Media Relations Release, December 4, 2002; David Mitchell, "Mangino Making Mark," *LJW*, December 4, 2002, C1; Chris Lazzarino, *Kansas Alumni Magazine* 1 (2002): 18–19. Prior to his three years with the Sooners, Mangino spent eight years on Coach Bill Snyder's staff at Kansas State.

50. Kansas Football Media Guide, 2013, 175, 194.

51. Ibid., 159, 175.

52. "Mangino Out at Kansas," *ESPN College Football*, December 4, 2009, http://sports.espn.go.com/ncf/news/story?id=4711389, accessed June 24, 2014.

53. "Kansas Fires Coach Turner Gill," *ESPN College Football*, November 28, 2011, http://espn.go.com/college-football/story/_/id/7287786/kansas-jayhawks-fires-coach-turner-gill-following-10-game-losing-streak, accessed June 24, 2014.

54. J. Brady McCullough, "Kansas Hires Charlie Weis as Football Coach," *Wichita Eagle*, December 8, 2011, Clippings File, 2011, University Archives, KU.

55. Kansas Football Media Guide, 2013, 194; KU Athletics Academic Support, Reports to Faculty Mentors, Team GPAs, 2013 and 2014. The grade-point average of the team, as well as the discipline and conditioning of the players, improved dramatically.

56. "Weis Relieved of Duties as Kansas Football Coach; Bowen Named Interim Head Coach," University of Kansas Athletics Media Release, October 8, 2014.

57. Ibid.

58. Matt Tait, "Beaty Takes Reins; Jayhawks Introduce 38th Coach," *LJW*, December 9, 2014; Clipping File, University Archives, KU.

59. Del Shankel, "Women's Sports Make Gains in Recent Years," *Kansas Alumni Magazine* (January 1983): 8–9; Patrick Thornton, Walter T. Champion, Jr., and Lawrence Randall, *Sport Ethics for Sport Management Professionals* (Burlington, MA: Jones and Bartlett Learning, 2012), 379.

60. Marian Washington as Women's AD, News Release, University of Kansas Division of Information, June 18, 1974.

61. Shankel, "Women's Sports," 8–9. By 1983, Vice Chancellor Del Shankel felt that "the University for all practical purposes had achieved its goal of equitable funding for men's and women's non-revenue sports."

62. Ibid.

63. Kansas Women's Basketball Media Guide, 2013–2014, 130; Marie Luce, "She's Got Game," *Kansas Alumni Magazine* 3 (1998): 6.

64. Kansas Women's Basketball Media Guide, 2013–2014, 169.

65. Ibid., 150–151. Booth Family Hall of Athletics Display, Decade of 2000–2010, Allen Fieldhouse, University of Kansas.

66. Kansas Women's Basketball Media Guide, 2013–2014, 70–73.

67. Ibid., 70–72, 151–152.

68. Ibid., 70, 152, 170.

69. KU Track and Field Media Guide, 2012, 133, 134.

70. Ibid.

71. Ibid., 134; Booth Family Hall of Athletics Display, Decade of the 1960s.

72. KU Track and Field Media Guide, 2012, 134.

73. Ibid., 135.

74. KU Track and Field Media Guide, 2014, 162, 166.

75. Ibid., 159.

76. Ibid., 158–159. McKnight still holds the Relays and Memorial Stadium record for that event.

77. Ibid., 158.

78. Ibid., 159, 162.

79. Ibid., 159.

80. Ibid., 56.

81. Brad Gilbert, Information Sheet, KU Athletics Communications, May 22, 2014.

82. KU Track and Field Media Guide, 2014, 169.

83. Ibid., 141.

84. Ibid., 141, 56. Both the 4x100 meter and 4x400 meter relay teams added important points for the Hawks, with fifth and sixth place finishes, respectively. The members of those teams were Paris Daniels, Tianna Valentine, Denesha Morris, Diamond Dixon, and Taylor Washington.

85. Kansas Cross Country Media Guide, 2013, 70–76.

86. KU Sports Information Press Release, February 15, 1977; KU Swimming Media Guide, 2000–2001, 17.

87. KU Men's Swimming Media Guide, 1980–1981, 4.

88. Ibid.

89. KU Men's Swimming Media Guide, 1984–1985, 7; KU Men's Swimming Media Guide, 1997–1998, 3.

90. KU Swimming and Diving Media Guide, 2013–2014, 80.

91. KU Men's Swimming Media Guide, 1997–1998, 3; KU Athletics Hall of Fame (online), Booth Hall of Athletics Hall of Fame, http://www.ku athletics.com/sports/2013/6/21/GEN_0621135435.aspx?id=11, accessed June 24, 2014.

92. KU Swimming and Diving Media Guide, 2013–2014, 54–56; Clark Campbell, interview by author, June 1, 2014.

93. Clark Campbell, interview; Records Display at Robinson Natatorium, University of Kansas, June 12, 2014.

94. Kansas Baseball Media Guide, 2013, 155.

95. Ibid., 180.

96. Ibid., 200.

97. Ibid., 147, 148, 180.

98. Ibid., 96–97.

99. Ibid., 202.

100. Ibid., 97, 147, 203.

101. KU Athletics Website, Baseball, http://www.kuathletics.com/index .aspx?path=baseball&, accessed June 23, 2014.

102. Kansas Baseball Media Guide, 2013, 99.

103. Kansas Softball Media Guide, 2014, 118–121.

104. Ibid., 118–121, 100.

105. Ibid., 121–124, 100, 97.

106. Ibid., 125–130, 97.

107. Ibid., 97; KU Athletics Website, Softball, http://www.kuathletics.com /index.aspx?path=softball&, accessed June 24, 2014.

108. Kansas Rowing Media Guide, 2013–2014, 36–37.

109. Ibid.

110. Ibid., 37, 45.

111. Kansas Soccer Media Guide, 2013, 64, 116.

112. Ibid., 64, 65; Brad Gilbert, KU Athletics Communications, interview with author and fact sheet, February 9, 2015.

113. Brad Gilbert, interview and fact sheet.

114. Kansas Soccer Media Guide, 2013, 66.

115. Ibid., 64–65.

116. Ibid., 115.

117. Brad Gilbert, interview with author and fact sheet.

118. Kansas Volleyball Media Guide, 2013, 88.

119. Ibid., 115–119.

120. Ibid., 58; KU Athletics Website, Coach Ray Bechard Biography, http://www.kuathletics.com/coaches.aspx?rc=704, accessed May 1, 2014; Alissa Bauer, KU Athletics Communications, interview with author and fact sheet, February 9, 2015.

121. Alissa Bauer, interview with author and fact sheet.

122. Kansas Volleyball Media Guide, 2013, 58–61; KU Athletics Website, Coach Ray Bechard Biography.

123. Kansas Volleyball Media Guide, 2013, 58.

124. Ibid., 58–61; Kansas Volleyball Banquet Program, January 26, 2014, 3–5.

125. Kansas Tennis Media Guide, 2001, 55–57.

126. Ibid., 51.

127. Ibid.

128. Ibid., 28, 30–32.

129. Ibid.

130. Kansas Women's Golf Media Guide, 2013–2014, 48; KU Athletics Website, Golf, http://www.kuathletics.com/index.aspx?path=wten&, accessed May 1, 2014.

131. Kansas Women's Golf Media Guide, 2013–2014, 45, 47.

132. KU Athletics Website, Golf.

133. Kansas Men's Golf Media Guide, 2013–2014, 37, 45, 49.

134. Ibid.

135. Wrestling History, 1924–1935, Wrestling Records, 66/21, Box 1, University Archives, KU; KU Sports News Bureau, Press Release, February 12, 1963; Wrestling Historical Folders, 1963–1966, University Archives, KU; KU Gymnastics Media Guide, 1979–1980; Gymnastics Coaches, 1963–1980, University Archives, KU; "Death of Gymnastics Leaves Team Hanging," *UDK*, March 18, 1980, 1; Tracee Hamilton, "KU Gymnasts Find New Life," *UDK*, August 26, 1980, 10. Wrestling was a varsity sport at KU from 1922 until 1935. The sport was resurrected in 1963 as a club sport under Coach Bob Lockwood; a year later the Jayhawks fielded a varsity team with Coach Terry Shockley in charge. About three-fourths of the wrestlers were KU football players. Matches were held in Allen Fieldhouse and Hoch Auditorium. The sport lasted only three years; after winning only one match during this period, it was discontinued following the 1966 season. Also in 1963, Lockwood, a former standout on the Jayhawk gymnastics club team, organized the first NCAA varsity team and became its head coach. Lockwood, who during his tenure on Mount Oread also coached wrestling, tennis, diving, and women's volleyball, remained at the helm of the gymnastics squad for 14 years, through the 1978–1979 season. His early teams were quite successful, regularly finishing third or fourth in the highly competitive Big Eight Conference, which was loaded with perennial national powers such as Nebraska, Iowa State, and Oklahoma. Lockwood also posted an impressive 88–60 career dual meet record. Some of his outstanding performers were Robert Pierson (floor exercises), Richard Schubert (pommel horse), Kirk Gardner (rings), Sean Williams (vaulting), Mark Joseph (parallel bars), Gerald Carley (high bar), and Ron Ortman and Kent Dobbins (all around). The women's gymnastics program was introduced in 1968 with Anise Catlett as its head coach and Ken Snow at its helm for the last six years of the program. Kathy Ross,

Angie Wagle, Sherry Hassler, Joan Smith, Sue Tagg, and Liz Phillips were excellent performers for the women's teams. In May 1980, Athletics Director Bob Marcum announced that both the men's and the women's gymnastics programs, with a combined budget of $70,000, were being discontinued as varsity sports, because of financial shortfalls within the Athletics Department. Marcum, however, decided to honor the scholarships for the seven male and four female athletes for the 1980–1981 school year.

136. "Longtime KU Director of Bands to End 30 Year Tenure," KU News Release, September 14, 2001; "Girls in the Band," *Kansas Alumni Magazine*, October 1972. Recipients of the Sudler Trophy are selected by the nation's intercollegiate band directors. In 1989, KU became only the seventh school chosen for the award. "Thirty High Schools to Participate in KU Band Day," KU News Release, September 12, 2014, http://news.ku.edu/2014/09/12/thirty-high-schools-participate-ku-band-day.

137. Williams Fund Brochure, 2014, 2. Men's basketball has a long history of being a major revenue-producing sport for Kansas Athletics. Allen Fieldhouse is filled to capacity for every game, year after year. However, football can and must be a difference maker. A consistent winning football team and a full stadium will enhance the athletics budget and be a huge boost for funding the university's nonrevenue sports.

138. Blair Kerkhoff, "Latest Round of Conference Income for Big 12, SEC Schools, Rival Ticket Sales," April 13, 2014, Kansas City Star Campus Corner Blog, http://www.kansascity.com/sports/spt-columns-blogs/campus-corner/article344995/Latest-round-of-conference-income-for-Big-12-SEC-schools-rivals-ticket-sales.html, accessed June 24, 2014.

139. After Nebraska, Colorado, Texas A&M, and longtime border rival Missouri left the Big 12 Conference, it looked as though the future of the conference was in jeopardy.

140. Four key staff members and a paid consultant were eventually convicted and imprisoned for their involvement in a ticket scam that began in 2005. "Federal Charges against Five Former Kansas Athletics Officials Accused of Selling Tickets for KU," *LJW*, November 18, 2010, Clippings Files, University Archives, KU; "Two in KU Tickets Scheme Sent to Prison Camps," *LJW*, May 5, 2011, Clippings Files, University Archives, KU. Over 19,000 basketball season tickets and 2,000 football season tickets were misappropriated and sold or distributed through brokers and others. Federal authorities said that the embezzlement of tickets cost Kansas Athletics at least $2 million. The five individuals received prison sentences ranging from 37 to 57 months and were ordered to pay restitution charges totaling $2.2 million. Two other Kansas Athletics employees received two years' probation for failing to inform authorities about their knowledge of the misappropriations and were ordered to pay restitution of $56,000 and $157,480, respectively. Kansas Athletics moved quickly as the investigation progressed in the summer of 2010 to institute measures to regain the trust and confidence of its donor base.

Sean Lester, KU's interim athletics director, commented in November 2010, "Over the past six months, we have implemented measures to strengthen our ticket protocols and make the entire process more transparent. I think our donors appreciate the enhancements we have made in transparency and accountability."

141. Paul Buskirk and Jane Widger Fulton, interviews by author, KU Athletics, June 11, 2014. In 2014, Buskirk's operating budget was about $745,000.

Contributors

J. MEGAN GREENE joined the faculty of the University of Kansas in 2002 and is associate professor of history and director of KU's Center for East Asian Studies. She teaches courses on modern Chinese history and performs research on the history of education and science and technology in the Republic of China, both in China and on Taiwan. Her publications include *The Origins of the Developmental State in Taiwan: Science Policy and the Quest for Modernization* (Harvard, 2008) and *Taiwan Enters the 21st Century: Aspects and Limitations of a Development Model*, co-edited with Robert Ash (Routledge, 2007), as well as a number of articles and chapters in edited volumes. She is a recipient of the George and Eleanor Woodyard International Educator Award. Before coming to KU, she taught at Gettysburg College and at the School of Oriental and African Studies, University of London. She earned her BA from Cornell University, an MA from the University of Chicago, and her PhD from Washington University in St. Louis.

FRANCIS B. "BERNIE" KISH is a lecturer in sport management in the Department of Health, Sport, and Exercise Sciences in the School of Education, teaching courses in ethics, facilities, events management, and leadership. He has won several teaching awards at KU, including the HOPE award (Honor for Outstanding Progressive Educators). His research interests focus on the history of sport, with emphasis on the history and tradition of athletics at KU and Notre Dame, plus the glory days of athletics at the Haskell Indian Nations University. A career military officer, he served in the US Army for over 29 years, was the executive director of the College Football Hall of Fame for ten years, and worked in the Kansas Athletics Department. He earned a BS in Education from Indiana University of Pennsylvania, an MPA from the University of Missouri at Kansas City, and a PhD in Higher Education from the University of Kansas. Dr. Kish has been a member of the KU faculty since 2005.

BURDETT A. LOOMIS (PhD, Wisconsin, 1974) is a professor of political science at the University of Kansas, where he has taught since 1979. In 2005, he worked as Kansas governor Kathleen Sebelius's director of administrative communication. He has twice been a Guest Scholar at the Brookings Institution in Washington, DC, and has served as a Fulbright Senior Scholar in 2006 (Argentina), and in 2013 he held the Fulbright Distinguished Chair in American Politics at Flinders University in Adelaide, Australia. He has written or edited more than 30 books in various editions. His scholarship focuses on legislatures, interest groups, and policy making. He has co-edited nine editions of *Interest Group Politics*, and in 2011 he edited *A Guide to Interest Groups*, an extensive set of original essays, as well as *The U.S. Senate: From Deliberation to Dysfunction*. Loomis won a Kemper Teaching Award (1996) and the Steeples Outstanding Service to the People of Kansas Award (2014). He has lectured extensively for the State Department in South America and Asia. Since 1984 he has directed KU's intern programs in Washington, DC, and Topeka.

JOSHUA L. ROSENBLOOM is professor of economics and courtesy professor of history and a research associate of the National Bureau of Economic Research (Cambridge, MA). From 2006 to 2012 he was associate vice chancellor for Research and Graduate Studies. From 2012 through 2014 he was director of the National Science Foundation's Science of Science and Innovation Policy program. His main areas of teaching and research are US economic history, labor economics, and the economics of science and technological change. He is the author of *Looking for Work, Searching for Workers: Labor Markets during American Industrialization* and over 30 scholarly articles. He earned a BA from Oberlin College in 1981 and a PhD from Stanford University in 1988. Professor Rosenbloom has been a member of the KU faculty since 1988.

JOHN L. RURY (PhD, Wisconsin, 1982) is professor of education and (by courtesy) history at KU. His teaching and research focuses on historical facets of education policy and social inequality. His published works include *The African American Struggle for Secondary Schooling* (with Shirley A. Hill, 2012), *Education and Social Change* (2002, 2005, 2009, 2013), and *Education and Women's Work* (1991), along with several edited volumes and more than fifty articles and review essays in academic periodicals. Professor Rury has been elected president of the History of Education Society (USA) and a vice president of the American

Educational Research Association. He has served as an editor of the *American Educational Research Journal* and also as a senior program officer at the Spencer Foundation. He came to KU in 2003.

KATHRYN NEMETH TUTTLE, associate vice provost emerita, came to KU in 1987 and was instrumental in efforts to improve advising, student academic support, and retention. She was named founding director of KU's Undergraduate Advising Center in 1997, after serving as associate and interim director of Admissions and director of New Student Orientation. She became associate vice provost for student success in 2003 and initiated KU's orientation course and the first learning communities and financial literacy programs. Her research focus is on the history of women in higher education, and she was awarded the NASPA Dissertation of the Year award. She is a co-author of *Reflecting Back, Looking Forward: Civil Rights and Student Affairs.* She has taught undergraduate and graduate courses for the School of Education. Kathryn received undergraduate and doctoral degrees from the University of Kansas. She was named to the KU Women's Hall of Fame in 1998.

WILLIAM M. TUTTLE, JR., is professor emeritus of American Studies at the University of Kansas. He joined the KU faculty in 1967, after being awarded a PhD by the University of Wisconsin. He is the author or editor of a number of books, including *Race Riot: Chicago in the Red Summer of 1919* and *W.E.B. Du Bois: A Great Life Observed;* coeditor of *Plain Folk: The Life Stories of Undistinguished Americans;* and coauthor of *A People and a Nation: A History of the United States.* Tuttle is also the author of *"Daddy's Gone to War": The Second World War in the Lives of America's Children,* which was named a Notable Book of the Year by the *New York Times* and nominated for the Pulitzer Prize. Tuttle has received KU's top awards for teaching, research, and service: the HOPE award, presented by KU's senior class; the Higuchi/Balfour S. Jeffrey Award for Research Achievement in the Humanities and Social Sciences; and the Steeples Outstanding Service to the People of Kansas Award.

SUSAN B. TWOMBLY is professor of higher education administration and chair of the Department of Educational Leadership and Policy Studies. Her main areas of teaching are qualitative research methods and postsecondary curriculum. She is author of numerous publications on higher education faculty and administrators. Her most recent scholarship, with colleagues Lisa Wolf-Wendel and Dongbin Kim, focuses on foreign-born faculty members' experiences in higher education. She is co-author of a 2012 monograph, *Study Abroad in a New Global Century*, with KU graduate Mark Salisbury (MA, American Studies) and current KU doctoral students Shannon Tumanut and Paul Klute. She served as president of the KU University Council in 2003–2004 and was a Fulbright Fellow to Ecuador in 1995. She earned a BA from Susquehanna University, an MS from SUNY Plattsburg, and a PhD from Pennsylvania State University. She joined the faculty at KU in 1985.

KIM CARY WARREN is associate professor of US history and director of graduate studies for Women, Gender, and Sexuality Studies. Her publications include *The Quest of Citizenship: African American and Native American Education in Kansas, 1880–1935* (2010), *The First and the Forced: Essays on the Native American and African American Experience* (2007, co-edited with James N. Leiker and Barbara Watkins), and articles that focus on Native American masculinity and athletics, separate gender spheres ideology, and African American tourism in West Africa. Warren's research has been supported by the National Academy of Education and the Woodrow Wilson National Fellowship Foundation. She earned her BA from Yale University and her MA and PhD from Stanford University. Professor Warren has been a member of the faculty at KU since 2004.

JAMES WOELFEL is a professor of Philosophy and of Humanities & Western Civilization, and was director of the Humanities & Western Civilization Program from 1985–2010. His main areas of teaching and research are modern European and American philosophical and religious thought and peace and conflict studies. He is the author of *Bonhoeffer's Theology, Borderland Christianity, Albert Camus on the Sacred and the Secular, The Agnostic Spirit, Portraits in Victorian Religious Thought, The Existentialist Legacy,* and *Patterns in Western Civilization* (co-edited and -authored; 4th edition), and of numerous journal articles and essays in edited volumes. In 1997 he received the 25th Anniversary Public Scholar Award from the Kansas Humanities Council, and in 1998 he was awarded a Kemper Fellowship for Teaching Excellence. He earned a BA from the University of Oklahoma, an MDiv from the Episcopal Divinity School, an MA from Yale University, and a PhD from the University of St. Andrews. Professor Woelfel has been a member of the KU faculty since 1966.

Index

415

Bogina, Gus, 101–103
Bohanan, Chris, 336
Bohnenstiel, Rodger, 313
Bold Aspirations (strategic plan), 33,
    74, 76, 79, 150, 153
  KU Core and, 153
  research and, 220–221
  student recruitment and retention,
    294
Bolton, Hannah, 302–303, 305, 308
Bolton, Kim, 341
Bond, Dick, 107
Bookman, Leo, 337
Boonraksasat, Thanuttra "Fhong,"
    353
Boots Adams Alumni Center, 65
Boozer, Nancy, 352
Boren Scholarships, 175
Boschee, Jeff, 316
Boston, Kara, 348
Bowen, Clint, 326
Bowman, Marilyn, 239, 267–268,
    281–282, 282 (photo)
Brady, Marilyn, 404
Branson, Andrea, 336
Brehm, Sharon, 127
Bricke, Hodgie, 174
Brigham Young University, 24
Brooks, Gwendolyn, 135 (photo)
Brown, Gilbert, 324
Brown, John, 4
Brown, Larry, 24, 314–315
Brown, Lorene, 233
Brown, Roger, 313
Brown, Terry, 316
Brownback, Sam, 86, 113
Bryant, Paul "Bear," 322
Bubb, Henry, 51, 366
Buchanan, Denise, 335
Buckingham, Jeff, 336
budget (KU), 15, 54, 69, 86, 88, 90,
    100
  athletic, 310, 311, 327–328, 356
  cuts, 64, 68, 77, 78, 112
  endowment and, 15, 34
  increases, 19, 59

legislature and, 95–97
  research, 193, 216
  tuition, 20, 30, 83, 89
Budig, Gene, 16, 25, 44, 63 (photo),
    65 (photo), 67–68, 78–80, 99
    (photo), 101 (photo), 103
    (photo), 106, 111, 142 (photo),
    192 (photo), 344 (photo), 356,
    367n53, 368n75, 374n24
  accomplishments, 12–13, 65–66
  athletics and, 344, 356
  background, 62
  Campaign Kansas, 15, 65, 80
  fundraising, 15, 80
  international studies and, 170–171
  Medical Center and, 217
  minority faculty and scholarships,
    14–15, 22, 212
  state legislature and, 97–104,
    112–113
  student protest and, 257–258, 261,
    393
  teaching professorships, 21
  values, 63–64
Budig, Gretchen, 67
Budig Hall, 65
Bunge, Tracy, 346, 347
Bunker, Chris, 259
Burcham Park Rowing Boathouse, 355
Bureau of Child Research, 189–191,
    193
Burge Union, 19, 296, 302
Burt Hall nuclear reactor, 182
Burzle, J. Anthony (Toni), 159–163,
    168, 175
Busch, Daryl, 217
Bush, George H. W., 14
Buskirk, Paul, 356
Bus 63 system, 291
Byrd, Isaac, 345
Bystander Education, 302

Caldwell, Matt, 305
Calipari, John, 318
Calmese, Sheila, 334
Cambodia, 242

THE UNIVERSITY OF KANSAS
WEST CAMPUS
2015

121

122

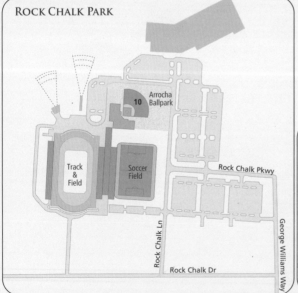

ROCK CHALK PARK

10 Arrocha Ballpark

Track & Field

Soccer Field

Rock Chalk Pkwy

Rock Chalk Ln

George Williams Way

Rock Chalk Dr

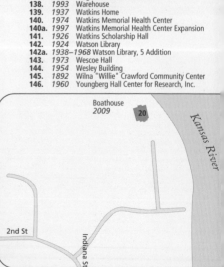

Boathouse
2009

20

Kansas River

2nd St

Indiana St